D1569678

UNIVERSITY OF WINNIPEG
LIBRARY
515 Portage Avenue
Winnipeg, Manitoba R3B 2E9

MATTHEW JOSEPHSON, BOURGEOIS BOHEMIAN

DAVID E. SHI

CT
215
.J85
S53
1981

MATTHEW JOSEPHSON, BOURGEOIS BOHEMIAN

NEW HAVEN AND LONDON / YALE UNIVERSITY PRESS

Copyright © 1981 by Yale University.
All rights reserved.
This book may not be reproduced, in whole
or in part, in any form (beyond that
copying permitted by Sections 107 and 108
of the U.S. Copyright Law and except by
reviewers for the public press), without
written permission from the publishers.

Designed by Sally Harris
and set in Linotron 202 Optima type.
Printed in the United States of America by
Vail-Ballou Press, Binghamton, N.Y.

Library of Congress Cataloging in Publication Data

Shi, David E
   Matthew Josephson, bourgeois bohemian.

   Includes bibliographical references and index.
   1. Josephson, Matthew, 1899–1978.   2. Authors,
American—20th century—Biography.   3. Intellectuals—
United States—Biography.   4. United States—Intellectual
life—20th century.   I. Title.
PS3519.079Z88   818'.5209 [B]   80-24493
ISBN 0-300-02563-7

10   9   8   7   6   5   4   3   2   1

Frontispiece: Matthew Josephson, 1940. Photo by Berenice Abbott.

TO EDWARD YOUNGER (1909–1979)

CONTENTS

ILLUSTRATIONS

ACKNOWLEDGMENTS

This study could not have been written without the information, advice, and cooperation provided by many people, starting with Matthew Josephson himself. On several occasions he and his wife Hannah offered me the hospitality of their home and responded patiently to my numerous, and occasionally impertinent, questions. They also gave me permission to examine their correspondence in the American Literature Collection at Yale University's Beinecke Library. After the Josephsons died, their two sons, Eric and Carl, continued such hospitality and assistance, giving me open access to their parents' personal papers at Sherman, Connecticut, and also filling in many details about their father's life and personality. Other relatives, including Murray Josephson, Eloise Segal, Felicia Van Veen, and Essie Weinstein Geffen, also aided me in my research.

I owe a special debt of gratitude to several of Josephson's closest friends, William Slater Brown, Kenneth Burke, Thomas Cochran, and Malcolm Cowley, each of whom found time to submit to repeated interviews, to respond to numerous written inquiries, and to read drafts of the manuscript with care and insight.

The following individuals generously agreed either to see me in person or to respond to my written questions: James Atlas, Miles Colean, Joel Freeman, Maxwell Geismar, Christine Griswold, Granville Hicks, Sidney Hook, Max Lerner, Jay Martin, Carey McWilliams, Lewis Mumford, Georgia O'Keefe, Paul Porter, Philippe Soupault, I. F. Stone, Paul Sweezy, Brom Weber, Alden Whitman, and C. Vann Woodward.

A number of scholars around the country, including Daniel Aaron, James Gilbert, Joan Givner, James Hoopes, Alfred Kazin, Walter Nugent, and Alan Wald, were kind enough to read the manuscript at various stages, and I have benefited immeasurably from their perceptive comments. In addition, my friends William Leverette of Furman University and Charles Cornwell and Malcolm Lester of Davidson College gave the manuscript a close reading and its author consistent encouragement.

Donald Gallup and his staff at the Beinecke Library went well beyond the normal courtesy in facilitating my research and in granting permission to publish material from its collections. Such was also the case at the Newberry Library and the special collections libraries at Boston University, Brown University, the University of Chicago, Columbia University, Harvard University, the University of Pennsylvania, Princeton University, and the University of Virginia. In addition I want to acknowledge the courtesy of Josephson's former publisher, Harcourt Brace Jovanovich, Inc., and specifically Rita Vaughan, who helped me locate correspondence in the company files. Excerpts of letters in the Harold Loeb Papers and the Allen Tate Papers are published here with the permission of Princeton University Library. For use of material from the Josephson and Allen papers and from the Alfred Stieglitz Archive, I thank the Collection of American Literature, Beinecke Rare Book and Manuscript Library, Yale University; for permission to use parts of the Alfred Stieglitz Archive I also thank Georgia O'Keefe. Passages from *Letters on Literature and Politics*, by Edmund Wilson, edited by Elena Wilson, copyright © 1957, 1973, 1974, 1977 by Elena Wilson, are reprinted by permission of Farrar, Straus & Giroux, Inc. I thank the University of California Press for permission to quote from *The Letters of Hart Crane*, edited by Brom Weber, copyright 1952, 1965 by Brom Weber. Quotations from *A Second Flowering* by Malcolm Cowley, copyright © 1973 by Malcolm Cowley, and *Exile's Return* by Malcolm Cowley, copyright 1951, © renewed 1969 by Malcolm Cowley, are reprinted by permission of Viking Penguin, Inc. "The Last Lady," by Matthew Josephson, © 1920 by The Modern Poetry Association, is reprinted by permission of the Editor of *Poetry*. I thank G. d'Andelot Belin and Brinton P. Roberts, Trustees under the Will of Amy Lowell, for permission to quote from her letters.

For the picture of the Dada party, I thank the Bibliothèque Doucet in

Paris. Kenneth Burke generously supplied the picture of himself in the 1920s; the picture of him dressed as an academic is reproduced here courtesy of Elspeth Hart. The photograph of John Brooks Wheelwright in the 1920s is reprinted with the kind permission of Brown University Library. For the shooting gallery picture I thank Richard Rychtarik. The frontispiece and picture of Matthew Josephson in 1940 are reprinted by permission of Berenice Abbott, and the photograph of Matthew Josephson in Sarasota is reproduced courtesy of Marcia Corbino. I thank Paul Porter for permission to include here the picture of Katherine Anne Porter. Prints of many of these photographs and the other illustrations were generously supplied by the Josephson family from its collection. Where possible I have indicated the name of the artist or photographer.

I also wish to express my appreciation to the Mellon Foundation and to the Davidson College Faculty Research Committee for providing me with a timely sabbatical and generous financial assistance. Ann Callahan and Ruth Wolf were indispensable in helping prepare the manuscript for submission. The staff at the Yale University Press, especially Chuck Grench, have been craftsmanlike in producing the book and patient in handling its author.

Much of the burden of this project has fallen on my wife, Susan, who tirelessly accompanied me on research trips and successfully transcribed my illegible handwriting on the typewriter. I am grateful for her help and understanding. Finally, I owe my greatest debt to Professor Edward Younger of the University of Virginia, a man devoted to the art of history and to the cultivation of young minds, who first suggested that I write a biography of Matthew Josephson. Unfortunately he did not live to see it completed. To his memory this book is dedicated.

MATTHEW JOSEPHSON, BOURGEOIS BOHEMIAN

1 INTRODUCTION

"My curse," Matthew Josephson wrote self-consciously at age thirty-eight, "has been extreme versatility; I began as a poet and belle-lettriste; have written one novel; numerous biographies; essays on political questions; journalism on the same; and for some years I have been a kind of historian, according to my own unacademic ideas." Josephson's curse has come back to haunt his biographer. A man of diverse interests and activities, Josephson was a prolific writer who took a generalist approach to the art of letters, much like his friends Van Wyck Brooks, Lewis Mumford, and Edmund Wilson. Starting out in the early 1920s as an experimentalist poet and editor among the Dadaists in Paris and Berlin, he later traded his typewriter for a ticker tape machine, serving for two years as a Wall Street broker during the peak of the Coolidge prosperity. Literature, however, remained his first love, and by the 1930s he had established himself as a successful popular historian, biographer, and journalist. Josephson is perhaps best known as the author of the best-selling *Robber Barons* (1934), *The Politicos* (1938), and *The President Makers* (1940), now classic muckraking studies that have shaped popular perceptions of American economic and political life during the Gilded Age and after.

But Josephson's significance extends beyond his numerous and influential writings. His career was representative of one major group making up the American literary Left in the interwar period, including such writers as Malcolm Cowley, Kenneth Burke, and Robert Coates, who changed from apolitical aesthetes in the early 1920s to fellow travelers in the early 1930s. Despite considerable differences in temperament and accomplishment, they shared a common pattern of alienation, return, and partial reintegration into conventional bourgeois American society. Born at the turn of the century, Josephson's generation of literary intellectuals grew up in an older, simpler America only to discover during adolescence that the country was rapidly becoming urban, complex, and mechanical. Education in eastern colleges and universities and in the bohemian cafes of Greenwich Village convinced them that America lacked a worthy cultural tradition and that literature should be detached from everyday life. The Great War and exile in Europe afterward accentuated this process of deracination.

By both training and inclination Josephson and his group of literary bohemians were artistic theorists rather than social theorists, preferring modernism to social realism. They spent most of their time during the twenties testing new literary forms and techniques. Josephson, for example, aligned himself first with Amy Lowell and the Imagists before becoming the "high priest" of American Dada. While in Paris and Berlin he was inspired by the European Dadaists to adopt a radical new approach to prose and poetry that praised machine-age America, and as editor of the controversial transatlantic reviews *Secession* and *Broom*, he urged that writers adapt literature to the dynamic rhythms of urban-industrial life in the United States. He thus set himself apart from most young writers of the so-called lost generation, who spent so much time lambasting American life and culture.

During the 1920s, however, the religion of art embraced by Josephson and his friends gradually began to lose its attraction. First the Sacco-Vanzetti affair, then the Great Depression persuaded them to end their artistic isolation. They made the transition from the artistic Left to the political Left, finally achieving a sense of social integration and responsibility by becoming Communist fellow travelers. Coalescing around the *New Republic* and its distinctive brand of Progressive radicalism, they superimposed Marxist rhetoric and teleology onto a foundation of pragmatic liberalism, thus unwittingly creating a political stance beset with internal tensions and contradictions. For instance, Josephson, Cowley, and other writers of similar views embraced the traditional Progressive emphasis on social engineering through economic planning and technocratic rule while at the same time they urged collectivization along Marxian lines.

They wrote passionately of the need and inevitability of revolution but shuddered at the thought of it; they lavished praise and sympathy on the working classes yet privately doubted the will and intelligence of the masses. Moreover, their preoccupation with social reform's tangible consequences occasionally blinded them to the fact that such a pragmatic orientation lacked a consistent moral standard. Thus they vigorously defended civil liberties in the United States but rationalized Stalinist terror in the Soviet Union.

For the most part, however, such ambiguities remained below the surface until late in the decade. In practice this meant that although independent of the Communist party, Josephson and others in his circle supported Communist political positions. They campaigned for Foster and Ford in 1932, sharply criticized Roosevelt for the conservatism of the early New Deal, and scoffed at the genteel approach to social change of Norman Thomas and the Socialists. Josephson joined many other literary fellow travelers who visited Soviet Russia in the early 1930s and came away convinced of the superiority of the Soviet system and in awe of its efficient ruler. As the decade wore on, he explained his support of Stalin and the Soviets as the only way to stop Hitler and fascism. He also endorsed the Popular Front, American aid to the Spanish Republicans, and American neutrality after the signing of the Nazi-Soviet pact. But he was never willing to submit completely to party control, nor was he ever comfortable with more orthodox Stalinist writers such as Granville Hicks, Bernard Smith, and Michael Gold who advocated a proletarian literature at the expense of pure art. He and other bohemian radicals like him preferred to support the Communists from a distance, hoping thereby to maintain their artistic freedom and to exert pressure on Roosevelt to move farther left in his response to the depression.

After the signing of the Nazi-Soviet pact and the outbreak of World War II, Josephson's relatively cohesive coterie of literary fellow travelers began to disintegrate. Some, like Cowley and Burke, turned inward, returning to more purely literary pursuits; others reversed themselves politically and became neoconservatives or Cold War liberals. Josephson, however, doggedly maintained his political stance and his involvement, convinced that a liberal Left movement, independent of the Communists yet supportive of an American rapprochement with the Soviet Union, must be maintained. His circle of friends changed accordingly, as did his association with the *New Republic*. After World War II Josephson aligned himself more with the *Nation* and its articulate staff and contributors—Freda Kirchwey, Carey McWilliams, Maxwell Geismar, Max

Lowenthal. They shared his hopes for a revival of an independent Left, as well as his fears of a conservative postwar reaction. During the Cold War era Josephson used the pages of the *Nation* to support Henry Wallace, the progressive labor movement, social welfare legislation, arms control, and civil liberties. He was one of the few liberals in the 1950s who openly attacked McCarthy and his supporters, thereby risking recrimination and loss of income. Until his death in 1978 he continued to advocate an active political role for writers and to espouse the basic tenets of Left liberalism—economic planning, democratic collectivism, and eventual democratic socialism.

Out of respect for the diversity of Josephson's career, I have sought to portray him as both a representative and a distinctive member of a literary generation notable for its talent, productivity, and political activism. As Alan Trachtenberg has maintained, it may have been the "last generation of Americans who believed in the power of culture, and in the qualifications of intellectuals to lead." But as was the case with so many of Josephson's peers, his transition from bumptious expatriate to literary activist and professional writer was neither smooth nor complete. He struggled during most of his career to strike a balance between commerce and art, literary freedom and social responsibility. As he explained in 1942, he had long been "absorbed in the problem of the relationship of the artist to society, the problem of his participation in public life." That absorption and those problems serve as the foci of this study. In the following pages I trace Josephson's transformation from Dadaist to fellow traveler and analyze how his attempt to assume the role of the writer turned public man affected his life and writings thereafter.

I have also tried to reveal Matthew Josephson as a person. Mark Twain once observed that every man "is a moon and has a dark side which he never shows to anybody." Like Twain, Josephson frequently was not as he portrayed himself in his published memoirs and among his family and friends. In public he projected himself as a confident, stable, happily married professional writer. Yet in private reflections and activities, he revealed a different personality—skeptical, anxious, even melancholy—more bohemian than bourgeois. Within himself Josephson struggled with what Van Wyck Brooks termed the "eternal dilemma of every American writer," the persistent clash between the impulse to create pure art and the impulse to vulgarize art for commercial gain. Throughout his career his creative and acquisitive instincts were at war; the struggle between living a life of art and earning a living and raising a family constituted one of the major hidden tensions of his life.

In writing this biography, I have examined how Josephson's ideas and behavior, and the cultural and historical forces that molded them, influenced his personal and literary development. This purpose dictated certain principles of selection and emphasis. I have written, not a literary biography in the strict sense of the term, but rather an intellectual biography of a literary figure. In probing the inconsistencies and paradoxes, false starts and second guesses that were a vital part of Josephson's life, I have relied extensively on his correspondence and his private journals. Moreover, in dealing with his major writings, I have concentrated more on the ideas, interpretations, and personal implications contained in them than on their intrinsic literary and historical qualities. These sources and emphases best reveal Josephson as he was: a man for whom the tense relationship between politics and literature, journalism and art, bohemian and bourgeois, provided the mainspring of his life and career.

2 GROWING UP IN BROOKLYN

Matthew Josephson's parents, Julius and Sarah, were among the millions of East European Jewish immigrants who arrived in the United States in the late nineteenth century. Julius Josephson's life reads like a Horatio Alger success story. He was born in 1870 in the town of Jassy in Moldavia, the "old kingdom" of Rumania. As a youngster Julius was apprenticed to an engraver, and by his teens he had attained the status of journeyman, traveling about Rumania, Austria, and Germany engraving invitations and wedding announcements for wealthy burghers. One day he was walking down a street in Jassy with another young printer when a Rumanian army officer approached and ordered the two boys off the sidewalk and into the gutter. When they failed to comply quickly enough, the soldier made the mistake of pushing them out of the way, whereupon Julius and his friend gave him a sound thrashing.[1]

Julius fled across the border. Soon thereafter his mother sent him a feather bed and other necessities, and he made his way to Hamburg, the nearest port where he could gain passage to the United States. There he and other Jewish emigrants were questioned, disinfected, labeled, and quarantined. The German authorities eventually allowed Julius to pay thirty-four dollars and board ship for America. But that was not the end of his tribulations. The crossing was not a pleasant one, especially for a six-teen-year-old separated from his home and family and aboard ship for the first time. A smallpox epidemic broke out on Julius's ship, and it was quarantined for several months off the coast near Staten Island. When in 1887 he finally arrived at Castle Garden, then the receiving center, he excitedly dumped his feather bed overboard and walked up Broadway, eager to begin a new life in an America rumored to be "paved with gold." [2]

Julius's printing background enabled him to get a job as a printer's devil earning four dollars a week. Ambitious and determined to make it on his own, he became a master printer within a few years and started a printing firm in the basement of a house at 1774 Pitkin Avenue, the main thoroughfare in Brownsville, the predominantly Jewish section in Brooklyn. Julius soon accumulated enough money to "acquire" a wife. The use of professional matchmakers was then common among the Jewish immigrants, many of whom had difficulty establishing social relationships because of their uprooted condition. With the aid of a matchmaker, whose commission was the profit she made from selling engagement rings and wedding bands, Julius met Sarah Rachel Kasindorf, a Russian Jew recently arrived in New York. On August 23, 1893, she and Julius were married at the Golden Rule Hall in Brooklyn.

Julius and Sarah were well matched, as they shared similar backgrounds and experiences. Sarah had grown up in Rostov, a city in southern Russia along the Don River. The area had traditionally been dominated by a Cossack population of Mongol extraction known as "khazars," who centuries before had adopted the Jewish religion. Sarah's high cheekbones bore witness to the Oriental strain in her family. Her father, Joel Kasindorf, imported wines from across the Black Sea. During the pogrom in Rostov, Sarah had had to hide for several days in one of the many hogsheads used for storing wine in her father's warehouse. Shortly thereafter, in the early 1890s, she and her family left for America.

Julius and Sarah Josephson had six children, only four of whom survived infancy. The first was stillborn, while another, named Moshe, died in infancy from diphtheria, a frequent occurrence in late nineteenth-century urban America. Matthew, the eldest son, born on February 15, 1899, was five years younger than his sister Essie. Two other sons, Archie and Murray, born in 1904 and 1909, completed the Josephson household. By the time of Matthew's birth, Julius was a successful printer, and the family lived in a small frame house above the printing shop. They later moved to a more spacious brick home on Jamaica Avenue near the Queens borough line.

Now that he had a family to support, Julius Josephson was determined to become more than just a successful printer. He revealed that sense of striving and indomitable will that characterized so many East European Jews who arrived in the United States. In the early 1900s, with the opening of the Williamsburg Bridge, Brownsville emerged as one of the most popular areas of settlement among the Jewish immigrants from Russia and eastern Europe. It was then regarded as a pastoral village where "Jews could live as in the old country, without any rush or excessive worries." Those who owned land in Brownsville benefited greatly as the community rapidly expanded. The resourceful Josephson took advantage of the promising commercial atmosphere and made timely investments in local real estate. He later converted his printing business into a small bank in order to take advantage of the inflationary boom.[3]

The Josephson bank grew with the community, and Julius emerged as one of Brownsville's civic leaders. Financial success eventually enabled him to move his entire family of twelve from Rumania to New York. Conscientious and unselfish, Josephson took an active part in local political and charitable organizations. He was a charter member of the Twenty-third District Democratic Committee and once campaigned unsuccessfully for a seat in the state assembly. Julius was a handsome man with pleasant dark eyes, a thick black moustache, and a bald pate covered with only a few strands of black hair. He had a kindly, unassuming personality and was remarkable for his sense of dignity and proud of his repute as a man of uncompromising integrity. Such qualities endeared him to his customers and associates.

In his business and public life, Julius Josephson was popular and frequently in the limelight. Yet toward his family he was shy, almost aloof. Young Matthew enjoyed a loving if somewhat distant relationship with his father, whom he remembered most vividly as a "noble fellow who was gentle and patient with me." The elder Josephson frequently took Essie and Matthew to political gatherings and business banquets. Matthew recalled going with his father to hear a stump speech by Theodore Roosevelt in support of Henry L. Stimson's candidacy for governor in 1910. While he thoroughly enjoyed such occasions, he felt less comfortable at home and later recalled feeling jealousy as well as admiration and respect for his father.[4]

Such jealousy may have been intensified by the strength of Matthew's attachment to his mother. Sarah was a proud, intelligent, and alert woman with a robust personality, and she dominated the Josephson household. At home she worked with compulsive energy, cooking, cleaning, and organizing the family activities. Her life was absorbed in observing the orthodox religious law and in overseeing the upbringing of the children. Matthew once stressed that in contrast to his quiet, gentle father, his "very possessive mother was the figure of authority," forceful yet protective and tender, as many East European Jewish mothers naturally are.[5]

Sarah Josephson's relationship to Matthew was that of a loving despot. She demonstrated both a warm temper and a tender affection. When he disobeyed or rebelled, she would punish him severely. Yet she would soon repent and offer a consoling embrace. Sarah spoiled Matthew, unwisely indicating to him at an early age that he was her "favorite." And he was quick to take advantage of his special situation. One summer at the beach, he and his mother had a sharp quarrel during which she threatened to whip him. He promptly ran away and spent the night under a nearby pier. After searching for hours, Sarah found him and led him back to his bed. Josephson later referred to this and other similar incidents with his mother as "lovers' quarrels." He portrayed her as "stormy, strong, headstrong and quick-thinking." The description is significant, for it captures Matthew's personality as well, both as a child and as a man. He once characterized himself as a "difficult, prickly child," willful and with a mischievous bent. Matthew inherited his mother's fiery, stubborn temperament and coupled it with a rebellious nature that made him the terror of the household.[6]

As a child of the new century, Matthew Josephson was fortunate to grow up during a period that Van Wyck Brooks aptly called "The Confident Years." It was a transitional age when the nation was clamoring to be modern while at the same time clinging desperately to the past. Change was the keynote of the era. By 1914 industry and technology had transformed the pace and tenor of American society. During Josephson's childhood, the automobile began to supplant the horse and carriage. Electric lights were installed along the main thoroughfares. American culture was fast becoming urban instead of rural, and Manhattan was setting the artistic and moral standards of the nation, for better or worse. Seemingly overnight the character of American life was changing. As Henry Adams observed, the "child born in 1900 would, then, be born into a new world which would not be a unity but a multiple."[7]

For much of his childhood, however, Matthew Josephson experienced more unity than multiplicity. His was a happily secure environment—almost too secure. Much like Walt Whitman, who reminisced in *Specimen Days* that the Brooklyn of his youth had been thoroughly rural and pleasant, Josephson remembered with a hint of nostalgia his youthful days in the "quiet and slow-moving world" of pre–World War I Brooklyn. It was a world that seemed "stable and peaceful . . . , still appearing very much as it did in the time of President Grant." The borough was then considered the sleeping quarters of New York, home for those who made their living in Manhattan. Brooklyn had an identity and character all its own. Unlike Manhattan, with its monotonous urban skyline and crowded tenements, it was a curious hybrid of urban, suburban, and rural areas.[8]

Brownsville, too, was a curious amalgam of old and new. It was a rapidly growing village surrounded by Long Island farmland. Its business and main residential districts throbbed with people and activity. A New York newspaper described it in 1899 as a "land of sweatshops and whirring sewing machines, of strange Russian baths, of innumerable dirty and tiny shops . . . , of anarchists, of Jew dancing schools and of a peasant market." Yet the open countryside was within walking distance. Two- and three-story houses, sturdily constructed, spacious and well kept, lined the streets. Although downtown Manhattan was only a few miles away, Brownsville seemed far removed from its noise and bustle. "When I was a child," Alfred Kazin remembered about Brownsville, "I thought we lived at the end of the world."[9]

Josephson recalled the Brownsville of his youth as a homogeneous, closely knit, dynamic community, a seemingly ideal environment in which to spend one's childhood. Not far from his home, in the direction of Canarsie, were neatly cultivated truck gardens and open fields where cattle, goats, and horses grazed. As a youngster, Matthew loved watching the burly Irish firemen working at the station next door to his house. On many occasions, unbeknownst to his mother, the firemen would take him for a ride atop their bright red fire wagon pulled by a team of massive, gray-white horses. He also relished walking with his father to the nearby beer garden at Trommer's Brewery on Bushwick Avenue, where he would drink lemonade and listen to a small brass band playing outdoors under the electrically illuminated trees. Occasionally on Saturdays his mother, especially proud of her eldest son, would dress him in new clothes she had sewn, and his father would lead Matthew through the Brooklyn Museum.

The Josephsons spent a great deal of time together. At the end of the school year, the family, except for Julius, would move from the stifling heat of Brooklyn to a rented Long Island beach cottage for the summer. Like most boys, Matthew loved the outdoors, and he lived for the summer months. Tall and thin, with raven black hair, a long face, and a prominent nose, he enjoyed a robust outdoor life. During the summer at the beach, when he was not swimming, he usually played in sandlot baseball games with tough Irish boys who lived nearby. He developed into a sinewy, pugnacious character, with the reputation to match. It was while playing with the Irish youngsters that he acquired the nickname "Matty."

In his neighborhood in Brooklyn, Matty Josephson engaged in most of the shenanigans typical of active young boys. Already a dominant personality, he emerged as the leader among his group of street friends. One day another boy induced the group to steal thirty cents' worth of candy from a neighborhood store. Matty felt sick afterward, remembering vividly the disappointed look upon the elderly storeowner's face as they ran away. He later expelled from the group the boy who had precipitated the incident. Such a gesture of conscience was not unusual for him. He had read of Frank Merriwell's exploits and identified with that character's crusading spirit. Once when Matty's best friend was accosted by an older, larger boy, he entered the fray, only to be badly mauled himself, receiving a broken nose for his efforts. His action was symbolic, however, for it dramatized the intense loyalty he felt for his friends—and his propensity for fighting—then and later.

Matty early revealed a shrewd sense of business acumen that also would remain with him throughout his life. When he was about thirteen, a local store selling candy near Public School 84 gave away coupons for every penny's worth of candy bought. The coupons were redeemable for various prizes, the most coveted of which was a magic lantern device which, like a stereopticon, projected a three-dimensional image on a screen. Young Josephson wanted that lantern. To acquire it, he convinced his eight-year-old brother Archie and his friends to turn over their coupons to him, so that they could obtain the toy. Matty soon amassed the required number of coupons and redeemed the lantern, which he then set up in the basement of his house. When Archie's friends turned out for the first performance, they were surprised to discover that Matty was at the door charging them admission.

Most of the testimony about Josephson as a child emphasizes his thoughtful, imaginative nature and inclinations. His family considered him a "dreamy" boy, given to great enthusiasms and possessed of a keen intellect. His childhood tastes ran toward artistic activities, which accommodated his self-absorption. His sister Essie recounted that at the age of about six, Matthew excitedly took up painting, leading the family to believe he was going to become an artist. Eventually, however, his interests changed, and he developed a passion for reading and a marked disposition for revery. From the outset literature filled him with an almost sensuous delight. Books fed his imagination and gave shape to his dreams. He read omnivorously and at high speed. At age ten he frequently stayed up all night reading Dickens. Three years later he had progressed beyond Keats, Tennyson, and Browning to the more recent and controversial works of Wilde and Dostoevski. The neighborhood's small branch library became his second home, and his playmates often had to drag him out of the building to fill out their baseball team.

For the most part, however, Josephson's pleasures as a teenager were more and more intensely solitary. As much as he enjoyed the companionship of his playmates and however heartily he was welcomed to their games, he began to feel consciously alienated from them, primarily because of the differing interests he had developed. As an aspiring poet, he increasingly held himself aloof from his friends. "I could at will," he remembered, "shut off the school, my classmates, in short the everyday world around me that seemed devoid of all beauty and romance." At home Matty occasionally read poetry aloud to his mother, and Sarah thoroughly enjoyed and encouraged such pursuits. Like many Old World orthodox Jews, she prized scholarship not as a "pure" activity but as a tool for a career in religion or business. Yet Matty would soon develop other career plans.[10]

Josephson's childhood as the son of East European Jewish immigrants was in some respects an exceptional one. Owing to his father's business success and popularity, Matty and his family never underwent the difficult struggle through years of poverty and anti-Semitic persecution so poignantly described by Alfred Kazin, Irving Howe, and other writers. Josephson once told Kazin that his parents were "the most compleat bourgeois you ever saw. Even when they had good money, they stayed very small middle class, living in a street that became a slum of Brownsville, until they could afford ten times the rent (when I was thirteen) and moved into our own detached brick house in the 'Arlington Avenue-Bushwick section.' And we always had Polish housemaids." Nor did Matthew inherit many of the East European Jewish cultural traditions or religious values. In fact, he consciously rejected them. A fervently pious woman, Sarah supervised her son's religious training, having him tutored at home in the orthodox Jewish tradition. According to Matthew, his mother feared and detested the Gentiles and tried to impress upon him his "Jewishness." But he would have none of it. Through his wide reading he absorbed all sorts of skeptical ideas which, to his delight, constantly challenged the pious dogmas of his family religion. Sarah's piety thus irritated rather than converted him. He even refused to answer his mother in Yiddish, which she frequently spoke to the children to "let them know they were Jews." Years later, Josephson admitted in his journal that he had failed to mention such perturbing episodes when he published his memoirs. He privately confessed that as a child he envied the Gentiles and desired to emulate them, not the Jewish world of his parents.[11]

As Matthew reached adolescence, he developed an independent frame of mind, rebelling against his mother and her religion as he eventually would rebel against nearly every other entrenched tradition or mode of thought he confronted. At age thirteen, shortly after his bar mitzvah, Matthew renounced religion. Although his action sorely disturbed his mother, there was little she could do. He substituted for religion an aesthetic justification of life; to create a work of art, to live a life of art, this alone seemed meaningful to him. By age fourteen Josephson had developed a consuming passion to be a writer. And like most young writers, he cultivated a sensitive ego and an antinomian opposition to restrictions on his artistic or personal freedom. Bible study by rote was irksome and boring to him. While at Boys High, the old public high school in Brooklyn, his devotion to literature increased, causing him to ignore the school's more popular activities such as the debating society or athletics and to concentrate instead on his own reading program and his own writing. As he later wrote: "I had numerous friends, and yet felt much alone. I was learning things by myself; neither my teachers nor my parents could be of help to me, I believed."[12]

Matthew learned a great deal about literature and life from one of the tellers working at his father's bank. Since many of the customers spoke little if any English, there were always several foreign tellers, usually young men recently arrived from Russia. Many of them were well versed in European literature, and Matthew spent fascinated hours listening to their literary stories and tales of personal adventure. One of these foreign tellers was Elias Ginzberg, later to become an accomplished Yiddish playwright, who had been forced to flee Russia because of his Socialist leanings and his Judaism. Ginzberg had a particularly strong influence upon the impressionable Josephson and undoubtedly instilled some of his revolutionary ardor into his young protégé.

Ginzberg remembered one of his first encounters with Matty Josephson, then age fourteen. One day after school Matty walked into the bank and found Ginzberg reading a Yiddish newspaper. "Why don't you get Americanized?" young Josephson asked condescendingly. "Why don't you read an American newspaper?" Ginzberg then asked what he meant by "Americanization." Josephson replied, "Well, it means to know English better, to get to know America and its ways better and to get a better education."

The precocious inquisitor next wanted to know why Ginzberg was so interested in the Jews. When he answered that since he was a Jew, it was only natural to be interested in his cultural group, Josephson retorted: "I'm a Jew, too, but I'm interested in America first and foremost."

Ginzberg then proceeded to take some of the wind out of his questioner's sails. He told Matty that he was ignorant and foolish, that he knew nothing about the treatment of the Jews in Eastern Europe. "If you knew," he sharply concluded, "perhaps your attitude would change." [13]

Matthew recognized the truth in the charge, and from that point on, he became Ginzberg's faithful pupil, stopping to talk almost every day after school and to learn about the plight of the Jews, the Russian people, Russian literature, and the Russian revolutionary movement. With his family Matthew exhibited a penchant for argument, but in the presence of Elias Ginzberg, he tended to be quiet and attentive, feeling something akin to adoration. From his Russian tutor Josephson developed an appreciation for the historical struggle of Judaism, even though he would always reject its spiritual message and would raise his own children as agnostics. He also learned about the lives and literary accomplishments of Dostoevski, Tolstoy, Chekhov, and others. And the more he learned about writers and writing, the more he wanted to know.

At Boys High Josephson met other students who were equally interested in literature. On opening day of his junior year, in the fall of 1914, as Europe was enveloped in war, he brought Oscar Wilde's *Secret of Dorian Gray* to class and read it behind his lesson books. After school the boy who had been sitting beside him rushed up, grabbed the book and tossed it to the floor, demanding: "What do *you* know about Oscar Wilde? Have you ever read 'The Ballad of Reading Gaol'? I know more than you do!" The agitated boy then proceeded to recite a number of Wilde's poems. But before he could finish, Josephson responded characteristically to what he considered a personal and intellectual assault. He slapped his challenger. Soon the two young aesthetes were engaged in a rather comic wrestling match, rolling around the floor of the classroom, bumping into desks and chairs, oblivious to the other children cheering them on. The teacher quickly ended the struggle, however, and the two combatants stood up and brushed themselves off. The stranger extended his hand, introduced himself as Percy Horace Winner, and invited Josephson to his home for tea and cakes. Thus started a relationship that had a great impact on Matty Josephson. With his association with Percy Winner, his childhood ended and his young manhood began.

Josephson encountered in Percy Winner his first thoroughgoing aesthete. Percy was quite the literary romantic, modeling himself after Poe. A short, stocky boy with a square forehead, a great mop of long black hair, and long sideburns, he dressed in a style of what might be termed Edwardian decadence. He wore a coat with a velvet collar and a Windsor tie and even sported a cane. Until meeting Winner, Matty had been a literary idealist. Life presented itself to him as full of possibilities for pleasure, enchantments, or noble actions that he read about. Now all was changed.[14]

Winner introduced Josephson to thoughts he had never before considered, ideas about the New Freedom, sex, self-expression, and the "hypocrisy" of the bourgeoisie. The precocious Winner's impassioned talk of fleshpots and secret sins and secret sorrows awakened him from his "tepid" dreams. His new friend's life seemed to be a perpetual, ever-changing drama. One day his great theme would be the virtue of suicide, the next it would be marriage without benefit of clergy. Percy's wild talk and violent moods kept Matthew in a constant state of bewilderment. "But they brought a new excitement to my formerly placid life," Josephson remembered, "for I was busily absorbing all sorts of notions, good and bad, which I had to sift very carefully later on." As firmly as Matthew was given to hope, Percy Winner was wedded to melancholy.[15]

Winner had histrionic gifts of a high order. He told Matty after having tea one day that he was a "neuropath" suffering from a permanent case of melancholia. His condition was complicated by insomnia that resulted from what he termed his "precocious" sexual development. After all, as he pointed out, he had been shaving since the age of twelve. Percy confided to Josephson that his Uncle Jack had taken him downtown to sample the services of "paid harlots" in the hope of relieving his insomnia. But such activity only produced further depression, and he assured Matty that suicide was a definite possibility. Josephson, who had known neither such great torments nor such satiety, found Winner captivating. Here was a boy no older than himself who seemed so mature, so experienced. Not only was Winner well versed in modern literature, he was also laden with sin and self-revulsion and suffered from a number of neurotic maladies deemed essential to the life of the true aesthete. "Never had I known anyone who was given to such towering passions, or such mercurial changes of mood," Josephson remembered, "or with the capacity to vocalize his emotion." Matty enjoyed "sharing his mental storms and 'tragic' moods and tried to give him help and counsel." Josephson initially argued for joy and optimism, but Winner easily brushed aside his sanguine reasoning and soon converted his inexperienced friend to his own gloomy outlook. Matty had never "realized before how pleasant it could be to bathe in melancholy thoughts, to sound the notes of despair instead of good cheer." [16]

As close friends the two young aesthetes did more than reinforce each other's literary orientation. Under Winner's tutelage Matthew sampled his first taste of cheap liquor. In 1915 Percy also introduced him to Freud's *Interpretation of Dreams*, which had just been published in English and was creating quite a controversy in the United States. Percy and Matty then invited two girls to relate to them their dreams, which they would interpret to their advantage. Their plan worked well. Winner fell madly in love with Helen Rosenberg, the daughter of the neighborhood doctor who had delivered Matthew. The Byronic Winner decided that his relationship with Helen would be enhanced immeasurably if he had a rival for her hand. So he suggested to Matty that he, too, fall in love with Helen. Josephson begrudgingly consented. "I was troubled," he recalled, "I wanted to be romantic and fall in love, but she had a squint. How could I get romantic?" After his date with Helen, he returned home only to be confronted by Percy wielding a knife. But the blade was not intended for Matty. Winner was going to kill himself if Helen had transferred her affections to his friend. Josephson assured him that such was not the case, and Percy and Helen were married a few years later. [17]

Josephson's association with Percy Winner provides insight into his attitudes and emotions during adolescence. As he later maintained, his head was "filled with bad poetry and gloomy Russian novels, such as Dostoevski's, whose sickly creatures we were probably trying to impersonate—while our parents knew nothing or could make nothing of all this." Matthew lived in a world of books and ideas, and he tended to model his life after what he read. As a result his values and attitudes were constantly changing, much to the chagrin and consternation of his parents. This was not an uncommon characteristic among his literary generation. Josephson was a member of a younger generation in the United States determined to go its own way, to set its own ideals and standards, but uncertain about what its ideals and standards were. Malcolm Cowley, later one of Josephson's closest friends, remembered that he and his high school friends in Pittsburgh were "disillusioned and weary." They loved change for its own sake, and they acquired and discarded enthusiasms with such rapidity that they soon lost sight of what they were rebelling against. They found themselves going through the motions of what Cowley called the "theory of convulsions." If someone began reading Wilde because everyone else was reading Tennyson, then he would have to change again, once everyone started reading Wilde. The goal was to be different, even at the cost of consistency. Cowley recognized that his youthful generation was not only derivative in its literary tastes, but also "spectatorial" in its attitude toward life. Matty also lived in a special world of art, a world that would shape his thinking for the next decade.[18]

During his high school years, Josephson began to display a certain imperious air, a sense of intellectual superiority and coolness that other people, then and later, took as a sign of haughty conceit. His arrogance probably resulted from the efforts of a literary boy to find status and security in his intellectual prowess. The more he read—and he read constantly—the more intellectual self-confidence he acquired. Matty prided himself on his discernment as a literary critic, and he developed a scathing invective style that made him the terror of his peers. When as a senior he served on the editorial board of the high school magazine, he demonstrated a devastating candor in discussing the merits or demerits of literary submissions. Aaron Copland, a classmate of Matty at the time, submitted a poem to the magazine for consideration. Speaking for the editors, Josephson treated the poem with such contempt, he later claimed, that Copland then decided to concentrate his energies on music. Josephson aptly described himself during this period as the "literary dictator" of the school.[19]

Josephson's intellectual precocity, literary bent, and youthful iconoclasm affected his behavior at home as well as at school. He was not one to keep his discontents to himself. He openly criticized his parents for being preoccupied with material concerns. Once, when his mother invited to supper her five brothers, all salesmen or small businessmen, Matthew insolently baited them, declaring himself a "socialist." On several occasions he was so brash as to proclaim at the dinner table that the conversation bored him. He then would retire to the security of his room and books, often reciting to himself poems or passages that he had memorized. Matthew had inherited his mother's stubborn streak and power of conviction, but he had applied such traits to the development of an artistic attitude that was anathema to the world view and value system of his parents.

Josephson's experience working as a teller at his father's bank during the summer after his junior year only helped to widen the breach between parents and child. While the rest of the family went to the beach as usual, Matthew and his father stayed in Brooklyn to work. He continued to enjoy his conversations with Ginzberg and the other tellers, but he did not like working in his father's bank. He detested his job "repeating the same gestures all day long in my cage. At the end of the day I would lie down on the floor of my room, feeling all washed up, unable to think or read anything and would sometimes weep with vexation." One evening, he later related, "I came back to our house, silent and musty at my mother's absence, lay down on the floor of my room and wept for hours." His father discovered him in such a state and, while sadly shaking his head, told Matthew he could quit his job and rejoin the family at the beach. [20]

Josephson's disheartening experience at his father's bank illustrates the continuing split between parents and child. Matthew's interest in literature and his association with romantic figures such as Elias Ginzberg and Percy Winner had cultivated in him a fervent desire to escape what he considered to be his mundane Brooklyn environment. He wanted to see the world, to live out his perception of the exciting life of the artist. The values of his parents, however, were in sharp contrast to their eldest son's artistic visions. Julius and Sarah wanted Matthew to pursue a more responsible career, to follow his father as head of the family bank. Since such a career was abhorrent to Matthew, parents and child were at an impasse; neither would compromise. Matthew began to hate his life in Brooklyn, for to him it had become a life dominated by "painful growth, self doubt and wild hope, and all the commonplace frictions of everyday life with my well-intentioned family." In his imagination he wished himself "as far away as possible from the Brooklyn scene." [21]

After much pleading Matthew convinced his parents not only that they should send him to Columbia University in Manhattan but also that they should allow him to live on campus instead of commuting from home. For young Josephson, this decision must have seemed like a dream come true. Living on his own he would be able to read and write whatever and whenever he wanted, unhampered by the strictures of his parents. Moreover, he would finally be able to balance his teenage bookishness with a firsthand knowledge of the "real" world. He had rebelled against his parents and had rejected the opportunity for a relatively safe and respectable career as a banker. His doing so indicates the rebelliousness of his spirit. It was an emotional stage through which he passed early in life and which set the course for his career. The young man of seventeen, full of ambition and restless energy, would leave behind his family, his religion, and the "quiet and slow-moving" world of Brooklyn, hoping to discover in Manhattan both himself and the world about him.

By rejecting the traditional transmitters of cultural continuity, particularly his family and his religion, however, Josephson became a creature separated from his past, uprooted, and dependent upon his contemporaries and his literary interests for support and sustenance. As he left Brooklyn, he was faced with the problem of rediscovering a sense of belonging and of coping with a strange new urban-industrial environment. It was a problem he would eventually solve, but only after years of false starts, punctured illusions, and internal struggles.

3 COLUMBIA AND GREENWICH VILLAGE

In the fall of 1916, when Matthew Josephson entered Columbia, the Morningside campus situated between the Hudson River and Harlem was visually unpretentious. A student remarked at the time that Columbia "makes no effort to seduce the eye . . . outwardly its ugliness is sententious, within it is brisk and businesslike." The university's lackluster physical appearance was deceiving; at its core the institution was a lively center of American intellectual life. The faculty included a host of stimulating, innovative professors, particularly in the social sciences. John Dewey, James Harvey Robinson, Franz Boas, J. McKeen Cattell, and Charles Beard provided a sharp contrast to the traditional academic conservatism exemplified by Columbia's domineering president, Nicholas Murray Butler. Their new approaches to the social sciences constituted a "revolt against formalism." They promoted an intellectual attitude that was freely experimental, openly skeptical of inherited values, and determined to subordinate the past to the exigencies of the present.[1]

Students at Columbia found such an intellectual atmosphere exhilarating; a spirit of experiment and adventure pervaded the campus. "At Columbia," Henry May has written, "students could encounter several kinds of radicalism, from the pragmatic innovations of Dewey and Beard to the elegant, antimoralist aestheticism of Joel Spingarn and others."

Max Eastman, who attended the graduate school, remembered that "ideas were sprouting up through the bricks at Columbia." Another student during the period was the brilliant, enigmatic Randolph Bourne. He wrote a friend in 1913 that he had encountered a number of professors whose "philosophy and science are not mere games, but real aids in understanding the world and living a worthy part of it."[2]

One such inspiring professor was Charles Austin Beard. In the years immediately preceding American intervention in the war, Beard was the most popular professor at Columbia. John Erskine, then a leading member of the English department, later maintained that there was "no one at Columbia in the second decade of this century who could rival Beard as an orator." During his freshman year Josephson was unable to enroll in Beard's American history course, but he frequently attended the lectures, often having to sit in the aisle. "As a lecturer," he recalled, "Beard was nothing less than a spellbinder. . . . In one moment he would be full of joy and pride, in the next he would be thundering with wrath, perhaps moved by some episode of chicanery or skullduggery, and using such violent invectives that some of his hearers would be frightened." Beard personified the rebellious, experimental intellectual mood at Columbia, and his enthusiasm was infectious. Irwin Edman, a student at Columbia with Josephson and later a noted philosopher, described in his memoirs the antiformalist atmosphere on campus, observing how much the "undergraduates enjoyed the sallies, the freshness, the irreverence." He remarked that many students, confronted with such an array of compelling teachers in the humanities and the social sciences, were torn between. "lyricism and Liberalism."[3]

For Josephson there was no such choice to make; he immersed himself in literary study. And he could not have picked a more stimulating time to do so. Scholars have characterized the period between 1912 and 1918 as the "joyous season," the "confident years," or the "little renaissance" in American literature. Such phrases capture the buoyant, energetic mood of the period. To that time, nineteenth-century Victorian gentility retained a strong hold over the arts in America. Literary life was "restrained, conventional, and excessively polite."[4]

By the end of the first decade of the new century, however, a rebellious spirit of adventure and experiment appeared in the arts. Its most common article of faith was the need for spontaneous, individual expression in "modern" terms. To many younger writers, Victorian literature seemed too elegant, subtle, and ornamental. "We had our own lives to live,"

Floyd Dell remembered, "—and all those classical utterances of the nineteenth-century literature had no relation to our lives." In 1912 the revolution in the arts began in earnest. In that year Edna St. Vincent Millay's "Renascence" appeared in *The Lyric Year*, and Harriet Monroe founded *Poetry* magazine. To be "modern," to attack bad art and bourgeois morality, was the unifying goal of the insurgent writers. The past was casually discarded; a new age was at hand.[5]

Within a few years the "little renaissance" was flourishing. Malcolm Cowley has written that the dominant theme of the period was one of "bustle and hopefulness. . . . Everywhere new institutions were being founded—magazines, clubs, little theatres, art or free-love or single-tax colonies, experimental schools, picture galleries. Everywhere was a sense of secret comradeship and immense potentialities for change." By 1916, when Josephson entered Columbia, the artistic rebellion against tradition, respectability, and middle-class values was in full swing. "Everyone was cooking up some sort of revolution," recalled James Oppenheim, poet-editor of *Seven Arts*, "socialism, sex, poetry, conversation, dawn-greeting—anything so long as it was taboo in the Middle West."[6]

Gradually, two almost mutually exclusive groups developed among the artistic rebels. One gathered around the *Seven Arts* and the *Masses*, while the other preferred Harriet Monroe's *Poetry* and Margaret Anderson's *Little Review*. The *Seven Arts* faction—Van Wyck Brooks, Randolph Bourne, Waldo Frank, James Oppenheim, Paul Rosenfeld, and Sherwood Anderson—believed that art must be used to help reform man and society. Similarly, the leaders of the *Masses* believed that politics was directly related to culture. They were sworn foes of monopoly capitalism. Max Eastman, Floyd Dell, and John Reed, however, went further than the cultural nationalists among the *Seven Arts* crowd. They wanted not reform but revolution.

At the other extreme of the artistic "renaissance" were the writers loosely grouped about the little literary magazines. Unlike Brooks, Eastman, and the other socially oriented rebels, these writers, including Amy Lowell, Marianne Moore, Wallace Stevens, and others, were not explicitly interested in the causes of liberal reform or socialist revolution. They were individualists, each engaged in artistic experiment and held loosely together by a common bond of aesthetic and moral values. The integrity of the self, not the salvation of society, was their utmost concern. Like their counterparts at the *Seven Arts* and the *Masses*, they revolted against the genteel tradition, but their revolt centered on developing experimental artistic forms and techniques. They preferred searching for the mot juste to writing uplifting editorials or staging radical demonstrations. Yet despite the differing artistic perspectives of the two groups, they shared a "will to see things afresh and a need for new ideas and genres."[7]

It was not long before Matthew Josephson, college freshman, acquainted himself with the new insurgent trends in literature. Joseph Freeman, a schoolmate of Josephson's both at Boys High and Columbia, recorded in his memoirs their days as underclassmen. He described Matty as one of the "skeptical minds questioning everything." The rebellious Josephson was attracted to those ideas and activities that went against tradition, that were new and controversial, that stressed individual creativity. In the fall of 1916 he discovered Amy Lowell and Imagism. Lowell, the rotund, blue-blooded spinster from Boston who smoked cigars and revered John Keats, rejected the traditional metrical forms and rhyming schemes as artificial. Her goal, she once wrote, was to "create new rhythms—as the expression of new moods—and not to copy old rhythms, which merely echo old moods. We do not insist upon 'free verse' as the only method of writing poetry. We fight for it as a principle of liberty."[8]

Such an open-ended approach to poetry fitted perfectly Josephson's own literary predilections. After attending a guest lecture by Lowell at Columbia, he emerged as one of her ardent supporters and was soon sending her his poems for critical appraisal. In his letters to her Josephson provided an illuminating glimpse of his personality and precious style at age eighteen. In February 1917 he wrote:

> I am emboldened to send you some of my work for perusal, if your time allows. It is because I have almost as high regard for your critical acumen as for your creative accomplishments, that I ask for your opinion. . . . I give you my assurance that I am a true lover of the art of poetry. . . . Peradventure, your criticism may be adverse; but remember, I am young and have great faith in myself.

Josephson's youthful ardor left a marked impression upon Lowell. She replied that as a rule, "I refuse to read manuscripts, but your interest in my lectures was so sincere that I shall be delighted to give an exception in your case."[9]

Several months later Lowell wrote a letter to Josephson in which she described some of his verses as having a "fine sense of colour and rhythm and a tenderness and feeling." She commented that while he had not yet found his own "particular style," he did display a "very distinct feeling for poetry and should go on and do better things." While one cannot know with certainty how Lowell actually felt about Matthew's poetry, the tactful nature of her remarks suggests that she may have been more impressed by his energy and enthusiasm than by his verses themselves. Josephson's failure to develop his own style would continue to plague his poetic efforts. He was so preoccupied with being modern, with experimenting with new forms and techniques, that he often lost sight of his subject matter or his inspiration. As a result much of his poetry was derivative and mannered, stimulated by his reading of someone else's work rather than by his own ideas.[10]

As a student at Columbia Josephson championed the New Poetry approach of Lowell and the Imagists. This set him apart from the distinguished but generally conservative English department. While most of the other English majors were writing sonnets about sunsets and roses, Josephson was reading Pound and Eliot. The English faculty at Columbia included a bevy of fledgling writers such as John Erskine, Carl Van Doren, Hatcher Hughes, and Clayton Hamilton. It also housed a number of older, more established professors such as George Woodberry and Brander Matthews, neither of whom could abide the other. Matthews, who held the chair in dramatic literature, was renowned for his artistic persona. He wore the Legion of Honor ribbon, was wealthy, traveled, meticulous, and snobbish, proud of his friendships with Stevenson, Kipling, Twain, and Howells. Urbane, full of prejudice, and frequently ill-tempered, he wore black capes and carried a cane, sported a reddish brown beard, silver-trimmed pince-nez, and always seemed to have a cigarette dangling from his lips. His American literature course was essentially a barrage of anecdotes so carefully timed that it was rumored the students could set their watches to them. Matthews had a passion for French culture, and to the students, he had the air of London clubs and Paris salons. Like his carriage and attire, his critical views were considered obsolete by Josephson and other young Turks among the majors. Yet Josephson found upon visiting Matthews in his home that the crusty professor was a delightful host, full of reminiscences, and thoroughly engaging in such informal settings. Erskine and Woodberry, like Matthews, were conservative in their approach to literature and were skeptical of innovation.

Soon after his arrival at Columbia Josephson had his first confrontation with Erskine, then the department chairman. At a meeting of the Boar's Head, the college's literary society, a student recited a poem about repressed sexual desire. When the young poet finished, Erskine launched into a tirade defending the genteel tradition and denouncing modern approaches to literature. Never one to ignore the casting down of a gauntlet, Matthew stood up and defended the student poet, stressing that "in light of Freud's teachings, we moderns could no longer write of love or sex in the terms of Elizabeth Barrett Browning." Such audacity from a mere freshman shocked Erskine, and he went into a rage, shouting that Freud was a charlatan out to corrupt the minds of the young.[11]

Although Josephson failed to win his first confrontation with Erskine, he did meet Kenneth Burke, the student whose reading had started the uproar. Burke, the future literary critic and respected theoretician of language, had transferred to Columbia from Ohio State, where he had studied under Lewis Lewisohn. Born and raised in Pittsburgh, he, like Josephson, had stood fast against parental pressure to forsake the life of the artist and start a career in banking instead. As the two defeated but undaunted literary rebels started out of the meeting hall, Josephson turned to Burke and suggested that instead of using the door, they go out the window as a gesture of defiance. Their doing so highlights the intensity with which they approached literature, even as undergraduates. Josephson then offered to buy his new friend an ice cream soda at the drugstore on the corner of Broadway and 116th. The more experienced Burke sardonically replied: "Ice cream soda! No, not ice cream soda; but I'll have a beer with you."[12]

Josephson and Burke quickly developed a close friendship that would last the rest of their lives. Years later Burke maintained that the "whole drift or tenor of my life was radically influenced by the opportunity to associate closely with Matty during the formative years of our faringforth." Josephson recalled that Kenneth was a "small, wiry young fellow with a great mop of black hair, large blue-grey eyes framed in spectacles, having what he himself described as a physiognomy of an interesting ugliness." Burke appraised Josephson shrewdly and early. After meeting Matty he candidly described his new comrade in a revealing letter to his hometown friend Malcolm Cowley, then at Harvard:

> I have met a most admirable jew here, who is anything but a jew religiously, but claims to be very proud of his nationality. . . . He is quite well read, and what delights me most of all, seems honestly attached to some of the old writers. He knows neither French nor German as well as I do, makes me howl with laughter when he dives, gets quite sore when I laugh at him, and has almost as stupid an expression as you, all of which endears him to me.

The philosophical Burke also noted that Matty had the habit of "cutting me off the midst of a cerebralization to comment on some girl's legs, and becomes meek and humble when I denounce him for it." But Burke admitted that as for his "commenting on girls' legs, you know I like that sort of thing." [13]

Josephson's association with Burke reinforced his own youthful and intellectual pretensions. Both were childish in their enthusiasm and petulant in their dislikes. Both of them had quick wits. And both were determined to become great writers. "When I first knew Matty," Burke remembered in 1979, "we were quite vigorously involved in a constant muddle of intimacy and scrappiness." Burke, an extremely witty and complex intellectual personality, abstract and analytical in his approach to literature, was the first person other than Elias Ginzberg capable enough to challenge Josephson's literary opinions, to threaten his precocious egoism, and to expand his intellectual horizons. John Brooks Wheelwright later perceptively observed that Burke "toughened Josephson. Josephson welcomed it as a theologian might welcome the onslaughts of a heretic whose animosity to his ideas made them stand out in clarity." Kenneth and Matty were constant companions, and they lived for literature. They were, as Josephson remembered, "adolescent egotists, now exalted by feelings of snobbish pride, now cast down by self-doubt, and pining to see our verses in print." Callow, presumptuous, given to posing, they were naive young litterateurs, full of fanciful dreams and longings and determined to achieve artistic success. In 1917 Josephson confessed to Burke that he was "doomed to write poetry or nothing else,—to slave for style and grandeur of expression. It saddens me to read dazzling poets, such as Hofmannsthal or Swinburne." His sadness resulted from his feeling that he could never be so brilliant in verse as those he read and studied. But he did not concede defeat. He affirmed that "by dint of sheer effort and arduous study . . . I shall conquer mediocrity. Thru mere contact with the great poets that I gather around me and thru rubbing against their divine poetry—grains of gold shall cling to me and I too shall gleam." What he lacked in talent Josephson was determined to compensate for with hard work and dedication. He also had no reticence about communicating with the most prominent artists of the time. [14]

Josephson revealed his youthful superciliousness in a letter to Theodore Dreiser in June 1917. After reading *The Financier* he decided to express his opinion of the book to the author. Dreiser must have been taken aback at what the college freshman had to say. Josephson began: "I have just completed reading the eight hundred pages of your book 'The Financier.' I look upon it all a little ruefully and feel slightly hostile towards you. Who would have thought that I should wade through it all?" He conceded that the novel was "a rather fair history of several decades, a rather efficient commercial or economic textbook. . . . In some ways it may be regarded as a novel." Like many fastidious critics then and since, Josephson attacked Dreiser's clumsy workmanship. "I was interested in noting," he commented, "how many rules of art were broken, how many errors of technique and crudities were committed. Their number are legion." After citing Dreiser's stylistic errors, Matthew finally began to point out the book's praiseworthy features, commending the author for treating sex "honestly and fearlessly," for displaying through his characters a "grandeur of vision," and for in general exhibiting an "unpuritanical, large-visioned and healthy" spirit. In concluding, he declared:

> You are grasping at some of the fundamental facts of American life. Thus I regard your work as the most important prose fiction being written here today. . . . I must seem the "insolent youth" to write this critically of you. And yet my conception of you leads me to believe that you will brook it. Am I right?

Dreiser never responded. But that did not deter Josephson. He would continue to communicate his feelings directly to those who inspired them. How else could he come into contact with the great writers?[15]

In 1917 John Dos Passos, then a senior at Harvard, confided to a friend that Columbia had "the merit of having no 'college life.'" Josephson must have agreed with such an assessment, for he and Burke increasingly isolated themselves from the mainstream of student activity and focused their attention on writing. Miles Colean, a classmate of Josephson, recalled his preoccupation with literature:

> I met Matty when I came to Columbia College as a sophomore and found him in the same English class. I considered him more advanced than I, particularly in his knowledge of contemporary poetry. One of his favorite avocations was engaging in sonnet writing contests, in which he excelled.

Colean also remembered that Josephson was "familiar to the circle around Edna Millay." Josephson and Burke had met Millay and her friends in Greenwich Village, a place they increasingly frequented. More and more they preferred the stimulating cultural environment in the Village to the dormitory life at Columbia.[16]

Greenwich Village in 1917 was one of the main centers of the revolution taking place in the arts. It was a bohemian's paradise. Impecunious but talented individuals eager to express themselves and to found new causes, from free love to socialism, flocked to the area around Washington Square. There was a warm, colorful atmosphere to Village life; it retained a small-town flavor. Floyd Dell pictured it as a mass of "little twisted streets that crossed and recrossed each other and never seemed to get anywhere." The Italian population was somewhat suspicious but friendly. Housing was cheap, and there were a number of good, inexpensive restaurants such as the Pepper Pot, the Mad-Hatter, Polly's, and Mother Bertolotti's. There were also art galleries, bookstores, and quaint shops of all kinds. Men could be seen walking around in smocks and sandals, while the New Women wore brightly colored outfits, bobbed hair, and long earrings.[17]

The varied and intense cultural activity in the Village strongly appealed to Josephson. The community not only served his intellectual interests; it also provided a sense of place, of belonging, to a young man detached from home and family. Although he had grown up less than ten miles from Washington Square, he first saw the Village early in 1917, when Burke took him to visit James and Susan Light, two of his friends from Pittsburgh, who lived at 86 Greenwich Avenue. Their rambling seven-room apartment was in the building in which Georges Clemenceau, the French premier, had once lived after fleeing France during the Paris Commune. Hence the house was referred to by Villagers as Clemenceau Cottage. The Lights acted in and directed plays with George Cram Cook and the Provincetown Players. Since their apartment was much larger than their needs, they rented out three or four rooms to friends. Djuna Barnes, the tall, striking poet, lived in one room. Berenice Abbott, later the renowned photographer, rented another. Other artists frequently visited Maison Clemenceau. Josephson recollected seeing Dorothy Day, then a newspaper reporter and ardent feminist who lived in an apartment below the Lights; Peggy Johns, the recently divorced wife of poet Orrick Johns, who lived nearby; Floyd Dell, coeditor of the *Masses*; and Eugene O'Neill, "a shy and silent man with a tense, dark face, who became very taciturn when he had been drinking." The articulate, cosmopolitan group that frequented Clemenceau Cottage impressed Josephson as "being not only brilliant in conversation . . . but also immensely 'sophisticated.'" They were contemptuous of anything that smacked of bourgeois conventions or Victorian gentility. In art, they espoused realism, not sentimentalism. The impressionable Josephson soon adopted this credo as his own. He emphasized to Burke in 1917 that they must "never be *sentimental*, must shrink from all manifestations of sentimentality." [18]

Columbia, Greenwich Village, and Josephson's new circle of friends provided him with continuous excitement and inspiration. During 1917, however, the prospect of American intervention in the Great War increasingly threatened to interrupt his education. At Columbia early in 1917 faculty members and students openly debated intervention. Many professors, including Henry W. L. Dana, Leon Fraser, and Carlton Hayes, signed petitions supporting the maintenance of strict neutrality. Randolph Bourne spoke eloquently against intervention, but with little success. By early February 1917, two months before war was declared, it appeared that most students supported intervention. The student newspaper, describing a mass rally on campus, reported that "pacifists have ceased their agitation and the feeling was expressed in no uncertain terms . . . that individually, every student was ready to protect the rights of the country." [19]

Even after the United States declared war in April, however, there were several Columbia students opposed to intervention. To Josephson and Burke the war seemed irrational. They were disturbed at the prospect of desecrating a German culture they had come to admire. As Josephson wrote: "We were skeptical when reading Allied propaganda about the alleged war atrocities committed by the countrymen of Goethe and Beethoven." He and Burke soon resolved to try to impede the American war effort. In the summer of 1917 they joined the Guillotine Club, a diverse group of socialists and pacifists in the Village opposed to the war. Very quickly, however, the two of them grew disenchanted with the organization's operating procedures. At the group's second meeting Josephson and Burke were stopped outside the door of the beer hall. The leaders then let them in one at a time. Burke went in first. Ten minutes later he returned, looking a bit flushed and shaken. They had asked him if he was willing to kill for the movement. When he said no they abruptly told him to leave. [20]

Josephson's turn was next. He went inside, was told to sit down, and then was questioned by a French anarchist. His interrogator explained that now that war had been declared, the club must go underground, become a secret society engaged in sabotage and subversion. He finally told Josephson that if he were not prepared to obey orders and do everything they asked, he had better drop out. Shaken, Josephson nervously admitted, "I didn't know much about such things." He insisted that he was a convinced revolutionist but did not know whether he could be a party to violence. He then was told that he, too, was not needed. Crestfallen, Matthew left the Rathskeller and rejoined Burke outside. His brief encounter with revolutionary orthodoxy was not a pleasant one, and it would serve as a reminder in later years for him to avoid such dogmatism.[21]

A few days later, in a letter to Burke, Josephson reflected on their experience with revolutionary socialism. He confessed that he had joined the group before its aims and structure had been clearly outlined, that he had been naive in not recognizing its radical nature. He stressed that "in a pinch if I am asked to do that which I do not believe in, my individuality has not been submerged enough to submit for the sake of a cause, and I must refuse in such a case. Thus I am a weak cog in the machine." This analysis is crucial to an understanding of Josephson's relationship to radical politics. He was first and foremost an individualist devoted to art, and this characteristic would always limit his participation in political affairs. He affirmed in conclusion that he would continue "letting my social consciousness develop. I think that what we want is an educational socialist society like the Fabians of London. That is for us. I don't think revolutionaries are the true type of moderns."[22]

From Josephson's letter to Burke emerges a picture of a young man sensitive to social and political problems, yet firmly committed to the preservation of his own individualism and freedom of action. Just as he resented the tedium of working as a bank teller, Josephson rebelled against the autocratic methods employed by the leaders of the Guillotine Club. Years later, as a fellow traveler during the 1930s, he would stage a similar rebellion against the Communist party's espousal of proletarian literature. At this point, however, Josephson's socialist leanings were more superficial than real, more sympathetic than ideological. He was exposed to the socialism that pervaded the Village, but if he was socialist at the time, it was by association, not careful deliberation. In 1917 Josephson was not ready "to obey orders by persons unknown to us nor were we prepared in our minds to join in any actions beyond the law." Thus his role as a political radical quickly ended, and he resumed his literary pursuits. For the next several years, his "social consciousness" would lie dormant. And within a few months, even his attitude toward the war would change.[23]

In the fall of 1917 Josephson returned to a campus embroiled in superheated patriotism. President Butler, supported by the board of trustees, arbitrarily dismissed three professors for participating in "unpatriotic" activities. One of those suspended, Leon Fraser, was Josephson's instructor in political science. Fraser's firing persuaded Charles Beard to resign in protest, even though he supported the war effort. During this reactionary period Josephson spent more and more of his time in Greenwich Village. Kenneth Burke, who had dropped out of Columbia in order to spend more time writing, had rented a room in Clemenceau Cottage and provided Josephson with a place to stay. In addition to Djuna Barnes and Berenice Abbott, the lodgers now included two old women with beards, an idiot boy, and an Australian draft evader. Such a menagerie provided continuous surprises and amusements. One of the bearded women took a liking to Matty, and he was forced to come up with ingenious ways of avoiding her or fending her off, much to the amusement of Burke.

At the end of the school year, in June 1918, Columbia closed down because of the war. Many of Josephson's later friends and associates, such as Malcolm Cowley, Slater Brown, E. E. Cummings, and John Dos Passos, were already in Europe serving in the Ambulance Corps. Josephson, however, remained in New York. While waiting to be drafted (he had now resigned himself to serving in the military), he took a job as a time clerk at a Staten Island shipyard, commuting each day from the Village. For the next six months, Greenwich Village replaced Columbia as his "university." In the many informal gatherings in the Village that he attended, Josephson heard "endless talk of being, above all, 'free' or 'expressing oneself freely.'" [24]

Perhaps the most intriguing, if somewhat frustrating, aspect of Village life to the nineteen-year-old Josephson was the group of New Women, the radical feminists who were determined to be treated as men's equals. They dressed in masculine clothes, bobbed their hair, dispensed with makeup, smoked constantly, and drank with gusto. Unlike most of the later chroniclers of Village life during the war, Josephson in his memoirs stressed that promiscuous behavior was not the rule. "Finding a respectable mistress with a college degree, who would pay for her own meals," he reflected, "seemed less simple the more one studied the question." He found that the New Women were determined to demonstrate their moral independence as well as their social equality. Josephson expressed his irritation at such behavior in a letter to Burke in 1918: "I am overwhelmed with disgust for 'intellectual women.' I enjoy conceits in poetry; but it riles my masculinity to find it extremely cultivated in a woman." He still retained a more conventional ideal of womanhood, an ideal "more *mignonne* than they usually were." [25]

Josephson's disgust at "intellectual women" may have resulted from a disheartening relationship he had with one of the New Women. In "The Last Lady," a poem written in 1918 and later published in *Poetry*, Josephson described his reaction to the affair:

> I have no love nor lady
>   Yet I do not wail bereft.
> There are many, many beautiful ladies,
>   And in the world there is much left.
>
> I have now no love nor lady;
>   I have made a brave good-bye.
> It is terrible not to have a lady
>   When the summer months run high.
>
> And the summer and the autumn
>   And the winter may be gone;
> But my mind is quite decided—
>   I shall have no other one.
>
> It will need a greener springtime
>   To seed new love in me.
> But in another springtime—
>   Ah—where shall I be?

Josephson later explained the circumstances behind the poem in a letter to Burke. He admitted his persistent shyness around women, noting, "I have been rather finicky and frail." The last lady in his life, he recalled, "was a very, very close call. . . . Then perhaps she was a bitch." [26]

Whether intended or not, the transition in the poem's tone from cool indifference to poignant anxiety clearly illustrates that Josephson was still searching for his own style, of both life and poetry. In 1917 he had warned Burke that they must never be sentimental. A little over a year later he had nearly reversed himself. When he submitted "The Last Lady" and several other poems to Harriet Monroe, the editor of *Poetry*, Josephson announced:

> As you will note they are in the manner of Blake, of the Seventeenth Century, and also of the modern English school of sophisticated naivete. They are in no measure what is in myself: a taste for the rococo and the *pathetically gallant old world sentiment*. On the edges of these faded and commonplace emotions I believe we may still find slight poses, faint hintings that are subtly different and quaintly novel.

His taste for the rococo and his interest in excessively intricate verse represented only a temporary phase. Within a few years Josephson would again reverse his emphasis and begin to imitate the modern experimentalists.[27]

By the fall of 1918 the increasing demands of the war effort forced the government to begin calling up nineteen-year-old males for military service. Josephson received his draft notice, ironically, signed by his father, who then was serving as chairman of the local draft board in Brooklyn. Young Josephson's sentiments about the war had changed a great deal since his experience with the Guillotine Club. While still opposed to the war in principle, he had decided he would participate in it if necessary. Earlier he had even volunteered for the Reserve Officer Training Corps, but had been rejected because of poor hearing, a disability from infancy that would plague him the rest of his life. Thus when Matty received his conscription notice, he was prepared to obey it. The armistice was declared a few weeks later, however, and Josephson never put on a uniform. His literary education could continue uninterrupted.

4 THE MAKING OF A WRITER

The United States in the aftermath of the Great Crusade was a nation in turmoil, as passions and convulsions born in war carried over into peacetime. An exaggerated fear of alien radicals, coupled with the frustrations over the difficulties of peacemaking and the problems associated with demobilization and the reconversion of the economy, combined to produce an unsettling atmosphere. In the year 1919 there were race riots in Chicago, the general strike in Seattle, the Red scare and the Palmer raids, the resurgence of the Ku Klux Klan, and the passage of the Volstead Act over the veto of a crippled president. The country's reactionary mentality dismayed many sensitive intellectuals, most of whom turned inward in response, divorcing themselves from societal concerns. George Jean Nathan, the drama critic, spoke for many when he remarked in 1919 that the "great problems of the world—social, political, economic, theological—do not concern me in the slightest. . . . What concerns me alone is myself, and the interests of a few close friends."[1]

Matthew Josephson experienced at first hand the postwar atmosphere of repression and enforced conformity. In the fall of 1918 he accepted the editorship of the Columbia literary journal. During the next few months he formed an editorial committee, gathered manuscripts, and prepared to raise funds for the first issue. The student council asked to see the material before deciding to fund the journal. They objected to several poems by Burke, finding them "immoral." One member asked editor Josephson whether there were any "Reds" among his contributors or if he himself was a Communist. Matthew grew livid and presented an eloquent defense of artistic freedom. But he also vigorously denied any personal attachment to Marxism or socialism. As he remembered in his journal, "My aesthetic principles since two years ago at the time forbade any tendency to socialism." But his appeal for funding was denied. The student council was not willing to sponsor his "radical" publication. Such a sanctimonious environment reinforced Josephson's conviction that he should remain isolated from the vortex of college activity and continue his concentration upon personal literary study. After completing the general curriculum requirements of the first two years, he concentrated his work in literature (his major), philosophy (his minor), and French. But he spent most of his time reading works of personal interest or writing poetry.[2]

In 1919 Josephson met other young writers with similar ambitions and backgrounds. In the summer, Malcolm Cowley, a high school classmate of Burke, arrived in New York after attending Harvard and serving in the American Ambulance Service in France. He lived in the Village at 16 Dominick Street in what he called the most battered and primitive flat in the city. Josephson remembered him as a "burly farm boy who wrote with a very light touch and a pleasant turn of wit." He was a handsome young writer with thick dark hair, piercing blue eyes, and a small moustache. Cowley decided to move to the Village because "living was cheap, because friends of ours had come already . . . , because it seemed that New York was the only city where a young writer could be published." In July 1919, Cowley wrote Burke, who was living at home in New Jersey, that he had met Josephson in Greenwich Village. "Chiefly Matty came to discuss poetry," Cowley reported, "and to tell me how good my verse was and how much like his." A week later Josephson commented to Burke that his "intercourse with Cowley has been the bright ray of a rather miserable month, whose leisure hours were spent mostly in the company of mediocre girls."[3]

That same summer Josephson also met William Slater Brown, a student at Columbia from Weston, Massachusetts, who, like Cowley, had served in the Ambulance Corps in France. While there, Brown was arrested along with his close friend E. E. Cummings and was imprisoned by the French, who suspected them of spying. In prison Brown nearly died of scurvy. This prison experience inspired Cummings to write *The Enormous Room*, in which Brown is represented by the character "B." Like

Josephson, Brown had developed a fondness for modern French literature, and the two of them often engaged in friendly contests reciting the
verses of Paul Verlaine. Brown was then writing prose and light verse in
the form of the Scottish ballad, which Matty told him he could not abide.

During the same period Josephson befriended the gifted Hart Crane,
who had come to New York from Cleveland to try to find a publisher for
his verse. Josephson met Crane when he delivered some poems to the
Little Review offices at West Sixteenth Street. Crane was living in an
apartment above the *Little Review* and was performing errands for the
editors, Jane Heap and Margaret Anderson. When Josephson arrived,
Crane answered the door and told him that the editors were away but
cordially invited him to come in and visit. Josephson later pictured the
"breezy and hospitable" Crane as having the "pudgy figure and ruddy
complexion of a butcher boy." Crane asked Matthew to read some of his
poems. His assessment was typically blunt. He advised Crane to burn
them and start over, this time writing in the modern style. Crane was suit-
ably impressed by his new, opinionated acquaintance. A few days later
he remarked to his close friend Gorham Munson that he had met "a real
poet the other day, someone at Columbia, a deep student of French
verse, a very strict judge." Munson remembered forming the impression
from Crane's letters that Josephson must have been of "aristocratic bear-
ing and most exacting taste."[4]

Josephson maintained and strengthened his friendships with Burke,
Cowley, Brown, and Crane for the next several years by frequent meetings or correspondence. Along with Cowley and Burke he formed what
they termed an "Anti-Logrolling Society," a mutual admiration club in reverse, the objective of which was to prevent each other from developing
too much self-esteem by ruthlessly evaluating their literary work. The
more intimate their friendship, the more unabashedly critical they became. They were, Josephson remarked, "loving little friends, who never
failed to say their worst for each other." Unlike older bohemians in the
Village such as Floyd Dell and Max Eastman, who had rebelled from society in the hope of changing the world, Josephson and his friends were
"convinced that society could never be changed by an effort of the will."
Too young to have been converted to the reform politics of Progressivism
and uprooted by the chaos of the war, they purposely ignored social and
political issues, preferring instead to develop their own literary skills.
Their "political opinions," if they ever had any, Cowley later remarked,
"were vague and by no means dangerous to Ford Motors or General Electric: the war had destroyed their belief in political action. They were try-

ing to get ahead and the proletariat be damned." Josephson, who in 1917 had attached himself to the Guillotine Club, found that in 1919 he was "far from a Socialist. . . . No thought of political-economic problems weighed upon me in those days."[5]

To understand this intense isolation from society that Josephson and others experienced in 1919, one must look beyond the disillusionment caused by the war and its aftermath. As Henry May and others have demonstrated, the transition from concern with society to preoccupation with self among literary intellectuals began before America entered the Great War. Various new artistic influences had already begun to transform attitudes prior to 1917. This was especially true in Josephson's case, for unlike Cowley, Brown, and others, he did not personally participate in the war. His postwar attitude, therefore, was as much a result of the revolutionary artistic ideas he encountered during his college years as it was a reflection of the impact of the war.[6]

Like everyone else in bohemia, Josephson was eager to find a style, and he turned first to the French. In 1918 and 1919 he began reading extensively the works of the Symbolists of the late nineteenth century. The Symbolists, including the earlier Baudelaire, tried to maintain their integrity in the face of the onslaught of positivism by sacrificing their lives to art. They were aristocratic, antisocial, aloof, and unconventional. They isolated themselves from society, retreating into an ivory tower existence in pursuit of art for art's sake.[7]

Josephson discovered the French Symbolists through his reading of Pound, Lowell, and the other Imagists. It was not so much the craft of the Symbolists as their unique view of art and life that impressed him. He and his literary friends emulated the intensity of the Symbolists, discovering for themselves, as Cowley noted, a "religion in art." The allusion to religion was significant. Cowley's later "Red romance," like his earlier search for an artistic way of life, can only be understood in a religious context. In a similar way, though with important differences, the quest for the certainties of religious faith seemed to play a role in Josephson's artistic development. His rejection of his family and religion had left him without a psychological gyroscope. This void was increasingly filled by his devotion to literature and the life of the artist.[8]

Poetry for Josephson and his group of friends became an ethic—it offered a way of protecting oneself from external concerns and commitments. As Josephson later commented: "We, who liked to consider ourselves young poetical and aesthetical rebels, assumed a pose that was more ironical and world-weary than ever, and, to the exclusion of almost everything else, gave ourselves to the pleasures of pure literature." From a somewhat superficial reading of the Symbolists, Josephson adopted an attitude of artistic effetism, of snobbish vexation at the commonplace world around him. "I was really on the threshold of life," he remarked, "with little experience of it, yet claiming vices I never had . . . and writing in a tone of 'despair' borrowed, no doubt, from Baudelaire or . . . Mallarmé." He and his friends assumed the role of decadents, pretending to be fascinated with the morbid and exotic when actually they were merely trying to ape the antisocial living habits of earlier literary rebels. They were imitators, and they were successful.[9]

By 1919, at age twenty, Josephson's adoption of a life-style similar to that of Mallarmé and the Symbolists was almost complete. In response to a dispirited letter from Burke, he wistfully observed: "I am bored with the world . . . , feel an exalted boredom. There is B. He too is bored. He is even more successful at it than I." The young aesthetes were virtually competing against one another to be like their decadent heroes, trying to appear terribly old and grave for their years. "We were nothing," Josephson remembered, "if not 'sophisticated.'" When they were not reading the Symbolists, they would turn to writers with similar outlooks—Wilde, Pater, Huysmans, Shaw, Russians such as Dostoevski, Tolstoy, and Chekhov, and the more salacious passages of Donne and Herrick. Their boredom, of course, was false. But for the moment their posturing seemed real, and it dominated their lives.[10]

Josephson revealed in his poetry the extent of his conversion to the Symbolist aesthetic. Early in 1919 he sent another group of poems to Harriet Monroe for publication in *Poetry*. "The group I am sending now," he explained, "is a study in modern sophistication and degeneration into insanity. They are written to theory. That you must know is a delightful occupation." Monroe must have disapproved of Josephson's aping of the Symbolists, for she returned the verses. Such setbacks, however, did not faze him. Matthew demonstrated a resilience that only youth or strong egos provide. He told Monroe that he was, like all poets, made of "hardy stuff." A few months later he sent virtually the same group of poems to Amy Lowell, announcing: "I disavow and repent of all that I wrote before 1919. . . . I have suffered a sort of 'sea-change,' or at least change of Gods." He explained that he recently had been influenced by the French Symbolists and their more contemporary French and American disciples. "Writing from an impetus of irritation and mocking dissent, and in the bewilderment of modern sophistication," he admitted, "it is clear that I need the criticism and appraisal of an older and riper mind."[11]

UNIVERSITY OF WINNIPEG
515 Portage
Winnipeg, Manitoba R3B 2E9
DISCARDED

Lowell's "older and riper mind," however, disapproved strongly of Josephson's conversion and his latest work. She likewise returned the poems, noting: "I do not think they are as good as your earlier ones. I do not like the note in them. It has a sort of 1890 decadence in it which seems to me out of date and rather feeble." One can see what Lowell meant by examining one of Josephson's poems written during this period. Entitled "Variations on a Theme of Baudelaire," it reflected the derivative nature of his poetry:

> What shall I do with this intelligent disgust?
> It is too valuable and instructive
> to permit itself to be so lightly lost.
> Again, it would be blankly ineffective
> to assume an interest in life;
> that is, in several of its petty atoms.
> Alas! how even a disgust can make one chafe
> to labor with the rigor of its canons.
>
> Let us sit home this evening with Debussy;
> let us pursue dust-specks along the floor;
> or tap prophetic walls expectantly;
> or from my window puff smoke-rings at a chosen star.

Lowell's distaste for his poems should not have surprised Josephson. She had admired the technical proficiency of the Symbolists but not their philosophical attitudes. Henry May has written that Lowell "espoused radicalism in the poetic form only, not in ideas. She detested the tendency of the public to associate free love and free verse, abjured decadent or 'sensual' poetic tastes." The Boston Brahmin poet had no appreciation for Verlaine, Oscar Wilde, or their youthful American imitators.[12]

Josephson described Lowell's "brief and almost vexed comment" on his latest work as a

> distinct disappointment to me. I thought that I had attained a much more modern note, a firmer and more craftsmanlike line. That their tone is disagreeable is simply due to current conditions, the harshness and rancour of city life. Possibly an attempted approach to beauty from a different angle, "tenderness and feeling" concealed yet potent. . . . Perhaps I must still find myself.

Yet the headstrong poet refused to abandon his latest artistic orientation. Instead of accepting Lowell's criticism he decided to transfer his loyalty from her to another prominent poet, one who would appreciate his modern style. Soon after his correspondence with Lowell, Josephson reported to Hart Crane that he had just "had a falling out with Amy Lowell, but a falling in with T. S. Eliot by way of compensation." He had recently read Eliot's "Prufrock" and had found the low-keyed verses and profound obscurities "haunting and jaded enough to suit my tastes of the season." Eliot's tone of world-weariness and impotence reinforced Josephson's own esoteric pose. In his usual impulsive manner he immediately wrote Eliot, expressing his admiration for the poem and his intention to travel to Europe and acquaint himself with the new movements in literature there. Eliot replied that he would be glad to see his young countryman and introduce him to Ezra Pound. He warned Josephson that it would be best for him to live in England, to maintain contact with the English language, rather than fall under the spell of the French.[13]

Perhaps because of his newly discovered interest in Eliot, Josephson began studying the Elizabethan and Tudor playwrights and poets. As always, he was eager to share his literary discoveries with his friends. Crane told Gorham Munson in 1919: "Josephson sends me a list of names for reading that you might be interested in. Marlowe is one of his favorites, John Webster and Donne." Crane then began reading the Elizabethans himself. During this period he greatly admired Josephson's literary taste and critical acumen. In fact, the relationship between the two aspiring poets was at its strongest during the years immediately following the Great War. Early in 1920 Josephson proposed to Crane that the two of them spend the summer traveling in Europe. Crane found his footloose friend's plan appealing. He confessed to Matty: "If you are bored and spleenful, we have much in common, though you are less impulsive and emotional than myself, and take it, I am sure, more lightly. Your suggestion of a flight to the walks of Chelsea or the Mediterranean tempts me exceedingly. I should like to be rash." But pressing family problems precluded such a foreign adventure for Crane. It mattered little anyway, for Josephson's plans were mere daydreams. He had no money for such an adventure and was forced to postpone his planned voyage.[14]

In a series of letters written in 1919 and 1920 Crane made several penetrating observations about his friend Josephson. He characterized Matty's letters, written in an imperial, self-confident style, as "charming, with a peculiar and very definite flavor to them." Josephson displayed a pretense of cool sophistication and superior intellect that Crane found altogether different from such other intimates as Sherwood Anderson. He once commented on the difference between Anderson and Josephson:

"He [Anderson] and Josephson are opposite poles. J. classic, hard, and glossy,—Anderson, crowd-bound, with a smell of sod about him, uncouth." The sensitive poet from Cleveland especially appreciated Josephson's pompous remarks about his literary work. His written opinions of Crane's poems were prompt, forceful, and impious, full of great derision and surprising approbations. Crane once boasted of a new poem he had written: "I am thoroughly confident about the thing itself since it has got by the particular, hierarchic Josephson, and I won't blush to show it to almost anyone now."[15]

During the years after the Great War, Josephson, as he had intimated in letters to Lowell, Eliot, and Crane, was becoming more and more impatient with his New York environment and his personal literary progress. He continued to find the atmosphere at Columbia unsatisfying. In a letter to Burke in September 1919, he wrote that he had "been up at Columbia recently. It seems to grow more stupid and sodden with the years, and is developing better football teams apace. I shall confront its activities with complete indifference and apathy." Like so many other aspiring American writers of the period, Josephson was eager to travel to Europe and expand his literary horizons. By taking extra courses at night at Columbia, he was able to graduate early in 1920, a half-year ahead of schedule. His academic performance at Columbia was conspicuously uneven, primarily because of the narrow range of his interests and his literary predilections. He did not spend much time on his studies. His only A's were in English, and his college transcript supports his candor when he described his Columbia experience as contributing "only a modest increment to my store of learning; the real profits were intangible and extracurricular." If Josephson retained anything from his education, it was a distaste for professional academics and academicians.[16]

Hart Crane told a friend that soon after graduating from Columbia, Josephson had again expressed an urge "to ramble toward the continent via a steamship or some vessel." Many of Josephson's friends had joined the migration of writers and painters to Europe, and he, too, wanted to learn at first hand the new literary techniques being tested there. Percy Winner, who was working for the *Chicago Tribune* in Paris, wrote Matty in May 1920 that soon "you will be coming or preparing to come to France. Everyone seems to be coming or preparing to come." But once again, money presented a problem. Josephson's only hope for reaching Europe was to find a job and try to save enough money for travel expenses. In the process he also found a wife.[17]

In 1920, while working for a subsidiary of Standard Oil, compiling and editing marketing reports, Josephson met and soon married Hannah Geffen, a vivacious nineteen-year-old reporter for Hearst's morning newspaper, the *New York American*. She was the next to youngest of a big family, mostly of girls, all music-loving. Her parents, A. D. and Anna Geffen, had emigrated to the United States from western Russia about 1880. In New York her father established a small bookstore. A scholarship winner in high school, Hannah attended Hunter College and the Columbia Graduate School of Journalism. She was an ardent feminist and resembled in many respects the New Women who earlier had confounded and irritated Josephson in Greenwich Village. Attractive, with long golden hair, she was well-read, full of energy and ambition, frequently temperamental, and sometimes overpowering. Yet she appeared different to him. Hannah understood his single-minded preoccupation with literature and offered continuous encouragement and support. In fact, Malcolm Cowley once insisted that she was the real driving force behind Matty Josephson. Her enthusiasm and spontaneity delighted him. Her quick wit diverted him. Her devotion to literature and his writing offered him reassurance and security. Hannah was a composite of old-fashioned charm, idealism, and generosity, a perfect complement to Matty and in many ways his superior.

Years later Hannah remembered her first impressions of Matty Josephson, with his "large smooth forehead, brown eyes perfectly matched and set, . . . long jaw and chin, [and] fine-cut lips open most of the time to breathe, but tender and strong when closed." She fell in love "with his way of saying things—he dressed his sentences up in fresh clothes everytime he opened his mouth, so that . . . when I hear him speak or write a commonplace it strikes me as particularly foreign to him, almost an affectation." In casual conversation, then and later, Matthew became known as quite a spellbinder. He liberally sprinkled his speech with gallicisms and literary allusions, ironical witticisms, and sweeping pronouncements, thus giving the impression of both cosmopolitanism and erudition. He learned early how to use such devices to gain control of a conversation and steer it to his advantage. "After a few months," Hannah recollected, "I would have followed him, (and did) anywhere in the world, knowing that he would always keep me amused." Matty and Hannah initially viewed their marriage as a temporary experiment (they had agreed to divorce after six months), but the two of them were quickly committed to each other for life.[18]

When Hart Crane learned of Josephson's rather sudden marriage, he was furious. He immediately wrote his "former" friend, cursing his marriage bed, calling him a "Benedict" and an "idiot." Josephson responded to the letter with equal furor, tearing it up in a rage and pledging never to speak to Crane again. Crane had apparently formed a personal feeling for his literary friend that was much more complex than Josephson had realized, and only later would Matthew come to recognize how much his early friendship had meant to Hart. But for now, in 1920, the two were no longer communicating.[19]

Hannah must have been a patient bride, for in the first six months of her marriage, Matthew changed jobs three times. He soon tired of writing market reports nine hours a day and turned next to newspaper reporting. Hubert "Red" Knickerbocker, a friend and former classmate at Columbia, had recently been hired as acting editor of the *Newark Morning Ledger* with the authorization to select a new staff. Josephson's literary background and "business experience" persuaded Knickerbocker to offer him the dual editorship of the literary and financial sections of the paper. Thus at age twenty-one Josephson began his short career as a newspaperman.

In his autobiography, Louis Untermeyer, the writer, literary critic, and tireless anthologizer, related an interesting encounter he had with young editor Josephson. At the end of 1920, Untermeyer, who then was the superintendent of a New Jersey jewelry factory, confronted a union organization crisis. During the period of labor unrest Josephson visited him at the plant. "He came in; a thin, not unpleasant young fellow," Untermeyer wrote, "even though he seemed to be carrying more chips than his shoulders would support." Instead of wanting to talk about the labor situation, as Untermeyer supposed, Josephson had come to discuss poetry. He intended to write a feature story about Untermeyer's dual role as poet and businessman. Josephson began the interview by expounding his views about poetry, supporting experimentation in modern forms and techniques, and vigorously challenging his host's criticism of T. S. Eliot and other modernists. "I felt I was contending with Young Anarchy," Untermeyer recounted, "while he was convinced he was doing battle with Old Fogey himself."[20]

The conspicuous iconoclasm and righteous self-confidence that Josephson revealed in his interview with Untermeyer and in his letters to Crane reflect his own perplexing attempt, as he had phrased it to Lowell, "to find himself." Ever since his childhood rebellion against his parents, he had acted the part of the assured aesthete, outspoken in his literary opinions and drawn to those activities and ideas that appeared new and shocking. He was a heady, ambitious young man with quite an ego. But his self-confident demeanor was deceiving; Josephson in all likelihood was unsure of himself and his direction. He was anxiously searching for a cause or movement or way of life to which he could wholeheartedly commit himself. Yet only rarely did he exhibit the patience to consider the philosophical implications of the various ideas he encountered or adopted. He was, like so many young aesthetes, the captive of ideas rather than the creator. As a result he found it difficult to remain in one place or to be guided by one literary school or occupation for extended periods of time.

Josephson at first found newspaper work exhilarating. But soon the novelty of journalism wore off, and the mechanical, devitalizing nature of the job began to tell on him. In several agonized letters to Kenneth Burke, he expressed his malaise. Only a few weeks after starting the job he wrote:

> I am working hard and doing all kinds of writing—also an asset. The other day I wrote a color story that was so degraded and cheap that when I saw it the next morning I could not believe my eyes. Of course it went very well. But usually I plug at financial stories.

Later Josephson described to Burke a recent interview with William Carlos Williams as one "of the bright spots in my rather dogged existence." Although excited at the prospect of editing the book review section of the paper, he concluded on a pessimistic note: "I seem to be planted in Newark for some months to come altho I still writhe at being a newspaper man. Night assignments are getting me crazy." About two months later he reported that he had quit his newspaper post and would "now enter the ranks of well-starved human beings again." He explained that newspaper work "had begun to deaden my brain for the last month or so. . . . I thirst for literary shop-talk again." [21]

Josephson missed the comradeship, frenetic activity, and color that he had experienced in Greenwich Village with his friends. By contrast he found the life of the business world prosaic. Not long after starting his next job at a commercial publishing firm in New York, he had reached the limit of his endurance. Together he and Hannah had managed to save 760 dollars, which "was designed for a holy cause—a year in France." The Josephsons decided to quit their jobs and move to the isolated back-country of Maine, where they would live for three months before sailing for Europe. In June 1921, the young couple boarded a coastal steamer and headed for Maine, destined for a summer of "delectable freedom."

Josephson's choice of a wilderness setting for a temporary retreat was premeditated. Two years before, he had spent a week in a remote forest cottage in upstate New York. During that stay he "promptly fell in love with country life," and resolved to repeat his Thoreauvian adventure. In Maine the Josephsons rented a small, broken-down house about a mile from where Kenneth Burke and his wife were doing the same. Although the roof leaked and the stove was broken, Matthew remembered that he and Hannah were "happier than we had yet been anywhere else, and I was free to write whatever I pleased." They were limited to a budget of seven dollars a week. Thus their new life-style required considerable sacrifice and ingenuity. Luckily for them, there was an apple orchard nearby. They had applesauce for breakfast, fried apples for lunch, and apple juice for dinner. It was monotonous, but it was "natural." That whole summer Josephson immersed himself in literature. When not writing or engaged in literary discussions with Burke, he was usually reading recent works by French avant-garde poets, sitting under an open sky in the backwoods of Maine, perusing a copy of the *Nouvelle Revue Française* or *Littérature*, the magazine of the madcap Dadaists. He thrived in his new environment. "In Maine," he recollected,

> I had become thoroughly at home in the country, and, though city bred, learned to relish even my solitude. My eyes were opened thereafter to the variety and subtle movements of natural things, and I would always miss the sense of physical well-being enjoyed in the country when city pent for too long.

The image of halcyon rural life was to retain a strong hold upon Josephson's mind, as he would later settle in the country.[22]

While in Maine Josephson renewed his correspondence with Hart Crane, but their relationship was still strained. Crane was critical of Josephson's admiration of the young French modernists. He recognized correctly that his friend was becoming more and more a prisoner of theory and method because of his constant emphasis upon them at the expense of intuition and spontaneity. In a letter to Gorham Munson, Crane elaborated on his deteriorating friendship with Josephson:

> I do not expect to hear from Josephson again. He wrote me several letters full of brilliant criticism and suggestions—but we do not exactly agree on theory and he has become so complex—that the lack of sympathy my last letter offered him will bring no response from [him] I'm quite sure. . . . this extremity of hair-splitting palls on one

after awhile. A little is interesting—but goes a long ways. He seems afraid to use any emotion in his poetry,—merely observation and sensation,—and because I call such work apt to become thin, he thinks me sloppy and stupid,—as no doubt I am. But after all,—I recognize him as in many ways the most *acute* critic of poetry I know of—the only trouble is he tries to force his theories into the creative process,—and the result, to me, is too tame a thing.

Josephson's overweening emphasis upon form and technique, upon theory rather than content, would continue to hamper his poetic efforts. Moreover, almost all his later works—poetry, biographies, and histories—would reflect his tendency to organize his material according to a single thesis or point of view.[23]

In September 1921, their summer of bucolic economy over, the Josephsons prepared to leave for Europe. Historians have traditionally characterized the American intellectuals who went to Europe in the early 1920s as a "lost generation," alienated by the war and its faulty peace, America's mundane business mentality, and its standardized mass culture. Frederick Lewis Allen in his classic study of the twenties, *Only Yesterday*, provided a typical example of the lost-generation stereotype. American expatriates, he wrote, "feared the effect upon themselves and American culture of mass production and the machine, and saw themselves as fighting to the last ditch for the right to be themselves in a civilization which was being leveled into monotony by Fordisms and the chain-store mind."[24]

Perhaps more than any other expatriate, Harold Stearns, a promising young journalist, has been portrayed as exemplifying the discontented intellectual of the 1920s. In 1921 he edited *Civilization in the United States*, a wide-ranging symposium of thirty prominent American intellectuals. The volume made a sweeping indictment of the country's culture, politics, business, and journalism. On July 4, 1921, after completing the manuscript of *Civilization in the United States*, Stearns sailed for Europe. His departure received widespread publicity, and a wave of Americans soon followed his example. The so-called lost generation began to flock to Paris, eager to escape an America characterized by Henry Ford, Prohibition, and the Ku Klux Klan.[25]

Frequently, however, historical stereotypes distort as much as they clarify. True, some Americans did turn their backs on America and did take up permanent residence in Europe. At the same time, however, there were many others who left for reasons less sweeping and who stayed abroad only temporarily. Josephson, for instance, went to great lengths in his memoirs to dissociate himself from the lost generation. He maintained that unlike Stearns and other disheartened expatriates, he had decided to go to Europe not because he was disgusted with life in the United States but because he wanted to expand his personal and literary horizons. As he told Charles Allen in 1944: "Many of us left for love of travel and adventure and the 'life of the artist.' I for one . . . never felt either pretended or real disgust with America." Josephson contended that for him, traveling to Europe represented another stage in his literary career. It was a youthful *Wanderjahr*, a way of improving himself, not a conscious protest against modern American life. In 1921 he had never heard of Harold Stearns.[26]

Josephson's published explanation, however, obscures the fact that he went to Europe also because he considered the United States in 1921 to be a cultural and intellectual backwater. He once wrote in his journal: "most of us, having no dean-of-letters (he was in London), no 'schools,' no continuous experience or memory of fortunes or retreats in culture, no masters to learn from or repudiate . . . , sought examples everywhere but the U.S.A." Literature was everything to him, and his literary idols were European, not American. Moreover, the political situation in the United States seemed increasingly oppressive. Josephson viewed Harding's election with consternation. "I saw in him only a fool of the Tories, and Toryism, following Wilson, as in a tidal wave. A wave, I should add, a colossal watery wave, which spelled ruin for all intelligent drinking." He felt he had to get away from such provincialism. Thus, even though he was not disgusted with American society in the sweeping or profound sense that Harold Stearns and others were, Josephson was critical of the artistic and political environment in the United States during the postwar era. But he was not "lost" in the sense of being cynical or disillusioned. As Frederick J. Hoffman has accurately observed, the writers of Josephson's group were naive rather than lost, "open to every new influence that came along." And in 1921 Europe was the magnet that attracted them.[27]

It was an emotional moment as Matthew and Hannah prepared to board the S.S. *Roussillon* at a New York pier in late September 1921. Josephson remembered that his father, mother, and sister were there to see them off. Since leaving home in 1916, Matthew had remained de-

voted, yet aloof from his parents, steadfastly determined to fulfill his literary ambitions with or without their approval. He was fond of his family,
but he did not intend to sacrifice his own freedom by conforming to their
standards. He remembered that he was glad to get away from "the exas-
peratingly dull meetings or dinners with numerous family groups, hospitable and gentle though they longed to be." He and his parents still communicated on different frequencies. "Like all others," he reminisced ten
years later, "these two, dear dead parents never 'understood' their son."
Although they may have wanted him to pursue another career, Julius and
Sarah always loved Matthew, and they wept as he said good-bye. Josephson related that his mother, "passionate egoist that she was" and "despite
all her censure of me in the last five years," held him in a tender embrace
and pressed into his hand an old family watch for good luck. At the same
time, Julius looked at his eldest son "with the curious detached gaze that
is accorded as a tribute to aviators tuning up their motors in preparation
for a transatlantic flight." It seems ironic that Josephson's parents, who
had arrived at the same harbor more than forty years earlier, were watching their son return across the ocean. Yet in one sense, the scene appro-
priately symbolizes the wide gulf that had emerged in their respective
attitudes about life.[28]

What sort of young man was this twenty-two-year-old poet as he sailed
for France? In appearance he revealed his mother's Oriental ancestry.
Thin, with an olive complexion, he had a long face with a large, twice-
broken nose and high cheekbones that, coupled with deep-set, dark
brown eyes and black hair parted down the middle, gave him a striking
physical appearance. As Malcolm Cowley once jocularly remarked,
Josephson looked like a "Mongolian horseman (or some would say, like
the horse)." He was attentive and charming to women, quite a conversationalist, and quite a wit. His jaunty demeanor, cloaking self-
doubts, reflected a personality that in many ways paralleled the description Wallace Stegner has applied to Bernard DeVoto at a similar age.
Stegner pictured DeVoto as being "precocious, alert, intelligent, brash,
challenging, irreverent, literary self-conscious, insecure . . . , sometimes insufferable." Josephson exhibited all of these qualities. At the
same time, however, there were other salient features of Matthew's character that would influence his later career.[29]

One is immediately struck by the youthful Josephson's fundamental
preoccupation with the world of art and ideas. Roy Nichols, the eminent
American historian, once admitted that growing up in the Progressive era

was "a great disadvantage because life gave you no sense of reality." In *Exile's Return* Malcolm Cowley expressed a similar view of his literary generation. He portrayed himself and his friends, including Josephson, as uprooted idealists. They were born into an age dominated by bourgeois convention and philistinism. In such an environment they felt forced to turn back on themselves, for only in themselves and in the world of literature was there any freedom or security. They rebelled against the middle-class standards of their parents, abandoned their hometowns, and attended universities that had trained them to belittle their own national culture and instead to admire European art and literature. If they participated at all in the Great War, they did so as observers, not as combatants. In fact, according to Cowley, his generation was "spectatorial" in its relation to life in general. They were, when scarcely out of childhood, censorious toward their elders, solemn and stiff-necked in their manner, eager to debate or reject all the conventions of life before having experienced them. They turned their backs on all aspects of tradition and convention and "yet could adhere to nothing new." As Cowley concluded, they ultimately "had been uprooted from something more than a birthplace, a country or a town. Their real exile was from society itself, from any society to which they could honestly contribute and from which they could draw the strength that lies in shared convictions." They were not so much disillusioned as disaffected. [30]

Josephson depicted himself in a similar light. Raised in a comfortable, middle-class household and later living on his own, he had been able from early adolescence to isolate himself in an antiseptic world of prose and poetry, esoteric discussions and bohemian culture. Like Burke, Cowley, and several others, he rejected any commitment to society and chose instead to live in a closed circle of mutually reinforcing ideas and attitudes. Josephson posed as a cold, reclusive aesthete, approaching life more through mind and art than through experience. Consequently, he easily assimilated the ingenuous assumption that literature was synonymous with life.

There is some danger, however, in taking at face value the ironic judgments that Josephson and his friends have made of their youthful selves from the perspective of the post-depression period. Were they really so vacuous, so empty of larger concerns? Or had not all this posturing, by which they later seemed embarrassed, some value in their growth? That they adopted the Symbolist aesthetic was a moral commitment and a social comment of sorts. Their emphasis on the revolution of the word, their absolute rage against the official order and established style, were implicitly moral attitudes. In this sense Josephson's artistic rebelliousness was a necessary first step toward what would become his social consciousness of the 1930s and after. Before social and political issues could be confronted he first had to establish his autonomy as a writer. For the moment he was intent upon establishing a new artistic order; later he would promote a new social order. In both cases he rebelled in order to rebuild.[31]

Despite what he would have us believe from reading his memoirs, Josephson's decision to associate with one artistic movement or another was reflective of his strong sense of moral conviction—he was never indifferent. His lack of interest in the commonplace world was more apparent than real. As strong as his literary idealism was his moral idealism. Daniel Aaron has perceptively noted that Josephson and Cowley were "moral even in their antimorality." They were "not nearly so detached from the moral imperatives of their fathers and their class as they imagined."[32] Vigorously nonconformist, Josephson demonstrated, much like his mother, an opinionated, combative nature, and he was capable of defending his beliefs with the zeal of an ideologue. He exhibited such qualities in an incident at Columbia in 1919, when one of his English instructors, Raymond Weaver, was threatened with dismissal for praising in class the works of Oscar Wilde. Josephson was outraged by such an invasion of academic freedom, and he circulated a petition calling for Weaver's retention. His efforts were apparently successful, for the expulsion proceedings were dropped. When sufficiently stimulated, Josephson did not hesitate to take to the ramparts in defense of principles he deemed inviolable. In the future he would display in the social and political realm the same moral indignation that he had witnessed in the lectures of Charles Beard or that he himself had demonstrated during his editorship of the Columbia literary magazine and in his ardent defense of Professor Weaver.

In 1921, however, Matthew Josephson successfully channeled such fervor into his own narrow literary interests. He remained preoccupied with the world of art. Later in his career, however, when he emerged from his self-imposed cloister of artistic egoism and confronted the reality of social problems, Josephson would transfer his moral passion for literature to the public sphere, and he would come to appreciate many of the bourgeois conventions he discarded. But such a development was still years away. First he had to go to Paris and live out his dream of being a "pure" poet. He was one of many Americans who sought in France both an artistic method and a way of life; he believed that discovering an aesthetic theory might achieve his vision of personal fulfillment. Going to Europe represented for Josephson the "culminating adventure" of his young life.

5   A EUROPEAN ADVENTURE

James Joyce once commented that Paris was the "last of the human cities." It was able to maintain its color and intimacy despite its large size. Josephson found there a congenial setting in which to live and work, and it did not take him long to learn to play the Parisian. Soon after arriving in Paris the Josephsons rented a room in a pension off the boulevard Montparnasse. They learned that living in postwar Paris had economic as well as cultural advantages. Josephson reported back to Burke that one could get soup, fish, meat, wine, dessert, and coffee for four francs. By occasionally writing translations for the *New York Herald* and by selling one of his literary pieces a month, Matthew discovered that he and Hannah could live quite comfortably. "The cheapness of living here," he noted, "makes a man much freer than elsewhere." Paris was freedom—freedom to dress, write, and travel as one pleased.[1]

Life in Paris was as exciting as it was inexpensive. The city was a constant hive of cultural activity. As Gertrude Stein remarked, Paris "is where the twentieth century is." After a few weeks of adaptation Josephson found "even the air of Paris stimulating." The bohemian cultural life on the Left Bank was much more varied and extensive than that of the Village. In addition to attending the satirical plays of Jean Cocteau and concerts by Erik Satie and Les Six, he and Hannah spent hours visiting art galleries where the latest works of the modern experimentalists were prominently displayed. They especially loved to stroll along the rue Bonaparte, with its colorful print and book shops. Matthew also enjoyed frequenting the Luxembourg Gardens and the student quarter of the boulevard St. Michel.[2]

The landmarks of the American colony in Paris were the three cafes at the corner of boulevard Montparnasse and the boulevard Raspail: the Dôme, the Rotonde, and the Select. After visiting the Rotonde, Josephson wrote Burke that the Americans were "so thick that the tendency is to forget all the French one has learned in the United States." He remembered watching from the Rotonde as Raymond Duncan, the brother of Isadora, walked past in flowing Grecian robes and open sandals in the dead of winter. He also occasionally saw Gertrude Stein and Alice B. Toklas, wearing dust hats and veils, ride by in their Model T coupe. Pablo Picasso frequented the Rotonde, and Josephson discovered the artist to be surprisingly approachable and found his casual conversation thrilling.[3]

On one occasion at the Rotonde Matthew ran into "a great big sodden boor named Harold Stearns" who insisted "on playing chess with me." Such a comment vividly illustrates the differing perspectives of the two young Americans. Josephson had arrived in Paris eager to improve his literary talent; Stearns had left the United States in disgust and disillusionment. Once in Paris he virtually abandoned his journalistic career. John Dos Passos once described Stearns's stagnation: "Even his pursuit of drink and women seemed to lack conviction. . . . He lived a pathetic barfly life eking out a living selling tips on the ponies to American tourists he picked up in the various ginmills he frequented."[4]

While Stearns and other expatriates were drowning their sorrows with aperitifs, Josephson immersed himself in the literary ambience of Paris. "[The] perfect ferment of activity around you is stimulating in itself. . . , he told Burke. "Paris, Berlin, or Europe present a milieu which is infinitely more sympathetic for the artist. Given the qualities I possess I could not help . . . writing myself to the ground in this city." Josephson met Jules Romains and the group of French writers associated with the *Nouvelle Revue Française* and saw as well numerous Americans in the Latin Quarter, including Helen Fox, his high school friend Percy Winner, Cuthbert Wright, James Light and Djuna Barnes, whom he had known in the Village, and Arthur Moss. He learned that the "*N.R.F.* was waning. That Huysmans was despised, de Gourmont rejected, Gide weakening." After meeting Gide, Josephson described him to Burke as being "far from what one would picture him. He is feline; his voice is caressing and insinuating; he is an utter scoundrel, but he too is rapidly losing his grip."

The boisterous Dadaists, as Josephson discerned, were undermining the dominant hold that Gide, Romains, and Valéry had exercised upon French letters. LaForgue was no longer esteemed; Rimbaud and Stendhal had replaced him. In addition, the tragic Guillaume Apollinaire, who had died three years earlier, was acquiring quite a following among the younger French writers. Literary fashions were rapidly changing, and Matthew found the tumult exciting.[5]

On the Left Bank Josephson met Gorham Munson, the young American writer from Long Island and Greenwich Village who was Hart Crane's friend. Pale, blond, and already balding at twenty-six, Munson was a minister's son known for his waxed and pointed moustache and for his intense devotion to modern literature. Like Josephson he had come to Europe for a year of "self-education." Munson later recalled meeting Josephson:

> I met a rather stiff young man, narrow in his interests, brittle in his thinking, and at moments charmingly pompous in speech. A certain pathos in his character was appealing. . . . He seemed to have escaped the muddle and ferment of 1916–1921 by excluding the elements of the muddle. He had no interest in liberalism, no interest in Brooks and the social approach to literature, no interest in philosophy.

About all that Matty did appear interested in, Munson remembered, was modern experimental poetry. He spoke enthusiastically of the work of Eliot and brought to Munson's attention the creative efforts of his friends Cowley and Burke. After learning that his two friends had met, Hart Crane wrote Munson that Josephson could at times be "cold as ice, having a most astonishing faculty for depersonalization,—and on the other hand, you have no doubt found a certain affectionate propensity in his nature that is doubly pleasant against the frigid intellectual relief of the rest of him."[6]

Munson introduced Josephson to Man Ray, the American Dadaist, who invited his two young countrymen to attend the opening of his exhibition and to meet the other Dadaists. Josephson had heard of Dada before leaving the United States, but he had never really understood the movement. His friend Percy Winner had reported from Paris in 1920: "Dadaism is here to stay. Of all the insane movements, it is the insanest." Several months later Josephson commented to Burke that Dadaism seemed to be "an attempt to throw Cubism into the discard, and is more amusing than important as a movement." Early in 1921 he and Crane had briefly discussed Dadaism in their correspondence, but to them it remained a confusing new approach to literature. Crane confessed that he could not "figure out just what Dadaism is beyond an insane jumble of the four winds, the six senses and plum pudding." Thus it was with both curiosity and trepidation that Josephson late in 1921 introduced himself to Tristan Tzara at Ray's exhibition.[7]

In his impetuous manner Josephson pressed Tzara with questions about Dada. When was it started? Why? What was its attitude toward literature? Tzara answered: Dada "is not anything, and it is everything." Josephson left the meeting confused and annoyed by Tzara's behavior. He had not been able to find out where Dada fit into the currents of modern experimentalist literature. Yet he was determined to learn more about the baffling movement. There was a certain mystery and audacity to Dadaism that fascinated him. Soon, however, he met other Dadaists who were not as ambiguous in their pronouncements as Tzara.[8]

Louis Aragon, Dadaist and Surrealist poet of the twenties, novelist and Communist party member during the thirties, and Resistance poet during World War II, exerted a particularly strong influence on Josephson, then and later. Aragon lived literature, and in Josephson he discovered a similar passion. Aragon explained to the eager young American that the Dadaists had been badly scarred by the Great War. They wanted to sweep away the debris of the past, to abolish the conventions and false pieties of bourgeois life and Victorian gentility, in order to create a new and pure artistic environment. To do so they employed radically new techniques such as automatic writing. They also took to the streets, the theaters, and the cafes in an attempt to put their artistic philosophy on public display. On one occasion Aragon led the Josephsons and several other attentive Americans to Montmartre to celebrate the unexplained receipt of 150 francs in his morning mail. When the money ran out after each guest had finished several glasses of champagne, Aragon simply shrugged his shoulders and sustained the spirit of intoxication by reciting verse after verse of Hugo. Then, the poetry over, Aragon led them off on a long walk through the darkened streets of Paris in early morning, declaiming the whole way on every conceivable problem of life or literature. Aragon's enthusiasm, erudition, and charm were infectious. Josephson identified with his fervor for poetry and his zest for life. He explained in a letter to Burke that Aragon was "a prince. His mind is all afire. He is absolutely on the square, and he and his friends are in the midst of a bitter fight. . . . he is the most potent artist I have ever met; I mean his brain functions beautifully, his intelligence is baffling, restless, old." Aragon, he remarked, "makes the language jump through hoops for him." His new French friend also pointed out the precursors of Dada: Stendhal, Rimbaud, Lautréamont, and Apollinaire.[9]

Besides Aragon, Josephson met several other young Dada poets, including Paul Eluard, Philippe Soupault, and Robert Desnos, who also impressed him with their talent and energy. Soon he was a Dadaist himself. He informed Cowley in December 1921 that "we have decided to attach ourselves to the Dadaists, of whom thrills may be wrested at the lowest cost." Josephson was initially drawn to the Dadaists not through a deliberate appreciation of their ideas or of the historical causes of the movement but instead because he found them carefree, exciting, talented, and rebellious. He thoroughly enjoyed Dada's rowdy public demonstrations and general "hell-raising" spirit. Although there were risks to be taken, he relished his new activist posture: "At least we writers would leave our sedentary lives in our studios, cafes, or the parlors where we used to read our poems to old ladies, and go forth into the streets to confront the public and strike great blows at its stupid face." During a large dinner gathering in January 1922 he demonstrated his conversion to the vulgar and contentious public activism of Dada. The meeting, attended by many of the Russian émigrés in Paris, quickly turned into a forum for Dadaist buffoonery, with the Russians serving as unappreciative foils. An inspired and somewhat tipsy Josephson climbed atop one of the tables and began reading a German tract on socialism to the Russians. They responded by hurling food. Josephson readied himself for combat, but fortunately for him, the proprietor intervened and declared the meeting adjourned.[10]

Although he enthusiastically participated in such activity, Josephson drew a distinction between the Dadaists' nihilistic public behavior and their artistic purposes. To the casual observer Dada represented the culminating attempt by artists to seek the freedom of the completely detached personality. But such a view was deceiving, Josephson believed, for the Dadaists were genuinely involved in the society they so heartily condemned. He eagerly embraced both their spirit of nonconformity and their active contact with society. The world was not to be ignored, as he had assumed during his Symbolist phase; instead it was to be "fought, insulted, or mystified." Matthew had discovered that beneath their facade of aggressive nihilism, the Dadaists harbored an affirmative spirit. They were driven by moral fervor in their assault on bourgeois morality. Josephson likewise pursued his immorality with great moral conviction. The Dadaists, he contended, destroyed in order to create; they broke away from tradition with the aim of developing new modes of expression, hoping in the process to bridge the gap between art and modern life. In this sense, therefore, Dada represented a means of producing constructive change; it was not simply destructive. Josephson felt that Dada's attitude of affirmative alienation provided an opportunity to express new and positive values through art. He realized that he had come to Dadaism with a set of intellectual baggage much different from that of the young Frenchmen. The war for him had not been the major turning point that it was for them. Thus it was only logical that he emphasized the affirmative side of Dada rather than its war-induced nihilism.[11]

In December 1921 Josephson launched a letter-writing campaign to win over his American friends to Dada. While admitting to Cowley that at times the Dadaists were childish, he asserted nonetheless:

> My claim is that these young men, when they break away from the rubbish of Dada, will be the big writers of the next decade. They are working at more or less the same problems that we are, although they abjure technique. . . . I find it all very stimulating; that is, I write here with ease.

He described the Dadaists to Burke as being "young, stimulating, and although looking at a mass of their revues gives you vertigo headache, I suspect that some of them will crawl out from under the rubbish and begin to write soon." Burke, however, failed to see the distinction Josephson made between the "rubbish" of Dada and its creative potential. He responded that the Dadaists were antireason and therefore should be damned, not praised: "I am scandalized that words of all things are used in a way that denies their essential property, the property of ideological clarity." Cowley, too, objected to Dada, primarily because it seemed intentionally obscure. Hart Crane, who continued to praise Matthew's writing while disagreeing with most of his attitudes, expressed an even stronger reaction to Josephson's latest pronouncements. He told Munson that Josephson "is, it strikes me, altogether unsteady. . . . Quite seriously, Matty is thrilling, in prose especially. His performance is agreeable despite my inability to sympathize with his theories."[12]

Josephson remained determined, however, to convince his friends that the Dadaists represented the wave of the future in literature. He insisted to Burke that Aragon, Eluard, and Soupault were "not incoherent; they do not murder the language; they really have no blague about them. The term DADA associated with them was partly to frighten off people, to indicate that they are under thirty." Josephson admired the defiant individualism and ardent experimentalism of the Dadaists and wanted his American friends to share his enthusiasm. It was the particular spirit of Dada that he found so exciting, a "certain 'audace,' absolute rage against the enemy, a flare for invective." Of course, these were the qualities of his own literary personality as well. Like his Dadaist friends, he also was reckless and fiercely polemical, constantly getting into fights, not always with good judgment. The danger, he warned Burke, was in being not audacious and aggressive enough: "In this respect I find the young Frenchmen inexhaustible." Not living in Paris, however, Burke, Crane, and Cowley found it difficult to appreciate the infectious effect that the Dadaists exercised upon Josephson and others.[13]

Josephson learned to his surprise that many of the French Dadaists were fascinated by modern American society and culture. Taking up where the Italian Futurists had left off, they imitated in their art and literature the fast-paced tempo of machine-age America. Unlike their Italian predecessors, however, they did not worship the violence of the machine age; instead they gloried in its aesthetic potential. Artists such as Marcel Duchamp and Francis Picabia had long displayed primitive machine-object constructions parodying American technology. French poets, led before and during the war by Guillaume Apollinaire and afterward by Blaise Cendrars and Philippe Soupault, expressed in their verse an enchantment with America's popular culture and its urban industrial ethos.[14]

The French fascination with American culture stimulated Josephson to revise his own artistic attitudes about his homeland. He related in his memoirs that he had come to France primarily to investigate the tradition of the Symbolists. "Instead," he wrote, "I was observing a young France that . . . was passionately concerned with the civilization of the U.S.A., and stood in fair way to be *Americanized*." Earlier, in imitating the Symbolists, Josephson had adopted a detached, exalted artistic perspective accompanied by a pose of fatigue and melancholy toward the everyday world about him. Now he discovered among the Dadaists a completely new mood. His new European friends, inspired by their images of modern American life, were animated, involved in life, and determined to destroy the pious reputation of art. They were the Keystone Cops of modern literature. As Josephson adopted the affirmative iconoclasm of the Dadaists, he found he could no longer give his loyalty or attention to such "old" schools of art as Symbolism. He emphasized to Burke that "the whole symbolist movement looks quite sterile. . . . *we* of course, are writing for *our* age." No longer did he view the United States as a cultural wasteland. He now began to see his native country as a source of inspiration.[15]

Josephson soon began integrating the tempo of contemporary American life into his own work, attempting to use the rhythm of the machine to artistic advantage. In a letter to Burke he called for "a more creative, more formal technique with subject. . . . The word, the sentence, the printed page should be used more daringly to create a formal composition detached from the relation of the original character of the material." He reflected the influence of Soupault and the earlier writings of Apollinaire when he argued that literature "should not hesitate to keep abreast of the time, to adopt and even foreshadow the influence of the cinema, the avion, the phonograph, the saxophone." An excerpt from his poem "Pursuit," illustrates his approach:

> O wheels that do not turn. O wheels in the brain cease to turn. Why don't they hurry I shall simply shriek to sit so steadfastly before an inert landscape.
>
> O whizzing dynamo set spinning the vast wheelbelts of this world the long rods inflight down the cool oiled cylinders.

Speed, energy, movement—these were the images Josephson attempted to convey, although the clumsiness of his effort is striking. He demonstrated in his prose another aspect of his Dadaist-inspired literary technique. Describing a short story he sent to Harold Loeb, editor of *Broom*, he explained that it "bears no positive ethical message, and locates at the opposite pole to the Sherwood Anderson, Russian realism, American-soil spirit." Josephson was not interested in writing social criticism. He casually accepted the reality of modern life and sought to make artistic use of it. From Paris he had stumbled upon an enthusiastic acceptance of his own machine-age civilization, and he was ready to sing its praises.[16]

To popularize his new artistic approach and to join together in a unified group his circle of young American literary friends, Josephson began looking for a review that would serve as an organ for his ideas. *Broom* appeared a logical choice, for Harold Loeb had started the magazine with a similar purpose in mind. A Princeton graduate and son of a Wall Street broker, he would later become the model for the character Robert Cohn in Hemingway's *The Sun Also Rises*. After selecting Alfred Kreymborg as his associate, Loeb announced in February 1921 the forthcoming publication of *Broom: An International Magazine of the Arts*. In *Broom*'s first issue, published in Rome, contributors from thirteen countries were represented, ranging from Conrad Aiken and Amy Lowell to Picasso and Juan Gris. Loeb received numerous congratulatory letters from around the world.

Among the correspondence addressed to *Broom* was a packet from Matthew Josephson containing several of his poems submitted for consideration. In a covering letter he wrote that he was "struck by the admirable first issue of *Broom*. It would seem to be a capital medium for the presentation of good American writing. I am of course an American. I have worked slowly, rarely published, found insuperable difficulties in getting a hearing." Josephson's praise, however, may have been intended more as an aid in getting his verse published than as a true indication of his feelings: only four days later he announced to Burke that *Broom* "came out in Rome, very handsome, well gotten-up, but rather indecisive. Kreymborg seems castrated. *Broom* was like very weak coffee after all the advance notices." [17]

The new transatlantic review was neither opinionated nor aggressive enough for Josephson, and subsequent issues only confirmed his disapproval. Loeb and Kreymborg differed sharply over editorial policies, and thus lacking any unified focus, *Broom* continued to publish a wide variety of material covering the whole spectrum of contemporary cultural trends. The magazine's catholic nature convinced Josephson that it would not be a suitable forum for the ambitious new literary program he envisioned. As he maintained to Burke in February 1922, *Broom* "has turned out untidy enough and is not doing much sweeping." Nor were any of the other literary reviews acceptable. Earlier, he had tersely summarized his opinion of them: "*The Little Review* is a thing of darkness, the *Broom*, from its first two issues, is Kreymborg flirting with the Drama League; the *Dial* is ———— ———— ————." [18]

Late in 1921 Josephson decided along with Gorham Munson to publish a new magazine. Low printing costs in postwar Europe made it relatively easy for anyone with enough time and energy to publish a review. Josephson told Burke in December that there "is a young man, with waxed moustache, named Gorham Munson, who has a fearful case of editorial nostalgia. He wants to run a magazine for les jeunes. He wants people like Cowley, Damon, Snow, Donald Clark, Hart Crane, you, me to compose it. None of the other kind." Josephson agreed to assist Munson by soliciting material from his young American and French friends. His intention was to "raise a great deal of thunder on the left, by publishing and championing the adventurous experimenters of America. . . . and vigorously assailing the Mrs. Grundies of literature." As he explained to Burke, the new review would provide "an excellent chance to skirmish, to create a diversion, to make an opening sally. All the enemies of LITERATURE can be attacked as such. . . . Some headway may be won against the ill-informed snobisme of the *Little Review*, the eclecticism of the *Dial*, the barbarousness of the others." Josephson viewed art as a battlefield, and his objective was to demolish the barriers of entrenched literary convention.[19]

Josephson and Munson received material from Burke, Cowley, William Carlos Williams, E. E. Cummings, Marianne Moore, Wallace Stevens, Louis Aragon, Tristan Tzara, Philippe Soupault, and Jean Arp. The first issue, printed in Vienna, appeared in April 1922. It included prose and poetry by Cowley, Aragon, and Tzara, as well as an editorial attack on the *Dial* and *Broom* for their eclecticism. In "A Bow to the Adventurous," Munson defined the review's purpose: "*Secession* exists for those writers who are preoccupied with new forms. It hopes that there is ready for it an American public which has advanced beyond the fiction and poetry of Sinclair Lewis and Sherwood Anderson, and the criticism of Paul Rosenfeld and Louis Untermeyer." Munson and Josephson considered Lewis and Anderson too socially oriented, Rosenfeld and Untermeyer too genteel.[20]

A provocative essay by Josephson dominated *Secession*'s first issue. In "Apollinaire: Or Let Us Be Troubadours," he surveyed the young Dadaists writers he had discovered in Paris. As he had done earlier in letters to his friends, Matthew took care to minimize the nihilistic aspects of their activities. The young Dadaists, unlike many of their French countrymen, he posited, had overcome the shock of the war and had displayed an unflagging zest for life and art. He took "much hope from their quick intelligence, their sensibility, their vigorous and fun-loving disposition." He praised inventive poets such as Aragon, Soupault, and Breton for being "bent frankly on unbounded adventures and experiments with modern phenomena." Josephson obviously chose to overlook the intense despair felt by some of the Dadaists. His emphasis was upbeat, reflecting his own background and interests.[21]

Josephson cited his hero Apollinaire as the guiding genius behind the young Dadaists. Before his tragic death, Apollinaire had urged "the poets of this time to be at least as daring as the mechanical wizards who exploited the airplane, wireless telegraphy, chemistry, the submarine, the cinema, the phonograph, what-not." And now his followers were heeding his advice. As an example of the machine-age art being created by the Dadaists, Josephson pointed to Tristan Tzara's poems as being "as naturally expressive of this age as Herrick's are of the 17th century. With an utterly simple and unaffected touch they employ all the instruments of the time, the streetcar, the billposter, the automobile, the incandescent light, etc." Tzara's technique was admirable not because he simply listed modern elements but because he fully integrated such material "into the very rhythm, form and texture of the poems." He also cited the prose of Aragon for displaying "the speed and vividness of the motion picture." [22]

Josephson called on American writers to open their eyes to the cultural possibilities inherent in their own urban industrial environment. His rhetoric soared as he proclaimed that Americans "need play no subservient part in the movement. It is no occasion for aping European or Parisian tendencies. Quite the reverse, Europe is being *Americanized.*" The rapid technological changes occurring in the United States, he claimed, gave American writers a strategic opportunity, and he challenged them to adopt a new artistic perspective amid their "daily existence in the big cities, the great industrial regions, athwart her marvelous and young mechanical forces." [23]

Josephson's European-inspired fascination with machine age America was not greeted with enthusiasm by many of his fellow writers in the United States. Edmund Wilson, then managing editor of *Vanity Fair*, assailed Josephson and the Dadaists for their unquestioning acceptance of the values of industrial America. While recognizing the constructive achievements of the young writers in Paris, he prophetically warned:

> Be careful that the elephants do not crush you! Do not try to make pets out of the machines. . . . The buildings are flattening us out; the machines are tearing us to pieces; our ideals are formed by the movies and our taste by the posters and jazz. Be careful how you fling away the rope that unites you with the past.

Wilson realized that the aesthetes in France, living in relative isolation from the daily turmoil of modern America, had not adequately assessed the destructive aspects of the technological revolution under way in the United States. He feared that they were discarding too quickly the achievements and lessons of the past. [24]

Josephson also continued to encounter opposition from his friends. Kenneth Burke lambasted him for implying that poetry should be guided by science and technology. Malcolm Cowley also expressed reservations about Matty's approach and reiterated his intention to write as a neoclassicist in the mold of Eliot. In answering Cowley, Josephson indicated the extent of his intellectual transformation since arriving in France. He argued that Eliot had been "born dead," and that his "Prufrock" was worthless. He pleaded with Malcolm to give up his "classical" orientation and become more modern: "The extraordinary age in which we live gives us much more to say, if we can, you and I—than the preceding periods, or almost any other." [25]

Hart Crane also remained skeptical of Josephson's proposals. In a letter to Munson he asked: "But what has happened to Matty!?! . . . Will radios, flying machines and cinemas have such a great effect on poetry in the end?" After admitting that Josephson's concept of relating literature to modern life was indeed stimulating, he concluded that it was much like coffee: "Twenty-four hours afterward not much remains to work with. It is . . . somehow thin,—a little too slender and 'smart'—after all." A few weeks later Crane told Munson that Josephson's

> present crazes are, frankly, beyond my understanding. They are so much so that I have still a great deal of confidence that no matter how wild and eccentric he becomes, it's just a phase which will be a practical benefit in the end. But, on the other hand, if one denies all emotional suffering the result is a rather frigid (however "gay") type of work. Let us watch and pray! [26]

Crane had perceived the obvious weakness in Josephson's latest artistic theory. His concept of incorporating the imagery and dynamism of the machine age into prose and poetry was too abstract to be of immediate use. He failed to specify how one should integrate the machine, the cinema, the billboard, and the rest into literature. Nor did he ever clearly delineate the values of such a popular-culture orientation. This lack of concreteness and depth was characteristic of his thinking during the period. As Crane had recognized earlier, Josephson's preoccupation with experimenting with modern forms and techniques prevented him from becoming a respectable poet because he suppressed the role of subjective inspiration, if indeed he ever possessed poetic genius.

Whatever the inherent weaknesses in Josephson's new approach to poetry, it is strikingly apparent that in the short span of a few months his attitude toward life and art had completely reversed itself again. Before leaving New York he had been a disciple of Pound and Eliot and had assumed a decadent, melancholy attitude. Now he displayed his more natural mien of the cheerful optimist, involved, opinionated, and controversial, eager to promote a radical new literary program. He revealed his rapid change of gods and his penchant for combative hyperbole in a letter to Harold Loeb. "Something must be done to stop Ezra Pound," he urged. "For God's sake don't print him! He is a pauvre idiot. He collects the *merdes* of French literature for the *Dial*." Josephson proposed that Loeb substitute Louis Aragon for Pound, describing his Dadaist friend as "a genius pure and simple over a stretch of prose." In another illuminating letter, this time to Burke, he admitted that he had earlier attempted to copy the mood of the Symbolists and other obscurantists, seeking refuge in an ivory tower of art. Now, however, all had changed, and he advised his friend in America to follow the same path: "Jettison all this leaky ballast for an heroic front of aggression, humor, vigor, and choler." When Burke frankly suggested that Matty grow up, he forcefully responded:

> I suddenly feel the need of eschewing the horribly serious air, with which so many unfortunates have practiced art. . . . I come forward definitely with a plea, nay I holler, for a whole department in *Secession* devoted to a regular overhauling of the contemporary best minds.

That his friends attacked him and his changing literary tastes did not faze Josephson. He told Burke that he was "cheered by your enthusiastic clamor against me." Matty fattened on antagonism and grew feeble when treated with indulgence. He was his insolent, combative self again, and the established American literary community would soon feel his full wrath.[27]

Although Josephson's American friends remained skeptical of his new literary proposals, in Europe his Dada-inspired ideas gained attention and support. By the spring of 1922 he had become one of the most prominent American expatriates in Paris. Edith Sitwell, commenting on *Secession* in *New Age*, remarked that she would subscribe to the new magazine "for the purpose of watching the career of Mr. Matthew Josephson." Early in 1922 Gertrude Stein inquired of Harold Loeb: "What is *Secession* and what do they do?" Loeb had begun to take an active interest in the new review and especially in its flamboyant editor Josephson. Kreymbourg had finally resigned from *Broom*, and Loeb began to revise the magazine's editorial policy.[28]

In an article entitled "Foreign Exchange," which he sent to Josephson for his comments, Loeb remarked that Americans in Paris were revising their attitudes toward their homeland. "America regarded from France," he maintained, "is not the same America that bustles from subway to elevator. The reevaluation is accelerated and assisted by the curious attitude of admiration among French artists." Loeb observed that Americans arriving in Paris expecting to find Frenchmen immersed in their rich cultural past would instead find spirited praise of American advertising, movies, jazz, comics, and skyscrapers. In his opinion, the transplanted young American writers in Paris offered a promising alternative to the "literature of revolt" taking place in the United States. Loeb cited Josephson, Cummings, and Munson as the most talented among the expatriates.[29]

After reading Loeb's essay, Josephson hurriedly sent him "Made in America," an article that began with an attack on *Broom*'s eclectic editorial policy, and then described in detail the program of the "youngest" generation in Paris. He noted that the Dadaists had adopted a style of prose and poetry substituting "humor instead of pathos, aggression instead of doubt, and complete freedom of method for the restriction of the previous age." They were ready to deal directly with their modern environment, to be at least "as daring as the mechanical geniuses of the age which has attained the veritable realization of the miracles forecast in primitive fables. To be prophets alike, the fable-makers for the incredible ages to come!" In direct reply to the warnings of Edmund Wilson, Josephson exclaimed:

> The machine is not "flattening us out" nor "crushing us." The machine is our magnificent slave, our fraternal genius. We are a new and hardier race, friend to the skyscraper and the subterranean railway as well. We are at home under the sea as well as in the air, and we can sing and laugh as heartily under these transformed conditions.

Josephson advised Americans to cease their imitation of a "discredited French naturalism" and react spontaneously to the panorama of modern American life. It was time for writers in the United States to cast off the self-imposed shackles of European cultural hegemony and develop their own native art.[30]

Despite its critical tone, "Made in America" delighted Loeb, and he immediately agreed to publish it in *Broom*. In his memoirs he recalled deciding that Josephson, "with this affirmative viewpoint, was a young writer with whom I could advantageously cooperate." A few weeks later, in July 1922, the Josephsons visited Loeb in Rome. They had been on a walking trip in southern France and planned to spend a fortnight in Rome before ending up in the Austrian Alps for the summer. Loeb remembered their first encounter:

Young Matty Josephson and his wife Hannah arrived in Rome, and I liked them immediately. Matty seemed a trifle brash, but then I could do with a little more of this quality. Of slender build, he was eager, earnest, energetic, and ambitious. With narrow, bent nose, high forehead and cheekbones, his features, and especially his eyes, were animated by a lively intelligence. Hannah's . . . yellow hair, and wistful eyes had an attractiveness. . . . She shared her husband's interests.

During their conversation Josephson suggested that *Broom* become an organ for the dynamic new modernists in literature and the plastic arts. He urged Loeb to relocate the magazine's headquarters to Germany, where cultural activities were experiencing a revival and printing costs were cheaper.[31]

Loeb agreed both to publish more material from the Dadaists and to move the magazine to Berlin. He also offered Josephson the job of associate editor. Matty was tempted to accept immediately. Personal and editorial quarrels with Munson had already begun to weaken his loyalty to *Secession*. Moreover, he would receive a small salary as an editor of *Broom*. Josephson described Loeb's offer as an admirable opportunity for him "to live easefully rolling in beer and wine, with plenty of freedom and time to write." Within a few weeks he accepted the position, even though he remained associated with *Secession*.[32]

After leaving Italy in July the Josephsons spent the next six weeks in the Tyrolean Alps. By all accounts they were finding their European experience thrilling. Matthew had written Burke a few months before, noting that he was enjoying a "second childhood" among the Dadaists. As co-editor of *Secession* and associate editor of *Broom* he had finally found his calling; he was much more effective as editor and critic than as poet. Eager to stimulate controversy, Josephson relished his mounting literary importance. Such prestige (or notoriety) enabled him to take the offensive, to impose his opinions and personality upon the two magazines and their reading public. In August 1922 Hart Crane told Munson, "Matty has developed a 'high hand' attitude in criticism that is . . . as effective and compelling as Pound's. I am beginning to see little Caesarian laurels sprouting on his brow."[33]

Wallace Stevens experienced at first hand young Josephson's growing intellectual arrogance. In a letter rejecting one of Stevens's poems for publication in *Secession*, Josephson remarked that the poem's first line "is frankly bad. Most of the others are merely neutral—and labored. The alliterations employed are quite obvious. Here and there are glimpses of your most personal method. The whole poem, then, offers the mechanics of your art and not the fruition thereof." Maxwell Bodenheim received a similar rejection notice from editor Josephson. He later asked Harold Loeb whether one of his poems had been accepted for publication in *Broom* in spite of the "ferocious Matthew Josephson, who knows so well whether a certain poem of mine is 'above average.' " [34]

Josephson's controversial editorial opinions expressed in *Secession* and *Broom* attracted the attention of a number of other writers and poets in the United States. On a couple of occasions, Waldo Frank expressed to Loeb a qualified admiration for Josephson's work. He "is intelligent and feels warmly," Frank observed in the summer of 1922, "and there is no other literary justice." Several months later he confided to Loeb that he considered his close friend Munson "in a far maturer intellectual state today than his brilliant friend Josephson, for whom however I have real attention." From another perspective, Allen Tate, then associated with the Fugitives, informed Hart Crane that he was "very much interested in Josephson's work. . . . I should like to get in touch with him." The sensitive Crane began to feel somewhat jealous of his editor friend's rising reputation. He admitted as much in a letter to Munson: "Allen Tate sends me a good poem, acknowledges myself and Eliot as his models—calls me mature and perfect—so that now . . . I feel vastly superior to Matty." Josephson thrived on such strong reactions to his work. Once you attack something, he advised Burke, "you get into the realm of action, you display a vertebra, you have fun. Let it then be a little more boisterous and adventurous." [35]

In late August 1922 Malcolm and Peggy Cowley visited the Josephsons in Austria. Cowley approached the meeting with some apprehension, for in the past several months, he and Matty had engaged in a caustic epistolary feud centered on Josephson's conversion to Dada. Cowley had reacted angrily to his friend's withering criticism and sarcasm. He told Burke that every time he read one of Matty's letters a second time, "it makes me boil. He has the habit of slipping in a superior sentence . . . and my answers are apt to be snotty." Such comments illustrate the seriousness with which the young writers approached their craft, as well as the size of their egos. The squabble reached a climax when Josephson wrote Cowley a letter on toilet paper. [36]

Cowley's apprehension at visiting the Josephsons, however, turned out to be unwarranted. He and Peggy thoroughly enjoyed their weekend in the Alps. They discovered that beneath Matty's brash exterior and sardonic wit resided a warm, sensitive, and entertaining young man. In the evenings, as the two couples took advantage of the favorable exchange rate to sample Austrian nightlife, Matthew was extremely gregarious, or "upstage," as Cowley put it. Although at times pompous, Josephson also revealed diffidence and charm, qualities that Cowley had not anticipated. He was, Malcolm remembered, "suave, polished, sociable, courtly." Josephson went out of his way to protest with his waiters about the food, fought with the innkeeper over the bill, and then reversed himself and tipped them extravagantly. During their conversation about literature and the little magazines, Cowley was impressed by his friend's ability to form broad conceptions and lay broad plans. He was also fascinated at Josephson's ability to live an unbohemian life-style. A few months later, after moving to Berlin, the Josephsons, thanks primarily to a monthly subsidy from his father, "lived in a duplex apartment with two maids, riding lessons for his wife, dinners in only the most expensive restaurants, tips to the orchestra, pictures collected, charities to struggling German writers." Josephson's brazen yet convivial manner was contagious, and he persuaded Cowley to revise his opinions of the Dadaists, whom he still had not met. After leaving the Josephsons in Austria, Cowley reported to Burke that "Matty was nicer . . . than we expected." He also confessed that he was beginning to agree with Josephson that while creating serious work, as writers they should at the same time "do stunts and polemify [sic] and all that." After being with Josephson, Cowley found it difficult to "resent Matty except in his letters." [37]

At the end of August 1922, Loeb transferred *Broom* to Berlin. On Josephson's advice he asked Cowley to serve as a contributing editor. Cowley accepted the offer, informing Burke that now he, Josephson, and Loeb were in agreement that the United States contained a wealth of new cultural material. Late in 1922 Cowley confessed his complete conversion to Josephson's ideas. After meeting and living with the Dadaists in Paris, he admitted to Burke: "Matty is right about them. They are the most amusing people in Paris." With Cowley's support Josephson was ready to transform *Broom* into an organ for their Dada-inspired ideas. Meanwhile, however, he was still connected with *Secession*, and this dual editorship soon posed problems. Josephson assumed at first that he could continue to serve both little magazines without creating a conflict of interests. He was wrong. It did not take long for Munson and Josephson to clash. And thus began one of the most famous literary controversies of the 1920s. [38]

Since the early days of *Secession*, Munson and Josephson had engaged in a continuous literary and personal feud, much of it petty. Both fiery editors had sensitive egos and strongly held literary opinions. Munson from the start had been wary of Josephson's paeans to the machine age. For his part Matty had never thought much of Munson's intellectual or literary ability. The turning point in their feud occurred in late 1922. It revolved around Munson's close friendship with Waldo Frank. Josephson, then speaking for *Broom*, rejected a favorable article about Frank that Munson had submitted. He then proceeded to write a caustic review of Frank's latest book. When Munson left for New York in the summer of 1922, leaving Josephson behind as official coeditor of *Secession*'s third issue, he anticipated trouble and asked Kenneth Burke to join the editorial board. Together they would gather material in the United States and forward it to Josephson in Europe for publication. Josephson resented this obvious attempt to weaken his editorial authority, and in defiance, he printed in *Secession* one of his own short stories that Munson had earlier vetoed. At the same time, Matty was moving closer to Loeb and *Broom*. As he did so, however, he still had in his possession the material for the fourth issue of *Secession*, scheduled to appear in January 1923. Munson expected the worst and asked John Brooks Wheelwright, the witty, eccentric Boston poet, who was then headed for Europe, to serve as *Secession*'s overseas agent.[39]

John Brooks Wheelwright has been an unnecessarily neglected figure in twentieth-century American literary history. The son of a prominent Boston family, he was educated at the exclusive Fay School, then at St. George's in Newport, and finally at Harvard, where he came to know Malcolm Cowley. Tall and thin, with blond hair, pale blue eyes, a wide mouth, and a big nose, Wheelwright was a wealthy bachelor who took great pride in his elliptical, unmelodic verse. A fastidious, eccentric dresser with a penchant for custom-made Italian suits, oversize fedoras, and hickory walking sticks, he had an imposing, aristocratic manner, but among friends he could be quite a clown. When Wheelwright arrived in Paris in the fall of 1922, with orders from Munson to protect *Secession* from Josephson's tampering, he arranged to meet the Josephsons and Cowleys at Les Deux Magots. Robert Coates, the young Yale graduate and aspiring novelist, was also there. "I liked the Josephsons immensely," Wheelwright remembered. They impressed him with their cosmopolitan manner and forceful opinions. Matty, he commented, had a habit of sprinkling his statements with gallicisms, and this added to his worldly persona. Wheelwright also enjoyed Josephson's ready wit and playful spirit.[40]

A few weeks later the same group met again at Cowley's house in Giverny, about fifty miles from Paris. There Wheelwright's fondness for Josephson and Cowley increased. From what he had heard about Josephson from Munson, he had come to France expecting to meet a "neurotic" aesthete. But such was not the case. He found Matty "surprisingly and delightfully sympathetic" to his own literary work. Josephson, he remarked, had a "full, rich and warm facility in taking in and giving out culture." Cowley told Wheelwright in private that Josephson "had grown up," thanks primarily to Hannah. Wheelwright remembered one of Peggy Cowley's observations—that Matty "had married a woman who thought him a genius and who in order to realize her thought had insisted to him that he was one. By gentle perseverance it was agreed she had advanced towards her desire." Wheelwright was especially taken with Hannah. She liked to argue and so did he. In a discussion about art Hannah sent Wheelwright into a rage: "I swore. I screamed. I beat the ground with my feet as I walked along. I clenched my fists and waved my arms in the air. I made faces at her and called her names and almost spat at her." Within a few minutes, however, his anger cooled, and he began singing the latest songs from Broadway for the "homesick" Josephsons. Hannah had much the same effect upon Wheelwright as she did upon Matty. She challenged them intellectually and in a way that made them hunger for more.[41]

After coming to know each other socially, Wheelwright, Josephson, and Cowley then turned their attention to *Secession* number four. Matty and Malcolm informed their new friend that they had already conferred about the makeup of the issue. They had received from Munson and Burke several poems by "Richard Ashton," the pseudonym of Donald B. Clark, at best an inconsistent American poet. The two American Dadaists found Clark's verse awful and decided to "edit" one of the poems, deleting nineteen of its twenty-one lines. The abridged version, entitled "The Jilted Moon," now read: "To me [you] are no more than Chinese, o moon, / Are no more than Chinese." After living with Cowley and Josephson for a few days, Wheelwright had assimilated their youthful, bumptious outlook and approved their editorial decisions. "Cowley and Josephson," he later recalled, "had devised what was, to them and me, a delightfully pleasing method of expression of their hatred for bad poetry, and I concurred with their obstinacy in holding fast to this expression; for in this expression all intellectual aspects of the case were to be found." To the three of them, the editing of the poem was no more than a literary prank, a Dadaist joke. To Munson, however, the butchering of Clark's poem was treason. He took his magazine seriously, perhaps too seriously. Munson removed the edited poem from *Secession*, and Josephson resigned from the editorial board. Thereafter, the two editors remained mortal enemies.[42]

Beginning with the October 1922 number, the Berlin issues of *Broom* reflected the magazine's change in editorial direction and Josephson's influence in particular. The October cover was a drawing of a huge turbine generator by Enrico Prampolini, one of the original Italian Futurists. The same issue contained a tribute to Robert Coady, editor of the short-lived *Soil*, which during the war years had pioneered the effort to create a uniquely American art and literature reflective of the country's popular culture and mechanical orientation. The November issue continued to stress a machine-age art. It included several stark photographs by Paul Strand of ball bearings, gears, ships, and factories. In an accompanying essay, Strand emphasized the aesthetic potential of machinery and encouraged American artists to make use of it.

Josephson and Cowley spearheaded the change in *Broom*'s format with their own contributions. In the December issue Cowley wrote "Young Mr. Elkins," a biting satire of those American writers who spent their time whining about the difficulty of living in the United States. He explained to Loeb that the essay comprised a "portrait of the American intellectual, the sort of person who wants to turn New York into a larger Paris. Venom and bile against the generation of Harold Stearns. Twelve hundred words of fine hate." Stearns's anthology *Civilization in the United States* had just been published, and he was determined to weaken its impact. In "Young Mr. Elkins" Cowley described how the abundant American economy provided for the literary intellectual: "It suckled him with Shredded Wheat. It draped Kuppenheimer Klothes about his shoulders. It gave him an Underwood typewriter (Model 5) and convenient magazines. It sent him to Harvard as a classmate of Walter Lippmann." But young Mr. Elkins did not appreciate such advantages. In fact he spent most of his time thundering against "billboards, Billy Sunday and Methodism, proportional representation, Comstock, elevated railroads. One year with special fulgurance he thundered against the commercial ugliness of the cities." But all the while, Cowley wrote, American civilization "howls outside his window." It keeps on moving, growing, prospering. "Young Mr. Elkins," he concluded, "annoyed by the racket, rose nervously and closed the window."[43]

Josephson was even more explicit in demonstrating his disgust at those writers who only found fault with their country. In "The Great American

Billposter" he warned that America would never have an indigenous culture if its intellectuals insisted on condemning their own national environment. Instead, American artists should appreciate the unique features of their homeland and start writing, rather than complaining. He
responded directly to the pessimistic tone of *Civilization in the United
States*:

> The problem is . . . to silence for a moment, the anguished voices of
> the Thirty Americans and to plunge hardily into the effervescent re-
> volving cacophonous milieu . . . where Billposters enunciate their
> wisdom, the Cinema transports us, the newspapers intone their
> gaudy jargon; where athletes play upon the frenetic passions of
> baseball crowds, and skyscrapers rise lyrically to the exotic rhythms
> of jazzbands which upon waking up we find to be nothing but the
> drilling of pneumatic hammers on steel girders.

Josephson pleaded for poets "who have dared the lightning, who come
to us out of the heart of this chimera; novelists who express for us its mad
humor." The irony of such comments is overwhelming. While in Europe
Josephson had fallen in love with modern urban industrial America, singing its praises from afar. Like the Dadaists he had succumbed to the image of America portrayed in its popular culture. He failed to recognize
that by blindly worshiping the machine, he was ignoring the deleterious
effects of mechanism upon the quality of life and artistic sensibility.
Moreover, he sacrificed the human qualities of experience that in their
unmechanical and unpredictable way give depth to art. As early as 1916
Waldo Frank had criticized writers who, "plunging into the American
maelstrom, were submerged in it, lost their vision altogether, and gave
forth a gross chronicle and a blind cult of the American Fact."[44]

Josephson now approached such an ingenuous attitude. He suggested
that the prose and poetry contained in American advertising slogans represented some of the country's best literature. As one of his examples he
favorably compared a line from Keats describing the qualities of good
wine—"The beaded bubbles winking at the brim"—with an excerpt
from an American soup promotion—"Meaty marrowy oxtail joints." He
concluded that American poets should imitate the style of advertising
slogans and thereby mirror the true values and dynamism of the nation.[45]

After reading Josephson's article on advertising as literary art, Waldo
Frank complained to Loeb about that "silly Billboard article." He dismissed Josephson as "simply another young man whose head has been

turned by the cerebrations of certain French artists he does not under-stand." Hart Crane also reacted strongly to his friend's latest controversial piece. In a letter to Munson he observed:

> Matty's "gay intellectualism" will eventually expose him to the jibes of a psychoanalyst if he continues in such loose estimates. . . . Some things he says may be true,—but how damned vulgar his rhapsodies become! I would rather be on the side of "sacred art" . . . than ad-mit that a great art is inherent in the tinsel of the billboards. Tech-nique there is, of course, but such gross materialism has nothing to do with art. Artistry and fancy will be Matty's limit as long as he is not willing to admit the power and beauty of emotional intensity— which he has proved he hasn't got.

Crane's continuing harsh assessments of Josephson's critical efforts no doubt reflected in part their deepening rift dating back to Matty's mar-riage to Hannah. This seems especially evident in his statement that Josephson ignored "the power and beauty of emotional intensity," a quality that Crane possessed in abundance. Yet despite the heat of his remarks, Hart was correct in recognizing that Josephson's overweening emphasis on form was inhibiting his performance as poet.[46]

American literary critics quickly noticed the change in *Broom*'s em-phasis under Josephson. Louis Untermeyer, writing in the *New Republic*, referred to the writers associated with *Broom* as the "new patricians." The new group, he remarked, "not only knocks at our doors but threat-ens to batter down the very structure in which we are just beginning to feel comfortable." He classified Josephson as the leader of the group, "straight Dada, accepting the Dadaists' denial of logic and their glorifica-tion of incoherence." Julius W. Friend, editor of the *Double-Dealer*, pub-lished in New Orleans, admitted that among the young American experi-mentalists in Europe, there was considerable talent. He cited Josephson as the "most prominent of those who will some day save himself from all this blather of 'new forms,' 'new ideas,' etc., etc., and, unless we miss our guess, do some very fine things."[47]

Josephson's experiment with *Broom* appeared successful, and he de-lighted in his growing reputation and literary influence. Cowley de-scribed to Burke their friend's sudden rise to prominence. Matty "has a great deal of vitality, conceit," Malcolm wrote. "He enjoys being decent, doing the right thing in the grand manner, also fighting with waiters and insulting people." Five days later Cowley continued his analysis:

> Perhaps there is something sound in Matty's instinct when he tries to shock people. Matty has several appealing qualities, chief of which is a lively interest in literature. I hate to admit it, but at present he is really less venial than either of us. He is uncompromising and compromising; I mean that he would compromise even the Holy Ghost or Charles Evans Hughes.

In a similar assessment Hart Crane commented to Munson in January 1923 that Josephson "appears to rest in clover and periwinkles, what with the Guggenheim millions and the international sweep of editorial authority." Crane's allusion to Harold Loeb's family connection with the Guggenheims was exaggerated. As the *Broom* group's notoriety spread, financial problems threatened to cut short the magazine's future. After four issues were published in Berlin, Loeb's resources were depleted. In an attempt to save the magazine he traveled to New York and appealed to his rich uncle, Simon Guggenheim, for financial support, but received none and returned to Europe empty-handed.[48]

Josephson remained determined to continue publication. After trying several schemes to reduce costs and acquire funds in Europe, he returned to New York in May 1923 and persuaded his brother-in-law, a young printer, to publish the magazine at reduced rates. With renewed optimism Matty informed Loeb from Manhattan that "the place for everybody is here; after all Europe is for repose, for leisure. But to put something over we have to be here." Thus, with a suddenness brought on by the threat of *Broom*'s collapse, Josephson's European experience was over, and after an absence of a year and a half, he was back in his native New York.[49]

How had his European *Wanderjahr* affected him? Certainly he had grown substantially in experience, knowledge, and self-assurance. Primarily, however, Josephson's experience abroad served to crystallize personality traits he had already displayed. In trying to explain to Burke the influence of Europe and the Dadaists upon Josephson, Cowley wrote a short biographical sketch of Louis Aragon, who had, according to Malcolm, "imposed all his ideas" on Josephson. Cowley spoke of Aragon:

> Suddenly at a certain age, he begins to reject all his family and social connections deliberately, and with a splendid disdain which he had acquired from his early successes, to tell everybody exactly what he thought. And still he was successful. He has so much charm when he wishes to exercise it, that it takes him years to make an enemy. But by force of repeated insults, he succeeds. He retains all

the hatred of compromise which is the quality of a youth he never wholly possessed. . . . He lives literature. . . . He judges a writer largely by his moral qualities, such as courage, vigor, the refusal to compromise. . . . He is unbelievably energetic. He is an egoist and vain, but faithful to his friends.[50]

Cowley, of course, was describing Josephson as much as Aragon, and he succeeded remarkably well in capturing the essence of the young editor's personality. Aragon was the teacher, Josephson the student. But Aragon did not "impose" such qualities upon Josephson. They were already inherent in his character. Aragon and Dadaism had provided the impetus for Matthew to recognize his own evolving philosophy of life and literature. Literature to him was indeed an ethical issue. As such there could be no compromise. And just as Aragon and other Dadaists would later transfer their moral intensity to the social and political sphere, Josephson would also redirect his artistic energies to the public arena in the 1930s. As the leading American Dadaist in Paris, he had shown little interest in politics. The meaning of Marxism, of Soviet Russia, of political pamphleteering, would assume importance for him only later, long after Dada had waned. But his association with Aragon and the Dadaists revealed a pronounced will to radicalism and activism that would eventually express themselves in political terms. In 1923, however, he arrived in New York determined to bring the spirit of Dada to the United States and to unveil his machine-age literary program to the country responsible for its inspiration. Yet he would soon discover that his transatlantic vision of America had been myopic, that his understanding of modern urban industrial life was superficial, and that he had yet to "find himself" completely.

6 DADA IN NEW YORK

Matthew Josephson returned to the United States with ideas that
bore little relation to the problems of living and and writing in modern
urban-industrial Manhattan. While abroad he had come to view his native country from an artistic perspective, oblivious to the fact that in most
cases, symbol, metaphor, and myth distort as much as represent reality.
From Europe he had praised the symbols and tempo of machine-age life,
not the objects behind the symbols. But it was with the objects that he
would have to live in New York. The change in perspective produced a
change in attitude. Malcolm Cowley has recently remarked that the sudden transition from tradition-bound Europe to modern America aroused
within himself and Josephson a "tension between our rural tastes and our
bravos for the spectacle of American business." In Europe such a tension
remained sublimated, since the young expatriates could rhapsodize
about machine-age America without daily experiencing the oppressive
aspects of mass urban life. In Manhattan, however, they came face-to-
face with the roaring machines, flashing neon lights, banal advertising
jingles, speeding automobiles, and ominous skyscrapers that they had invested with vital artistic and spiritual qualities. As a result Josephson
would begin to recognize the simplistic nature of his worship of the mechanical process. He eventually would learn to probe beneath modern

society's superficial gloss, to go beyond just dealing in metaphor and symbol, and would begin to ask the more profound questions about man and machine, artist and society, that he had earlier ignored.[1]

When he arrived in Manhattan, however, the twenty-four-year-old Josephson was far from such a realization. He was convinced that his homeland, with its thriving culture, its machines, factories, movies, and jazz, provided the artist with an ideal working environment. Matty fully expected to transplant the spirit of Dada in New York, and he intended to serve as its high priest. His initial activities in Manhattan served only to reinforce such plans. On the surface, New York in the early 1920s seemed frivolous and hedonistic. The popular arts were flourishing, and New Yorkers were intent on enjoying their growing prosperity. Josephson was quick to sample the city's varied cultural offerings. After watching the Marx Brothers he compared their antics to those of the European Dadaists. He told Loeb in May 1923 that he had just seen "*Merton of the Movies* and really enjoyed it. See Al Jolson tomorrow and Ted Lewis in Greenwich Village Follies after that. . . . New York is very lively and drink is plentiful and varied."[2]

Josephson quickly renewed his association with Kenneth Burke, who now was ready to overlook his friend's Dadaist eccentricities and support *Broom*, although he still disagreed with some of his more radical views. Josephson informed Cowley: "The most profitable company I have found has been Burke's. We reconciled very speedily because as he put it there is so little good company here. Upon this modest basis of comradeship we have been drinking good Jersey beer and stout together and managed to have some fine times." Burke, he reported, "still has an extraordinary gift for definition, and great stability. . . . He has become even more likeable than before and very resourceful when drunk." The Josephsons enjoyed spending weekends at the Burke homestead in Andover, New Jersey, where they rededicated themselves to obtaining their own rural retreat one day. As Josephson told Cowley, "I agree that you ought to live in the country. We all ought to, but beware of Burke's scheme of starting a Platonic republic in Andover." With Burke in the fold Matthew was more optimistic than ever about *Broom*'s fortunes in the United States. "America," he wrote Cowley, "is getting nuttier and nuttier. The country is falling our way. Burke laments it as the danger of too much quest of subject matter. But I incline to think that Burke will remain interestingly wrong on some of these symptoms. . . . the most colorful and preposterous life in the world is being lived in America."[3]

Hart Crane had also begun to move closer to the ideas espoused by Josephson and Cowley. A few months earlier, in March 1923, he had announced to Munson that he felt himself "quite fit to become a suitable Pindar for the dawn of the Machine Age, so-called. I have lost the last shreds of philosophical pessimism during the last few months." Despite Crane's new appreciation for the literary potential inherent in machine-age America, however, he still could not get along well with Josephson. The latter's opinionated, forceful nature overwhelmed the hypersensitive Crane. He simply could not stand up to Josephson's overbearing personality and withering sarcasm. As he told his friend Alfred Stieglitz, "I'm in a low state of reactions towards everything, following an evening with Mr. Josephson." Their relationship was strained even more by Matty's continuing, intense feud with Gorham Munson, one of Crane's closest friends. But as John Unterecker has pointed out, the conflict between Josephson and Crane centered primarily on a fundamental difference in literary perspective. Hart was a visionary idealist; he wrote poetry with his heart and soul. Matty was a Dadaist determined to take the wind out of such mystical visionaries.[4]

A few weeks after returning to Manhattan, Josephson went to the posh *Vanity Fair* offices on Fifth Avenue and introduced himself to Edmund Wilson, who earlier had sharply criticized the Dadaists. He remembered that Wilson had a "trim figure, looked spruce in a brown Brooks Brothers suit, and wore a brilliant yellow necktie; his hair was reddish brown, his eyes dark brown and keen looking, his manner shy but sometimes brusque." Josephson had come to convert Wilson to his new literary program and brought along a one-act playlet by Soupault for him to read. When Wilson had finished he looked up at Josephson, flashed a broad grin and said: "But they are just pulling our leg, aren't they?" The two young editors then began arguing about Dada, Wilson contending that it was purely destructive; Josephson responding that it destroyed in order to create a new and better art. Wilson wanted to see examples of the Dadaists' "constructive" art. After thirty minutes of discussion Josephson gave up trying to explain Dada to Wilson. He decided that the Ivy League editor took his art too seriously.[5]

Josephson's failure to win Crane's and Wilson's support did not deter him from his plans for *Broom*. He soon found other writers and artists who were interested in his ideas and the magazine's American adventure. Among them were Edward Nagle, a young artist from Boston who agreed to serve as an adviser on painting; Glenway Wescott, a promising, golden-haired novelist from Wisconsin; Jean Toomer, the gifted Negro poet and novelist; Charles Sheeler, then one of America's leading modernist painters; and Allen Tate, the young poet from Tennessee. Josephson, Burke, Slater Brown, Tate, and other members of this group would regularly meet for lunch at an inexpensive Italian restaurant in the Village. There they would "sit in the sun in the late afternoon drinking 'California Chianti' from coffee cups, while little children play nearby, and a policeman comes in to sit beside us and sip wine peacefully." The group's activities were not always as mellow and serene as Josephson indicated. The Prohibition era had its seamier side as well. In June 1923 he reported that he, Nagle, Brown, and Burke

> escaped with our lives from a gang on Sullivan Street after midnight, leaving a bootleg joint that is always our common meeting ground. Brown's influence, when he has money, is very demoralizing. So far I have only been to two parties. Stuff is perfectly all right, but in the bootleg age you drink fast, when you get it.

As he told Loeb they were all having a "pleasant" time, even though the pace "is fast and desperate." [6]

Buoyed by the interest and support of these artists, Josephson proclaimed that the "young generation has come over solidly." He suggested that *Broom* focus even more upon developing an American emphasis, and he advocated an American civilization department that would discuss musical shows, popular song hits, movies, and other elements of the national culture. Burke wanted a timely "kick" section devoting to directing salvos at the "liberal" and established magazines. In other words, Josephson stressed to Loeb: "We think *Broom* has been too sedate. This would give the air of an aggressive group of individuals behind it, which *Secession* has only been able to do socially here." [7]

After setting up an office for *Broom* at 45 King Street on the southern border of the Village, Josephson began putting his ideas into action. Loeb, who had grown tired of the continued demands of editing a transatlantic review, remained in Europe and began writing a long-planned novel. Malcolm Cowley would soon leave France and join Josephson in New York. Slater Brown also joined the editorial staff. In the first New York issue, printed in July 1923, Loeb introduced the group associated with *Broom* to American readers. He emphasized their attitude of optimism and affirmation:

> The men of this group are not shocked by the disclosure that stockyards are congenial hangouts for neither man nor beast. They cannot

confess even to surprise when told newspapers occasionally mis-
represent the facts. Although interested in the social customs of
Main Street, they are dubious whether a reformed Main Street, with
Little Theatre, Community Pageants, Modern Book Shop and Birth
Control Club would be more attractive and happier. . . . they may
like billposters no more than does Van Wyck Brooks, but they do not
contend that such things are done better in Europe. Rather they hold
that there is a great deal to be said for the American system of going
the limit if you are going to go it at all. They keep an open mind
toward the phenomena of contemporary industrialism, and devote
themselves to the more immediate task of men of letters: writing
well.

Loeb concluded that *Broom* was finally in the country to which it
belonged.[8]

Broom's New York numbers clearly reflected Josephson's desire to
stimulate an appreciation for American cultural life in all its facets. The
September *Broom*, for instance, contained a series of essays on American
movies. In addition there were poems by Cowley and Isidor Schneider, a
short story by Jean Toomer, and a selection from what would become
William Carlos Williams's impressionistic history of the United States, *In
the American Grain*. The October issue was even more American in emphasis. It featured E. E. Cummings's "Five Americans," a handful of
poems about American prostitutes. In addition there was another install-
ment of *In the American Grain* and a tribute to Charles Sheeler emphasizing his literal depiction of American subjects, from Bucks County
barns and Shaker furniture to modern machines and factories. Despite its
heavy American emphasis, however, *Broom* continued to publish European artists. Virginia Woolf contributed a short story, as did Louis Aragon. Josephson also translated in serial form Apollinaire's *The Poet
Assassinated*.[9]

Josephson's opinions and personality dominated the American phase
of *Broom*. Many of his comments in 1923 about the role of the writer in
America's mass industrial society appear remarkably ironic when viewed
in light of his later historical works and political affiliations. In the August
issue he argued that the "large, imaginative, daring, formidable people
in America are mostly found on the vaudeville stage, in the movies, in
the advertising business, prize-fighting, railroads, Wall Street." The modern age, he concluded, "demands hardier poets, such as can straddle the

language of the people as well as the vaudeville comedian or an advertising copywriter, positive, voluble, sententious, and yet by their own form and attitude defining the very nature of their age." The central thrust of his argument was clear: literature and writers must accept present-day realities and stop trying to change or wish them away.[10]

In the September *Broom* Josephson praised even more explicitly the inspirational quality and positive achievements of American industry and business. Again he castigated those who criticized modern America, finding their "resistance and sense of oppression curiously misguided." He continued in the same vein:

> Nor is it true that the artist in modern times has been cast into the ditch by industrialism. Abhorring Spengler I find it more plausible to liken this age of mechanism to the Renaissance, by virtue of its vast physical triumphs over nature. . . . Our Drakes and Marco Polos are in the laboratory or at the salesmanager's desk. . . . Whatever we may think of the social injustice wrought by the machine, it has certainly turned up an amazing store of fresh artistic material.

In a review of Stuart Sherman's *The Genius of America*, Josephson asserted that the country's "genius" resided not in its moral idealism, as Sherman maintained, but in its "economic organization, and expresses itself in quantity production and national sales. It creates an inspiring enough spectacle for poets and novelists to ruminate over."[11]

Matthew Josephson was in love with America's business civilization. He had succumbed to the gospel of efficiency and mass production, and he was determined to integrate such values in art. In a poem dedicated to Henry Ford, he employed the automotive king as a symbl of the machine age, gleaning phrases from advertising copy to provide a dynamic tone:

> With the brain at the wheel
> the eye on the road
> and the hand to the left
> pleasant be your progress
> explorer, producer, stoic, after your fashion.
> Change
> CHANGE
> to what speed? to what underwear?
> Here is a town, here a mill:
> nothing surprises you old horse face.

>   Guzzle guzzle goes the siren;
>   and the world will learn to admire and applaud your
>   concern about the parts, your firmness with
>   employees, and your justice to your friends.

This "poem" illustrates the shallow but energetic and persistent way in which Josephson sought to infuse the elements and energy of the machine age into literature. His verse represented a series of random impressions and jumbled phrases rather than a logical sequence. The result was typical of Dada—a poetry more cute than profound.[12]

As a result of Josephson's aggressive editorial leadership, *Broom* began to attract considerable attention in New York literary circles. The editors of the *Dial*, the most successful of America's little magazines, referred to *Broom*'s contributors as "skyscraper primitives" preaching an articulate form of Futurism. The *Dial* commended them for recognizing that the "machine is the dominant factor in contemporary life, and that America is the most highly mechanized country in the world, so that for better or worse, the course of society for the next era is most likely to be settled in America's terms." Josephson's reputation as the controversial leader of the "skyscraper primitives" was also growing, although not always to his credit. Edmund Wilson still disapproved strongly of the *Broom* group. "I can't hand the *Broom* crowd very much," he told John Peale Bishop, "Cowley, I think, has some ability but is sort of an ass, and Josephson is an ass with practically no observable ability."[13]

Wilson illustrated both the importance and the naivete of Josephson's ideas in an imaginary interview he published in the *New Republic* between *Broom*'s editor and Paul Rosenfeld, an exemplar of a more genteel approach to literature. Wilson has Josephson proclaim that the literature of the past is worthless, that only Dadaists can "appreciate the gigantic, the gorgeous, the fantastic world of the twentieth century." The compelling genius of American civilization, he contends, is not its art, but its advertising, automobiles, factories, movies, Irving Berlin, Krazy Kat cartoons, and Wall Street mania. Rosenfeld counters that such a view is simplistic and juvenile. He accuses Josephson of wanting people not only to "appreciate the vulgar but also to forget the fine." Advertising copywriters, he insists, do not write out of sheer joy; they write ads because they have to make a living. The truly sensitive artist, according to Rosenfeld, should attack the degrading and dehumanizing impact of the machine.

The human spirit is what is important, not artificial inventions of the human mind.[14]

The hypothetical Josephson finds such sentiments laughable. Wilson has him sarcastically reply:

> The honor of the human spirit . . . the principles of justice and humanity . . . Liberty, Fraternity, Equality . . . the dawn of a new day . . . Workers of the world arise! you have nothing to lose but your chains! . . . E. E. Cummings could make a very amusing poem by mixing them all up together and sticking in the Paris urinal and the venereal affiches.

He assaults Rosenfeld for taking life and literature too seriously. Dada, on the other hand, can show Americans how to be gay, to enjoy the "delightful idiocy" of modern life. He cites comedians Joe Cook and Ed Wynn as coming closest to expressing the Dada spirit in the United States. Speaking through Rosenfeld, Wilson pointedly warns Josephson of the dangers of his glorification of the machine age. The age of mechanism has no place for critics or poets: "You can only prostrate yourself before the monster in amazement and awe of his strength."[15]

Other observers, however, were not as critical of Josephson as Wilson was. Alfred Stieglitz told Hart Crane in October 1923 that Josephson is "certainly youthful and very important." *Broom*'s editor was soon important enough to warrant a lengthy interview with Burton Rascoe, literary editor for the *New York Herald-Tribune*. Although Rascoe described Josephson as a "courteous and well-mannered young man" who had a "proper respect for my years," the tone of the interview revealed a somewhat different personality. "First of all," Josephson abruptly informed Rascoe, "we are against all the dead lumber which critics like you have been touting." He then asserted:

> We think that Anatole France, Thomas Hardy, Joseph Conrad, Sherwood Anderson, Sinclair Lewis, Willa Cather, Joseph Hergesheimer, Edna St. Vincent Millay, Elinor Wylie and all these writers voicing a worn-out, conventional, sentimental, romantic despair and disillusionment are all bad writers. They do not express their time; they have nothing to say of any value, they are imitators, following an outmoded tradition. "Diamond Dick" is better writing: there at least you get something of the quickened movement, the rush and vitality of modern life.

Rascoe reasoned that Josephson belonged to that generation of writers too young to have been greatly affected by the war and therefore able to adopt a favorable view of modern life.[16]

Josephson basked under the limelight he was receiving and the controversy he was creating. At the same time, however, he increasingly found the mundane chores involved in editing *Broom* exhausting, both mentally and physically. Although his friends offered encouragement and occasional contributions, he received little tangible assistance in editing, printing, and marketing the review. Cowley did not return from Europe until August, and when he did, financial considerations immediately forced him to take a job as a copywriter for *Sweet's Architectural Catalogue*. Consequently, he had little time to devote to *Broom*. Kenneth Burke, meanwhile, remained virtually secluded on his New Jersey homestead. As a result, Josephson found himself working ten hours a day trying to attend to a variety of editorial duties. In mid-July he explained to Loeb his debilitating situation: "You will never know what a terrible time I have had—consider it as if I have been doing all the work of the New York and Berlin offices combined. . . . all alone, my own stenographer, business manager, office boy, editor, etc., etc."[17]

Personal concerns soon compounded Josephson's malaise. Since returning from Europe he had begun to regret his estrangement from his parents. Like many rebellious sons he had never felt completely comfortable in his role as family dissident. Immediately after returning from Europe he had visited his parents in Brooklyn. Sarah Josephson, he remembered, was "unreserved both in her display of affection and her reproaches to me for the harum-scarum life I led." His father, partially disabled by a recent heart attack, welcomed his son warmly. Possibly because he was an avid reader and fancied himself somewhat of an intellectual, Julius had always been less critical of his eldest son's literary activities than Sarah. He told Matthew that although his literary tastes seemed a bit odd, he continued to be "amused" by him, drawing some pleasure and pride from his son's growing notoriety.[18]

The sight of his father in a semiparalyzed condition shocked Matthew. He "felt some pangs of remorse at the thought that I had never been able to enter his business and learn all about it and give up writing, as he would have wished me to." A few weeks later he revealed to Loeb his concern for his parents:

> I have been forced to take $100 a month from my father which I
> cannot count on much longer, as he should retire from business and

try to save his health. The old man has been terribly nice to me and I am worried about him. While I was in Europe he was nearly counted out on two occasions. My real obligation to him and myself (this is my real position without sentiment) is to go into business and provide for myself so well in the next year or two, that he can retire . . . and live on a small income without fear about me and the other two boys.

Josephson's opposition to pursuing a career in business obviously had changed a great deal since his high school days. Several months earlier, while still in Europe, he had told Cowley that if their experiment with *Broom* failed, he would probably return to New York and join his father in the banking business.[19]

In addition to his nagging sense of filial obligation, Josephson realized that he and Hannah would soon be starting a family, and they would need a regular income. The two of them, despite the supplement from Julius, were barely surviving financially. Even when Hannah finally obtained a job as an assistant editor of *Telling Tales*, a pulp-paper monthly specializing in "true confessions," they remained relatively poor. Matthew thus began looking for a job in the business world. In April 1923 he informed Loeb, "I like America so much, that I shall go to work soon and try to make heaps of golden dollars in order to 'see America.'" Several months later he confessed that he was "still looking for a lucrative business to go into. Because neither Hannah nor I have advanced one step toward the solution of our problems."[20]

By the fall of 1923 Josephson still had not found such a business position, and he viewed both his personal situation and that of *Broom* with growing pessimism. Much to his dismay he discovered that Americans in the jazz age were indifferent to his new approach to literature and the plastic arts. *Broom*'s printing debts mounted and its resources dwindled. But the most disillusioning aspect of the whole affair was his friends' lack of support. He described to Loeb their declining enthusiasm:

> After I got well into the job and I saw nearly everybody possible, all in diverse ways fell upon my neck, avowed that *Broom* was a Moses come to lead them out of the wilderness, that all else was ashes. I secured enough for three numbers. But the "group" which is roughly associated with *Broom* is in a remarkably sterile mood. The absence of any real cooperation . . . on the part of the younger generation is highly discouraging.

Matthew then expressed both his personal plight and his devotion to *Broom*: "I for one am tired. I must get a job and go to work. We are penniless, clotheless, furnitureless, and are moving to another $80 apartment. Cannot even pay for a bed. Remember I have tried my best."[21]

As he had demonstrated before, however, Josephson would not abandon *Broom* until literally forced to do so. Crane observed to Munson, "Matty is not going to let go of his sheet until it is either so dead as to be hopeless or else so loaded with debts that its successor would be crushed under them." To his reading public Josephson continued to sing the praises of his magazine. At the same time that he was telling Loeb of the mounting problems facing himself and *Broom*, he was writing Alfred Stieglitz, "Prospects for BROOM are excellent, especially since it is published in New York." In early October 1923 Josephson met with Cowley to discuss their editorial alternatives. They could reduce *Broom* to a quarterly issue, thus allowing Matty to take a business job and edit the review in his spare time, or they could simply cease publication altogether. Cowley suggested that before deciding, they should call a meeting of all the writers and artists associated with *Broom* and *Secession* to discuss common problems and arrive at a joint solution. Still at odds with Gorham Munson, Josephson reluctantly agreed, even though he saw no real chance of cooperation. In October he reported to Loeb: "Cowley believes *Broom* should have a spectacular end. . . . He has some great ideas, such as calling a meeting of all the friends and enemies of *Broom* for a grand powwow out of which he hopes the air might be cleared, and perhaps another magazine. . . . *Moi, je m'en fiche.* I am looking for a job as ever."[22]

The now famous *Broom-Secession* meeting took place on October 19 at a small restaurant and speakeasy on Prince Street. About fifteen writers and artists attended, as well as several spouses. Munson, who was ill, remained at a friend's house in upstate New York. Nor were many of his close friends and supporters there. Neither Waldo Frank nor Jean Toomer could attend, both of whom sided with Munson. Hart Crane, therefore, was understandably anxious before the affair. As he admitted to Munson, "I seem to be the only delegate from the higher spaces at the *Broom* conclave." Crane especially resented allowing wives to attend. "Very likely," he told Munson, "I'll play the most contrary role—make a scene or something before we get through."[23]

The meeting began with Malcolm Cowley reading a letter from Munson, ostensibly addressed to the group, but essentially comprising an invective against Josephson. Munson referred to his former associate as dishonest, cunning, treacherous, and a "fake-artist." He urged the group to separate themselves from Josephson. As he read the diatribe Cowley grew more and more impressed with the comedic aspects of the scene: "I began to read it seriously to my audience, but . . . I was overcome by a sense of absurdity and began to declaim it like a blue-jawed actor reciting Hamlet's soliloquy." At that point the gathering erupted into a chaotic mélange of insults, shouting, and persistent drinking. Josephson gave Loeb an account of the meeting a few days later:

> It turned into a riotous party after a while. Attempts by Cowley and me to control it were pathetic. Attempts by the members to discuss their common problems concertedly failed through the inertia of intoxication. Yet many things were clarified. Principally that if anything is to be done here (Cowley admits), three or four of us must go ahead and then tell the others about it. Artists, like humans, are sheep, only controversial and ill-controlled sheep.

Josephson compared the meeting to a "Tzara-Breton (Dadaist) affair." Americans, he concluded, when they engage in such literary quarrels, "have more sense of humor (too much always) and drink harder than Frenchmen—very emotional and less logical than Dadas." After the meeting broke up Josephson and Crane nearly had a fight in the street. But the two were so drunk that they could not even hit each other. Matthew swung but instead struck James Light, the dramatist. And so the evening ended.[24]

As a result of the now open split between Munson and Josephson, the young writers associated with the two magazines aligned themselves either with *Broom* or *Secession*. Burke resigned from the editorial board of the latter, saying that he would contribute impartially to both. Hart Crane sided with Munson, as did Waldo Frank. Brown and Cowley, on the other hand, told Munson that they would no longer contribute to *Secession*. "The reason I prefer Josephson," Cowley admitted to Munson, "is because he has infinitely more talent as a writer."[25]

Josephson was furious after the meeting. Munson's personal attack had impugned his literary reputation. A few days later he decided there was only one "honorable" way to settle this festering dispute—with fists. He arranged a visit with Slater Brown at his place in the country near Pawling and then one morning made the short trip to Woodstock, where Munson was staying with William Murrell Fisher. Munson later recalled his day of reckoning with Josephson:

> I had heard rumors of his coming . . . but dismissed the reports as only bluster. . . . I was mistaken. Here he was knocking at the door, after traveling 100 miles to avenge himself. . . . I had some guest for tea, when Josephson burst in shouting for battle. The guest dispersed hastily, leaving Josephson and my host William Murrell Fisher to parley. . . . Fisher said there was nothing to do but fight.

The two tempestuous editors then adjourned to a marshy meadow chosen specifically to cushion the expected falls. With great solemnity Munson made the following shrewd pronouncement before the struggle commenced: "It may be that I shall be forced to retract what I said about you. In case I do have to retract, I want it understood in advance that I don't retract a single word." [26]

Accounts of the "fight" vary according to the sympathies of the observers. What is known for certain is that it was one of the worst exhibitions of the pugilistic arts ever staged. After throwing several wayward punches, the two editors began to wrestle on the wet ground, rolling in the mud like wallowing pigs. Murrell Fisher, who was serving as referee, watched for five minutes and then stopped the bout out of sheer boredom. He later referred to the fracas as the "worst fight I ever saw." Munson described it as an inconclusive draw: "The scuffle was brief, but not bloody, and at one moment exceedingly funny." Josephson remembered "drawing the claret with a right hook to the mouth." He also testified that when the match was stopped, he was sitting atop Munson's chest. Munson said he was the one on top. Josephson told Loeb that he had beaten Munson "severely," undoubtedly a poetic exaggeration. The only reason he failed to knock his opponent out, Matty explained, was that "I don't know enough, but I did other things, and at the end he and I were quite a muddy sight." [27]

Malcolm Cowley has provided the most humorous, if inflated, description of the scuffle between his two proud associates. In an ode composed after the bout he wrote:

> Know, Muse, that heroes yet exist
> Whose anger brooks no intercession,
> And tooth meets tooth and fist meets fist
> And "Up," cries Munson, "with *Secession*!
> Down *Broom*," he snarls, and warriors pant
> Each to defend his literary slant.

All afternoon the battle wavers;
Now fortune smiles on Josephson,
Now frowns, and now stout Munson quavers,
"*Broom* is unswept. I've almost won."
The other sneers, "Almost how splendid!"
As deep in mud both heroes lie up-ended.

Yet battling on, till strength and light
Together failed. Then Fisher rose,
Grimly dividing weary wight
From bleary knight and fist from nose:
So, on another fateful day,
Half-dead Achilles by half-living Hector lay.

Whatever the outcome of Josephson's struggle with Munson, it was now glaringly apparent that the group of artists associated with *Broom* and *Secession* was more divided than ever. Soon after the fight Matthew reported that he had definitely decided to be either a "financial reporter or the branch manager of a bank. I am more convinced than ever that a career in business with independent and detached position in literature is my cue." Meanwhile, the problems confronting *Broom* remained unresolved, and they were soon multiplied.[28]

In *Broom*'s January issue Josephson printed a story by Kenneth Burke that referred to a woman's breast in the plural, a reference that was contrary to the rules laid down by the postmaster general. On January 14, 1924, the New York postmaster informed Josephson that the January issue was "unmailable." Burton Rascoe discussed the censorship decision in the *New York Herald-Tribune*:

> I am mindful of the fine and courageous things among some otherwise *Broom* has published, for it has published Pirandello, Apollinaire, Lautréamont and the letters of Dostoyevsky for the first time in English; it has given space to many excellent things by unknown writers, and its editorial policy has been refreshingly unorthodox. The suppression of *Broom* . . . amounted to an invasion of privacy and should be denounced, for the circulation of *Broom* is almost cipherous. No one who has the perseverance and curiosity to read beyond the first several pages could possibly be of the mental age which might be injured by anything printed there.

Others also protested the censorship decree. Eugene O'Neill wrote a let-ter to the postmaster general criticizing the decision, and the American Civil Liberties Union offered free legal aid to appeal the decision. But Josephson and Cowley decided it was not worth the effort. They were frustrated, exhausted, and penniless. The group soon dispersed, taking jobs in business or fleeing to the countryside. As Josephson remembered, it was time "to make a home, beget a child, and plant a tree." [29]

The *Broom* group's attempt to promote in the United States their mod-ern literary program failed largely because Josephson and the others had naively assumed that they could recreate in New York the stimulating at-mosphere of artistic creativity and righteous indignation they had dis-covered among the Dadaists. As Cowley has remembered, they had "at-tempted to write and publish a new sort of literature celebrating the picturesque qualities of American machinery and our business civiliza-tion, and we found that American businessmen in the age of machines were not interested in reading poems about them." In a similar comment Josephson recalled the simplistic nature of their movement:

> We had bravely announced our "acceptance" of the Machine Age without much analysis or thinking through the matter. . . . We had the effect of a few people firing off peashooters at the unbreakable glass and steel facade of our civilization. . . . We ourselves, in effect, were being flung to the machines.

While in Europe Josephson and Cowley had been able to idealize the "picturesque" qualities of modern American life from a safe distance. From Paris, New York's anonymous crowds, soaring skyscrapers, neon lights, billposters, and automobiles seemed exciting; from Manhattan they seemed frightening. [30]

Josephson's disappointing experience after his return to New York illus-trates the conflict between rural and urban values and personal and artis-tic needs that has persistently characterized American literary history, a conflict that was a significant theme in his life and career. Josephson found the problem of adjusting to his homeland "harassing." Soon after his return he told a reporter that he had to "get away from the noise of New York . . . in order to enjoy it." Others among the group shared his shock and dismay. Manhattan, Cowley observed to Kenneth Burke, had become "more than I could bear." In Europe among the Dadaists, Jo-sephson and Cowley had crusaded against separating literature from modern life, but they were unable to adapt to the modern life they encountered in New York. Indeed, within a short time after the collapse of *Broom*, they would follow the lead of Burke, Slater Brown, Allen Tate, and several others who had bought or rented houses in the countryside.[31]

That Josephson and the others had a superficial understanding of the complexities of modern society is obvious. True, twentieth-century man was no longer the charge of a benevolent nature but the orphan of technology, and he had to develop some sense of spiritual and cultural intercourse with his new urban-industrial environment. Josephson, however, went too far in his emphasis upon the inspiring quality of man's artificial creations and began to worship them without seriously considering their effect upon humanity. Gorham Munson correctly described Josephson's "blurbing of new phenomena" as going "no deeper than the romantics' thrill upon finding stranger material to exploit." Much like the skyscrapers he praised, Josephson's machine-age aesthetic constituted an extrinsic structural framework of ideas devoid of internal substance.[32]

There is no question that machinery and other products of the industrial age possess significant aesthetic qualities. As Charles Sheeler, Charles Demuth, Paul Strand, and others have demonstrated, the clean lines, geometric beauty, and effortless precision of machinery can certainly be employed to artistic advantage. The danger in developing such an orientation, however, is that in focusing solely on the form, or symbol, of the mechanical object, and ignoring the idea behind the creation of the machine or its practical effects, one tends to forget the human impact or human involvement. Amy Lowell, Josephson's early mentor, recognized that he had become a prisoner of his emphasis on form. She wrote in 1923 that the object of the Josephson group

> is science rather than art; or perhaps it is fairer to say that to them art is akin to mathematics. They are much intrigued by structure, in a sense quite other than that in which it is usually employed in poetry. They have a host of theories, and are most interesting when stating them, but the doubt arises whether a movement which concerns itself more with statements about poetry than with the making of poetry itself is ever going to produce works of art of a quality to justify the space taken up by pronunciamentos.

For all their talk about integrating the machine age into prose and poetry, Josephson and his friends had produced little solid work. His poetry was more impressive for its zaniness than its substance. He conceived and composed poetry more with his wit, unable to recognize that genuine poetry is written in the soul.[33]

In spite of the weaknesses and excesses in Josephson's approach, however, he and his group did perceive the importance of relating language and the plastic arts to the contemporary environment. They sought to rescue art from the romantic prejudice that technology is necessarily hostile to the world of feeling. They also attempted to help create a national cultural identity. In pursuing such goals they represented an advance guard in the revolution taking place in the arts in the 1920s. In the pages of *Broom* Josephson provided a forum for some of the most important experimental writing of the day. Kenneth Rexroth has maintained that *Broom* was "certainly the best of all the avant-garde magazines. It introduced to America the most exciting and innovative literature of the time." Josephson was thus in the vanguard of an intellectual movement dedicated to modernism in form and technique. In the process he helped break down the sentimentalism of the genteel tradition. Dickran Tashjian has pointed out that Josephson "stood as a prophet of the present day, anticipating many of McLuhan's ideas and boldly envisioning the new extensions of man that were henceforth available to the artist." Josephson had made his mark as editor of *Broom*; now he would try to make his million.[34]

7 FROM GRUB STREET TO WALL STREET

At the beginning of 1924 Matthew Josephson, American Dadaist, entered the turbulent world of big business as an account representative and statistician with Steiner, Rouse, and Stroock, Incorporated, a brokerage firm on Wall Street. Such a career, he remembered, seemed to offer "a short cut to some of the folding money I had long dispensed with, but now required in the most immediate manner." His intention was to make enough money to provide for his family needs and to permit his return to a literary career. At that time the economic boom of the Coolidge years was well under way, and to Josephson, Wall Street exuded a certain glamorous "wickedness." There, he believed, resided the real power in modern American life. For several years he had been praising the creativity and dynamism of American capitalists. Now he would try his hand at money-making.[1]

Josephson was hired as a "customer's man." He dealt with both buyers and sellers of stocks and bonds, usually on a small or moderate scale. With the rapid increase in securities transactions in the 1920s, literally hundreds of such positions were newly created. Matthew took a two-week course in stock market activities and techniques and then began handling accounts worth thousands of dollars. In his study of Wall Street during the twenties, Robert Sobel has pointed to Josephson's experience as an example of the careless manner in which the securities industry conducted itself during the period. "Thirty years earlier," Sobel observed, "a person with his background would never have achieved such a desk, or received more than an interview from a member firm." In effect, uninitiated brokers like Josephson were selling stocks on a massive scale to an uninformed public.[2]

Josephson was oblivious to such concerns. Initially, the chaotic, exciting atmosphere of Wall Street finance fascinated him. He immersed himself in his new role, poring over the moving ticker tapes, memorizing the numerous company abbreviations, and watching for the slight price fluctuations that could have significant implications. His diligence soon paid off, and he began to garner profits for his customers, his firm, and himself. "It looked like a beautiful sort of game," he remarked, "and it impressed me as the most painless and quickest way of making money I had ever heard of." Within only a few weeks, his salary, based on a percentage of his commissions, was raised, then promptly raised again. "These were strenuous and exciting days when fortune seemed to smile on me." His first victories were intoxicating, and he developed a dangerous overconfidence, blithely assuming that the upward trend in the market would be permanent.[3]

Josephson spoke to his friends with enthusiasm about the ease with which he was making money. At the same time, however, he recognized that in pursuing his new career and enjoying its material advantages, he was losing contact with his literary comrades. In a letter to Kenneth Burke he discussed his perplexing situation:

> I have made so many hundreds of dollars, have been going so much faster recently, getting so much rottener, while the moving tape has been a growing drug, or fever. . . . The pace is very hard. The truth is that I do suffer successive shock from the imbeciles I deal with, and the absence of my particular cronies of Paris, Berlin, and New York is still a raw wound.

Matthew longed for the time when he could resume his literary life, unhindered by financial concerns. Writing was everything to him, and his forced absence from his artistic activities and associates frustrated him. "For God's sake," he scolded Burke: "I want you, at least, to write. . . . I envy you. I envy you. I envy you. I shall turn on you, if you keep hacking. You are the only one of us who hasn't been cornered." Burke, then leading a frugal life on his farm in New Jersey, was one of the few economically self-sufficient members of Josephson's group of friends. It distressed Matty that Kenneth was not taking better advantage of his situation to write more.[4]

Inevitably, a sharp, though temporary, decline in the stock market wiped out Josephson's initial triumphs. Without warning most of his speculative ventures began a downward slide in the late winter of 1924. "I looked on in bewilderment," he remembered, "as most of my stocks— those on whose rising movement my livelihood as a broker depended— fell at least three points." The first "bear" market is indeed the harshest for the uninitiated, and it was a sobering experience for young Josephson. As he sat at his desk, stunned by the sudden collapse of his clients' holdings, he was shocked to see many of his fellow brokers celebrating the decline. Unknown to him they had been selling "short" the whole time. At the end of the disastrous day Matthew headed for a nearby speakeasy, where he spent the rest of the afternoon and evening. The next morning his superiors confronted him as he walked into the office. Josephson, who had not wanted to disturb his clients at such a calamitous time, found that his bosses wanted him hurriedly to secure more margin from his customers. "Don't worry about your customers too much," one senior broker advised, while the elder partner in the firm told him he needed to find some "new blood." Josephson glumly swallowed his pride and obeyed their orders. "This side of a Wall Street man's life," he commented, "I had never heard of; I could never learn to like it." The game was not so much fun anymore.[5]

The ambience of Wall Street is not, of course, congenial to believers in the brotherhood of man. A chilling coldness pervades stock market activities; the transactions are carried out with impersonal and frequently ruthless dispatch. When Josephson finally perceived this reality, his business outlook changed. He began to acquire "a specifically Wall Street character. I was growing to be tough, calloused, indifferent to the blows of chance as to the plaint of the unfortunate. Emotions were dying within me, as a certain immunity developed." Wall Street now resembled a jungle in which the combatants observed no rules in their daily struggle for quick profits; it was a "perpetual war of predatory creatures, with each man's hand turned against each other."[6]

The thought of leaving such an unsavory environment passed more than once through Josephson's mind. But he had not yet made enough money to resume his literary career. Consequently, he steeled himself to continue working in the stock market, but only after adopting a new attitude. He now realized that he could trust no one, not even his superiors, for they were known to pass false rumors to stimulate sudden buying or selling. The only way to survive was "to plunge into a deeper and deeper scrutiny of the ticker tape, to learn all that I could from the course of market events themselves."[7]

Josephson also learned to operate in the market with a greater degree of patience; he realized that the "insiders" never hurried. He began to watch the "long-pull" movements in selected stocks, waiting for a discernible trend before buying or selling. His superiors, however, frowned upon such prolonged tactics. They wanted quick turnovers, not long, delayed transactions. Thus he was forced to stress to his customers "the virtue of taking a sure profit of whatever size rather than waiting through whatever troubles the future might bring." With his own funds that he occasionally invested, however, Matthew chose to be more conservative and patient.[8]

As stock prices pushed upward again during the summer of 1924, Josephson began to enjoy moderate successes. "Mistrustful, furtive, skeptical, chastened by defeat," he later said, "I acquired steadily the larger, truer view of the stock market from the lessons of the old traders and the ticker tape itself." In July he explained his activities to Harold Loeb:

> In the market I guide my clan steadily, taking a few lickings now and then, but eking out small wins steadily, and once in a while making a major move. I haven't a bad eye for the tape you know, and they say that it takes a fool to win at the races and a poet at the market.

Within only a few months Josephson had become an experienced, successful broker. Malcolm Cowley visited him at his office and found his friend no longer penurious and threadbare. Matty now dressed in conservative business suits and looked the part of the earnest speculator, surrounded by telephones and ticker tape. But Cowley knew that Josephson's mind was divided, that he still dreamed of escaping the urban financial world and retreating to a more pastoral literary existence. Cowley wrote a poem about his friend, "Buy 300 Steel," in which he captured Josephson's divided loyalties:

> Buy 300 steel at the
> market, buy 300 steel
> at the market, buy 300
> steel.

His face melted into the telephone,
his lips curled with hello, and dreamed
his vulcanized-rubber eyes,
with a hello . . . there was a lake beneath
with Bowling Green 6000 trees,
and hello, Bowling Green, the noise of waters

under a curdled sky, hello,
I dove into the lake, hello,
into the lake as green, hello,
as green as Bowling Green.

I'll make a note of it, good-by, and rain
suddenly falling, down fell railways, coppers,
motors, industrials, Rebecca Steel,
Calumet, Monkey-Ward, and Chrysler falling,
rain steadily falling, public utilities
. . . always a good buy,

a good, I'll make a note of it,
buy, good-by, good-by[9]

Josephson, who only a few months before had been glorifying urban-industrial life, still looked forward to the time when he could leave Wall Street and New York City and move to the country, where he could take up the creative life again. The poet within him, he told Loeb, was being "beaten down. No poems for a year gone. I only write in the country." He was obstinately trying to earn enough money to buy "that little nest in the country, 1 hour by train, where alone we can be happy and I can write again. Ultimately the germ will kill off market talents, and I am to be knocked loose from Wall St. by Christmas or early Spring." Hannah was expecting their first child in the fall, and Matthew was determined that they have a home of their own in the country for the raising of a family.[10]

Ever since returning from Europe Josephson had sought to move to the country, as many of his friends had done. Occasional visits with the Burkes or the Slater Browns only heightened his interest. In a letter to Kenneth in August 1924, he reaffirmed his literary interests and outlined his future goals:

For literature I have an overweening weakness; if I should [sic] lei-sure I would succumb to literature constantly. . . . To create a period of leisure is what concerns me most, a leisure to which literature and its kindred arts are associated. I suppose it will not harm me for the while to work over the essentials, the primary facts: a child, a family, a house in the country. This leisure, although it will surely include certain hardships, I look for in the early part of next year. Once attained I shall not hesitate to yield to my agreeable weaknesses at every possible occasion.

His career in Wall Street remained a temporary expedient, a necessary stage in his quest for a life devoted to literature.[11]

While working in New York in the fall of 1924 Josephson developed a schizophrenic lifestyle. From ten o'clock in the morning to four in the afternoon, he would labor in his office on Wall Street, preoccupied with material concerns and dealing with "crass," single-minded businessmen. In the evening he would experience a complete change of mood and activity, spending most of his time reading or writing in a small study in their apartment. As well as working on a novel, *Lionel and Camilla*, he had begun writing book reviews for the *New York Herald-Tribune* and the *Saturday Review*. Josephson reported to Harold Loeb that he had "settled into my Wall Street shackles, and am now seeking to exert my voice in the medium of criticism (meaning book reviews) since there is, frankly, little other outlet."[12]

Once or twice a week, while Hannah stayed home with their newborn son, Eric, Matthew would meet with his old group of literary friends for a drink at Poncino Palace or for dinner at Squarcialupi's, a nearby Italian restaurant on Perry Street in the Village. Cowley, Burke, Brown, Crane, and Tate were usually there, along with several others. Cowley has recollected that at such affairs they would sit around the table after dinner and take turns reading their latest poems or listen to Crane bang away at the old upright piano. They were festive, colorful occasions, full of jokes, laughs, and heated arguments, all of which ended amicably, thanks in part to the plenitude of bootleg gin. In one of his poems Cowley described the scene:

> All of an age, all heretics,
> all rich in promise, but poor in rupees.
> I knew them all at twenty-six,
> when to a sound of scraping shovels,
> emerging from whatever dream,
> by night they left their separate hovels

as if with an exultant scream,
stamped off the snow and gathered round
a table at John Squarcialupi's
happy as jaybirds, loud as puppies.

On several occasions at the restaurant, a different literary crowd would hold its own meetings at the same time. This was the group of "radical" writers associated with the *New Masses*. Among them were Michael Gold, John Dos Passos, and Joseph Freeman. One evening, Cowley remembered, Dos Passos yelled over to their table: "Intellectual workers of the world unite, you have nothing to lose but your brains." Usually, however, the radicals ignored Josephson's group, considering them too unpolitical. Little did they know that eight years later they would all be working for the same political cause.[13]

Although Josephson still enjoyed the comradeship of his old friends, it seemed to him that the group had lost the energetic, iconoclastic spirit that had been its trademark. In a note to Loeb in October 1924 he described one of their recent parties: "We had a crowd, the other Friday night, even Waldo Frank and Munson attending. It was such a sad fizzle that I decided to devote the balance of my extra-office energy to cheering at football games." Josephson deplored the group's loss of its combative spirit, its apparent unwillingness to appear foolish or to attack the literary establishment anymore. He expressed to Burke his disgust at their apathy and reaffirmed his own commitment to an active, irreverent literary stance:

> I do not understand what has become of everybody. I have never felt such a woeful lack of stimulus of any kind. After a period of some months, I suddenly realize how lost everything and everybody is. . . . And when I think of you, oh my spiritless friends, I am even more grief-stricken. When will you crawl out of your woodchuck holes, when will you be unafraid to appear ridiculous, when will you consent to compromise yourselves?
>
> What I mean, in all candor, is that the situation, the momentary American scene whips me into such a horrid spleen that if we don't get together, I shall revile you all with my last breath. The protracted silence and the smugness have really given me more chilling fright than I have received in numerous years.

In his opinion the literary life was meaningless unless one was involved, committed to a cause or point of view and capable of group action.[14]

In a casual comment in the same letter to Burke, Josephson revealed that his desire to lead a life of commitment was beginning to extend beyond purely artistic concerns. "At the last moment," he confided, "I suffered an emotional *vire-volte* and cast my ballot for LaFollette." The 1924 election had just been held, and Senator Robert LaFollette had run as the candidate of the Progressive party. Josephson's decision to vote for LaFollette, a candidate whose platform explicitly condemned big business and Wall Street finance, was curiously ironic, for he was at that time making his living in the citadel of corporate power. A few years later he remembered the election night and recognized his own ambivalent position: "Election day. Hurrah, Cal Coolidge and Mellon were in the saddle; stocks rose almost vertically so that by New Year's Eve we had good reason to get drunk among our friends." [15]

Josephson would always remain essentially a bourgeois intellectual with a strong sense of social concern and a disdain for corporate power. He was not a revolutionary. His vote for LaFollette was a demonstration of disgust at the "system" all the while he remained a part of that system. Such inconsistency was typical of writers on the left, then and since. Josephson would again demonstrate it in 1932 when he campaigned for William Z. Foster, the Communist candidate for president, while at the same time he owned a considerable amount of securities and was enjoying a thoroughly bourgeois living under contract with a major publishing firm. Josephson's seemingly contradictory behavior in 1924 and later in the 1930s illustrates well the peculiar, vexing problem confronting the writer with social concerns. As a social activist, he is opposed to the prevailing capitalist order. But to succeed as an artist, to gain recognition as well as in order to subsist, he must be a part of that same capitalist order. Thus inconsistencies in thought and action result. It was this perplexing dilemma, the question of defining one's role as artist and as citizen, that would come to dominate Josephson's career.

Josephson's voting for LaFollette, or voting at all for that matter, marked a distinct departure from the apolitical stance of his earlier days among the Dadaists. He was slowly acquiring a sense of social responsibility and awareness. First his own penurious state and then his revealing experiences on Wall Street had forced him to confront in a personal way the everyday realities of living in modern America, and that confrontation began to have a sobering effect upon his previously carefree outlook. Yet this transformation was far from complete or even well advanced in 1924. Josephson's maturation and social sensitivity progressed at an

arithmetic rate. Much of his characteristic naivete and bohemianism remained, as well as his zaniness. Furthermore, his dream of owning a
home in the country betrayed a deep-seated desire to escape from his
urban environment and view modern society again from the outside. In
the fall of 1924, through the benevolence of his father and with some
money he had earned on Wall Street, Josephson's dreams were fulfilled,
and he bought a country house in Katonah, New York, about forty miles
above Manhattan. "With no rent to pay," he remarked to Harold Loeb at
the time, "I hope to become another and better man." He realized that
he would soon be able to leave Wall Street and return to a career of creative writing.[16]

The twenty-five-year-old Josephson was beginning to show signs of
settling down. Yet he still retained his youthful, iconoclastic temperament and his aggressive personality. He still wanted to go on the attack,
to organize group manifestos, to raise American eyebrows in the hope of
stimulating controversy and breaking down literary conventions. In
November 1924 he made overtures to his friends about combining again
for a project designed to assault the ruling literary circles. "I am sorely
overworked in the market these days," he told Burke, "and I want to stop
writing book reviews, or writing anything for 'worms,' and devote the little sap I have left every day to an outlet of our own making." What he
had in mind was an all-out attack in pamphlet form against Ernest Boyd
and H. L. Mencken, two of America's leading literary critics who had in
the past year caustically satirized the American "aesthetes" associated
with *Broom*.[17]

Boyd had been particularly scathing in his polemical attacks. He had
written an essay for the *American Mercury* entitled "Aesthete: Model
1924," in which he presented a "composite portrait" of the younger generation of avant-garde writers in the United States. According to Boyd,
the typical "aesthete" was a not-too-masculine graduate of an Ivy League
university who had avoided serving in World War I, had lived both in
Greenwich Village and Paris, and had published "nonsensical" prose
and verse in his own little review.[18]

Boyd's caricature enraged Josephson, Cowley, and many other young
writers associated with *Broom* or *Secession*, each of whom believed that
the portrait was intended to represent himself. Soon after Boyd's satire
appeared, Cowley, Crane, and Burke gathered at Josephson's apartment,
where they took turns calling Boyd on the telephone, cursing and threatening him profusely. Boyd took the threats seriously and locked himself

in his apartment. It was not long before the literary press in New York got wind of the farcical dispute. Burton Rascoe's account of the affair is illuminating, albeit inflated:

> Two hours after the edition of the American Mercury appeared on the stands, Greenwich Village was in an uproar. The whole literary left wing, which had hitherto been disorganized by internecine strife, solidified against the perpetrator of the article. . . .
>
> East 19th Street swarmed with younger poets and when the venerable Boyd set out on his morning constitutional, he was greeted with a fusillade of ripe tomatoes, eggs, sticks . . . and barely escaped with his life back into the house.
>
> There he was kept prisoner for three days while the Dadaists pushed his doorbell, kept his telephone abuzz, scaled the walls to his apartment and cast old cabbages and odor bombs through the windows. Barricaded behind his books, subsisting on depleted rations, grown wan and weary under the assaults . . . Boyd called Heaven to witness that he had never heard or read anything of the assailants who besieged him.

Since the publication of Boyd's incendiary article in December 1923, Mencken had occasionally joined in the assault against the "aesthetes." In March 1924 he had reviewed Josephson's translation of Apollinaire's *The Poet Assassinated*, abruptly dismissing both the work and its translator's introduction as a "barbarous" joke. According to Mencken, the book "turns out to be a dull pasquinade in the manner of the rather atheistic sophomore, with a few dirty words thrown in to shock the booboisie."[19]

Josephson reacted angrily to Mencken's diatribe against Apollinaire, his literary hero. He suggested to Cowley that they organize a group response to Mencken, Boyd, and the other "stuffed shirts" of the literary world. Cowley told Wheelwright in November 1924 that there are "wars and rumors of them; Boyd thwacks at us girlfully; Munson runs off to discharge his poisoned jellybeans from ambush. . . . Everything points to our getting out some sort of single-issue venture, a revival of *Broom* or *Secession*, anything to startle, amuse and answer back." They decided to entitle their broadside *Aesthete 1925*. William Carlos Williams responded positively to Josephson's call to arms: "Aesthete 1925? what t'ell—seems to promise fermentation. I'll be in the city Friday afternoon. . . . Do you really make any money on the rise in stocks? And is that why you now are talking Aesthete 1925—I ask you." Josephson had indeed been making money in the stock market, enough for him to defray part of the printing costs of *Aesthete 1925*.[20]

Josephson and his friends decided to focus their artistic energies in an attack upon Boyd and Mencken. Their efforts resulted in a thirty-two-page pamphlet edited by the mysterious (and fictitious) Walter S. Hankel. Collaborators on *Aesthete 1925* included Josephson, Cowley, Burke, Tate, Crane, Wheelwright, and William Slater Brown. They wrote the entire pamphlet in a day and a half filled with riotous laughter and good fun. A warning on the inside cover indicated the nature of the broadside's contents: "Every article contained in this issue . . . is guaranteed to be in strictly bad taste."[21]

Aesthete 1925 represented the youthful literary rebels at their inane best; the spirit of Dada was still alive and well in New York, at least for a day or so at a time. In one of their fictitious advertisements, supposedly paid for by the "Mencken Promotion Society," Burke urged: "Get Self-Respect Like Taking a Pill/MENCKENIZE!" Josephson contributed a review of Boyd's latest book, an anthology of his articles, including the one aimed at the *Broom* group. With a pen dipped in irony, he commended Boyd's notorious article:

> Mr. Boyd, beyond question, must be complimented for importing into American letters the spirit of controversy. His blows fell upon the heads of the generation of Younger Writers at a moment when they had become far too smug, far too happy in their eccentricities, and were basking much too luxuriously in the warm sunshine of the public's approval. Here in America, we are too gentle and soft-spoken among ourselves. How much more bracing is the atmosphere of combat which the irrepressible Mr. Boyd brings.

Josephson asserted that he did not "wish to speak ill of Mr. Boyd; rather to point out that you can be an uninteresting conversationalist, have very little concern for ideas or clear thinking, and still write an epochal essay like 'Aesthete: Model 1924.'" Matthew's review reflected the tone and substance of the entire issue; it was a typical performance—contentious, sarcastic, and aimed at a prominent adversary.[22]

Organizing, writing, and publishing *Aesthete 1925* with his friends invigorated Josephson. But his excitement quickly subsided. *Aesthete 1925*, he confessed to Burke, "has been the outburst, the exasperated retort of a harassed set of young men who might have been much more mellow in their persuasions under a happier climate." It was fun working together, fun attacking the literary elites, but his personal situation had not improved. The aesthetes again split up and went their separate ways. Moreover, working on Wall Street continued to have a debilitating effect on Josephson's state of mind during the first half of 1925. He was doing remarkably well financially, having advanced in a little over a year from 30 dollars a week to much more than 10,000 dollars a year in salary. Even though his business prospered, however, Josephson found the atmosphere in the boardroom more and more stifling. In February he admitted to Burke that he was "a little saddened by my labors as a financial coal-heaver. . . . I should after all be doing something that makes me happy, and you should be doing more of the same thing." It would not be long before he would be free to do what he wanted.[23]

Eventually events combined to convince Josephson that he could no longer remain on Wall Street. His second "bear" market, much more severe than the first, provided the occasion for his decision to leave. In midsummer 1925 stock prices fell rapidly under a wave of sensational selling. Panic spread as brokers began indiscriminately dumping their holdings. "The unbelievable thing happens again," Josephson recounted, "I watch my star customers whom I thought in an impregnable position, smashed to pieces, compelled to make hurried decisions, closed out with the shreds of their fortunes of yesterday." He quickly began calling his clients, pleading for margin, urging them to buy while prices were abnormally low. But he had little success, largely because he hated bleeding his faithful clients and looking for new "suckers."[24]

When the closing bell signaled the end of the calamitous trading day, Josephson found that "only a handful of my battalion are still alive. . . . My large customers are out of the market, the gains of some eighteen months' campaigning destroyed in a few hours." That night he slept very little as he tried to figure out what had gone wrong, where he had made mistakes. When he returned to work the following day, his bosses again urged him to keep searching for more margin and to close out his weakened accounts. Their pleadings were to no avail. Josephson had lost his business spirit:

> The conviction comes to me finally that nothing my bare hands or sleepless brain may contrive will save us from our fate. . . . I suffer inwardly over the destruction among my circle of customers. The mere fact, in short, that I am feeling a certain moral degradation, that I feel my character compromised in any way, is a tell-tale sign that I am not the stuff of which great brokers are made. . . . I longed to escape from the impermanence of the Street, from its shifting

scenes of intrigue and artifice, from its miles of tape dotted with ciphers, utterly remote from life, and in the ultimate moral sense, completely futile.

While entertaining new clients one evening during July 1925, Matthew caught a cold in the rain and fell seriously ill when it developed into an acute ear infection. Upon his doctor's advice he took a leave of absence from his job in the market and spent several weeks convalescing at his home in the country.[25]

In his novel *The American* Henry James has the hero, Christopher Newman, renounce a successful career in the stock market. "What I wanted to get out of," Newman explains, "was Wall Street."

> I told the man to drive down to the Brooklyn ferry and to cross over. When we were over, I told him to drive me out into the country. . . . I spent the morning looking at the first green leaves on Long Island. I was sick of business; I wanted to throw it all up and break off short; I had money enough. . . . I seemed to feel a new man inside my old skin, and I longed for a new world.

With much the same attitude, Matthew Josephson left New York City and journeyed to Katonah in the late summer of 1925. He would not return to Wall Street. After a month in the country he decided that he could never go back to the beehive of corporate America. He told Malcolm Cowley that he was "filled with inertia at the idea of going back to the Street. There are some great issues or questions which upon being stared at in silence simply go away unanswered. I shall probably be here, then, for the next month and the month after that." A year and a half of hectic transactions and crass money-making had been enough for Josephson. It was time to resume his literary career.[26]

Josephson's short career on Wall Street represented a critically formative experience in his intellectual development. As he once admitted, "Only later did I realize how much I had struggled to conceal the depression I felt while working there." For the first time in his life he had participated in an American economic system that seemed to care little about the social welfare of the people. His revealing experience awakened in him a broader social vision, an ethical sensitivity and anticapitalist bent that gradually would come to dominate his ideas and actions as a writer. The transition in perspective was neither complete nor immediate; other events and influences were needed to make him completely aware of his changing attitude. But the seed of social awareness had been planted. All that it needed to grow was time and nourishment.[27]

During the early fall of 1925 Josephson spent much of his time recuperating from the ear malady in a hammock near his garden. He recalled that his son Eric would usually be in a crib beside him, "the wind blowing on his cheeks and the rustling of fallen leaves keeping him constantly amused." Matty was at home in the country and his spirits revived. The frenetic pace of life on Wall Street had worn him down; his refuge in the country provided a much-needed respite. The isolation and serenity of rural life, then and later, was like a balm to him, and he began working in earnest on his novel. But he could not remain in total isolation for long. Josephson sought to live in what Leo Marx has labeled the "middle landscape," that border area between rural and urban life. He needed to have the best of both worlds, the pastoral virtues of the country and the cultural offerings of the city. Occasional contact with his circle of literary friends was vital to him. Thus, although he would eventually make his permanent home in the country, he would also live intermittently in Manhattan and Greenwich Village.[28]

In October 1925, after visiting his doctor in Manhattan, Josephson returned to Katonah to find a telegram waiting for him. His father had just suffered a severe heart attack. By the time Matthew arrived in Brooklyn his father was dead. It was quite a blow, for in recent years father and son had come to know and appreciate each other far more than ever before. In a letter to Burke, Josephson confessed that attending the funeral "was hard, especially the public displays of grief—much more trying than the immediate loss which is of course unreal." Compounding Matthew's grief was the fact that Hannah only a few days later underwent a minor operation. Allen Tate informed Cowley that Josephson was "surely having a hell of a time; and there's apparently nothing any of us can do. Matty is in Brooklyn; Hannah, with her mother."[29]

But worse was yet to come. No sooner had the Josephsons returned to Katonah than Matthew began receiving notices from publishers rejecting his first attempt at a novel. He confided to Cowley: "I shall now write for the wall again." Ever since childhood Josephson seemed to harbor a feeling of insecurity that he revealed in his self-consciously opinionated, combative, and assertive personality. While he was in Europe, in all probability, he had begun to realize that his poetic talent was inferior to that of his close friends and associates. For this reason he turned increasingly to writing critical essays and controversial editorials. After returning to New York he decided to write a novel, apparently believing that he could better apply his abilities in that genre. But his first attempt was a failure; his novel was a bust. As Allen Tate told Cowley: "Matty's novel, which I have just read, couldn't be worse." Slater Brown had a similar opinion, observing that it was "the most God-awful thing I have ever read." He suggested that they should encourage Matty "to put his novel in a lead casket, weight it down with rocks, and set it afloat on the East River." Josephson was extremely wounded by the candor of his friends, even though he himself was known for being woundingly frank in his assessment of their work. The juxtaposition of the two tendencies betrayed his sensitive ego, at once both defensive and offensive. "Never have my friends," he wrote Cowley, "plunged me into such an utter stinking darkness and confusion." He wondered whether he was really meant to be a creative writer. Josephson was nearing a critical turning point in his literary career. His confidence in his artistic ability and in his friends had been shaken. The "mystery of identity," he admitted to Cowley, "becomes deeper and deeper." Then disaster struck again.[30]

Shortly after Julius Josephson's funeral, Sarah, who had earlier developed cancer, collapsed and was confined to her bed. Within a few months her condition sharply deteriorated. In February Matthew returned to Brooklyn and maintained a vigil by her bedside. "I, who had been much away from her," he remembered, "was now often by her side; she talked with me calmly and with good sense about my future and of the duties I owed the other children." The sight of Sarah slowly losing strength deeply affected him. His strong love for her, so long suppressed, now came to the fore. He told a friend at the time that Brooklyn was an "uncommonly depressing place."[31]

In March 1926 Sarah Josephson died, only four months after Julius. The mental anguish of the event seemed to affect Matthew physically. His ear infection returned and developed into mastoiditis, requiring several operations. He recalled this time as the most unhappy period of his life, his nadir. Life on Wall Street had made him a sick man. His novel was a failure and his parents had died in quick succession. Now he was losing his hearing. In a letter to Jane Heap, he painfully described his state of mind at the end of 1926: "I am finishing up a rather disastrous year: for many weeks my office was at the Polyclinic where I was operated on from time to time for mastoiditis. As soon as I can get on my feet again I shall pack off to some high dry place in France. My mother is dead too. I sound pretty blue, don't I." The eighteen months after July 1925, when Josephson's second "bear" market began, thus represented a major turning point in his life and career. As he returned to the country after his ear operations he was ready to renew life, but that life and his outlook would be markedly different. The new Josephson was more serious, more mature. He was ready to settle into hard literary work, for in hard work there is escape from memory.[32]

This traumatic succession of events in 1925–26 not only transformed Josephson's personal perspective, it altered his artistic outlook as well. In his youthful exuberance over the wonders of the machine age, he had ignored the negative, seamier side of America's urban industrial revolution. By the spring of 1926, however, he was developing a more balanced perspective. "My two years on Wall Street," he later admitted, "had taught me to think in terms of power; as a result I became more rather than less social minded." Josephson had begun to look at literature and society from a different point of view. Until now he had employed prose and poetry to alter one's perception of the world; within a few years he would use literature to try to change the world.[33]

8   THE POET TRANSFORMED

Matthew Josephson's transformation from Dadaist poet to com-
mitted social critic and historian was not immediate; it occurred in stages
during a period of several years. He first demonstrated a changing outlook upon life and literature in the *Little Review* in the spring of 1926. In
"A Letter to My Friends" he attacked the European Surrealists (formerly
his Dadaist companions) for their antisocial and irrational tendencies. He
now had no use for their abstruse literary works that relied upon dreams
for inspiration: "Of what value are these tedious and tepid dreams, these
diffuse poems in prose, these wearisome manifestos couched in an habit-
ual imagery and an inverted syntax. They have begun with logic; let
them cast off their literary robes; let them speak reasonably." The withdrawal of his French friends into the inner recesses of the self seemed like
a retreat, an act of cowardice, an abdication of responsibility.[1]

Josephson's artistic attitudes had obviously changed. Only four years
earlier, writing in *Broom*, he had proclaimed that with "the nullification
of human reason, the mind abandons itself to a sort of destructive sincerity, whereby all may be denied or posited, and nothing is impossible."
Now he questioned the value both of pure literature and of the subconscious imagination. He urged his European friends to involve themselves in the pressing problems facing modern society rather than retreat
into esoteric irrelevance: "Sell the French franc until the government falls

again and again. Betray the country! Go over to the Riffs! But no, they cannot quit being littérateurs." Josephson noted that in America, writers could not afford the luxury of pursuing art for art's sake. "In America we live in storm cellars or country retreats. It is bitter to survive; it is bitter to find ears." Yet he insisted that the struggle of the artist in the United States constituted a "thrilling" experience, requiring "vitality and courage" to overcome the public's indifference to artistic endeavors. "For this reason," he concluded, "one may be happy here, although the consuls in our skyscrapers still turn their thumbs down for us and our position remains desperate and precarious enough."[2]

Josephson's critical message to his European friends was prophetic. By the time his open letter was published, the Surrealists had shifted their energies to political revolution. Most of them turned Communist, while a few joined the French fascist leagues. Upon learning of this remarkable turn of events, he remarked to Kenneth Burke, "We have veritably grown up. . . . Breton and Aragon are heroic when they renounce literature and become Bolshevists at this moment in France." Josephson had developed a self-conscious view of himself as maturing; he had come to respect the writer who committed himself to a social cause, something he would have scoffed at a few years before. No longer did he believe that the poet should remain indifferent to great public issues and concentrate solely on perfecting literary form. It was time to "do a great deal of thinking through of our relation as human beings and artists with the real world, with the world of modern industry and power politics, with our swiftly changing society."[3]

Josephson had changed not only artistically but personally as well. In November 1926 he confessed his transformation to Burke:

> Kenneth, I have decided to be middle class; I am glad that we live on W. 104th Street rather than Hudson Duster Street. I loathe the Village. I promise to be a good husband, a good student, a good gardener, a good friend; but I also wish to be middle class. Soon I shall try even to have a middle class income. Forgive me! Bear with me!

For all his Dadaist zaniness Matthew had remained fundamentally a bourgeois. He had since childhood subconsciously desired to be a part of middle-class America, without its Victorian gentility. Just as he had earlier shed his Jewishness and asserted his Americanness, he now sought to lose the mantle of the bohemian aesthete and to gain social acceptance, economic security, and professional recognition. He soon achieved all three.[4]

Late in 1926, while at a literary gathering, Josephson met the owners of the Macaulay Company, a new publishing firm. In the course of their conversation, the publishers offered him a commission to write a literary biography. He accepted the offer with alacrity, for he was eager to produce a "serious" book, one with a direct impact upon the greater reading public. At a meeting the next morning he and the head of the company agreed upon a study of Emile Zola. In choosing Zola as his subject Josephson again demonstrated his recent conversion to a new artistic attitude. He had earlier vilified American writers such as Dreiser, Lewis, and Anderson for imitating the "discredited" French naturalism of Zola. Now he was planning a full-length biography of him. Two years later, in 1928, Josephson explained his change of heart:

> I returned to writing late in 1926, this time with the intention of concentrating upon a larger canvas, something that would move the great public. Up till now I had never desired public success. My critical work thus far always seemed either too outspoken or too "obscure." I desired, therefore, that the new work I planned reach the public; and I was led, naturally, to the record of Zola's life. Zola's fearlessness, and above all, his admirable power of indignation, seemed the perfect antithesis to the mass life of the modern age. He was the heroic type who resisted the mass life, addressed it directly, and had the strength to resist it.

Josephson had long been concerned about the role of the writer in modern society, and in Zola he found a compelling example to follow.[5]

In the spring of 1927 Matthew sailed again to Europe, this time to begin research for his biography. After traveling around France interviewing relatives of Zola and examining family letters, he arrived in Paris, where he spent most of his time cloistered in the Bibliothèque Nationale. Occasionally he saw his former Dadaist friends, reporting to Cowley that he had spent pleasant hours with Jacques Baron, Max Ernst, Robert Desnos, Benjamin Peret, Jean Arp, and Tristan Tzara. André Breton, he commented, was "cool" toward him because of his recent swipe at them in the *Little Review*. Josephson also saw Harold Loeb, who seemed to be acting "more and more the part of Robert Cohn."[6]

As Josephson dug into his project, examining Zola's correspondence, diaries, and writings, he found himself more and more attracted to his subject. "For me," he recounted, "Zola began to assume grandeur. He left his study at one of the bitter moments of history; and the picture of a man against the mob, of an Odysseus in quest of 'truth' which leads to the cross of earthly suffering in an ideal cause, illuminated the sublime trait in Man which justifies his questionable existence." Zola's career, widely regarded as the classic example of the writer turned public man, strongly appealed to his own emerging sense of social responsibility.[7]

While in France Josephson took an active interest in the Sacco-Vanzetti affair taking place in the United States. The impending execution in Boston of the two convicted anarchists bore a striking resemblance to the Dreyfus scandal at the turn of the century, in which Zola had played such a significant role. Outraged at the prejudicial manner in which Sacco and Vanzetti had been convicted, writers in America, led by Edmund Wilson, John Dos Passos, and Edna Millay, organized mass protests against the executions. Josephson wrote Burke of his admiration for those writers taking part in the protests. "I am thrilled, Kenneth, at the notion that we are in promising line for electrocution. To be sure, we haven't formulated our dissent, we haven't labelled it, but we are none the less dissenters, the safety and tranquility of whose existence in the United States is a measure with our passiveness, shyness, or our candor and responsibility. The sense of this danger, as I see it, gives me an authentic and long-absent thrill." He concluded by affirming his own activist bent as writer: "the playing-with-words, the belief that words have an independent character of their own, I begin to renounce, as a passé stage of bourgeois culture."[8]

A month later, in September 1927, Josephson directed an impassioned appeal to Burke to abandon his own artistic isolation and assume a more socially active stance. He felt that Kenneth was theorizing too much, losing himself in abstractions. Burke had already developed a reputation as a writer intensely devoted to his craft at the expense of social or political involvement. Thus Matthew was forced to be blunt:

> I wonder . . . whether you have at all, or have ever felt inclined to explore the cleansing, the revivifying aspects of the combined action-and-utterance (I think not only of *J'Accuse!* I think of Areopagitica, of Les Illuminations, of Blake's Prophetical Poems). . . . The play-of-words really seems done for me, purely poetry and all. I have seen Joyce's latest work-in-progress, and I shudder. . . . Ah Kenneth, do you not become aware that your concern over "aesthetics" is monstrous; MONSTROUS. For Aesthetics has been always more or less under a disrepute similar to metaphysics in the modern age. And the *Hauptfrage* is whether you should be silent or speak.

Josephson's contact with Zola had provided him with a heroic writer to emulate, and he wanted his close friends to share in his discovery. Burke, however, would prove to be as stubborn as ever.[9]

In many ways Josephson's method of researching and writing his biography of Zola established a precedent for his later works in the same genre. His life studies were as much autobiographies as biographies. Malcolm Cowley once described his friend's approach to biography as that of immersion in the subject: "He *became* Zola until the book was finished in 1928." Josephson later admitted as much: "In a measure, I lived Zola's life vicariously."[10]

Josephson's unbounded enthusiasm for Zola gave his biography an exuberant quality that helped make it a truly distinguished study. Published in the fall of 1928 it was by far his best literary effort to date, and in many respects would remain the best work of his entire career. *Zola and His Times* is a thoroughly researched, forcefully written, and skillfully conceived study of Zola and his literary age. Still, at times Josephson's rhetoric gets out of hand, as when he writes: "How roseate was the interior of this rapturous starveling." Or later, when he breathlessly observes that Zola "clutched at his foothold of safety with hysterical fingers." Moreover, Josephson falls into a pattern of sprinkling his narrative with gallicisms that eventually seems pretentious. Such stylistic flaws, however, are more than compensated for by the book's masterful dramatic structure. Josephson carefully organizes his portrait around Zola's dual transition from romanticism to naturalism and from aestheticism to activism, a transition he himself was undergoing. Zola's story is one of colorful events and heroic actions, and Josephson effectively uses it to express his own emerging literary philosophy.[11]

The overriding theme of Josephson's study of Zola is that a writer is "heroic" if he emerges from his cloister to confront the reality of modern mass life, if he retains his individuality while committing himself to a great public cause. And in a larger sense, this view of the writer turned public man would come to dominate Josephson's thinking throughout his career. With this theme in mind, it was thus logical that he chose Zola's intervention in the Dreyfus affair as the dramatic climax of his biography. Beginning in the late 1880s when he wrote *Germinal*, Zola the naturalist, who heretofore had viewed society as the product of impersonal environmental forces and had attempted to describe natural phenomena dispassionately, began to emerge as a committed, humanitarian idealist. As a measure of his own priorities Josephson devoted three chapters to Zola's intervention in the Dreyfus affair, when suddenly Zola the naturalist became Zola the social activist. "For some fifteen or twenty years now, he had been a worthy bourgeois; he had withdrawn from 'controversies.' All that was stubborn, courageous, combative in him reawoke." [12]

With his famous polemic *J'Accuse!* Zola aroused the public from its smug indifference and eventually helped cause the case of Dreyfus to be reopened. Zola's broadside, Josephson writes, was "written in a tone of supreme indignation; anger, bitterness, hope had crystallized into a protest of such insight and eloquence that the very stones would be moved, the whole universe would crepitate." Zola, of course, paid a high price for his heroic action. He was scurrilously attacked in the national press, burned in effigy, accused of treason by many of his countrymen, and finally forced to flee the country after being convicted of libel in a rigged trial. To Josephson, however, Zola's action had been necessary: "It had been a question of submitting to the existence not only of one abominable social crime, but a succession of them, a possible reign of darkness." Josephson's energetic, passionate narrative of the events surrounding the Dreyfus scandal betrayed an extraordinary involvement. He wrote the lengthy section in forty-eight hours, without sleeping, supported by moderate portions of wine and much coffee. Initially he had hoped that his presentation of the event "might be of some little help to the victims [Sacco and Vanzetti] of what I believed to be a miscarriage of justice." But alas, as he concluded in the biography, there are no Zolas today. [13]

Both the literary critics and the general public deemed *Zola and His Times* a success. Malcolm Cowley characterized Josephson's first biography as "vigorous, absorbing, . . . superbly documented, and rich, amazingly rich." Van Wyck Brooks insisted that this book "must rank among the conspicuous biographical works of our generation." After reading *Zola*, Herbert Gorman, critic for the *New York Times*, recognized the change that had taken place in Josephson's literary perspective. He commented that the author had been known "as pretty much of a left-wing intellectual," who has now, "curiously enough, submerged his esthetic and literary theories in an excellent biographical presentation of a man whose life was a long struggle." Josephson himself confirmed the change in a letter thanking Brooks for his kind review. He recalled an intense argument they had had in 1923 over the ideas he was espousing in *Broom*. "I had all the impetuousness of my years then," Josephson confessed, "while you were quite tempered. In the four or five years passed, my point of view has apparently changed in important respects; and I must say that you have finally won the argument." [14]

Zola and His Time, meanwhile, was attracting the wide public following that Josephson so badly desired. It quickly went through a first and second printing. An edition was readied for sale in England, and the Book League selected it as its monthly offering. The biography would continue to attract widespread praise. In his history of American biography, Edward H. O'Neill described the book as "one of the best literary biographies of modern times." Such success and acclaim helped Josephson decide that biography and criticism were to be his genres from now on. His choice of biography rather than creative writing reflected his temperament—Matthew Josephson was greatly inspired by people he read about. He felt at home with biography, making characters come alive, finding the unifying themes binding together a great life, and speaking through his subject to contemporary issues. Through biography, he believed, "I could communicate with my readers on a variety of ideas—on art and life, love and death, on human freedom and justice— and could feel myself in contact with a real public." [15]

While he was working in Paris in 1927 Josephson met Eliot Paul and Eugene Jolas, the editors of *transition*, a new and ambitious transatlantic review. Jolas, then under the spell of the Surrealists and the literature of the subconscious, found Josephson's stringent criticism of their esoteric art interesting. Jolas was attracted by his optimism and his strongly held opinions, and after a second meeting he asked Josephson to serve as a contributing editor to the review upon his return to the United States. Josephson was an editor again. [16]

Josephson soon began planning another group project for his literary friends back home, which would be published in *transition*. He wanted to demonstrate to Europeans and Americans that there were writers who did not flee their country but stayed and attempted to cope with their machine-age society. He hurriedly sent letters to his friends, explaining his project and telling them to be ready for an all-day session when he returned. The response was typically enthusiastic. Kenneth Burke saluted Matty's call "for joint action, salute it all the more since it is so typically yours: deciding upon the spirit before going in search of the job." [17]

After arriving in New York and finding an apartment on the East Side, Josephson, along with Cowley, organized a marathon writing session similar to the one that had produced *Aesthete 1925*. In January 1928 Burke, Slater Brown, Cowley, and Robert Coates joined Josephson in a suite at the old Broadway Central Hotel. They arrived at nine in the morning and worked all day, stopping only to laugh at what someone had written or to argue a point. By late afternoon they had finished, and they picked up their wives and went to the Savoy Ballroom in Harlem for an evening of dancing. The result of their efforts, "New York: 1928," a collection of poems, essays, and witticisms, was typically contentious, replete with ironic satire. Slater Brown set the tone for the group manifesto with his poem "Observation":

> 'Tis said all poetry must and can
> Resolve the ways of God to Man
> And yet when Ford or Morgan raise their face
> Poets paddle off to some French watering place.*
> *Or to Rapallo.

Although the tone of their writings was satirical and witty, their message was quite serious. Josephson and his friends savagely attacked American expatriates, even though he, Cowley, Brown, and Coates had once lived in Europe themselves. Now, however, they were determined to separate themselves from those American artists in Europe who still made a religion of art at the expense of society.[18]

   Josephson made this point even more explicit in "An Open Letter to Ezra Pound, and Other Exiles." After speaking of the pathbreaking contributions of Pound, Eliot, Stein, and others, he admitted: "For a time we went adventuring along the same trails, it was helpful to find your baggage a little everywhere. But in the end, we grow tired of our aesthetic wanderlust; we demand constants. . . . most of us who count on persisting are in search of an *active principle* for the artist." He and the others of his group were no longer satisfied with art for art's sake; they wanted to apply "what may have been discovered within tangible or living forms, rather than in those with which 'life cannot co-exist.'" Josephson dismissed the whole game of "making words play with each other" as worthless, a waste of time and talent. Even though he described the United States as a "cruel mistress," he called on Pound and others to return to their homeland:

> We may become centurions of Soap for a time, proconsuls of hydro-
> electricity; we may sing before the microphone; dance before the
> television box. A period of training, a phase of discipline will elapse,
> and in the end the force of mind will leaven this society which has

known only material preoccupations. . . . A spiritual equilibrium will have been reached in which we shall have been active factors.

Josephson had recently been reading the works of John Dewey, and the impact of that scholar's instrumentalist philosophy upon his thinking is obvious. To the young biographer of Zola, it was the duty of American artists to stay in their country, even if it meant temporarily taking a job in business, and provide a counterbalancing force to the country's rampant materialism. Ideas had power, if writers would employ them.[19]

After reading Josephson's essay, Ezra Pound grew indignant and wrote his close friend William Carlos Williams to find out why Josephson and his group were attacking him. Williams, who knew Josephson and the others, tried to reassure Pound that their criticism of him was unwarranted and misguided: "What *transition*—per Josephson—wants to say is that you are conservative. You are, what of it? It's just a class of radicals which wants to sell what it has high." Williams went on to say: "As to the Hart Crane–Josephson group—to hell with them all. There is good there but it's not for me." But Josephson, who still thrived on contention and controversy, had accomplished his objective; he had attracted Pound's attention and raised his ire. He remarked to Burke in 1928 that after looking at a batch of old letters from the *Broom* days, he was shocked at how "*passive* we have become."[20]

Throughout 1928 and 1929 the question of the artist's role in modern urban industrial America continued to dominate Josephson's thoughts. He had returned from France to an America at the height of the Coolidge prosperity. When Henry Ford introduced the first Model A in 1927, more than half a million people made down payments without having seen the car or the price. It was also in that year that the Great Bull Market began, as thousands of Americans rushed to join the speculative boom. Mass production was the keynote of the period, and the masses were eager to take advantage of it, buying luxury items that an earlier generation could only dream about.

In the fall of 1928 Josephson wrote an essay in which he discussed these economic developments and commented on the effects of widespread prosperity upon the political and cultural situation in the United States. Society, he predicted, could continue to progress through improved social organization and applied technology, provided that its leaders acted in behalf of the individual human being rather than out of any special or selfish interests. He revealed again his strong individualist bent, even though he admitted that the execution of Sacco and Vanzetti the previous year had demonstrated the "perfect impotence of Individualists in the face of mass realities." Yet he noted that communism offered little hope for America's problems. The material prosperity of the United States, he remarked, had undermined any mass support for collectivist alternatives to the American capitalist system: "The people vote for General Motors!" Like many other literary intellectuals at the time, Josephson revealed what Daniel Aaron has described as the "political uncertainty of the still-uncommitted writer out of sorts with capitalism yet very suspicious of the Russian state." Josephson concluded his essay by surmising that those artists alienated by America's form of "social collectivism" would find life in Russia just as frustrating.[21]

By late 1928 it was obvious that Matthew Josephson no longer identified with the concept of the isolated aesthete, passively watching the world rush by, concerned only with his privatist art. In a letter to the editor of the *New Masses* he demonstrated his change of attitude:

> It occurs to me that if the highbrows, the intellectuals and their cohorts were willing to come out in the open and assert aggressively that they were in favor of more intellect and less ignorance or superstition and were ready to fight for their beliefs, more honor would be attached to the epithet: *intellectual*.

This was the Zola in Josephson speaking. He was now beginning to combine a life of ideas with action in support of them. In the fall of 1928 he toured the Midwest preparing a series of magazine articles for the *Outlook and Independent*, profiling modern life in several large American cities. "In my own way," he recalled, "I was trying to get out of the Ivory Tower in which most American men of letters still confined themselves and learn at first hand what sort of country we were living in." Like the careful Zola, Josephson wanted to be objective in his role as social observer. In his new role as journalist he decided to tour slums, walk through factories, and interview the people themselves in order to be as accurate as possible.[22]

In each of the articles he wrote for the *Outlook*, Josephson expressed concern at the decline of individualism in industrial America. How could one speak of individualism, he asked, when gigantic trusts dominated the economy? While admitting the general rise in the standard of living, he insisted that "nowhere in the world did men seem more *automatized*, submissive, and monotonous." While in Detroit Josephson visited the famous Ford automobile plant in nearby Dearborn. Although he found the gigantic factory complex impressive and efficient, "the stunning noise and heat continued to oppress me." In Chicago he toured the headquarters of Sears and the Swift Meat Packing plant. He discovered that while the great business leaders were brilliant at making profits, they displayed "blind spots towards all the human issues not immediately under their charge." In another article he discussed the same problem and again displayed a mixed attitude concerning America's industrial leaders. On one hand, he expressed admiration for the "brilliant constructive achievements" of the powerful capitalists and even applauded the "process of combination which gathers all our wealth and energy into a few great phalanxes." On the other hand, however, Josephson resented the tendency of businessmen to neglect their "social responsibility to the masses whose total lives hang on their leadership." Yet he still professed an optimistic belief that the modern mass media provided an unlimited opportunity "for artists of heroic mold to communicate with and lead the blind multitudes." [23]

While in Chicago Josephson's pugnacious jauntiness and barbed wit got him embroiled in another tussle. While at a bar in the Wrigley Building he began declaiming about the foulness of the city's air. When a man walked up and introduced himself as the smoke commissioner, Matthew, with his usual finesse, told him that he found the air in Chicago unbreathable, the foulest of any city he had visited. The tipsy smoke commissioner, a rather rotound man, thereupon threw a wild punch. According to a story in the New York World, eyewitnesses reported that the smoke commissioner "landed in the well-known heap, not, however, without taking toll of Mr. Josephson's front teeth." [24]

Back in New York Josephson continued his close association with his literary friends. Kenneth Burke reported to Allen Tate in March 1929 that "things have changed little. Matty seems a little more prosperous, Malcolm a little more bohemian, Brown a little more subdued." During the spring there were frequent parties and get-togethers in the country, usually at Slater Brown's or the Josephsons' cottage in Katonah. They tended to be noisy, often boisterous affairs, with bathtub gin available in large quantities. In the fall the Josephsons would return to Manhattan and live in a rented apartment for the season, a practice they continued most of their lives. In New York the cocktail parties would continue unabated. [25]

At one of the literary gatherings in New York, Hart Crane showed up, just off the boat from Paris. Robert Coates was there, and he had brought along his close friend James Thurber, then on the staff of the New Yorker.

Thurber and Crane did not mix well from the start, the former taking a
lighthearted view of Crane's serious artistic persona. Crane, who tended
to be unruly at such occasions anyway, began shouting at Thurber, and a
fight soon erupted. While others rushed to separate the two ineffective
combatants, Thurber proceeded to step in a bucket of ice water. The mis-
step not only cooled his feet, but the heated tempers as well. Walter
Mitty had come to life. A short while later the Josephsons hosted another
party. Again, Crane was there, and after several hours of drinking, he decided it was time to start throwing furniture. Josephson then threw Crane
out. He was not mad at Hart, but after all, he was just renting the place;
the furniture was not even his to destroy. The party finally broke up
around midnight, and the Josephsons retired to bed. Then, at about four
o'clock in the morning, Hart reached the contrite stage. He phoned
Matty, waking him up to apologize for his unseemly behavior. "That's the
stage," Josephson wryly remembered, "that you can't forgive."[26]

In 1929, at age thirty, Matthew Josephson was quite a successful professional writer. "You know," he confided to John Brooks Wheelwright in
April,

> I do get a good deal of work these days and being extremely busy
> keeps me happy in a way. I help at a publishing house once a week,
> I write magazine articles, book reviews, translate, and carry forward
> one or two books, new ones, which I am writing. Outside of this I
> play the stock market and occasionally go to parties.

One of the books he was completing was *Portrait of the Artist as American*, a study of the writer's dilemma in modern America. It was a theme
that Van Wyck Brooks and Lewis Mumford had earlier addressed, but
Josephson intended to look at the issue from a different perspective. Ever
since his contact with Zola he had been trying to clarify in his own mind
the obligation a writer has to his art and to his society. Now he was ready
to put his thoughts on paper.[27]

Josephson began his second book as a rebuttal to Brooks's *The Pilgrimage of Henry James*. In that work Brooks had described expatriation
as a frustrating and futile experience; he who quits his native land dooms
himself to absorption in the sterilely aesthetic. Brooks therefore had little
respect for James's later works, *The Ambassadors*, *The Wings of the
Dove*, and *The Golden Bowl*. Josephson strongly disagreed with such an
interpretation. He noted that the "later work of Henry James must be

placed among the finest literature of the time and signalizes him as the great American novelist; then his expatriation seems a very successful adventure."[28]

Josephson's attack on Brooks sets the stage for the bulk of the book, which is primarily a group portrait of the generation of writers after the Civil War, including James, Ambrose Bierce, Stephen Crane, Emily Dickenson, and Lafcadio Hearn, who deemed themselves "exiled." Alienated by industrialism and mass democracy, they either fled the country or turned inward, isolating themselves from modern life. Josephson suggests that a similar situation existed in 1929. In his introduction he argues that the "present confusion in human values may be blamed largely upon the immeasurable changes ordered by the industrial revolution." Mechanization was warping the natural emotions and transforming men into automatons. "Under mechanism," he observes, "the eternal drama of the artist becomes resistance to the milieu, as if the highest prerogative were the preservation of the individual type, the defense of the human self from dissolution in the horde." The moral of his story, it seems, is that the sensitive artist, like James, must flee in order to save his sanity and his soul. Most of Josephson's book, therefore, comprises a melancholy account of frustration and defeat, of genius crushed by an insensitive society, of talented men and women fighting for their artistic integrity and finally being driven into exile.[29]

In the book's concluding chapter, however, Josephson takes a strangely contradictory view of the subject. He reverses the tone and complexion of his thought. Earlier he had denounced the callousness of machine-age America and then detailed the individual struggles of representative artists. But he concludes his study on an optimistic note. Josephson, himself returned from expatriation, again criticizes Pound, Eliot, Stein, and their disciples in Europe. He satirizes them as being "solitary or nervous groups spinning like fretful midges between two worlds . . . , those forlorn wanderers, those fugitives, those exiles." Josephson seems confused. Was expatriation justifiable in the nineteenth century but not in the twentieth? He answers that there is a significant difference between both the two historical eras and the artists involved. The modern exiles like Pound and Eliot fled not only from the American scene but also from the American subject, something that James had carefully avoided. Moreover, he contends, the situation in the twentieth century made physical escape impossible. "Americanization" threatens the world, and "no serious artist who now retraces the journeys of his youth, or even of a few years previous, but gathers in an abiding sense of the threatened failure of old Europe as a last resort of leisure, individualism, personal freedom—as a place of escape."[30]

At this point the whole discussion seems confused, and it becomes more so as Josephson addresses the issue of the impact of the machine age upon writers in the 1920s. He concludes with a gospel of hope and good cheer for the future, noting that it "is startling, once we leave the plane of ideas and sentiments, to perceive the rigorous discipline, what organization, implacable energy, novelty, prevails in the world of modern business and industry." Josephson still retained a fascination for the form and energy of the industrial process. Eventually, he predicts, the progress of the machine would reach a saturation point. At that time, a humanistic revival, a determined cultivation of new values would follow. Rejecting the liberal and equalitarian views of Mumford in *The Golden Days*, he visualizes a kind of Platonic state, where artists would utilize the resources of the mass media to give the masses moral and aesthetic leadership. As he theorizes: "The humanizing force of art may work best through example and symbol, upon the larger scale envisioned, reaching numberless crowds through the magnificent new machines." Instead of preaching "resistance to the milieu," as he had done earlier in the book, he ends with the assertion that the "salvation and the strength of artists lies in their ability, hereafter, to *incorporate* themselves within the actual milieu."[31]

Josephson's *Portrait* reveals much about his changing attitudes. In fact, Burke criticized the book for being too autobiographical. Intellectually, Josephson was still far from his later role as fellow traveler. In *Portrait of the Artist as American* he forcefully demonstrated his individualist bent. His primary concern remained the plight and salvation of the artist, not the plight and salvation of the masses. And his proposed method of salvation for the writer was artistic and spiritual. A humanistic revival would best be accomplished, in his view, not through collective social and political action but through "example and symbol." Murray Godwin, a prominent New York literary critic, perceived the weakness inherent in Josephson's proposal. He remarked that for Josephson,

> there is a great attraction in the attitude of the individual who has a firm conviction that thought, exhortation and example can make a fundamental change in the character of society. From my point of view, this indicates something quite different. . . . It indicates a

failure on the part of the individual to comprehend the nature of the force at the bottom of the social and political whirl.

Godwin was right. Although Josephson had come a long way since his days as editor of *Broom*, he still suffered from a tendency to look at life through the rose-colored glasses of metaphor and symbol, a tendency he never completely eliminated.[32]

Late in 1928 Josephson accepted an offer from the Macaulay Company to serve part-time as one of its book editors. In this position he assisted many of his friends and associates who had hitherto rarely published. Macaulay soon published on his advice novels by Robert Coates and Hamilton Basso (his first). Josephson also assigned writing, translating, or editing jobs to Burke, Cowley, Slater Brown, William Carlos Williams, James Thurber, and E. B. White. He also secured Susan Jenkins Brown, Slater's wife, a job as an editor at Macaulay and found them an apartment in Manhattan.

Josephson's assistance to his friends was not limited to his efforts at Macaulay. He was always, as Cowley once remarked, extremely "loyal" to his comrades. Under his hard, critical exterior Matty had a boundless capacity for encouraging and assisting those close to him. He also retained his fondness for practical jokes. Toward the end of 1925, for instance, Allen Tate took a job as a janitor in order to pay his rent. When Josephson heard about the situation, he asked a newspaper to send a reporter to write a story about the plight of a young poet forced to sweep floors in the prosperous United States. He later explained in his memoirs that he had hoped a sympathetic reader might take it to heart and offer to subsidize Tate's literary endeavors, as Otto Kahn had done for Hart Crane. Actually, however, he was pulling another one of his Dadaist pranks. Josephson knew that Tate was a sensitive and proud young artist who would not appreciate such an invasion of his privacy. When the reporter arrived, Tate was furious and refused to allow the story to be written.[33]

Josephson's efforts on behalf of his friends were in most cases genuine, despite his role in the Tate affair. At the end of 1925 he had rushed to the aid of Hart Crane. Marianne Moore, the editor of the *Dial*, had accepted one of Crane's poems for publication. She then proceeded to rearrange and eliminate many of the verses. Crane was hypersensitive in such matters, but he needed the money so desperately that he grudgingly consented to the revisions. He immediately regretted his action. After hearing the story, Matty told Hart he would try to buy the poem back from Moore. In his letter to her he characterized her actions as "perfectly preposterous, brutal, and tyrannical." He then asked what right she had to butcher other people's poems:

> If I paint a portrait, even though you are acknowledged the greatest portrait painter . . . you have no right to alter a single stroke of the brush, nor a single line. You either suffer my picture to be seen as I painted it, or spurn it completely. BUT YOU DO NOT exhibit something which is neither mine nor yours, but which is some bastard product of the two of us.

Josephson had apparently forgotten his own earlier editorial tampering when he and Cowley had destroyed one of Donald Clark's poems submitted for use in *Secession*. More probably, he now believed himself above such youthful pranks. That it was a friend's poem that was revised certainly influenced his action as well. Whatever his reasoning, Josephson's efforts on Crane's behalf failed. Moore reacted angrily to his "meddling" and printed the poem as amended. Despite the mixed results, Josephson's repeated attempts to aid his friends revealed both a sincere concern for them and an unflinching devotion to the cause of literature.[34]

Of his efforts in behalf of his friends and other struggling young writers, Josephson was proudest of his contributions to the career of Katherine Anne Porter. In September 1928, while working at the Macaulay office, Josephson was introduced to Porter, then a relatively unknown Southern writer down on her luck, who had just been hired as a part-time editor. After reading some of her stories, Matthew was quite impressed, and he persuaded Harcourt, Brace and Company to publish a collection of them under the title *Flowering Judas*. As he told the editors, Katherine Anne Porter "is one of the bright 'promises' of the surrounding scene. Her short stories have really caused underground admiration and murmur." He also proposed that they engage her to write a book about her experiences in Mexico during the 1920s.[35]

Josephson's enthusiasm for Porter, however, went well beyond an appreciation of her literary abilities. For several months during 1928 and 1929 they were lovers. Hannah was pregnant at the time with Carl, their second child, and Matthew found in Porter an attractive, vivacious distraction. "She gave me the impression," he wrote later, "of intelligence and sensitiveness, with her huge dark eyes and iron grey hair held back in a simple bun." He remembered that she spoke in a low, soft, and somewhat husky voice that was especially sensuous. Although nine years his elder, she displayed the spirit and restlessness of a much younger woman. Her figure was small and fine, her conversation charming and accomplished. And she was fanatically dedicated to the art of writing. Porter obviously stood out among the staff at Macaulay. To Josephson she was "quite polished, quite lady-like." [36]

Several days after their first meeting, Matthew asked Katherine Anne to dinner, ostensibly to celebrate the publication of his *Zola* and its choice by the Book League as a featured selection. Porter accepted but told him that she would have to shift her commitment to baby-sit for a friend, Holger Cahill, whose wife had deserted him. Josephson was to call for her at Cahill's apartment. When he arrived Cahill was about to leave with his date, Marjorie Spencer, the attractive young sister of painter Niles Spencer. On the spur of the moment, Josephson invited Cahill and Marjorie to join Katherine Anne and himself to eat dinner and then go dancing in Harlem. His intentions were less than honorable. "I had some vague scheme," he later recalled, "for enjoying the esprit of Katherine Anne and contriving to sleep with the beautiful, rosy-cheeked Marjorie." [37]

As the evening progressed, however, it was Porter who attracted Josephson more. "As I remember she deployed great charm—and quite carried me away." Porter was well traveled and experienced and had, as her close friend Glenway Wescott once commented, lived a "maximum life." At age sixteen she had eloped; she was divorced nine years later. She had lived in Chicago, Denver, and Mexico, where she had witnessed the Obregon revolution. Her past was an interestingly active and diverse one, and she captured Josephson's imagination with her colorful stories. Witty, intelligent, and attentive, she also displayed qualities that he shared: Porter, too, questioned many of the values she had inherited; moreover, she could be opinionated and downright cantankerous. In Matthew, Katherine Anne saw a promising young author on the move, already prominent in New York literary circles. With women, as Malcolm Cowley once observed, he was especially "suave, polished, sociable, courtly." His magnetism partly reflected his conscious cultivation of French mannerisms. For these reasons and others, at the outset, the two writers delighted in each other's company. While Hannah remained at home in Katonah, initially unaware of his activities, Matty and Katherine Anne went dancing in Harlem, met for lunch, and spent occasional evenings together. [38]

As their relationship progressed, however, Katherine Anne wanted to see more of Matthew and wanted a commitment from him. Although he thoroughly enjoyed seeing her, he had no intention of sacrificing either his marriage or his career. Soon Katherine Anne became frustrated and bitter: "It's unaccountable, yes, simply, the way you have gradually wangled me into the place you wish me to occupy; that of a loving and mistreated woman who, in spite of all, pursues you. Ah, God, with one tenth of your adroitness I should have done wonders with this world." [39]

Yet when Josephson wrote from Chicago in December 1928, reporting his fight with the smoke commissioner, Katherine Anne still felt able to tease him:

> The trouble is, you are entirely corrupted by civilization and the humanitarian tradition. . . . When he came up, you should have been heartily ready to sock him again instead of shaking hands. You'll be getting a cauliflower ear next, my love and my angel. Why did I let you go to Chicago alone?

Two days later she added impatiently: "Will you come home or must I come after you? My very love, shall I weep for joy at the very sight of you, or pull your hair? I could do both. . . . Damn it, if you run away and get into any more scrapes, I shall go to the West Indies." And in conclusion: "I do not forget you, my good soldier. . . . It is possible that the days pass, I don't count them; tell me when you will be here, come to me first." [40]

When Josephson returned from the Midwest, however, he did not go to Katherine Anne first. Instead he went home to see Hannah and Eric. By now Hannah had learned of the affair and made it plain to him that he could not have her and a mistress as well. He chose Hannah and then sought to transform his relationship with Katherine Anne into a platonic friendship. She responded with anger and bitterness, noting (with truth, he later agreed) that he depended on Hannah's maternal qualities even during his pursuit of other women. [41]

The affair did not end there, however. Shortly after the initial rift Katherine Anne left for Bermuda to recover from tuberculosis. From the Caribbean she wrote repeatedly to Matty, beseeching him, in letters sometimes pathetically insistent, to reconsider his attitude. [42] He continued to correspond, but without a change of heart. The inevitable break did not occur until Katherine Anne returned to New York late in 1929, when there was an emotional confrontation. Katherine Anne remained cool toward Josephson thereafter. Looking back in later years, Matthew himself recalled the relationship without warmth. "I did feel, after a few weeks of intimacy, an overwhelming need to get away from her," he wrote on one occasion.[43]

The liaison with Katherine Anne Porter was not Josephson's last indiscretion as a husband. Affairs with attractive, intelligent women occurred intermittently throughout his life. He did attempt to be discreet, but Hannah's willingness to overlook his infidelity nevertheless proved remarkable over the years. Despite periodic lapses, their marriage remained strong.

Matty and Hannah did not linger long over the Porter affair. External events almost immediately diverted their attention to more pressing concerns. On October 23, 1929, the stock market suddenly collapsed. By the end of the year, stock prices had fallen by more than 35 billion dollars. In the first quarter of 1930 the market had experienced a substantial recovery, but by June, it had dropped again, and thereafter steadily declined. When the Wall Street collapse occurred at the same time that overall consumer demand was slackening, the entire economy came down with a resounding crash.[44]

Matthew Josephson was not a neutral observer of the catastrophic events taking place on Wall Street. He owned securities, gained largely through inheritance, that he had been counting on to provide an independent source of income. In a few short days in late 1929 his portfolio was reduced by more than fifty thousand dollars. As he recalled in his memoirs: "I had shared for a while the hopes and illusions of the American middle class, and now I suffered their common fate." Fortunately for Josephson, however, he had recently negotiated a long-term contract with Harcourt, Brace and Company which helped ameliorate somewhat the effects of the Great Crash, allowing him to retain most of his stock holdings in the hope of an eventual return of prosperity.[45]

Money, however, soon became the least of Matthew's worries. In late January 1930 the Josephsons were living in a third-floor apartment at 218 East Fifteenth Street in Manhattan, preparing to sail again for France, where Matthew planned to spend several months researching his next book, a biography of Rousseau. Lewis Mumford had been so impressed with Josephson's *Zola* that he had suggested to Harcourt that Matty was "primed" to do a study of Rousseau. The choice of Rousseau for his subject was logical, reflecting Josephson's continuing affection for French writers and especially for those who, like Zola, were sensitive to social concerns and active in public causes.[46]

In the early morning hours of February 1, the day they were scheduled to sail, Matthew was suddenly wakened by the shouts of the apartment building's janitor. The building was on fire. Quickly grabbing his infant son Carl while Hannah led Eric, Josephson herded his family out the window and down the fire escape as flames roared around them. Without thinking he deposited Carl in the arms of a woman standing nearby and ran back into the burning building, frantically trying to save his papers and paintings. It was much too late for such heroics. He soon found himself trapped, surrounded by a wall of flames and unable to reach the fire escape. Forced to retreat to the ledge outside, he was stranded, too high to jump and with no firemen in sight. For nearly thirty minutes he held on to the scorching building as flames licked out the window, burning his legs, arms, neck, and head. Finally, a fire truck arrived with a ladder long enough to reach him, and after several near misses he was rescued.[47]

Josephson was listed in critical condition after being admitted to Bellevue Hospital with first- and second-degree burns covering his body. The treatment he received, however, was remarkably effective, and he left the hospital six weeks later with permanent scars showing only on his hands and neck. He was lucky to have survived at all. Kenneth Burke remembered visiting Josephson at the hospital and being shocked by the ghastly appearance of his friend, who was obviously in much pain. Matthew recognized his sensitive comrade's shock and discomfort. "And you're supposed to be a philosopher," he said to Kenneth, "you should be taking this like a Stoic, yet you cringe like a Romantic." Burke left the room and immediately began to weep in the hall. Matty, he thought, was a very courageous man, tough and as strong-willed as ever. Hannah, too, was shaken by Matty's condition. The fire, tragic though it was, did serve to restore the close bond between them. For the moment they forgot their recent difficulties and, as Matty said, "fell in love again."[48]

Josephson's brush with death in 1930, coinciding as it did with the Great Crash on Wall Street and the onset of the depression, provides a symbolic turning point in his career. Just as the country had been on a youthful spree during the 1920s, so, in a way, had been Matty Josephson. Now, both were chastened and ready to enter a much more serious and significant period in their development, a period in which Josephson would make the final step in the transition from aestheticism to activism. "For better or worse," he later wrote, he and his generation of writers "were becoming more like men of reason. For many of them the thirties were to be the years of fruition." And so it was for the nation as well.[49]

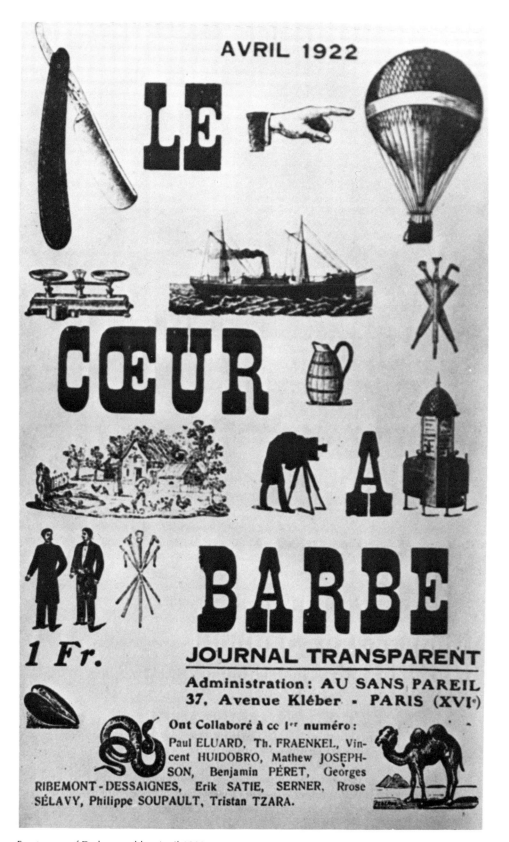

Front cover of Dada pamphlet, April 1922.

Dada party in Paris, 1921.

Left: Matthew Josephson and Tristan Tzara in the Tyrolean Alps, 1922. Photo by Jean Arp. *Below*: Tristan Tzara, Jean Arp, and Max Ernst, 1922.

Right: Kenneth Burke, 1920s.
Below: John Brooks Wheelwright, 1920s.

Right: Kenneth Burke as a zany academic, late 1920s. *Below*: Hart Crane, Allen Tate, and William Slater Brown at a New York shooting gallery, 1925. Photo by Richard Rychtarik.

Left: Katherine Anne Porter in Hilgrove, Bermuda, July 1929. *Below*: Matthew Josephson in his converted corncrib study, Sherman, Connecticut, 1930s.

Left: Hannah Josephson in Katonah, New York, 1925. *Below*: Matthew Josephson in Sherman, Connecticut, 1930.

Malcolm Cowley at the *New Republic*, 1934. Photo by Morton Zabel.

Above: Portrait of Matthew Josephson by Henry Billings. *Right*: Matthew Josephson, 1940. Photo by Berenice Abbott.

At home in Sherman, Connecticut. Matthew Josephson in 1930 (*left*) and in 1938 (*below*). *Far below*: Twin Willows.

Above: Matthew Josephson, 1962. Photo by Kenneth M. Swezey. *Below left*: Matthew Josephson and Kenneth Burke in the country, early 1950s. *Below right*: Matthew and Hannah Josephson in Italy, 1949.

Above: Matthew Josephson, late 1960s. Photo by Mary Jane Shields. *Right*: Matthew Josephson, undated. *Below*: Hannah Josephson, 1960s.

Right: Matthew Josephson in Sarasota, Florida, 1970s. Photo by Marcia Corbino.

Matthew Josephson in Sherman, 1977. Photo by Marge Josephson.

9 FELLOW TRAVELER

In May 1930, after spending several weeks convalescing at the house of the artist Peter Blume in Charleston, South Carolina, Josephson and his family sold their cottage in Katonah and moved to Sherman, Connecticut, where he had for 12,000 dollars bought an isolated, two-hundred-acre farm in the foothills of the Berkshire Mountains near the New York state line. There, in the pastoral atmosphere of the Housatonic River valley, he was able for a few months to isolate himself from the outside world and begin writing again. His physical condition forced him to cancel his planned trip to France. Josephson's new home was once a thriving tobacco farm called Twin Willows. The well-situated house, built in the early nineteenth-century and renovated in 1848 in the Greek revival style, rested on a knoll overlooking a gentle valley divided by a small, meandering trout stream. Although Twin Willows had fallen in disrepair, it had character and grace. Matthew and Hannah fell in love with country life in Sherman. "I found myself in full accord with Thoreau," Josephson wrote, "who said that if he had not gone to the woods he might have died with the feeling that he had never really lived." They busied themselves repairing and painting the house, planting bulbs, and tending a kitchen garden. Within a few months Twin Willows was transformed into a beautiful country homestead.[1]

Josephson's spirits were further lifted by the favorable reception given his recently published *Portrait of the Artist as American*. John Chamberlain described it as "the best work we have on American post–Civil War cultural pilgrimages since Mr. Mumford's 'The Golden Day.'" Gamaliel Bradford, the noted biographer, complimented Josephson "on the great advance in style from the Zola. . . . surely one who can progress so much in a short time has a future before him." Josephson's neighbor from nearby Amenia, Lewis Mumford, told him that he had written an "excellent" book, parts of which "no one could have done any better." After reading *Portrait* James Thurber wrote Matty that "I haven't in years so greatly enjoyed a book. I go around beseeching people to buy it, buying it myself to give to people. . . . It is really a splendid thing. . . . I loved to hear the whanging of your blade around old Van Wyck's throat—them passages were like a cool drink of water (don't let my metaphors get you down)."[2]

It was left to Burke's incisive critical eye to pinpoint the maturing Josephson's strengths and weaknesses as a writer as demonstrated in his new book. Kenneth objectively commented:

> As a biographer you are gratifyingly competent. As a critic you show yourself to be a man of taste, but your impatience with codification seems to have worked against you. You are good at the penetrative glimpse, you are discerning in obiter dicta, whereas the implications of your underlying thesis are not dialectically ramified. You give a sense of persons, of acts and emotions, of lives rather than a critical scrutinizing and translation of the material.

Burke, like Bradford and others, realized how well Josephson's talents were suited to biography, how effective he was at making characters come alive and at capturing the imagination of the reader. But he also correctly recognized that Matthew had not been completely successful in adopting both a biographical and a thematic approach. In addition he noted the lack of depth in Josephson's thought, a weakness that would continue to hamper his effectiveness as critic.[3]

It was in the summer of 1930 that the Josephsons first met Charles and Mary Beard, who lived in nearby New Milford. The two couples were introduced at a village square dance and became "fast friends from the start." During the next decade and a half, in numerous discussions with the erudite Beard, Josephson would learn a great deal about history, economics, and politics. Much as Louis Aragon had been during the early 1920s, Charles Beard became a major source of inspiration for Josephson. The character and integrity of the man made a deep imprint upon his thinking. Max Lerner has recalled how close Matty "felt to Beard, how he defended him when most of the rest of us were impatient with him." They both were iconoclasts—opinionated, argumentative, and capable of great moral indignation. In 1932 and 1933, while writing *The Robber Barons*, Josephson frequently talked with Beard about the project. In fact it was Beard who inspired him to write the book. In his memoirs Josephson remembered their discussions:

> This honest and forthright man was greatly exercised over the scandals about our financial leaders just then being reported in the newspapers. His was a nature often swept by gusts of moral passion; at such moments his blue eyes would blaze up, he would flail his arms wildly and launch into a truly purple passage of vituperation. "Oh those *respectable* ones—oh! their *temples* of respectability—how I detest them, how I would love to pull them all down!" he cried out one day.

One suspects that Josephson could have written the same description about himself.[4]

In the summer of 1930, however, Josephson was not yet thinking about the corrupt practices of American businessmen. Instead he immersed himself in the study of Rousseau and the Enlightenment. He told Burke in August that he had "learned to love the French eighteenth century, not so golden as the preceding one, but talkative, humane, moralizing and theorizing, libertine and disputatious, winding up with a melodramatic last act." Josephson admired the rational, optimistic spirit that permeated the age, as well as its rebellious temper. He felt at home in such an intellectual environment, and the Age of Reason became his guiding historical framework. More and more during the 1930s he would come to identify with the spirit of the Enlightenment and the literary activism of Voltaire, Swift, Condorcet, and Diderot.[5]

While Josephson read about Rousseau and the eighteenth century amid the pastoral beauty of Twin Willows, many American intellectuals were advocating socialism or communism as necessary alternatives to the nation's depressed capitalism. In an article written for the *New Republic* in September 1930 Matthew commented on such schemes. He first noted the evidence of such "social documents" as *Babbitt* and *Mid-*

dletown, which demonstrated the loss of individualism in modern America, the tendency of the masses toward uniformity and "herd-mindedness." The philosophes of the eighteenth century, he argued, would have risen up "in splendid indignation against whatever despot, church, aristocracy had bred these conditions." But modern America had no despots to focus upon. Instead, intellectuals confronted the tyranny of the mob. The problem facing the liberal mind was therefore twofold: "First, it is obliged to resist the majority, the *vox populi*, the great crowd which for two centuries it has entertained as sovereign. Second, it is reluctant to resort to power or violence to gain its end, something which the crowd is always ready to use against dissenters and also liberals."[6]

Josephson went on to say that liberals should not be shocked when they discover that most people care less for liberty than for prosperity. Yet he retained his optimistic belief that society could progress: "If we are good determinists we may recognize the present obscure moment as one of transition to that which Dewey and Beard have called a 'technological-rationalist society,' a society which developing . . . a still more valid equality, must inevitably sacrifice the liberties of the individual." Beard and Dewey, while both critical of America's worship of materialism, had been suggesting that through education, planning, and experiment, the economic and political systems of the country could be vastly improved. Catastrophic events like that of October 1929 would be averted; society would progress from chaos to stability. If such a new society resulted in "order, enthusiasm, harmony," Josephson concluded, then the sacrifice of individual liberties would be worthwhile. This Progressive vision of a rational social order run from the top by "experts" continued to dominate Josephson's imagination. Within a few years he would demonstrate his instrumentalist faith in social engineering as he came to admire the efficiency of the Soviet experiment under Stalin. Like so many other pragmatic liberals turned fellow travelers he would rationalize the brutal collectivization of the Russian peasants as the only way to promote social equality.[7]

In the mind of most Americans 1931 was *the* year of the Great Depression. That twelve months was "the period of the headache, the grim reality, the struggle to see a ray of light in empty skies." Most Americans no longer looked to the captains of industry and finance for leadership. The public was distraught and confused, searching for new sources of guidance and inspiration, and many of the nation's literary intellectuals attempted to provide such leadership. The depression sensitized them to the reality of life at the bottom of the social order. Increasingly, the sufferings of the unemployed and uprooted made capitalism appear all the more disgusting; conversely, collectivism became all the more appealing.[8]

Early in 1931 the New Republic published a series of articles by various "progressive" intellectuals in which the authors analyzed the contemporary American situation and offered suggestions for its improvement. In "An Open Letter to Progressives," Edmund Wilson announced that the capitalist system was about to collapse, and he looked with hope to the example of the Soviet Union and its constructive program based on national economic planning. He warned American radicals that if they expected to achieve tangible social change, they would have to "take Communism away from the Communists, and take it without ambiguities, asserting that their ultimate goal is the ownership by the government of the means of production." Wilson addressed intellectuals with uncharacteristic fervor:

> So American intelligentsia—scientists, philosophers, artists, engineers—who have been weltering now for so long in a chaos of prostitutions and frustrations: that phase of human life is done! Stagger out of the big office, the big mill—look through those barren walls— look beyond your useless bankrupt fields and pastures! Remember that discovery and freedom which you enjoyed for a little while— the discovery of humanity and the earth has only begun!

It was time for American intellectuals to quit thinking about radical solutions to the economic crisis and begin applying them. Communism based on democratic principles was Wilson's plan of action.[9]

Wilson's appeal found warm acceptance among writers who were not yet Communists but who were disenchanted with the capitalist system and with conventional liberal reform. In the next week's issue of the New Republic George Soule presented his diagnosis of the crisis and his prescription for improvement. Where Wilson called for taking communism away from the Communists, Soule spoke for a planned, collectivist society based on American democratic traditions. He emphasized that the general populace was hostile to Marx and revolutionary socialism. People still wanted private property. Moreover, he expressed concern about the loss of individual liberties under Communism. Thus he echoed Dewey, Chase, and other middle-class liberals who advocated tighter government control of the free enterprise system rather than its abolition.[10]

The third writer in this series was Matthew Josephson. For the past several months he had been struggling to decide what his role should be in the growing crisis. In late January he had told Wheelwright that he was "disoriented," that in recent weeks he had grown "inwardly, secretly dissatisfied with the furnishings of my head, and have set about revising them in a great many ways." His long-time friends Cowley and Burke were going off on separate literary tangents that had little appeal to him. Burke was beginning to develop his brilliant, if obtuse, theories of literary criticism, and Cowley was moving closer to the party line in his political thinking and literary opinions. "What, for instance," Josephson asked Wheelwright, "have Burke and I now in common? And Cowley is a *soi-disant* Communist in his criticism. I am troubled enough in my conscience upon many issues." He indicated that his primary interest was still artistic rather than political: "I think we should stay here and work together and separately to build the conditions of a culture."[11]

Then Josephson read Wilson's passionate statement in the *New Republic*, and he began to change his direction. He later claimed that Wilson's article "did more to turn intellectuals leftward than any other pamphleteering of that time." In his own article in the *New Republic* Josephson praised the realistic concerns expressed by Soule, but he placed his own support behind Wilson's more radical program and his admirable sense of "moral anger." The current social crisis demanded radical change, not mere tinkering. Like Wilson, Josephson was acting out of a sense of moral outrage. He described himself as a utopian rather than a cynic and advocated the immediate socialization of the means of production. Of course, the Communist blueprint must be adapted, as Wilson had argued, to the native American situation; it must be implemented through evolutionary democratic practices, not through violent revolution. To do so would require educating the public on a mass scale: "Far from shunning propaganda we must use it more nobly, more skillfully than our predecessors, and speak through it in the local language and slogans." Josephson was self-consciously beginning to emulate Zola's role in the Dreyfus affair. "The driving power," he concluded, "as in all great social movements, must come from the high quantity of *moral* certainty and moral passion."[12]

Josephson's transformation from writer to activist was proceeding apace. Only a few months before he had reaffirmed his faith in the liberalism of Dewey and in the efficiency of American technology to save the country; by early 1931 he was starting to move further left in his attitudes. He clearly demonstrated this shift in a review of Stuart Chase's *The Nemesis of American Business*. Chase was an articulate spokesman for middle-class liberalism; he was a critic of Russia and was devoted to saving capitalism by the implementation of national planning and rule by technocratic experts. Josephson agreed with a number of points Chase made in his book, especially those concerning the potential for social improvement through the application of technological expertise. But while Josephson agreed with Chase, Dewey, Beard, and others that technocratic rule in theory is beautiful, he observed that in practice the engineers in America had succumbed to the selfish lure of big business. Consequently, he could no longer go along with liberals like Chase who continued to put their faith solely in enlightened planning from the top. The liabilities of Chase's proposed system of national economic planning, he wrote, "must lie in its not being radical enough: radical, I mean, in the original sense of going down to the roots." Planning to him now represented only a superficial remedy. What was needed, Josephson emphasized, was a new system "whose first object must be the simple one of leveling economic inequality as far as possible. For we need not surface changes, but a new economy to inform, to revivify the whole American system." As yet, however, he was not ready to specify how these radical changes should be implemented.[13]

As the summer of 1931 progressed, however, Josephson's economic and political attitudes began to crystallize, and it was during this period that he began to commit himself to a more active personal role in promoting radical social change. As late as May 1931 he still preferred the cloister to the ramparts. He had told Wheelwright several months before that he looked forward to the spring in Sherman. "I am going to live in the country among books and Victrola records." During that spring he was a happy, contented man, living in the country, watching the dogwoods blossom, busily writing the final chapters of his biography of Rousseau. His little valley seemed immune from the problems and turmoil of the outside world. At that time he reported to Burke: "I cannot adequately explain to you how I became instantly, then lastingly happy here. . . . I seemed to want nothing more than to be here, for the strain to fade away from the region of my head, above my eyes." In the next few months, however, a series of events combined to bring him out of his peaceful, rustic literary existence.[14]

Early that summer, while in Manhattan to discuss the publication of his study of Rousseau, Josephson witnessed for the first time a mass public demonstration by unemployed workers. It was an enlightening experience for a man accustomed to discussing social problems in the parlor while sipping a cocktail. "There were very nice people walking down Sixth Avenue," he recalled, "probably led by Communists, but who cared?" The sight gave Josephson "quite a shock that I have never forgotten. . . . Anger rose within me . . . because good, able-bodied American citizens were forced to walk the street and cry out for food and shelter." His anxiety over the impact of industrialization had finally passed from the level of abstraction to the realm of stark reality, and he began to point to the business leaders as the villains responsible for such desperate conditions.[15]

Personal setbacks further contributed to Josephson's hardening attitude toward big business. As the effects of the depression spread, his relatively secure literary existence in the Connecticut countryside disintegrated. "Everything seemed perfectly arranged for us," he later commented, "until the heavy repercussions of the Depression hit us." Since the end of 1930 stock market values had continued to drop sharply. Finally, when the Bank of England devalued the pound sterling, Josephson decided in the summer of 1931 to sell his remaining holdings, at an average price 80 percent below 1929 values. Such an economic loss, he remembered, "threw a pall over our cheerful acres."[16]

That same summer Josephson joined the staff of the *New Republic* on a temporary basis as a contributor of editorials and general articles. Malcolm Cowley, the magazine's literary editor since the fall of 1929, had taken a leave of absence and had suggested to Bruce Bliven that Matty be asked to fill in for him. During the early 1930s the *New Republic*'s offices in the Chelsea district of Manhattan at 421 West Twenty-first Street were hives of cultural and political activity. Alfred Kazin has recalled that the magazine was "not merely a publication but a cause and the center of many causes. . . . there was a heady sense of involvement with every movement in the air, a spirit of literary crusading, the sense of a movement." In the back of the brownstone building was a garden patio where, after working hours, the staff and others would congregate for cocktails and conversation. At one dinner gathering, Harold Laski, recently arrived from England, spoke optimistically about the future of democratic socialism. Josephson brought Charles Beard to the dinner, and the intense discussion lasted well into the night.[17]

Life at the *New Republic* was filled with excitement and important personalities. Like Kazin, Josephson was attracted by the sense of group purpose that pervaded the magazine's staff, and he was soon drawn into its spirit. In doing so he became more and more absorbed in the subject of political economy and less in pure literature and belles lettres. His circle of friends and associates widened accordingly. At the *New Republic* he met George Soule, Stuart Chase, Leo Wolman, and Bruce Bliven, as well as many other writers, economists, and intellectuals who visited the offices. Josephson also saw a great deal of Edmund Wilson during this period. He remembered him as "*the* inspiring leader of the left literary movement of that era." Wilson no longer dressed in a flashy, Ivy League style; now he wore dark suits and a broad-brimmed black Stetson. He took his revolutionary politics seriously, although he soon would grow disenchanted with orthodox Marxism.[18]

Josephson's initial writing assignments at the *New Republic* were articles and editorials on unemployment relief and Hoover's handling of the economic and social crisis. He reported on hunger marches and strikes taking place around the country, as well as violent incidents brought on by hunger and frustration. In preparation for a series of articles on the relief problem, Josephson visited Hoovervilles, municipal shelters, and abandoned factories taken over by the Salvation Army. He found the Hoovervilles to be repulsive, unsanitary by-products of the capitalist system, with its haphazard agencies for private charity and relief. As he wrote in the *New Republic*:

> There is being created in our midst another nation, in the sense that Lord Macaulay meant when he wrote long ago of the dark industrial towns of England. . . . The morale of those who were on the dole, as of those receiving work relief, was no better than their low purchasing power. They seemed bewildered at being thrust down toward an unbelievably low standard of living; weak, disheartened, apathetic, their whole spirit has been altered. Theirs is a sickness that is spreading.

Josephson, who had for so long dealt with society from an artistic perspective, now discovered the bleak reality behind the images. That summer, in describing to Malcolm Cowley the situation in New York, he remarked that it is "an exceedingly strong summer. On some days your ears throb so hard you cannot indignate properly even over massacred hunger marchers."[19]

In August Erskine Caldwell, then no more than twenty-eight, visited Manhattan seeking a small advance for *God's Little Acre*. Josephson took the lanky Southern writer out to lunch and was shocked to discover that the impecunious Caldwell had spent the previous night sleeping on a sofa in the lobby of a fashionable Fifth Avenue apartment building. That afternoon he visited Alfred Harcourt and asked for 100 dollars to tide Caldwell over until his book appeared. Harcourt replied that he could not afford to bail out every young writer down on his luck, especially during a depression. Matthew's pleading, however, won out, and Harcourt gave Caldwell the money. This incident provided Josephson with further direct evidence of the human impact of the economic situation. People were struggling; their plight was indeed real and compelling. Something must be done.[20]

As Josephson's social awareness and indignation increased during the summer of 1931, his critical opinion of American businessmen also hardened. He wrote "Confessions of a Customer's Man," a detailed account of his career on Wall Street, intended for serial publication in the *New Republic*. In the manuscript Josephson revealed his growing interest in the business leaders of the past. He observed that recently published documents, monographs, and memoirs had disclosed "how treacherously the cave-men of finance invariably dealt with each other in the past." His own experience had demonstrated that

> force alone, that is sheer money power, could exact loyalty and obedience by the fear it generated. The big speculators fought with each other almost continually. . . . The same morality . . . is absorbed by the rabble of brokers, traders, agents, and spies, who live uneasily in the market place, in the arena of the financial gladiators.

By chance that fall, Harold Ross invited Josephson to write several profiles of Wall Street figures for the *New Yorker*. His subjects included Richard Whitney, "Sell 'em" Ben Smith, and Harold Content. Observing Wall Street activities again and talking to the financial wizards led Josephson to studies of their more famous and picturesque forerunners, the "robber barons" of the Gilded Age. It was during this period that he decided to write a history of the great men of industry and finance who emerged after the Civil War and transformed the structure of American society. "My concern with the fate of our culture," he later wrote, "led me to focus on the Robber Barons who, I was convinced, had given the unmitigated materialistic mold to our civilization."[21]

For all his anxiety over the deteriorating social and political scene in 1931, Josephson still found time for more lighthearted pursuits. During the summer, he, along with Malcolm Cowley, organized another group retreat for their old literary friends. This time, however, their purpose was not to publish another witty broadside but to write recollections of the early 1920s in the form of a symposium to which each would contribute a chapter. Cowley arranged for them the exclusive use of the Trask mansion at Yaddo, near Saratoga Springs, which had come to serve as a refuge for writers and artists. Wheelwright, Burke, and Robert Coates joined Josephson and Cowley at the mansion. Also in attendance was Evan Shipman, a poet who had been a close friend and drinking companion of Ernest Hemingway in Paris and whom Josephson had met and liked in New York in 1929. After arriving at Yaddo the group discovered to its dismay that no one had seen to the liquor supply. Evan came to the rescue. While Josephson and the others began writing their memoirs, Shipman went to nearby Saratoga to play pool. He played well, winning sixty dollars, with which he bought a case of Gordon's gin that had been smuggled across the Canadian border. The crowd at Yaddo appreciated Shipman's efforts and immediately set about drinking the gin. "After that," Josephson later recalled, "we wrote no more, but debated joyously day and night—save for Cowley, who began to write *Exile's Return* and did not stop." [22]

In the fall of 1931 Josephson's biography of Rousseau was published, and the book demonstrated his continuing maturation as a writer. In it he successfully assaults Irving Babbitt's critique of Rousseau, noting that to ascribe to the Citizen from Geneva all the ills of modern society, from romanticism and revolution to pragmatism and Freudianism, was facile. In a thinly disguised swipe at Babbitt and the neohumanists, he praises Rousseau as a man of feeling and compassion, a man whose "impulses were in the direction of life, where so many others move naturally toward coldness or silence or death." Josephson's most impressive achievement is in relating all the temperamental chaos, all the irrationality and contradictions in Rousseau's life, to the guiding principle of a man struggling against himself, overcoming by virtue of his own fortitude and integrity the limitations of his personality. This interpretation of the philosopher's life did a great deal to restore Rousseau's character and reputation in the 1930s. [23]

As Josephson studied Rousseau and the eighteenth-century Enlightenment, his still unformed social philosophy seemed to coalesce. Voltaire, Diderot, Condorcet, and the other philosophes had been fundamentally men of reason, skeptical of inherited assumptions and traditional institutions, determined to break the hold of entrenched convention upon society and culture. Most of them believed in virtually unlimited social progress through the innovations of science and technology. They agreed that man had the capacity for self-improvement through educational and environmental changes. With the exception of Rousseau, they also tended to be intellectual elitists, scornful of the mob, and convinced that they could provide moral leadership and direction for the masses. Josephson found such personalities and attitudes attractive. He, too, was urbane, cosmopolitan, and witty. Satire came naturally to his pen. Moreover, despite his characterization of Rousseau as a man of the common people, Josephson himself preferred to associate with intellectuals who shared his interests and concerns. Several years later he admitted to Burke: "Once I studied Rousseau, but Voltaire left the stronger mark on me. He carried the Enlightenment with him." During the 1920s Josephson had suggested to Cowley that they form a literary "salon" in New York, modeled after Voltaire and the philosophes, so that they would have someplace where they could meet "with a pretence of breeding and a reality of conversation." Although he sympathized with the masses, he preferred to identify with intellectuals of his own stripe.[24]

The parallel between Josephson and the philosophes can also be seen in their similar ideas and attitudes. As noted earlier, the triumphs of the machine had seduced Josephson into an ingenuous idealization of science and technology. He also thumbed his nose at crusty traditions and Victorian morality; he was determined above all else to be "modern." Josephson was never more typically a man of the Enlightenment than in his conviction that reason and skeptical inquiry could lead man away from whatever was false or fleeting. In his memoirs he admitted his affinity with the philosophes and the ideas of the Enlightenment. His vision of progress, he insisted, "was based on the long historical notion of *homo faber*, of belief in man's courage and will to liberate himself in the face of a hostile nature and evil circumstances." Like so many liberal intellectuals he cherished the illusion that reason properly applied could solve most problems. Thus, in his ideal society, scientists and engineers would enjoy the fullest scope in seeking to advance technology, while writers and artists would also be free to achieve the highest expressions of man's creative impulse. He said little about the average American.[25]

In addition to identifying with the rational, optimistic philosophy of the Enlightenment, Josephson shared with the philosophes a belief that during social crises the artist must play an active role in stimulating constructive change through education and exhortation. After admitting in an essay that social revolution could not occur without general public support, Josephson pointed out that as more and more men of letters "leaped into the fray," the consciousness of the masses would be raised. Among many instances of dramatic changes," he observed, "I think of that phase of the eighteenth century when the Catholic Church, declining a little in stature, was suddenly set upon by Voltaire with a sustained fury that visibly hastened its downfall as a temporal power." Now that capitalism was declining, the time was ripe for similar efforts by American intellectuals. He thus shared with many writers on the Left an abiding faith in reason and an exaggerated conception of the power of the pen to promote radical social change on a mass scale. He would come to discover that such assumptions were less than adequate for dealing with modern developments in the twentieth century. Within the next decade world developments would reveal the weaknesses of a purely humanistic perspective. Force would trample ideals; idealists would rationalize force. For the moment, however, Josephson began putting his ideas into practice.[26]

By 1932 American writers had gone far beyond the rest of the nation in feeling that the contemporary crisis demanded fundamental social and political changes. Matthew Josephson, for one, had decided that the intensity of the depression required more than the halfway measures proposed by liberal reformers. Early in 1932, in responding to a questionnaire from the Soviet newspaper *Pravda*, he revealed his excitement at becoming involved in radical politics: "For my part, I enjoy the period thoroughly. The breakdown of our cult of business success and optimism, the miraculous disappearance of our famous American complacency, all this is having a tonic effect. One feels infinitely closer to reality in 1932 than one did in 1929. And in the deeper sense the moment is a far more hopeful one." He noted with obvious approval the movement of American writers toward social and political activism. Josephson indicated that he was now convinced that "no patchwork of 'reform' can be of any avail." A fundamental change was required for American society, and the Russian model provided the best example. "The freedom of the U.S.S.R. from our cycles of insanity is the strongest argument in the world for the reconstruction of our society in a new form that is as highly centralized as Russia's and as clearly dominated by the representatives of the producing classes." Writers, he stressed, had a key role to play in encouraging such a transformation, "even if it takes them far from their studies." In March he said much the same in a letter to John Dos Passos, observing that he had given up any hope of repairing the capitalist system. "I for my part, am frankly happier in going over to the party of destruction." The situation required patient vigilance: "Edmund Wilson says let's play a waiting game, publish whatever we can manage to squeeze in, get whatever we can, then wait some more to see if something won't crack soon."[27]

Josephson caused a controversy among the New York literary community when in March 1932 he discussed in the *New York World Telegram* the growing movement of writers toward the Left. He noted that they were generally following one of two paths: national economic planning or communism. Josephson flippantly dismissed planning as a viable alternative, remarking that it required the support of the big industrialists and bankers, men who were not yet willing to hoist themselves by their own petard. "I am not optimistic," he commented, "about the chances of Beard, Chase, Soule, and Co." Josephson expressed more interest in those writers who were coming to support collectivism and who have "no intention of asking the big capitalists to cooperate with them." The problem with such a radical scheme, however, was that American workers, with their "petty bourgeois class consciousness," would not permit revolution. He suggested, therefore, that the writers on the Left should "launch a revolutionary party of their own, if only for the sake of preserving their sanity and peace of mind. By banding together into a solid and enterprising organization they might work more efficiently—they might try at least—to overcome the combined resistance of the capitalists and working men of this country." He was frankly proposing a literary "vanguard of the proletariat." [28]

Josephson's comments brought quite a response from the readers. Most of the letters to the editor were critical, and most of them correctly pointed out the simplistic and elitist nature of Josephson's political thinking. He had suggested the formation of a writers' party because the blue-collar workers were too "petty bourgeois" to go along with radical change. Yet the literary intellectuals were certainly as "bourgeois" as—if not more so than—the American working class. Charles Yale Harrison referred to Josephson's idea as "puerile and silly." After stressing the irony of writers calling for revolution in the name of the working class but refusing to allow the workers to participate, he suggested that what the eighteenth-century-oriented Josephson needed was "not so much a new party, but a little solid, revolutionary reading. Not Rousseau, Diderot, Blanqui or Voltaire, but Marx, Engels, Plekhanov, Lenin, Bukharin and Liebknecht." [29]

Josephson complained that he had been misunderstood. His intention had been to satirize those writers who professed to be political radicals, those who talked about revolution but had no appreciation for the immense labor required to conduct one. "This country," he stressed, "is still made up of capitalist and proletarian sheep who are ready neither for revolution nor for real progress. Presumably, misery has not made enough headway yet." He emphatically denied that he had criticized the

Communists. After all, they were "the most courageous and mentally consistent group visible on the horizon; they have troubles, problems enough. As I see it, they present a real potential danger, because they have so much logic and so much truth on their side." But Josephson could not give his personal loyalty to the American Communist party (CPUSA). He still did not feel comfortable around political ideologues. That is why he suggested a revolutionary party of writers. He wanted to become politically active, but he was not ready to step outside his traditional role as writer.[30]

The Communist ideal, however, grew ever more attractive to Josephson as the depression wore on. In March he displayed again an admiring attitude toward the Soviet Union. In a review of Trotsky's history of the Bolshevik revolution he wrote:

> All those who are within the church of Communism must regret or condemn his opposition and the notes of bitter criticism occasionally evident in his "History," on the ground that the Russian state is still in peril. Others may take satisfaction in the fact that the "electric" Trotsky of the civil war is replaced by the methodical and persistent Stalin of the reconstruction period.

To Josephson and other writers on the Left in the early 1930's, Stalin represented the practical visionary, a man who had abandoned the wild-eyed revolutionism of Trotsky in favor of "building socialism." He appealed to them less as a representative of Marxism than as an example of a successful social engineer in the best tradition of Enlightenment rationalism or, more recently, Progressive liberalism. Edmund Wilson illustrated this same attitude in 1932 when he wrote of his admiration for Russia's leaders "because they are men of superior brains who have triumphed over the ignorance, the stupidity, and the short-sighted selfishness of the mass." Russian society was being transformed from the top by an enlightened and efficient leader, just as Josephson had earlier envisioned his ideal state. Stalin's Marxist philosophical base, in his eyes, served as the justification for such a hierarchical social program. The Russian leader's actions were in the best interests of the general populace, whether they knew it or not. Stalin was certainly "methodical and persistent," as Josephson noted. He had yet to realize how much so.[31]

Josephson was not alone in his infatuation with the Communists in 1932. More and more writers were placing their support behind the CPUSA. In September 1932 he joined fifty-two other writers and artists, including Wilson, Cowley, and Dreiser, in signing an open letter accusing the two major political parties of being "hopelessly corrupt" and expressing support for the Communist party. "We believe," the manifesto proclaimed, "that the only effective way to protest against the chaos, the appalling wastefulness, and the indescribable misery inherent in the present economic system is to vote for the Communist candidates." A month later the group organized the League of Professional Groups for [William Z.] Foster and [James W.] Ford, the Communist candidates in the 1932 presidential campaign. On October 13 the league sponsored a mass meeting at the Manhattan Lyceum. More than a thousand artists, writers, and academics attended. Josephson and Cowley joined Michael Gold and Scott Nearing in giving speeches. They all emphasized that the leftward movement of writers and intellectuals revealed that the overthrow of capitalism was a cultural as well as a social necessity.[32]

In his address Josephson spoke at some length about the frustrations suffered by "honest" writers under capitalism, where their output was measured in terms of quick profit rather than lasting quality. He suspected that cultural life would be improved under a collectivist form of government, and if so, writers had a direct stake in supporting a radical social program. Josephson concluded his address by noting that two momentous decisions had been made by literary intellectuals. "First they had to resolve that they had no stake in the present order. The second decision was easier: to recognize that the fight against capitalism must be mainly fought by the working class under the leadership of the C.P." Josephson had within a few months' time come to accept the primary role of the working classes in fomenting a social revolution. But whether he truly identified with the proletariat or really felt comfortable in his new role as fellow traveler was another matter.[33]

To Josephson, Cowley, Lewis Corey, and James Rorty fell the assignment of writing a campaign brochure appealing to artists and professionals to vote for Foster and Ford. The resulting pamphlet, *Culture and Crisis*, argued that American capitalism had disintegrated and called on intellectuals to support the Communist ticket. In one passage Josephson penned an emotional appeal:

> It is important that the professional workers realize that they do not constitute an independent economic class in society. They can neither remain neutral in the struggle between capitalism and Communism nor can they by their own independent action effect any social change. Their choice is between serving as the cultural lieutenants

of the capitalist class or as allies and fellow travelers of the working class. That for them is the historic issue which cannot be straddled by the multiform varieties of personal escape or settled by flying to the vantage points of above the battle moralists.

This is a significant, ironic statement, for within a few years his own active involvement would diminish considerably. In fact he himself would become, in his own phrase, *au dessus de la mêlée*. Years later he would describe his decision to support the Communist candidates as "innocent and by and large well-intentioned. It was, as we see now, Quixotic." In 1932, however, he rushed enthusiastically into his role as fellow traveler. He had a cause and a sense of direction and again was part of a group literary movement. Josephson's spirits soared; he was finally the writer turned public man. After attending a rally for Foster and Ford at the Cooper Union in New York, he wrote Hannah that the intellectuals "are not acquitting themselves badly at all these days." [34]

As the decade of the 1930s progressed, the chilling specter of fascism provided another issue around which American leftist intellectuals could unite. Reports from Germany describing the anti-Semitic policies, book burnings, and expansionist rhetoric of Hitler and his henchmen suggested a new and bloody reign of terror. Many American writers rallied to organize antifascist protests and demonstrations. Matthew Josephson was one of the first literary intellectuals to warn of the danger of Hitler to Western values. Early in 1933 he joined the Committee Against Fascist Oppression in Germany, an organization designed to aid German refugees and publish pamphlets. [35]

Incensed at the tactics and objectives of Hitler and the Nazis, Josephson published in 1933 a prophetic pamphlet entitled *Nazi Culture: The Brown Darkness over Germany*. In discussing the essay with Wheelwright, he indicated how successful he had been in detaching himself from his Jewish heritage. Josephson remarked that he "was not touching much on anti-semitism . . . , although I for my part am quite proud of my Jews, always getting in the way of history, the butt of fierce feudal, military, and nationalistic revival-passion! A great deal of yammering, however, has been done for them by now." In the pamphlet he contended: "Fascism is called forth by the threat of a growing trade union or communist movement. We know that the purpose is to change nothing in the social picture, no element of ownership or exploitation, but instead to stir up against the impending revolt of the masses a reactionary

fury that Moderate governments are never equal to." After citing numerous examples of Nazi terror, he concluded his broadside with a plea for
action:

> If the future is to the Brown monster, then we are victims all! We
> must take sides. We must take our stand before it is too late. We can-
> not face the new Vandals with the Bill of Rights in our hands. To halt
> their terror we must raise the terror of world opinion, of universal
> anger and ill-will. . . . It is wrong to believe that nothing can be
> done. In all times, even the men with white hands, used to holding
> nothing but books, have shown a burning courage to defend civi-
> lization. Once convinced that "they could not live in a world where
> such things can be" they have been able to move heaven and earth
> in a good cause.

He again clearly demonstrated his optimistic faith in reason and the
power of the written word to neutralize evil. He also displayed his capacity for moral indignation. Josephson was now in his element, speaking
out in support of a noble cause and producing polemical prose worthy of
a Voltaire or a Zola.[36]

In the course of writing *Nazi Culture*, Josephson for the first time came
into direct contact with the Communist party—and it would be his last
formal dealing with the CPUSA. Joseph Freeman, a party member, promised Josephson that the CPUSA would subsidize the printing of his pamphlet. After he wrote the broadside he sent it to Freeman and awaited its
publication. Six weeks later he finally learned that some of the party ide-
ologists had disapproved of his effort. He had not given sufficient attention to the activities of the "heroic" German workers or to the "inevitability" of Communism. This episode, Josephson later remarked,
"marked the end of my brief efforts at direct collaboration with the Communists." Thereafter, he would continue to support the goals of the party,
but at arm's length.[37]

More orthodox fellow travelers recognized and disapproved of Josephson's detachment. Bernard Smith, the Marxist literary critic, wrote early
in 1933 that both Josephson and Cowley "are uncertain at the present
time of their philosophical and political objectives." Several months later
Smith surveyed the burgeoning movement of writers toward the Left.
Writing in the *Saturday Review* he reported that Edmund Wilson, Granville Hicks, Clifton Fadiman, and Newton Arvin "have moved over, with
varying degrees of emphasis, from the dwindling center toward the

swelling left, while Matthew Josephson is not far behind and Waldo Frank, vehement as ever, is far ahead." Kenneth Burke mystified Smith as much as he did Josephson. He noted that the solitary literary critic from New Jersey occupies "an indeterminate or unclarified position." Smith was obviously pleased that writers of such caliber were moving left in their politics. But he was disturbed that they insisted on retaining their artistic independence. He picked out Lewis Mumford and Josephson as examples of important young writers who had yet to realize the benefits of a Marxian literary perspective. In neither of them, he asserted, "is there the bite, the poise, possessed by men who know exactly what they want and are sure of getting it. No, these liberals are no longer fighting for the satisfaction of their needs as men, but pleading for privileges as intellectuals."[38]

Smith was right. Although Josephson was willing to support most of the policies of the Communist party, he was not about to give up his artistic freedom. He realized that literature had great political power, and he fully intended to use his literary skills to express his political convictions. In a letter to John Chamberlain, a *New York Times* book reviewer then completing a disenchanted study of the Progressive reformers, Josephson highlighted their role as literary activists. "We must be good agitators," he impressed upon Chamberlain, "We must bring steady, unremitting pressure to bear upon the establishment *from the left.*" A few weeks later, in April 1933, Josephson spoke of the exciting opportunities available to the younger generation of writers, "opportunities to go into battle for a more generous social order. There will be need, then, for unstinted moral enthusiasm. . . . There will be need enough for eloquence, and for rhetoric, too, as courageous, as efficient as possible.[39]

Josephson insisted, however, that it was possible to write both political literature and artistic literature without necessarily sacrificing one to the other. In a 1933 review of a new study of Zola he maintained that writers should certainly take part in politics and social action. But in doing so they must avoid compromising their artistic standards. Long before the great debate among the literary Left over proletarian literature, Josephson emphasized that he was opposed to it. He could not tolerate hack writing, for the party or otherwise. "In a novel," he wrote, "the mere quantity of class-consciousness is not enough. It is the amount of dramatic power engendered by the novel and the degree in which it fulfills esthetic requirements that determines its interest and success as a novel." He cited Zola as the foremost example of a writer who served both his craft and his conscience well. Josephson assumed that the writer could simply alternate between his study and the streets, carefully avoiding immersion in either context. As he himself would discover, however, it was not easy to lead such a double life.[40]

At the same time that Josephson was trying to stimulate writers to become involved in political action, he was gaining increased recognition as a professional writer of some note. The literary critic of the *Boston Evening Transcript* wrote an article early in 1932 in which he highlighted the rising young American literary critics, especially Austin Warren, Cowley, Burke, and Josephson. He cited Josephson as "the most substantial among them." Other critics also praised Josephson's talents. Austin Warren reported in 1933 that Cowley and Josephson have both "joined the staff of *The New Republic*: and though they have not, like Wilson, Arvin, and Hicks, gone Communist, they have acquired 'liberal' political and economic interests, great fluency at sociological description and exposition." Even more indicative of Josephson's growing reputation was his receipt of a Guggenheim Fellowship in 1933. The other winners that year were E. E. Cummings, Louise Bogan, and George Dillon. In an account of the awards one literary critic referred to Josephson as "the most important writer" among the group. He went on to say that Josephson, "biographer, critic, and essayist, is one of the alivest intelligences writing today in the critical manner. . . . his critical writing for *The New Republic* is both sound and reasonable journalism."[41]

During the early 1930s author Josephson continued to split his time between Sherman and Manhattan, taking the train into New York for two or three days a week to do research for his articles and books. He also regularly reviewed books for the *New Republic* and continued to visit Cowley and others there. Increasingly, however, he came to dislike the gloomy atmosphere in New York during the depression. He preferred to get his work done as quickly as possible and return to the country, where his mood almost immediately became more refreshed, restful, and optimistic. By 1932 the Josephsons had made considerable progress in renovating and refurbishing their country home. They dammed up their brook to provide the boys with a swimming hole, and during the summer months it became their chief recreational area. Matthew found the noise created by their cavorting a distraction, so he soon abandoned the study in the main house and retreated to an old, run-down corncrib about two hundred feet away as his place of work. While visiting the Josephsons, E. B. White remarked that he had never seen a country house so well situated in the midst of a broad lawn, under towering maples and elms, and overlooking a gracious valley and babbling stream. It was an ideal location for a writer, and he envied his associate's good fortune.[42]

Although Josephson's standard of living certainly suffered during the depression, he was far from Grub Street. His stock holdings in 1933 were valued at 30,000 dollars. He also received regular advances from Harcourt for *The Robber Barons*. In addition his free-lance journalism contributed significantly to his income. But he also had more mouths to feed. In the early 1930s the Josephson household swelled to six. In addition to himself, Hannah, Eric, and Carl, it now included a young Finnish woman named Walma who served as live-in maid and nanny. During the summer months Hannah's niece Eloise joined the household. The Josephsons added another resident in the spring of 1932 when Montgomery Schuyler, a middle-aged unemployed engineer, appeared one day asking for work in exchange for food and shelter. They took him in, and Schuyler served as a handyman for several months.

The Josephsons still managed to maintain an active social life during the depression. Numerous parties were held at Twin Willows on Friday nights. A barrel of applejack brandy and a keg of bootleg whiskey provided liquid refreshment, and the servings were liberal. Frequent guests included Robert Coates, to whom Josephson had sold an adjoining piece of property, the Cowleys, who lived down the road, Peter and Ebie Blume, who lived across from the Cowleys, Robert Cantwell, Slater Brown, Gladys and Henry Billings, Hamilton Basso, and Evan Shipman. Jack Wheelwright was also an occasional visitor to Sherman in the early 1930s. Matthew enjoyed his company and his eccentricity. At Twin Willows Wheelwright would try to compensate for his room and board by helping around the house, mowing the lawn dressed only in "soiled, scant undershorts, looking like an unclad Ichabod Crane." One day Hannah took an old bedstead out to the terrace and began removing the paint. Wheelwright saw her laboring and yelled: "You poor woman! What a long business, I must help you." Whereupon he went inside, grabbed a volume of Dante Gabriel Rossetti, pulled up a chair, and proceeded to read aloud from the *House of Life* for Hannah's edification as she continued to labor.[43]

At Sherman Josephson could think and write in an ideal setting. As spring began its stately advance he could observe from his corncrib study as the buds appeared, first on the pussy willows, then on the shadblow and the lilacs. The swamp maples down in the valley would appear as a red stain. Orioles would encamp in a thick grove of maples behind the house and provide a daily serenade. Here he and his family were well insulated from the turmoil and ugliness of the depression. He did not have to confront daily the sight of masses of human beings agonizing in the cities. His physical detachment reflected his mental detachment. And this inevitably affected his perspective as a writer on the Left.[44]

There have been numerous attempts to explain why so many bourgeois writers were attracted by Marxism and aligned themselves with the Communist party during the thirties, either as official members or, more often, as fellow travelers. Conservative critics and former leftists such as Peter Viereck, Daniel Bell, Sidney Hook, and Leslie Fiedler have attributed the phenomenon primarily to the self-doubt, conformity, and naivete of the writers. According to this view, the leftist writers were romantic idealists, political innocents duped by the alluring rhetoric of Marxist theory and the sense of group solidarity promised by communism. The net result of their activities during the thirties was that they helped serve as unknowing accomplices in the international Communist conspiracy.[45]

Other commentators, however, have explained the attraction of communism in a less critical light. Malcolm Cowley, for instance, has compared his acceptance of Marxism and support of communism to a religious conversion. Suddenly after years of wandering in a bohemian wasteland, he and his friends, including Josephson, "saw the light" during the early years of the depression. Their religion of art of the 1920s, the artistic individualism of Dada and the lost generation, was no longer relevant. They sought new spiritual and intellectual satisfaction, a role to play *in* society, and communism seemed to provide it. Communism offered salvation not only in the future but also in the present, by making life meaningful and by giving intellectuals a sense of constructive involvement in society. As Cowley noted, they chose to replace the religion of art with the class struggle. And in doing so, many discovered an escape from their déclassé existence, the loneliness and insecurity of literary life. By allying themselves with "the people," they could eliminate "the desperate feeling of solitude and uniqueness that had been oppressing artists for the last two centuries." Other literary fellow travelers, including Edmund Wilson and Kenneth Burke, have utilized a similar religious analogy to explain their political conversion. For them communism did seem to provide a sense of religious certainty during a period of social upheaval.[46]

Matthew Josephson's assumption of the role of fellow traveler certainly followed a pattern similar to both of these interpretations. At the same time, however, there were important differences. In his memoirs Josephson attacked both the conservative critique of the literary Left and the "religious" analogy provided by Cowley and others. He emphasized that he saw no conspiracy at work during the early thirties. The writers on the Left were "often sharply demarcated individuals in their opinions and were in no sense regimented." He stressed that although he sympathized with the Communist ideal, he was never a helot to the CPUSA. His description of his relationship to the Communist party was remarkably similar to that of Waldo Frank, who explained his position in his memoirs:

> I was in a dilemma. I could not join a party that had doctrines and methods I considered not only wrong but dangerous. Yet so long as I was convinced, in those early 1930s, that the Communists were the sole organized instrument for the transformation of the capitalist into a socialist society, I could not oppose them. . . . In brief, I must somehow act. Conviction without deed is bad ethics. . . . I devised a plan. I could not join the Party; but I accepted its fundamental aim, the creating of free persons; even if its doctrines of the contingent nature of man and necessity . . . barred free persons and suppressed them. . . . I collaborated in a limited form with the Party: defending Russia's right to its own way, speaking at open meetings where that way was explained, participating in protests and strikes.

Like Frank, Josephson portrayed himself in his role as fellow traveler as a man at the edge of the crowd more than at the front. He insisted that he always made up his mind independent of party influence.[47]

But there is more to be said on this issue. True, Josephson never inclined toward membership in the party. And as he emphasized time and again in later years, he frequently and openly disagreed with party policies concerning cultural matters. In addition, both The Robber Barons and The Politicos were attacked in the party press for not being "Marxian" enough. Nevertheless, on most major political issues in the 1930s and after, Josephson pretty much followed the Communist line. Like so many fellow travelers he pragmatically fastened upon the utopian promises and immediate relevance of communism without recognizing or admitting the gross vulgarities and human inequalities of communism in practice. His own idealism at times betrayed him and his critical faculties.

Josephson also later insisted that he did not experience something akin to a sudden religious conversion to communism, as Cowley and others did. "I was not," he wrote, "one who experienced a religious conversion to Marxism and read *Das Kapital* as a breviary, but I found Marx wonderfully timely and apposite in those days." On the surface, however, Josephson's transformation from Dadaist to Marxist did indeed seem to represent an incredible reversal of attitudes, a remarkable about-face analogous to a religious conversion. After seeing Josephson at a Communist rally during the early 1930s, Murray Kempton remarked with astonishment: "There was Matthew Josephson, the playboy of the revolution of the word in the twenties . . . previously identified with . . . *Secession, transition* and Dada." Josephson's change of roles and attitudes, however, was not so much revolutionary as evolutionary, not so much a religious conversion as a sequential intellectual progression. There was an underlying unity of values at work behind such a spectacular transition in ideology.[48]

In some respects Josephson was attracted to communism for the same reasons he had earlier been attracted to Dadaism. His basic intellectual outlook had been shaped by the modernist literary attitude he had adopted as a college student in Greenwich Village, an attitude that meant great esteem for those writers who were most revolutionary in their artistic approach: Pound, Eliot, Joyce. Josephson later found the Dadaists appealing because they, too, went to extremes. Now he embraced the Communist position at least in part because of its radicalism. He clearly preferred it to the socialism of Norman Thomas, which he derided as an "educational or evolutionary socialism, devised by our granddaddies." The Communists, on the other hand, did not compromise or temporize in promoting revolutionary change. And such dynamism was what the contemporary crisis demanded. As Josephson exclaimed in 1932, "My disgust, my pessimism . . . , leads me to support, if anything, those extremists who disturb our inert society a little." Whether as Dadaist or as fellow traveler, Matthew Josephson was by nature a disturber of the peace, a man capable of great indignation and oriented toward group action. "No Protestant liberalism for me," he told Cowley, "not in these times, anyway."[49]

In this sense Josephson fits the description that T. B. Bottomore has applied to the fellow travelers in his study *Critics of Society*. He points out that literary intellectuals were attracted to Marxism not primarily as a complex social theory but more as a means of continuing, "in another fashion, that alienation from American society which had begun toward the end of the nineteenth century." During the twenties Josephson was alienated from the conventions of genteel literature and the philistinism of bourgeois life; in the thirties he was alienated from the callousness of Western capitalism. As Dadaist and as fellow traveler Josephson was both a distinct individual and part of a group. In both roles he was involved in society yet also detached from it; he cherished his involvement and his detachment. Thus, in both Dadaism and communism he found a haven, a sense of community and involvement, that served as an antidote to the alienation he felt. His attachment in each instance, therefore, was relatively superficial. In neither case did he develop a thorough understanding of the historical or theoretical bases of the movements. Nor did he ever give himself totally to them, as did his friend Louis Aragon. He was, in the literal sense of the term, a fellow traveler, both as Dadaist and as Communist.[50]

In addition to his being attracted to communism from a continuing sense of social alienation, Josephson also found in Marxism a system compatible with many of the ideas he had been developing during the 1920s. By the early 1930s he had already developed the major strands of his personal philosophy, what he referred to as twentieth-century Enlightenment humanism, a secular devotion to social progress through rational inquiry and constructive skepticism. Thus, with the onset of the depression and the incumbent social crisis, he turned naturally to Marx, not as a savior, but as a "true heir of Humanism and the eighteenth-century Enlightenment as well as the intellectual son of the French Revolution." To him Marx was simply one of a long line of humanist critics, from Voltaire to Zola, who had sought to improve the social order through rational, "scientific" inquiry. Nor was Josephson alone in approaching Marxism from this perspective. As David Caute has demonstrated, fellow-traveling provided "a return to the eighteenth century vision of a rational, educated and scientific society based on the maximization of resources and the steady improvement (if not perfection) of human nature as visualized by objective, unprejudiced brains."[51]

But like the philosophes, Josephson's admiration for reason and scientific method was at times simplistic. John Dewey perceptively recognized the susceptibility of writers like Josephson to the scientific claims of Marxism when he wrote that "literary persons have been chiefly the ones in the country who have fallen for Marxist theory, since they are the ones who, having the least amount of scientific attitude, swallow most readily the notion that 'science' is a new kind of infallibility." In the 1930s Marxism appealed especially to those who respected science, but who were not trained in science, to those who were primarily interested in ideas and culture and who tended to have little contact with the daily social scene. It also offered to literary intellectuals a significant role to play in the social process, a chance to leave the cloister and put their idealism into practice as the vanguard of the proletariat. It is in this sense, then, that Josephson seems to have been attracted to Marxism and fellow-traveling. His conversion reflected values and interests he had developed long before 1929. That his political transformation was evolutionary rather than revolutionary also helps explain why he, unlike so many of his peers, did not renounce his leftist convictions after the depression and the war.[52]

10   A WRITER ON THE LEFT

After the publication of his biography of Rousseau in 1932, Joseph-son began research for *The Robber Barons*, visiting public and college libraries along the East Coast and spending several weeks at the Library of Congress. One would like to imagine that he pursued his research systematically, sifting through the dusty primary sources, newspapers, diaries, Congressional hearings, and personal correspondence, then turning to secondary accounts to determine how businessmen built up their commercial, industrial, and financial empires, then studying the economic theorists to determine why they acted as they did. But in his first attempt at historical research, Josephson read and thought in somewhat haphazard fashion, mingling theory and practice, contemporary authors with past records, not distinguishing between European and American theorists, professional scholars and polemicists. As a result, his scholarly labors tended to reinforce his already critical attitude toward American capitalists.

Almost all of Josephson's material for the book was gathered from secondary sources. This in itself is not surprising. The Gilded Age businessmen did not leave many records of their activities. For insights into economic theory Josephson relied most heavily upon Marx's *Capital*, various works by Thorstein Veblen, Henry George's *Progress and Poverty*, John A. Hobson's *The Evolution of Modern Capitalism*, Werner Sombart's *The*

Quintessence of Capitalism, and R. H. Tawney's *Religion and the Rise of Capitalism*. For information about the individual "robber barons" in American history, he utilized primarily Gustavus Myers's *History of Great American Fortunes*, Charles and Mary Beard's *Rise of American Civilization*, Henry D. Lloyd's *Wealth against Commonwealth*, Lewis Corey's *House of Morgan*, John Flynn's *God's Gold*, Burton Hendrick's *Life of Andrew Carnegie* and *Age of Big Business*, and John Moody's *The Masters of Capital* and *The Railroad Builders*. In addition, he read a number of the few available memoirs, autobiographies, and diaries of the businessmen themselves. As is obvious, however, nearly all of Josephson's main secondary sources could be classified under the general heading of "anticapitalist." They included orthodox Marxists, socialists, utopian reformers, and economic determinists. Most of them shared in one degree or another a personal animus against big business. Thus, Josephson's research confirmed rather than challenged his own views.

Josephson derived most of his ideas about the writing of history from his close association with Charles Beard, to whom *The Robber Barons* is dedicated. His contact with Beard introduced him to the Progressive school of history, an approach to the past that coincided neatly with his already developed attitude toward the role of the writer in encouraging social reform. In the early 1930s Beard, along with Carl Becker, spent a great deal of time challenging the claims of "scientific" historians that history could and should be written from a detached, objective point of view. History, according to Beard, was not an abstract discipline designed for contemplation. On the contrary the historian had a duty to play an active role in trying to develop a better world. By uncovering and explaining the historical roots of contemporary problems, historians could provide the information necessary to produce reform and progress. Beard believed that historians necessarily reflect in their writings their own social and cultural milieu; they cannot be totally detached and objective. "Any selection and arrangement of facts," he wrote in 1933, "is controlled inexorably by the frame of reference in the mind of the selector or arranger." Beard thus considered history inevitably to be, at least in part, an instrument of propaganda. The challenge, therefore, was in making sure that the propaganda was for a good cause, for peace and progress, for justice and humanity. In his frequent discussions with Beard, Josephson undoubtedly adopted a similar viewpoint as he prepared to write *The Robber Barons*. He also assimilated the bipolar view of society that Beard and other Progressive scholars stressed, with its clear-cut conflict between haves and have-nots, robber barons and workers, politicos and reformers. In addition he adopted the "realistic" methodology of Progressive scholarship, pointedly dismissing the public utterances of politicians and capitalists in order to get at their true motives and conduct. And inevitably he would find such "reality" in the selfish personal quest for political power or economic gain.[1]

Josephson revealed the historical perspective he brought to *The Robber Barons* in a letter he wrote to Alfred Harcourt in April 1932. The purpose of the study, he explained, was to describe the emergence of the giant industrial combinations in the United States after the Civil War. He then discussed the structure of the book:

> My theory is that the Robber Barons of industry and finance built up this country, at great speed, by their speculations and colossal ambitions. But how they built, or jerry-built is another matter, involves a judgment which I want to leave for the present generation to make. I am not going to be sentimental; I am to mass up the facts themselves, the stories, as amazing as anything in modern history. . . . Against their great constructive labors, I shall lay up all the destructive tendencies which were implicit in their class.

After making some pretensions to objective history, Josephson made clear to Harcourt what he really had in mind in writing the book. He told his publisher that his new study would be "factual, but like Gibbon's *Decline and Fall of Rome*, also colorful and dramatic. . . . After I have my facts I want to turn it into a piece of literature." He intended to provide a dramatic portrait of the American businessmen, focusing on "the whole character of their construction, rotten at the core by virtue of the profit-making motive that fixed its character, and the inevitable maldistribution that brings successive waves of disaster." Such a remark clearly reveals that Josephson studied the past with one eye fastened on contemporary concerns. He believed that the greedy, irresponsible activities of the Gilded Age "robber barons" bore a direct causal connection to the stock market crash of 1929 and the ensuing depression.[2]

In concluding his letter to Harcourt, Josephson left no doubt about his primary purpose in writing the book. "In short," he stressed, "I wish to place the brand of obloquy squarely upon the masters of capital in 1870–1890: what they did; how they did it; what heritage they left us." He guardedly admitted his relativism in the introduction to the book. After maintaining that he had "tried insofar as possible to write of them without anger, to paint them as no more 'wicked' than they or their contemporaries actually were," he noted that he was living "in another moral climate and in the midst of a new generation which carries the vast and onerous social responsibilities bequeathed to it." In this vein he saw *The Robber Barons* as more than a simple history; it was also a polemic against the capitalist order in the United States, past and present. Its message was directly relevant to the crisis at hand. In May 1933 he told Harcourt: "If I were a prestidigitator of some kind I would bring my book out next week. What things these eyes behold in the morning papers every day." Several weeks later he described *The Robber Barons* as the "most 'timely' work" he had yet written.[3]

Josephson was certainly right about the timeliness of his subject. As William Leuchtenburg has observed, the American businessman by 1932 "had lost his magic and was as discredited as a Hopi rainmaker in a prolonged drought." Thus when *The Robber Barons* appeared in March 1934, it found a public eager to read about the machinations of the captains of industry and finance. Within a week the book appeared on the best-seller list and was selected as a Book-of-the-Month Club offering. Josephson's national reputation soared, as did his income. The immediate success of *The Robber Barons*, however, resulted more from its intrinsic merits than from the favorable temper of the time. The book would not have evoked such a broad, sustained response had it not been so carefully conceived, so forcefully written, and so filled with high drama and colorful characters. Josephson wrote with the verve of a pamphleteer and the style of the romantic novelist. As in his biographies of Zola and Rousseau, he aimed his book not at a small segment of the literary public or at academic historians but at the general readers, the economically depressed middle classes, the professional men, artists, and workers who could relate to the lives and stories he portrayed. In this sense one must examine *The Robber Barons* on its own terms, assess it from both a literary and a historical perspective, for Josephson effectively combined both arts.[4]

As the organizing theme of *The Robber Barons* Josephson chose the development of monopoly capitalism in American industry and finance in the latter half of the nineteenth century. For his theoretical approach to the process of monopoly formation, he relied extensively upon the first volume of Marx's *Capital*. One capitalist, Marx observed, "always kills many." With the general increase in social wealth that accompanies industrialization, more men emerge as capitalists, but they systematically "expropriate" one another, thus accelerating concentration. This theory of monopoly formation was essentially the only element of Marxian economics that Josephson overtly utilized in writing *The Robber Barons*. As he later admitted to Lewis Corey: "I am not a compleat Marxist. But what I took to heart for my own project was his theory of the process of industrial concentration, in Vol. I of *Capital*, which underlay my book." [5]

Despite his use of Marx, Josephson told his story primarily in terms of human drama and conflict. In his preliminary outline of *The Robber Barons* he had observed that he was concerned with the Industrial Revolution's "human documents rather than its quantitative character." *The Robber Barons* comprises a group portrait, a collection of biographies intertwined around a common theme. Through the lives of Cornelius Vanderbilt, Daniel Drew, Jay Gould, Jim Fisk, Henry Villard, Phillip Armour, James J. Hill, Collis P. Huntington, Leland Stanford, Andrew Carnegie, John D. Rockefeller, J. P. Morgan, and several other leading businessmen of the era, Josephson constructs a dynamic narrative in which the characters develop as they attempt to monopolize their respective industries. He concentrates on the backgrounds, attitudes, activities, and relationships of the personalities themselves rather than on the institutional changes they made. The "robber barons" appear as a group of devious, ambitious, scheming economic giants frequently engaged in open combat, occasionally working together as allies, but most often plotting to stab each other in the back. By brute force and overwhelming personality they install themselves in the citadels of industrial America, without regard for public interest, private right, or social morality. They bribe judges and legislatures, blackmail their competitors, and milk the public. While effectively centralizing the American economy, these great captains of industry and finance do little to increase its efficiency.

There is caricature in many of Josephson's characterizations of the individual barons, a tendency to draw out certain features with a view to making them ridiculous. They all seem to have small, beady eyes, are shrewd, calculating, surreptitious. His description of Rockefeller is typical: "His long, fine nose, his small bird-like eyes set wide apart, with the narrowed lips drooping a little, and the innumerable tiny wrinkles, made up a remarkable physiognomy. But his mouth was slit, like a shark's." Jay Gould, he writes, was "small, dark, of a somewhat furtive and melancholy cast." He tended to be "tight lipped, secretive, alert." Later, Josephson highlights Gould's "curly black beard, his piercing dark eyes, his hooked nose." Another example of Josephson's effective descriptive style occurs in his account of the notorious struggle between Jay Gould, Vanderbilt, and others to gain control of the Erie Railroad:

> A Molière, a Balzac alone could paint the strong passion, the glittering eyes of greed, which Gould, Circe-like, aroused in the swine, jackals and wolves who pursued him: the Dixes, Belmonts, Astors, Goldschmidts and others who figured in the dissenting stockholders' faction.

Josephson thus conveys a general impression of the appearance and character of the "robber baron" type. With their personalities thus sharply delineated, he next outlines in detail the unprincipled methods employed by the barons in their rise to power.[6]

Throughout the book Josephson insists that most of the tycoons were neither innovative nor visionary. The career of Cornelius Vanderbilt "shows little of that triumphant enterprise or 'vision' for which he has been applauded for so long. As a master of sailing vessels, he despised the newly arrived paddle-wheelers of 1807, holding that they were merely good enough for Sunday picnics." Just as Veblen had portrayed the captains of industry as parasites growing fat on the technological innovations of other men, Josephson depicts the barons as crafty capitalists who stole the accomplishments of the true innovators. Inventors like Cyrus McCormick were "used and flung aside by men of ruse and audacity who had shown gifts for the accumulation of capital, who were skilled at management . . . and who, far from sharing the hazards of applied science, tended to enter an affair only when its commercial character had been established beyond a doubt." As in the case of Vanderbilt, Josephson pictures Andrew Carnegie as a reluctant, if not recalcitrant, innovator in replacing iron rails with steel:

> It is a sly or tardy agent of progress that we see in Carnegie. . . . The man who was all spirit-of-enterprise had waited too long—indeed one wonders much in this connection at the significant lag between the interests of technical progress and those of business enterprise. Had not the rickety iron rails and bridges been collapsing everywhere for years with horrendous accidents as a commonplace for the time? . . . Did not numerous contentious factions cling to the small lines, having different track gauges, so that passengers and freight must be transferred after short hauls—a system obsolete decades before it was abandoned? *One wonders if another form of society, one that was not dependent for its innovations upon the providential "blind hand" of commercial struggle, would not have moved more rapidly in matters which affected the general population so deeply.* [Emphasis added.]

Josephson was convinced that some type of collective social organization would have been preferable to the unpredictable and chaotic free enterprise system of the late nineteenth century.[7]

In highlighting the reluctance of many of the "robber barons" to experiment, Josephson effectively marshals evidence to support his conviction that on balance they were more destructive than constructive in their actions. While admitting that, as Marx said, the industrialists moved upon the crest of centralization and thereby hastened their own downfall, he insists that "often their profit seeking seemed to be served best by resisting or restraining the historic process, by combating the very constant advance of the 'state of the industrial arts' wrought by innumerable technicians and workers." Following Veblen, he portrays them as not only lacking innovative daring, but also as being immensely wasteful, both of human and natural resources. He notes, for example, that the work of constructing the transcontinental railroads was "carried on with heedless abandon . . . [which] caused a waste of between 70 and 75 percent of the expenditure as against the normal rate of construction."[8]

In the chapters dealing with the social activities of the industrialists and financiers, Josephson's tone lightens considerably, and he gives full play to his masterful wit and sense of irony. One is struck by the sheer vulgarity of the proceedings as the barons seek to outdo each other at conspicuous consumption and pecuniary emulation. In one of the book's funniest passages he describes J. P. Morgan's sudden decision to become a connoisseur of the arts despite his apparent lack of cultural sensibility. After several years of buying art treasures from around the world, he was still forced to ask: "Who is Vermeer?" Others surrounded themselves with the best European paintings and sculpture, even though they little understood or appreciated their exquisite acquisitions. In a hilarious portrait Josephson imagines that for the business barons, "sleeping in priceless Renaissance beds once occupied by kings and their concubines, and in boudoirs decorated with Fragonard murals, softened them in no way, apparently. Sometimes they had the droll aspect of the aborigine who decorates his person with the *disjecta membra* of Western civilization, with pieces of tin can for his earrings, or a rubber tire for a belt."[9]

The Robber Barons is not a completely one-sided assault on the great capitalists, as some critics have implied. Josephson frequently gives credit to the "constructive virtues" of the Gilded Age business leaders. They were at least, as Marx pointed out, "agents of progress." They did provide the nation with a much-needed array of industries and services while at the same time unconsciously preparing the way for an eventual socialist revolution. At times Josephson's descriptions of the shrewd, ingenious practices of the industrial capitalists take on an admiring, almost envious tone. It is not uncommon in *The Robber Barons* for him to assert that Jay Cooke displayed a "strain of genius" and that James J. Hill was an "able administrator," "sounder" and "more efficient" than his contemporaries. Furthermore, he concedes that Rockefeller was indeed a "great innovator." He admires his "unequaled efficiency and power of organization." [10]

Yet in almost every instance where Josephson commends the moguls, his praise is qualified. In his estimation the "robber barons," though at times constructive, were interested only in private profit and oblivious to any human or social concerns. Although they did build up great industrial combines, the business leaders were "guided by purely pecuniary motives, as Veblen points out, and it remains always a matter of doubt if the mightier industrial combinations improved their services to society at large in the highest possible degree." [11]

In the book's conclusion Josephson explicitly judges the past in light of the present. The attitudes and methods of the captains of industry, he insists, did not end with their generation:

> Ever since the end of the century the form of our economic organization was virtually crystallized; the ownership of the means of production, the method of exploiting labor and natural resources, were fixed. . . . The successive periods of plethora and complacency, the intervals of tragic disillusionment, the waves of infantile reform launched by middle-road politicians, the recurrence of public corruption, financial madness and renewed crisis—all this would seem so much ironical and wearisome historical reiteration of a familiar system, did we not begin to perceive at last in this system all the fatal signs of a shortening rope. . . .
>
> Extremes of mismanagement and stupidity would make themselves felt, as the more advanced cycles of the industrial revolution were attained and the economic organism became less susceptible for control. The alternations of prosperity and poverty would be more violent and mercurial, speculation and breakdown each more excessive; while the inherent contradictions within the society pressed with increasing intolerable force against the bonds of the old order. Then in the days when the busy workers of our cities were turned into idle and hungry louts, and our once patriotic farmers into

rebels and lawbreakers, there would arise hosts of men and women, numerous enough, who knew that "they could no longer live in a world where such things can be." [12]

The Robber Barons was history written in the mood and ambience of a turbulent, angry decade, history that reflected perfectly the spirit and needs of the times. Its conspicuous merit was in its vividness of portrayal. Josephson wrote with a cumulative dramatic power that gave to the story such intense reality as to make the personalities live again and grip the mind of the present generation. The crisis atmosphere of the depression years demanded that the past be made relevant, that history promote and buttress social and political reform, that the public be informed of past and present injustices. Fairness therefore might be sacrificed to readability, objectivity to the author's controlling emotions and socioeconomic convictions. In the way of Zola, his hero, Josephson had produced a stirring social tract. Viewed in this light *The Robber Barons* was a stunning success. In almost all the leading newspapers and periodicals the book was treated with high praise. Lambert Davis, editor of the *Virginia Quarterly Review*, listed *The Robber Barons* as "required reading for anyone interested in American history or American life." Henry Hazlitt agreed, noting in the *New York Times* that Josephson's new book "ought to be read by every one who wants a genuine insight into our national history." After reading the book, Hazlitt observed, Americans would better understand the activities and attitudes of the modern day "robber barons"—the Insulls, the Mitchells, and the Wiggins. [13]

Allan Nevins, destined to become one of America's foremost historians and Josephson's chief antagonist, wrote a lengthy review of *The Robber Barons* for the *Saturday Review*. He described the work as a *"tour de force . . .* a swiftly moving, vividly written, factually detailed panorama of the more aggressive and unscrupulous side of American business from 1865 to 1901." Nevins attributed to Josephson "the force and eloquence of a born pamphleteer; and this interesting book is a pamphlet or polemic as well as a vivid picture." More negatively he noted that *The Robber Barons* was obviously written "by a man not expert in either history or economics. Its consistently critical and hostile tone makes little pretense to balance or impartiality." Nevins also criticized Josephson for failing to credit the business leaders with "imparting superior efficiency to the American economic system." But it was hard for Josephson to stress such efficiency in 1934, and Nevins seemed to recognize that fact. "Anyone who believes in the New Deal must wish it the widest possible reading. It shows how evil the worst side of the Old Deal, the Raw Deal, actually was. To that phase of laissez-faire we should never return."[14]

For six months after its publication *The Robber Barons* headed the nonfiction best-seller list. Josephson remembered hearing in the 1930s that his work was considered required reading among New Deal bureaucrats. Even more important, in the long run, was that high-school and college teachers used the book in their American history courses. In addition, many general textbooks incorporated Josephson's interpretations in their treatments of the Gilded Age, thus insuring that a generation of young adults would be acquainted with the robber barons. *The Robber Barons*, therefore, is more than just a period piece. Its literary merit and moral tone, in addition to its persuasive indictment, have given it a universal appeal that goes beyond the situation that brought about its creation. Its basic statement about human nature and economic behavior transcends particular epochs. As a result, for well over a generation, *The Robber Barons* remained the standard work in its field. Even today, despite numerous revisionist attacks, it dominates the popular perception of the subject. One scholar, speaking of the impact of *The Robber Barons*, observed in 1958 that "perhaps more than any other single volume, it served to disseminate the phrase, 'the robber barons,' through American historical writing. It was, in a sense, the culmination of the idea expressed in its title."[15]

When *The Robber Barons* was published in March 1934, Matthew Josephson was not in the United States to enjoy its success. Several months before, he had again boarded ship for Europe. This time, however, he was headed not for France but for Soviet Russia. The years of the Great Depression were also the years of Stalin's first Five-Year Plan. As faith in capitalism sank among Western intellectuals, the contrasting success of Russian state collectivism convinced many of the superiority of the Soviet system. "The contrast," wrote Arthur Koestler, "between the downward trend of capitalism and the simultaneous steep rise of planned Soviet economy was so striking and obvious that it led to the equally obvious conclusion: They are the future—we, the past." While the West struggled through the Great Depression, Russia flaunted her budget surpluses, full employment, scientific agriculture, roaring factories, and general atmosphere of hope and security. It is not surprising, therefore, that Russia in the early thirties was a mecca for Western intellectuals.

They flocked to visit the country that seemed to have solved the fundamental problems plaguing capitalism.[16]

Josephson likewise found the Russian experiment alluring. To him, the Soviet Union "seemed like the hope of the world—the only large nation run by men of reason." As a self-proclaimed twentieth-century philosophe, he admired the spirit of a coherently planned society. Arriving in Russia in December 1933 he was given a guided tour of the country, visiting steel mills and shoe factories, attending banquets and official ceremonies, and conversing at length with several Russian artists and writers. His first impression of the Russians was that "they are extremely sympathetic people, as fine as I have seen anywhere in the world, and very fine looking too. In fact they have a special charm of their own." A week later he wrote home to Hannah that when one remembered what Russia had been under the czars and how the Bolsheviks had lifted the country from "a wasteland to the status of a great power and a civilized socialist state, surviving among great armies, I understand the cry eternal for machinery, for industrial power, and the minimization of the 'finer things in life.'" The Russian writers were informed, intelligent, and gracious hosts. "I like their life and their spirit," he observed in a letter to his editor, Charles Pearce. "They are completely sold by the way on the present political program. The intellectual class in any case is remarkably well off in Russia. It has work up to the neck, but gets everything it wants." Although he found everyday life in Russia difficult, with few modern luxuries or conveniences, Josephson urged: "Before people pass judgment on Comrade Stalin they ought to come here and see his Works, his Opus Major, in many volumes with their own eyes. It is very impressive; and few other statesmen in all history have so much to show."[17]

In his impetuous enthusiasm for Russian collectivism, Josephson tended to overlook or minimize Stalin's ruthless methods and instead focus on the Soviet ruler's alleged devotion to the long-range welfare of the commonweal. Years later, with the benefit of hindsight and historical perspective, he admitted that his admiration for the position of Soviet writers was probably overenthusiastic: "Perhaps (considering how ephemeral their security proved to be) I spoke with excessive optimism of the superior economic status and prosperity of Soviet authors." As David Caute has demonstrated, fellow travelers like Josephson made the mistake of visualizing Stalin as a "dispassionate surgeon wielding the social scalpel with scientific detachment." Collectivization and rapid industrialization in Russia were achieved only through the suppression of large segments of the population by the secret police. Civil liberties were violated with abandon. Not only kulaks but entire peasant communities were deported; livestock and property were seized. Those who resisted were arrested, tortured, exiled, or executed. Josephson in 1934 seemed oblivious to such realities.[18]

After leaving Russia in March, Matthew joined Hannah in Paris. There, in the early spring of 1934, he first learned of the success of *The Robber Barons*. He began receiving reviews of the book that, he said at the time, "amuse me a great deal, to tell the truth." Two reviews, written by Louis Hacker and Lewis Corey, both of whom had recently broken with the Communists and were inclined toward Trotskyism, sharply criticized the theoretical economic framework of the book. Josephson found these attacks by fellow "comrades" confusing: "One would think they would help me to undermine the bourgeoisie, rather than parade their knowledge gained from a too hasty reading of my one work on this interesting subject." Combative as always, he admitted that he probably should have stayed in New York while his book was coming out, so that he would be "right there in the ring." In general, however, he had little to worry about; almost all the reviews were favorable and the public was reading *The Robber Barons* in large numbers.[19]

In April 1934, after vacationing in France and Spain, the Josephsons returned to the United States, and Matthew began writing free-lance articles and book reviews. In the *New Republic* that summer he published an account of the literary life in Russia. At that time there was considerable discussion among the American literary Left about the cultural situation under the Soviet regime. The disenchanted Max Eastman, now intensely anti-Stalinist, had recently authored a series of articles in *Modern Monthly* in which he tried to expose Stalin's control of thought and letters in Russia. In the spring of 1934 the articles were published as the book *Artists in Uniform*. Eastman referred to Soviet writers as soldiers serving the revolutionary cause with blind obedience and thereby sacrificing their artistic standards. What was happening to culture under Stalin, he wrote, represented "the crude humiliation of arts and letters, the obsequious and almost obscene lowering of the standards of the creative mind."[20]

In his own account of literary life in Russia Josephson disagreed sharply with the dismal picture presented by Eastman and others. The writers, painters, and dramatists whom he saw were not "artists in uniform." They "seemed neither to suffer nor to have regrets." They discussed their creative work with "so much genuine enthusiasm and earnestness that the notion of their being coerced seemed more and more mythical." Josephson had temporarily put his critical faculties in mothballs. He had seen in Russia what he and his Russian hosts had wanted him to see. Since he had encountered no unhappy Russian artists, his logic went, there must not be any. In his conversations with Russian writers and painters he "felt the universal enthusiasm for the Russian adventure."[21]

To intellectuals in Russia, Josephson maintained in his article, the social revolution had assumed a romantic and heroic character. They were proud of their great public works achievements, just as Americans had been proud of their amazing engineering feats after the Civil War. "But in our case," he argued, "the great public works were directed by plunderers for their own private profit." Mechanization under the Soviets, unlike the American experience, "is not a blind, uncontrolled thing; it has a creative, purposive character and is imbued with a moral atmosphere totally different from and far superior to that known in the West." Josephson praised the superior moral atmosphere of the Soviet system without commenting on the methods employed by Stalin in implementing the Five-Year plans. He had fallen for the official Soviet image hook, line, and sinker, and his enthusiasm was infectious. From Provincetown Edmund Wilson wrote to a friend in 1934, "Matty Josephson has been up here for a few days, rendered surprisingly agreeable and entertaining by his Guggenheim trip—he regaled us with such lively news of Russia, France and Spain that it made me decide to apply for a Guggenheim myself next year."[22]

After returning from abroad, Josephson grew increasingly disenchanted with Roosevelt's New Deal. In the summer of 1934 he spent several weeks in Washington writing a lengthy profile of Hugh Johnson, director of the National Recovery Administration. His contact with such government officials convinced him that the "Roosevelt regime in its second year was an affair of cross-purposes, ill-humored discord and glaring contradictions." He judged Roosevelt's attempt to conciliate and unify the conflicting class interests, rather than restructure them, as a technique typical of fascist statesmanship. "Under the Roosevelt revolution," he wrote, "the rich grew richer and the poor grew poorer, as ever." In his journal Josephson castigated the president as the "great compromiser, the left hand taking away what the right hand gives." Roosevelt was vainly trying to save capitalism and restore the status quo rather than revolutionize the economic order. "The whole venture groans under the weight of its contradictions and errors."[23]

As Josephson's opinion of Roosevelt and the New Deal deteriorated, he continued to call for a more radical solution to the depression. He also participated in several demonstrations. In the summer of 1934, for instance, he joined with Burke, Cowley, Sue Jenkins Brown, and Isidor Schneider in a protest against the Macaulay Company, his former publisher. The firm's editorial and clerical staff had called a strike after a bookkeeper had been fired for supposedly being a union organizer. Urgent calls from New York went out to writers to join in the demonstration. Josephson rushed to Manhattan where, placard in hand, he joined the picket line in front of the Macaulay offices. He later remembered:

> It was a sunlit day of spring; and for us, who habitually worked alone, it was a joyful occasion to come together outdoors and give expression to our public spirit and our fellow feeling for the Macaulay clerks. The laughter, slogan-shouting, and singing made it one of the merriest parties I had ever attended.

Josephson then admitted that his devotion to the oppressed workers at Macaulay was less than complete: "I had only forty minutes to donate to the class struggle that day, since I had a prior appointment the same afternoon and had to catch a train home after that. I therefore surrendered my placard to a fellow agitator and hailed a taxi which took me uptown." Only minutes after Josephson left, the police arrived and arrested the writers for illegal picketing. A few hours later, as he perused the *New York World Telegram* on the train heading back to Sherman, he was shocked to read an account of the arrest of his fellow picketers: "I was just then sitting in the train's club car enjoying a very bourgeois cocktail—and I laughed out loud." According to the news story, one Matthew Josephson was among the writers arrested.[24]

This incident provides a characteristic example of the ironic nature of Josephson's radical politics. An ardent supporter of the Communist party platform, he at the same time lived unabashedly the life of a bourgeois intellectual. While he was roundly condemning the capitalist system as unjust, calling for the socialization of the means of production, joining in strikes and protests, and writing influential histories critical of American businessmen and politicians, Josephson was himself a best-selling author, world traveler, country squire, and proficient stock speculator. This paradoxical existence typified many of the fellow travelers of the 1930s. Indeed, in a broader sense, it has typified the position of the American liberal throughout the twentieth century. Writers on the Left have persistently attacked class distinctions, yet they have also insisted upon maintaining their own distinctions as individual artists and cultural spokesmen. The sympathies of fellow travelers like Josephson, Cowley, and Wilson were outwardly with the proletariat, yet their backgrounds, professions, and tastes were nothing if not bourgeois. They were sincere Marxists but also sincere professional artists, committed to literature as well as to collectivism. At times such dual loyalties were compatible; more frequently they were not.[25]

Josephson was painfully aware of the inconsistencies in his artistic and personal life and his politics. In his journal during 1934–35 he candidly reflected on his role as fellow traveler. On October 1, 1934, he noted that the honest writer could not avoid confronting the moral and political issues of his time. "How can I continue to write books merely for a living," he asked, "when the form of society in which I live is repugnant?" What his part should be in the social process, however, remained a difficult question. He observed that many of his literary friends "have confessed themselves and entered the 'church' of communism." Josephson could not follow the same path: "I who believe in the communist or Marxian solution, I who deeply admire and believe in the leadership of the Russian revolution, am nevertheless beset with doubts concerning the immediate efficacy of yielding myself to the Comrades in my own country."[26]

This was a comment typical of many American fellow travelers. Although supportive of the party's goals, Josephson and others viewed the CPUSA as essentially a crude and ineffective organization. The American Communists seemed to lack the sincerity and congeniality of the Russian and Spanish revolutionaries he had met abroad. Moreover, he had found many of the American comrades to be full of hypocrisy and duplicity. He could not join the party because he was determined not to be hypocritical himself. "Had I a true faith," he confessed, "I should give up everything I own, stocks, bonds, property, to the cause of humanity; I should spurn the privilege of living in comparative bourgeois ease and embrace poverty, hardship, danger toward the great end." Yet he could not bring himself to do so because, looking at the American Communists, "I see almost none of them who by his example of self-denial or selflessness encourages me to such measures." On the contrary, they appeared to give precious little to "the cause." Furthermore, their actions "do not inspire confidence, do not bespeak generosity, candor, nobility, such as the heroic revolutionary movement implies."[27]

Josephson recognized that he was not by nature an ideologue; he did not even like speaking in public. "If I were fitted for politics," he maintained, "I might feel some hope of working out my own salvation in such activity. I for my part have a deep-rooted, instinctive aversion for the catch as catch can of political struggle." Even more important, he disclosed, was that at heart he harbored an intellectual's distaste for associating with the masses. "In a mass," he reflected, "I always feel an aversion for people, which I cannot overcome. I feel instinctively a great hostility." Josephson recognized the irony of intellectuals like himself who were concerned about the plight of the masses but who could not overcome their class bias. Thus he saw very little "hope for escape from all manners of contradiction, stupidity, injustice, for 'outsiders like myself.'" He agonizingly confessed that "I am not a pure altruist, this is the trouble, rather than want of courage." He had his own life to lead, his own family to feed, and his own books to write. He could not completely abandon such freedom or responsibilities for the sake of communism or any other political ideology. By the mid-thirties he was beginning to recognize that the dual role of writer and activist he had mapped out for himself was a difficult one at best.[28]

Josephson anguished over the contradictions he saw in himself and his public position, as indicated by the number of times he reflected on the subject in his journal during this period. At heart, he finally conceded, he was a skeptic about American Communism. In his public statements, however, he suppressed doubts and distinctions. His misgivings about the American Communists were confined to his journal. He felt that he could not admit his skepticism openly, that he must "refrain from criticizing my Red comrades, or opposing their narrower views for diverse reasons: 1) to avoid being accused of 'unconscious capitalism,' defeatism or even fascism; 2) to avoid adding to the weight of their difficulties, they having more at stake, more woes, than I in my still comparatively detached position, somewhat remote from or 'above the battle.'"[29]

Despite his desire to stay out of the thicket of ideological debate, Josephson became embroiled in the controversey over proletarian literature that emerged among left-wing writers in the mid–1930s. Under the leadership of Granville Hicks and Michael Gold, the Communists demanded that artists completely subordinate their professional work to the needs of the party and the proletariat. They advocated a literature devoted to "one class, the proletariat, and to one task, the destruction of capitalism." According to Hicks there was no longer any need for "pure" literature, no longer any point in experimenting in new forms and techniques, no longer any reason for an artist to try to convey a nonpolitical personal feeling or experience. The writer succeeded, he believed, not to the extent that he mastered modern technique but to the degree that he assimilated the life of the proletariat.[30]

In January 1935 the *New Masses* issued a "Call for an American Writers' Conference," a mass meeting intended to mobilize liberal intellectuals against the growing threat of fascism. The Comintern had recently begun to modify its policies. Instead of emphasizing a strict orthodoxy and attacking middle-class intellectuals, it now put forth a program of openness and toleration. All liberals were now welcomed into a "Popular Front" against fascism. One of the most important questions to be discussed at the gathering was the role of literature in America in promoting such a revolution.[31]

Josephson looked forward to the meeting because he wanted to speak out against the advocates of proletarian literature. As he told Burke, "There has been so much idiotic confusion about 'Marxian literary criticism' that it is high time to clear the air." In an article in the *New Masses* Matthew proposed that at the upcoming conference the assembled writers try to establish the basis for a united literary front that would "embrace people of various persuasions." Many other fellow travelers shared Josephson's distaste for Marxian criticism and proletarian literature. John Dos Passos wrote in February that he would have liked to attend the upcoming congress in New York but could not because of prior commitments. Nevertheless, he wanted to express his support of Josephson's position against the orthodox proponents of social realism:

> I'm entirely with you about the Marxian critics—in some mysterious way American communist agitation seems to have dropped the industrial workers and farmworkers and become part of the revolt of the white collar class. It's a damn funny phenomenon and I can't pretend to understand yet—this is a time when you wish you really knew something about history.

Dos Passos referred to the Marxists in Union Square as having a "sort of methodist-rabbinical sectarianism that rapidly becomes a racket." He concluded that "independent thinking is more valuable in the long run than all this copying out of manifestoes already discarded in Moscow. God damn it, a man has no right to save his soul at public expense. If he wants to save his soul then let him go to church where he belongs."[32]

More than two hundred delegates attended the first American Writers' Congress held in New York at the Mecca Temple in late April 1935. Josephson delivered a paper in which he lashed out at those Marxist literary critics "of the most dogmatic stripe" who acted as "detectives, pros-

ecuting attorneys and judges." He had no patience with those who criticized such authors as Dos Passos, Erskine Caldwell, Edward Dahlberg,
and others for not being "dialectically sound" or for failing to sympathize
explicitly enough with the proletariat. The "honest writer," he maintained, "a writer who is not a tory or a capitalist at heart, can no longer
approach his material without being directly, profoundly influenced by
revolutionary necessities and hopes, in short by the Marxian conception
of society and its inherent conflicts." It appeared inconceivable to him
that a writer should not take the side of the masses in the present crisis.
Yet, he warned, the writer must not submit to the doctrinaire guidelines
of those advocating a proletarian literature. American writers who felt a
sense of social duty, he concluded, "should not feel it necessary to adopt
the more transient theories or restrictions of Russia's *littérateurs.*" [33]

In addition to discussing the weaknesses of proletarian literature,
Josephson also commented on life in the Soviet Union. He reported that
the 100,000 men and women who dug the impressive Bielnostroy Canal
were "former thieves, vagabonds, rebellious kulaks, saboteurs." Despite
the loss of hundreds of lives, these workers labored through the summer
and winter to produce an amazing physical achievement. In the process,
he noted with admiration, "Great numbers of the former rebels and
thieves were converted, honored, decorated, restored to citizenship,"
primarily because "they had been infected by their teachers with the
conquering spirit of the whole socialist army." Josephson's romanticized
account of this event glossed over the fact that these workers were also
prisoners. He also failed to mention that the "teachers" responsible for
the remarkable conversion of the workers were none other than the Soviet secret police, the GPU. Whether such omissions were intentional or
merely resulted from his ignorance of the true situation is difficult to determine. One would like to think that Josephson simply did not realize
the true nature of the forced labor system. Whatever the case, his roseate
view of the construction of the canal reveals again the myopic manner in
which he and others observed the Soviet Union. [34]

Josephson's performance at the Congress illustrated the divided nature
of his political commitment. On cultural issues he was willing to oppose
openly the party line; on most political issues he remained silent, admitting his doubts only in private. In the fall of 1935, for example, he wrote
a lengthy letter to Burke in which he discussed his divided feelings:

> Properly seen, communism *is* but a step further—not a new begin-
> ning—but a rigorously logical continuation of social and thought

processes of the 18th and 19th centuries. . . . But again and again I would return to the proposition: Does the becoming condition, above-named, justify devotion (perhaps immolation) of the intelligence to a strict partisanship? Or, does the intelligence have rights, prerogatives, needs, of its own, which at all costs must be retained in the long run and without which the capacity for backward and forward viewing, highest desideratum of Marxism itself, would be weakened and ruined?

They must retain their individuality and freedom of criticism, he stressed, without endangering the success of the Communist issue. "We may work with the Marxist 'school,' and we must look beyond it. Our usefulness would always reside in our ability to look further ahead. If ever it becomes dishonorable to doubt, to reflect for ourselves, or use disinterested judgment, then it will be too late for everything."[35]

Josephson's struggle to develop a satisfactory attitude toward the Communist party in particular and Marxism in general led him again and again during the thirties to reflect frankly upon his personal situation. His ruminations in his journal provide a fascinating glimpse of a writer trying to come to grips with his own nature, confronting himself in order to develop a sense of inner balance and literary direction. Much of Josephson's self-questioning in the 1930s resulted from his growing feeling of isolation from the New York intellectual community. It was especially disconcerting to see his close friendships of the 1920s dissipate during the Great Depression. He, Cowley, and Burke had begun to go their separate ways, both artistically and politically. Although all three had "gone left," they had done so at different speeds along different paths. Cowley was forever busy with the book department of the *New Republic*. Unlike Josephson he was, as he wrote later, "interested in day-to-day tactics and in problems of political behavior." Cowley enjoyed the intense partisan wrangling that went along with fellow-traveling; he relished his significant role in the "movement." As the decade wore on, however, Josephson began to feel that his friend was getting too immersed in politics, sacrificing art to ideology. In late 1935 he gave Cowley some pointed advice:

I feel like admonishing you sometimes, by the right of having been an old crony: I have liked very much the review-pieces you have been doing, better than those of any one else I know who is doing such work as a regular job. . . . But I would like to see you, putting it bluntly, do some criticism, enfin. For this, hard as it seems, you will have to read, or keep up reading, books other than those currently published. . . . In this way one would be less an instrument of immediate contingency and the contingent would become the instrument of a purpose. I think your real talents for criticism, which are probably not being sufficiently exploited now, would flourish under the condition I have in mind.

A decade later Malcolm would take such advice to heart. At present, however, he was too committed to the politics of the literary Left to heed Matty's suggestion.[36]

Kenneth Burke was also attracted to Marxism and communism, but in a much more esoteric sense than either Cowley or Josephson. He was always the independent theorist of language and literary form, persistently withholding his complete allegiance from all political organizations. "Marxism does," he wrote Josephson in 1935, "provide some necessary admonitions as to our faulty institutions—but as I understand it, it is exactly 180 degrees short of being a completely rounded philosophy of human motivation." He admitted that socialism was a necessary first step toward solving the material problems facing the West, but it did nothing to alleviate the spiritual crisis. For his own part he felt more comfortable in Andover, chopping wood and studying literature. When Josephson criticized him for his unwillingness to use his pen for "the cause," Burke replied: "As for writing on current topics, I don't know by what route you came to think that I abhorred the thought of so sullying my lily-whites. How I should love to have a column, in which I could comment each day, hot on the heels of news. But I lack influence. I don't know anybody to ask. That's all. No, that's not quite all. I get tied in knots, too. I still don't know wholly why."[37]

As a result of such differences, Josephson, Cowley, and Burke saw each other less and less. "As I grow older," Matthew reflected in his journal, "I find it more difficult to confide in or converse with my contemporaries. Nor can I in discussing my doubts or discoveries with them advance the more easily toward certainties." The atmosphere of creative exchange and frivolity that had characterized Josephson's relationships of the twenties was displaced by ideological debate and personal rancor. He no longer felt the same esprit de corps, nor did he experience the constructive give and take of the previous decade. "Instead," he confessed, "one is alone and must proceed alone. Hence one falls into moods of immitigable self-questioning and doubting."[38]

A practical problem contributing to Josephson's malaise was his deteriorating hearing. His incipient deafness became a "blight" that adversely affected his personal relationships and his social confidence. In November 1935 he admitted the effects of the physical handicap:

> Narcissus-like, I should like to examine in detail the nature of my melancholy. . . . Like other deaf persons I am hypersensitive with respect to all the inadequacies produced by my disability: I resent that people are not audible, and am tormented when they are compelled to shout with absurd effect. Then I have a reaction and fear that they will find the effort too arduous and will cease attempts to communicate with me. My mischance has wrought confusion in my hopes.

Josephson had always tended to be a great talker and a bad listener, but now his hearing problem compounded his social mannerisms. He became a compulsive talker, unconsciously terrified that no one was listening. In social settings he found himself shouting, trying to dominate the discussions in order to compensate for his inability to hear others. He would contradict, shock, or rail at his listeners. Josephson's close friends increasingly found him quarrelsome. Malcolm Cowley wrote him a letter in March 1936 in which he addressed their faltering relationship. He wanted to discuss "the difficulties of communication aggravated during these last years by your deafness and my dumbness—but also partly caused by our own inability to think at the same time along the same channels (though we often think at different times along the same channels)." He suggested that they get together and "talk about some of my present ideas and make a plea for better understanding and cooperation between us." But the planned discussion never took place, and the split between the two friends widened.[39]

One of the major factors contributing to the widening gulf between Josephson and his old friends Cowley and Burke was their divergent literary activities. Matthew, far more than either Malcolm or Kenneth, embraced commercial journalism, writing at times purely for profit. Malcolm and Kenneth came to feel that by doing so he was compromising both his craft and his ability. Josephson privately recognized that there was at least some truth to the charge. Although he was quite successful in his role as free-lance journalist, Matty was persistently troubled by a sense of guilt about doing such "hackwork." In his journal he disclosed "my own intellectual uncertainty or want of conviction with reference to the partly 'commercial' task at hand." The problem of making money, of earning a living as a professional writer in a capitalist society without at the same time compromising one's artistic or personal principles, has frequently been a nagging concern of American writers. Then and later Josephson agonized over writing for such "slick" publications as the *New Yorker* and the *Saturday Evening Post*. Yet how else could he earn enough to maintain his family's comfortable life-style and allow himself the freedom to write something of his own choosing? In January 1935 he became so frustrated that he called a temporary halt to his commercial writing: "Now I must bring my attempts at money-winning magazine articles to an end. . . . I am filled with revulsion and that is that." He needed to return to history and social commentary.[40]

During the mid-1930s Josephson was also plagued by several physical setbacks. He developed an asthmatic condition that would worsen as he grew older, eventually forcing him to take lengthy sojourns to more temperate regions. In addition his chronic hearing problem became acute in 1935, when he again contracted mastoiditis. His doctors finally decided that major surgery was necessary, surgery that carried only an even chance of survival. With such a prospect facing him, Matthew wrote a revealing letter to Hannah in July 1935, just before he entered the hospital. The letter was in the form of a last will and testament, instructing Hannah about the condition of the family finances and about legal counsel. After covering such mundane matters, Josephson adopted a much more personal tone in advising his wife of fifteen years. If he died, he wrote, she should marry again. Matty warned, however, that she should choose carefully: "I must confess that I have long had the greatest contempt for the weakness and essential dishonesty of most members of my species. I would warn you to take thought and judge well for a second choice."[41]

Matty then offered an intimate assessment of their marriage, noting that Hannah had made "a wonderful wife," putting up with him for so long with such grace:

> I cared for you in the manner of a deep, habitual friendship rather than of a passing attachment. And though I have been moderately frail and have at times been attracted by other women, in a gallant or sensual way, being human, I think I have never met one whom all in all I rated up to your qualities. I have said "friendship" because nobody really knows what "love" is. Your friendship then was rare, noble, unstinted, profound. Insofar as one could be helped by a woman to be happy I was tremendously and consistently helped.

Any sense of hindrance I may have suggested at moments was only transient. I thank you and salute you. I think you should have confidence and pride in yourself.

Josephson was not through settling his accounts; his confessional continued. He admitted that in the past ten years he had "known intimately" seven or eight other women. Although "certain of them appealed to me remarkably," he observed, "I may say that not one reconciled me to the idea of losing you or being separated from you." It was a remarkably candid testimony. Whether or not Hannah ever saw it remains a mystery. Matthew's surgery was successful, and the need for such a document disappeared.[42]

Despite this surgery, Josephson continued to be bothered by ailments in the mid-thirties. In 1936, after suffering a respiratory illness that resulted in pneumonia, he left for Key West on the advice of his doctor. His intention was to stay a week or so until he had recovered. Once there, however, he fell in love with the balmy climate and bohemian atmosphere of the Keys, and he decided to stay and work. After renting a seven-room stone house situated among palm trees, poinsettias, and hibiscus, he then sent word for his family to join him. As he wrote Hannah, Key West was "full of variety, character, charm, busy seaport life, unpretentious, cheap to live in, marvelous climate, sea and beach. . . . I like it greatly. I am crazy about it in fact, and feel better every day." A few days later he repeated his request that she and the children join him: "I find it awfully hard to dig up men who talk as well or understand as much or are as well informed as you. I too am spoiled for others. . . . How can I enjoy all this beauty without the whole three of you to share it?" A week later Josephson described to Charles Pearce his life in Key West:

> After staying with a friend here, Canby Chambers, an old soak of a pulp writer, I established myself very comfortably in a large house sitting in a sort of jungle a few minutes' walk from the beach. Sobered up and received my family on Xmas Eve. We reconstitute our forces on this line, in full sunlight, with a cabana, a battered old sailing skiff for the boys, and as much New York social life (Winter colony) as we might need. Colonies have their uses, you know, to mitigate the effects of a circumambient barbarism. But I was especially surprised to find that the Florida species of barbarism which I dreaded much was not present in this island seaport. . . . Absolutely nothing fake here. I like it, and I am well.

The only drawback to the place, Josephson observed, was that it was peopled with "lousy writers, of more or less wounded physique, hard-boiled lotus eaters. I miss the keen, strong, healthy people of the old North among whom I really belong. (If I see one more novel attacking New York intellectuals I shall go haywire; why not 'New York' intellectuals?)" [43]

Late in 1936 Josephson met Ernest Hemingway, and the two writers quickly established a close rapport. In a letter to Hannah, Matthew described Ernest and his wife. Pauline, he remarked, "is a peach, both good and intelligent. Ernest Hemingway got back from Cuba, a mellow and lovable giant nowadays, with an inspirational tone in his talk much like Bob Cantwell." Hemingway was then completing his first novel aimed at raising social consciousness, *To Have and Have Not*, and he asked Matty to read the manuscript. "With some embarrassment," Josephson remembered, "I expressed my reservations about the second half of the novel, but spoke with enthusiasm about the opening scenes at Havana and the descriptions of the sea journeys. Hemingway received these observations with good grace, though I sensed he was unhappy about them." During the first few months of 1937 they met two or three times a week to go fishing, swimming, or to play badminton. On Saturday nights they would adjourn to Sloppy Joe's cafe, which offered a rumba band and all-night dancing. [44]

While much of their conversation concerned mutual friends like Harold Loeb and Evan Shipman, Josephson did his best to encourage Hemingway's interest in the domestic political situation. But he had little success. As he told Burke, he had to "go slow in bringing Hemingway around. They [American Communists] have certainly gored and maddened him." Josephson discovered that Hemingway was even more opposed to ideological squabbling with other writers than he himself was. This shared aversion may have been a cementing link between the two writers. Josephson informed Burke that he liked Hemingway "more than I ever expected to. He has certainly shown integrity about his craft, and you feel an overweening interest in that when you talk with him." He saw no need to alienate Hemingway by forcing him to discuss literary politics. Whenever the subject came up, Ernest expressed only contempt for Marxist writers, at one point mocking Dos Passos as a man whose heart was bleeding for the proletariat but who always traveled in Pullman sleepers of the Orient Express and stopped at first-class hotels. The only contemporary political subject that Hemingway responded to with real interest, Josephson learned, was the Spanish Civil War. [45]

The civil war in Spain represented an intellectual and emotional climax of the 1930s. It was a major test of Western will against fascism. For many American literary intellectuals, including Josephson and Hemingway, the cause of Republican Spain symbolized the "brightness of the Enlightenment's vision, or, at least, a beacon of hope in a continent darkened by increasingly ominous clouds." For antifascists around the world, the events in Spain provided a crucial chance to demonstrate Western will. The Republicans represented the forces of light, of liberty, reason, and progress; the Nationalists represented the forces of darkness, of anti-intellectualism, clerical superstition, and reactionary militarism.[46]

Josephson had developed a keen interest in Spain ever since he visited there in 1934. When the civil war erupted in 1936, he was intensely moved by the struggle. "The fight for the liberation of the Spanish people," he wrote in his journal, "is to me the last contest in decades (probably) under the old banner of human rights." And tragically, it appeared, the Western nations were unwilling to accept the challenge. "It is our last chance to cry out," he warned prophetically. In August 1936 Josephson proclaimed in the *New Masses* that the Spanish people "are giving us magnificent lessons, not only in heroism, but in the 'making' of history. . . . We must now protest everywhere against the crudely conceived intervention by fascist Germany and Italy in Spain."[47]

Hemingway developed such a consuming interest in Spain that he decided in February 1937 to leave Key West and go there himself. His departure took some of the color and attraction of the Keys with him, at least as far as Josephson was concerned. He remarked to a friend, "Now that Hemingway is gone, I shall let the sailfish alone." More and more, however, political developments intruded upon Josephson's idyllic retreat. The continuing sensational show trials and purges in Russia dominated the headlines of the leftist press, and a factious dispute erupted between Stalinists and Trotskyites. Josephson told Charles Pearce that he never thought "the differences over Soviet policy between a Stalin and a Trotsky should concern us in any immediate way in the United States." He sharply criticized those who engaged in what he considered to be a virulent, self-defeating debate. Early in 1937, speaking of the Stalin-Trotsky controversy, he wrote that he was "practically poxed on both houses." A few weeks later he made a similar comment: "I don't like Trotskyism; but I'm not carrying any water, either, for Mr. Stalin." Although he did not like to take sides in the Stalinist-Trotskyite dispute, however, he generally tended to identify with the Stalinist point of view, believing that the Soviet Union, despite its problems, would one day provide a beacon for all mankind to follow.[48]

After returning to New York in the spring of 1937 Josephson discovered the literary Left increasingly divided over events in Russia and Spain. For many of the fellow travelers, enthusiasm for Soviet Russia soon turned into disillusionment and disgust as more and more evidence appeared of Stalin's terrorism and duplicity. A spate of "jeremiad" books appeared in 1937 written by various European and American intellectuals who now viewed Russian communism as the "God that failed." In a lengthy review of four such books, written by Eugene Lyons, Max Eastman, André Gide, and Victor Serge, Josephson expressed his personal attitude toward the situation in Russia. Writing in the *New Republic* he characterized the Soviet Union as a society of violent contrasts. Tremendous social gains were achieved, but only at great cost to civil liberties and human rights. The capitalist exploitation of the masses was replaced by a massive, impersonal bureaucracy. Josephson commented that the Moscow show trials "shock the faith of Western democrats more than anything else, more even than gruesome tales of GPU dungeons or mass expropriations." The trials symbolized Stalin's "fierce intolerance" of dissent and individual rights.[49]

Thus it appeared that Josephson was indeed concerned about Soviet methods. Yet he did not summarily turn his back on Russia, as he accused the four authors of doing. He criticized American intellectuals for assuming that the social revolution in Russia could be achieved without some sacrifice of human liberties. "Moving Day," he blithely insisted, "is never peaceful or pleasant." He urged that instead of abandoning Russia, leftist intellectuals should engage in constructive criticism. As he contended, "to voice one's wish of mitigation of the harsh Soviet system of justice is one thing; to despair altogether of Russia, as some of our mercurial friends are doing, is another point which does not follow." In 1937 Josephson was worried more about the danger of fascism than the evils of Stalinism, and he justified his continued support of Soviet Russia on the basis of *Realpolitik*. In foreign affairs, unlike domestic life, the Russians seemed above reproach. After all, they had supported the League of Nations, they had called for sanctions against the fascist aggressors, they had repeatedly urged collective security among the Western nations. Josephson could not abandon Russia because he considered Soviet support of Republican Spain vital. He concluded his review essay by stressing that the "sane view would be to hold Russia our ally, while reserving our freedom of criticism."[50]

Josephson's essay understandably provoked a number of responses from the readers of the *New Republic*. Upton Sinclair expressed strong approval of his position: "I yield to the temptation to tell you how much I appreciate your review of the books on Russia. It seems to me you have struck the balance exactly right." Others did not share Sinclair's enthusiasm. In a letter to the editor Eugene Lyons called Josephson's position a "shocking example of moral bankruptcy." Matthew responded with his own letter to the editor:

> Nowhere have I condoned or apologized for the violence of Russia's system of justice. I stated in so many words that the situation admitted of no apologetics. . . . the authority of modern "civilized" states rests, in the last analysis, upon force of some kind. . . . If American hands were lily-white I might be quicker to offer some confident prescription to the Soviets for abolishing their police system and disarming their Red Army. But with Russian Socialists looking into the teeth of the two huge military machines on either side of them, just now, I feel humbler about judging who is guilty and what to do than Mr. Lyons.

While some might agree with Josephson that foreign policy considerations justified continued support of the Soviet Union, it is nevertheless evident that he had succumbed to an apologetic relativism. During the early thirties he had praised the Soviet system on moral grounds. Now he defended it on the basis of practical politics. His shifting position, like that of Malcolm Cowley, revealed what Daniel Aaron has described as the dilemma "of a man of good will straining to preserve the illusion and parading his uncertainties and unfirm convictions."[51]

Josephson spent much of his time between 1935 and 1938 writing *The Politicos*, his second historical work. It was intended to be a companion volume to *The Robber Barons*, detailing the activities of the national political system during the Gilded Age. As the writing of *The Politicos* progressed, Matthew grew increasingly confident about the book's impact. He remarked to Charles Pearce in the summer of 1936: "I shall have to leave the country as soon as this thing appears. If everything works out there should be one long howl of rage at me from all sides—or I shall be a very discomfited young historian." Josephson believed that he was writing a book that would provide a significant insight into both the past and present operations of the national party system. As he told Harcourt in 1938:

> Among other things it seems "timely" or "news" because our country, our business, is falling more and more into the hands of "politicos" after being run, more or less by Big Business. Thus it refers not only to the recent past, with its lines running solidly into the present, but to the future. As to its radicalism, I have been, I maintain, truthful, undogmatic, rather than vociferous.

Josephson concluded that the book "is by my own sense, the best thing I have ever done." He was also prepared for any adverse reaction to *The Politicos*. In his journal of 28 June 1938, he admitted, "I expect to be assailed as 'unjust'—'biased'—'distorted'—poisonous—unfit to be read save by vigorous minds." [52]

Josephson believed that by revealing the methods and objectives of the earlier "politicos," he could help explain the apparent lack of purpose and imagination in contemporary national politics. As in the case of *The Robber Barons*, he wrote *The Politicos* as much to condemn the present as to explain the past. Soon after the book was published he confessed to a friend:

> My big object was essentially, by giving the "inside story" of special interests and political groups during a whole long generation, to throw as strong light as possible upon the fierce political struggles of the present hour. In other words, *The Politicos* was intended to give the story behind the great struggles of today.

Through writing *The Politicos*, he sought to attack the deficiencies of Roosevelt's New Deal political philosophy. Political parties in the Gilded Age, he once wrote, "embodied no consistent political ideas, but only the functioning of an army of opportunists in the local ward as on the national level." This was essentially the same criticism he applied to the New Dealers. Roosevelt's program, he insisted, had the "fatal flaw of abjuring belief in any distinct body of social doctrines and of improvising curative measures without an over-all plan." [53]

Published early in 1938, *The Politicos* is a splendid, compendious dramatization of Gilded Age politics. The lengthy book is rich in details and alive with personalities; it opens the doors to the smoke-filled rooms and private homes where major political decisions were made and party conventions were planned and directed. Josephson paints with a firm brush the pitiful picture of Grant, incarnation of administrative ignorance and mundane outlook:

> We see the hero and the fool; the kind father, the loyal friend, the hapless victim of flatterers and knaves; we see him ever obstinate and ever indecisive; dignified and slothful; now indolent, now roused to fury; but always no more than half intelligent; ever silent from agonizing uncertainty, and no wiser than the mythical man in the street. Essentially he was comic; not one of Plutarch's soldier-citizens, but rather a character out of nineteenth century satire, out of Trollope or Mark Twain.

Zachariah Chandler, one of the leading Stalwarts, appears as "a huge, stout, bibulous fellow, bediamonded with an imposing array of side-whiskers." Josephson also brings to life the stubborn honesty and individualism of Grover Cleveland, the soaring idealism of John Altgeld, the messianic evangelism of William Jennings Bryan, and the cruel efficiency of Mark Hanna.[54]

Yet unlike *The Robber Barons*, the emphasis in *The Politicos* is balanced between a treatment of personalities and an analysis of the inner workings of the party machinery and the political mentality of the participants. For the interpretive framework of the book Josephson again relied heavily on the writings of Marx and Beard, as well as on those of social scientists such as Veblen, Max Weber, Robert Michels, and Karl Mannheim. Josephson later admitted that Marx's "method of historical analysis, as an instrument, was of powerful aid to me in the study." Josephson particularly emphasized Marx's treatment of the conflict between ideology and interest in political affairs. After reading *The Eighteenth Brumaire of Louis Bonaparte*, he recorded in his research notebook that the "first thing we must perceive in the orations of politicians is that they do not mean what they say." Josephson thus discovered in his reading of Marx and Engels the ruling idea for *The Politicos*—he would study the contrast between ideology and interest, between political rhetoric designed to win votes and the underlying socioeconomic interests of the politicians themselves. "In a preceding work," he observed in the preface, "I wrote of men who spoke little and did much. In the present work . . . I write of men who, in effect, did as little as possible and spoke all too much."[55]

From this Marxist-Beardian concept of political ideology, Josephson derived two important assumptions that served as the unifying threads of

The Politicos. The first corollary was that to understand the inner workings of the political parties in the Gilded Age, one must first discover "the
differences between that which men say and that which they mean in
politics." His second assumption was that a political party possessed two
functions. Initially it must carry out its "assignment," catering to the interests of its "shareholders" who grease the party machinery with their votes
and money. "The statesman and the captain of industry," he posits,
"complement each other well: one talks, the other acts." Once this obligation has been met, however, the party must concern itself with self-
preservation and perpetuation. It must "institutionalize" itself. Thus the
interests of the politicos and of the robber barons were not always identical. While for the most part the actions of the politicians and the desires
of big business coincided, Josephson stresses that political survival always held sway over the economic alliance.[56]

Like Henry Adams and James Bryce before him, Josephson highlights
the corruption and blandness of Gilded Age politics, emphasizing that
the two major political parties failed to deal with the fundamental social
and economic issues of the day and instead spent most of their time dividing the spoils of office. That the two national parties during the Gilded
Age were so evenly balanced "was undoubtedly the result of their common nullity of program, their identity in objective and group relationships, and the degrading character of public leadership." The indifference of the politicians toward pressing social and economic issues
was contagious. Josephson observes, "The veritable indifference of the
public seems as marked as the excitement of the professional seems
feigned."[57]

In *The Politicos* Josephson presents a convincing case in support of his
critical view of Gilded Age politics. Yet his repeated application of the
Marxian-Beardian concept of political ideology serves to dilute the
book's effectiveness. He again allowed his susceptibility to such neat,
all-explaining theories, as well as his contemporary concerns, to cloud
his historical vision. His thesis that politicians act not out of ideals but
out of crass economic and political self-interest is effective and in many
cases correct; but it also tends to be reductionistic. He pushed his thesis
too hard. And in doing so he at times ignored the complexity of human
behavior, often exaggerated or distorted the influence of pecuniary and
partisan motives, and occasionally compromised the genuine ideals of
several political figures.

Josephson knew before the book was published that it contained a number of distortions and factual errors. He confided to Beard that "in spite of all my precautions there might be a good many historical inaccuracies in my book." Beard replied: "All works of history are inaccurate. Hegel, who wrote the most important book in our field, for all time, is one mass of historical inaccuracies!" Still, Josephson simply did not have the scholarly precision, objectivity, or patience of the professional historian. He was concerned primarily with bringing characters to life and with conveying the dramatic sweep of historical events. He sought to interpret basic human motives as he saw them and to organize his work around a unifying thesis or interpretive scheme. But in doing so he again allowed himself to be carried away by theoretical speculations, the weakness that Hart Crane had sensed almost twenty years earlier.[58]

Several reviewers resented Josephson's heavy-handed Marxist interpretation. The critic for the *New York Sun* admitted that interpretation plays an important part "in any broad political history, but Josephson thrusts it forward in an offensively dogmatic manner at the start, and mingles it inextricably with the narrative at every possible opportunity." Henry Steele Commager criticized Josephson's cynical attitude toward politics and politicians. In the *New York Herald Tribune* he wrote:

> At all times Mr. Josephson puts the worst possible construction upon the words or actions of the Politicos, and he is inclined to put the worst construction upon the words of those who have written about the period as well. He has a low opinion of human nature, knows that men respond only to "pecuniary interests," and is inclined to think that those who pretend otherwise are hypocrites.

Even more critical was Louis Hacker's assessment in the *Nation*. Hacker argued that *The Politicos* was "not nearly so good" as *The Robber Barons*. He implied in his review that Josephson was an adherent to the "current line of the Communist Party." After noting that the book's thesis was scarcely "original," Hacker concluded sarcastically that Josephson "has told this not very complicated story in a richly documented narrative of seven hundred pages." Hacker, however, was so preoccupied with an ad hominem attack on Josephson's supposed Stalinist connections that he actually missed the main themes of the book.[59]

During most of his career Josephson took such criticism in stride, possibly because of his own considerable experience as a reviewer. In the case of *The Politicos*, however, he reacted angrily. He considered Hacker's "red-baiting" review to be part of a smear campaign by the Trotskyite

faction of the literary Left. In a letter to Max Lerner at the *Nation*, Josephson maintained, "I don't hold my writings sacred in any sense, and think
I am fair game for polemics . . . , but if controversy is going to be carried
on at the rather degraded level which the *Nation* in this instance has
chosen then we had better review our accounts." He vigorously protested Hacker's insinuation that he was merely a party propagandist. "Of
course," he told Lerner, "everyone knows that I am a bloated capitalist
and land-owner; as for my knowledge of the C.P. 'line,' the *New Masses*
this same week officially reproves me for not sharing their view of the
Civil War and Reconstruction." Josephson was referring to a review in
the *New Masses* that criticized *The Politicos* for not emphasizing enough
a class interpretation of the Civil War and Reconstruction. In concluding
his letter to Lerner, Josephson remarked that as for the *Nation*, "I hereby
resign and kiss her good-bye; I also resign from New York's intellectuals'
pitiable parlor quarrels over Trotsky and Stalin." He felt that he had been
caught within an ideological crossfire that only served to distort his latest
book and to defame his literary character. He had never felt comfortable
among the orthodox literary radicals on the Left, and such incidents only
confirmed his unease.[60]

Despite the mixed initial reception of *The Politicos* Josephson retained
a staunch belief in the book's importance. He received support for this
conviction from Charles Beard. In April 1938 he recorded in his journal a
conversation with Beard about the book. "Talking to 'Uncle Charlie' at
New Milford," he wrote, "stimulated me as always. I had been despon-
dent at the stupid or stupefied ('shell-shocked') reaction to 'The Politicos.'" Beard told him that if critics like Hacker had "liked your book it
would have proved there was something wrong with it." He went on to
tell Matthew that he felt the style of *The Politicos* was decidedly "French"
in its clarity and irony. While he had known of most of the characters
"pretty well," he had never seen them "so naked." Beard assured Josephson that the new book was "a finer and better thing" than *The Robber
Barons*. Such praise from his mentor restored Josephson's confidence. He
told Charles Pearce that Beard "finally confided to me the other day that
The Politicos was the best thing I had ever done." A few months later, in
another letter to Pearce, Josephson reaffirmed that he "believed and do
believe in that book. I mean . . . it's the only thing of its kind in the field,
an important field, with so many dunderheads and 4th of July orators taking up the field, that it's not pretentious to say this."[61]

Josephson then offered his explanation of the book's disappointing
sales:

An author has poor facilities for finding out what his public's reactions were or even *who* they were. Now in this case most of the squirts who pass for book critics made it hard to reach out to the public; meanwhile the academic squirts, as I finally piece it together, must have been badly jarred or shaken up by the very appearance of the book. Why do I bring this up? Because whispers and rumors reach me all the time which indicate that the whole body of younger scholars even in the grand old universities is with me rather than agin. (Truly it revives one's faith in our youth.) Last month, through Vann Woodward, I heard of the upheavals among the younger men at Chapel Hill (probably our best university now) at the Nation review. This week I got a long letter from a Harvard man asking me to come up and lecture there on "The Politicos," on certain theories incorporated therein which appear to them of scientific value.

C. Vann Woodward had written Josephson in August 1938 to "express my genuine admiration and enthusiasm for your *Politicos*! I thought it masterly, and quite up to the *Robber Barons*. The feeling among my friends down here is that you were done a grave injustice by such men as Hacker and Henry Commager."[62]

Such comments buoyed up Josephson's faith in his latest book. He continued to stress to his publisher that the book was beginning to catch on, that reports from several colleges and universities indicated that the volume "was slowly taking root." In December he waxed philosophical about the fate of *The Politicos*:

I refuse to be disappointed. After all, in addition to the advance sales, about a thousand hardy readers have bought *The Politicos*, in the first six or seven months. Maybe it will continue steadily, if I continue to survive or grow. As to the lean earnings, I knew of that risk when I decided not to arrange myself to write for Hollywood or Collier's, just now, but to "write as I please." I gave nearly three years, part of the earnings of other books and movie rights to what I felt was my best work—and appreciate the fun of it. (You will learn how mad and "impractical" and obstinate we authors can be.)

Josephson's predictions were correct. It was indeed on the academic level that *The Politicos* eventually "caught on." Whatever the reason for the book's failure to attract widespread public attention, it did have a significant, lasting impact upon the historiography of American politics in the Gilded Age. Within a few years *The Politicos*, like *The Robber Barons*, was generally considered the standard work in its field. Despite numerous scholarly attacks on *The Politicos* since the 1950s, a recent survey of history textbooks emphasizes that Josephson's portrait of the period still dominates the general studies.[63]

11   THE FORKED ROAD TO WAR

As the decade of the thirties came to a close, the threat of war in Europe grew ever more real. Hitler and the fascists, sensing the disunity and irresolution infecting the Western democracies, became more bold in their aggressive actions. Americans could no longer view the European situation with detachment; the Atlantic Ocean seemed to narrow as Hitler's expansionist program progressed. What role the United States should play in the growing crisis increasingly occupied the attention of Matthew Josephson and other members of the literary Left between 1938 and 1941. On the surface the situation seemed clear. The United States should stand up against Hitler, Mussolini, and the forces of aggression in the world. But how this should be done was a more complex issue, one that served to divide and frustrate American intellectuals.

After the Munich settlement in the fall of 1938, several of Josephson's' friends, just back from Europe, reported that they doubted the will and ability of France and England to resist German advances. They expressed little hope for a rational approach in the face of the irrationalism and violence practiced by the fascists. Josephson castigated his friends for adopting such a pessimistic attitude. He emphasized that it was time for intellectuals to start a propaganda campaign to arouse the West from its lethargy and reveal the threat of Hitler's ambitions. In his journal he categorically denied the "counsels of despair. . . . The people who bear petitions, who march, who picket, who gather pennies for Spain—they help. Have steady nerves." Matty retained his sense of optimism and his faith in reason; he was convinced that Western democracy, with its industrial capacity and technological genius, would meet the challenge of totalitarianism. Hamilton Basso, a thorough pessimist, attacked Josephson for maintaining such an idealistic philosophy in the face of Hitler and Nazism. "The trouble with you," he stressed, "is that you believe in reason, in economic determinism, in the quantitative strength of the Western nations; whereas Hitler and Mussolini are 'irrational' and so are able to defy your laws of economics." The criticism was a telling one, but Matthew held firm to his convictions. Reason, he emphasized in responding to Basso, was the only recourse for men of intelligence. Beyond reason "lay madness, pseudo-mysticism, all forms of mental bondage and torture, the Foot of the Cross, etc." Josephson had yet to be convinced that he was being naive or that he should abandon the humanistic approach that had guided him for so long. As he explained to Basso: "I cannot make myself over." [1]

The Munich settlement and the collapse of the Popular Front in France were ominous signs for Josephson and many other writers on the Left. He was still not willing, however, to support American military intervention in Europe. "We must concentrate on the home-front," he reflected in his journal late in 1938, "and endeavor to influence other nations by our example." He shared with Max Lerner and others the belief that Americans must oppose fascism by affirming their democratic values and procedures, by shoring up the Popular Front, and by moderating the revolutionary rhetoric of the Left. This would mean, he admitted, "a retreat from socialism for a time—perhaps for long years—in the face of a greater menace that must be beaten off first, if the essential democratic conditions permitting renewed future action should not be lost." [2]

When Hitler betrayed the Munich Pact in March of 1939 and took control of all of Czechoslovakia, Josephson realized that the need for action was imperative. Another outpost of culture, democracy, and humanity had fallen to the "brown darkness." He feared that "our people will become shell-shocked, numbed by the barbarous tempo of events." In an essay written for the *New Masses* in April 1939, he addressed the rising danger posed by Hitler and tried to encourage the will to resist. He charged that some Western intellectuals were now cowering before Hitler's swift action:

Some wonder even if the Fascists do not possess some unknown magic or wizardry which helps them to victory both in the economic and military fields, and makes resistance vain. Others have begun to entertain doubts about the rule of reason itself, and about the humanistic doctrine underlying democratic and socialistic societies.

He argued, however, that the Nazis may have reached the limit of their success. Hitler's clever coup in Czechoslovakia may have provided the catalyst needed to reveal to the Western world the immediate menace at hand. Westerners, he stressed, should not give up hope, even after the collapse of Republican Spain and the sacrifice of the Czechs. There was still time to stop Hitler:

> Every so often the fight against the barbarians and bookburners must be fought all over again. What liberties, what human rights were ever won without being fought for? Instead of turning from this experience with a sense of defeat, I hope that the friends of democracy . . . will keep always with them an awarenesss of the potential strength they showed when unified in defense of a great cause.

Josephson noted that there were numerous examples of writers in the past who had successfully helped fight tyranny and injustice, men such as Zola, Voltaire, and Rousseau. In doing so they "reached their highest point of self-realization." Stopping Hitler, however, would take more than a few writers sounding impassioned warnings. This was a reality that Josephson had yet to confront.[3]

As part of his own campaign against Hitler, Josephson wrote a lengthy pamphlet in 1939 entitled "No Panic before Fascism." It represented an attempt "to measure, by the lights we have had—rather than by hysteria or passion—the force and the implication of the Fascist development from the point of view of an American progressive." The general spirit of the piece, he remarked to his publisher, would be "constructive and hopeful," a polemic directed against the "prevailing pessimism." Josephson admitted that in a "restrained way, it is fairly emotional, too." In the broadside he discussed the disillusionment and withdrawal of many literary intellectuals from the Popular Front. But he himself was not willing to succumb to such pessimism and resignation, not willing to abandon "the rational, materialistic, meliorative idea of political action by whose lights both liberal-capitalist democracy and socialist thought are guided." In fact, he reaffirmed his faith in the power of ideas and the role of writers in time of crisis. "We need more rather than less intellectual effort applied to the questions of the time." For writers "to wait passively for an 'inevitable' Fascism to arrive and burn our books, not only reflects an extremely narrow, fallacious notion of the play of free action within the frame of the determined; it is a posture of suicide." [4]

Josephson urged intellectuals to continue to work for progressive social change at home and thereby prevent fascism from taking root from within. They must maintain their support of the united labor movement in its effort to create industrial democracy. When the working class was organized, he insisted, then the United States would not only begin to make the "fullest use of our existing mechanisms for production and distribution of goods and services, but also to promote the politics of peace, of human liberty, and human dignity." His pamphlet was typically emotional, optimistic, and uplifting. The pace of world events, however, made his effort at pamphleteering obsolete before it could be published. In the late summer of 1939, Americans first learned of the Nazi-Soviet non-aggression pact signed on August 23. A few days later Russia and Germany began carving up Poland. Aggression was no longer the exclusive sin of fascism. Josephson would have to revise his pamphlet accordingly. [5]

The Nazi-Soviet pact had a shattering effect on the literary Left. Carey McWilliams referred to the period between the signing of the pact and the German invasion of Russia as the "nightmarish season" on the Left. The Popular Front had been built on the foundation of antifascism, and now that foundation had been destroyed. Most writers who were still members of the CPUSA hastened to resign. Granville Hicks remembered hearing news of the Nazi-Soviet pact on the radio. "When I was able to speak, I said, 'That knocks the bottom out of everything!'" The casualties were even greater among the fellow travelers like Josephson and Cowley, both of whom withdrew from the League of American Writers because of its close Soviet ties. For Josephson the Nazi-Soviet pact was a shock that muddled his thinking. Only two weeks before he had joined 400 other intellectuals in signing an open letter staunchly defending the Soviet Union. At one point the document asserted that Russia "continues as always to be a bulwark against war and aggression and works unceasingly for a peaceful international order." Now Matthew did not know what to think. "My poor head," he noted, "is bursting with anxiety of all sorts and confusion." [6]

In his journal Josephson reflected on the chaotic state of the literary Left in the wake of the Russo-German alliance:

> We must struggle to collect our thoughts. . . . At all events the European democracies have not capitulated as at Munich last year, but have taken up arms "to save the world from lawless aggression." So far so good. But Soviet Russia which yesterday worked to the same end has turned to . . . alliance with Nazi Germany. Hitler has joined hands with the Bolshevists!

He then noted that Stalin's action was not entirely surprising. Other political leaders such as Lenin and Lincoln had concluded alliances and made compromises in order to pursue ultimate objectives. Obviously, he found it hard to abandon the country and social system that had for so long inspired him. "The addiction to the Soviet myth," Arthur Koestler once remarked, "is as tenacious and difficult to cure as any other addiction." Yet Josephson begrudgingly severed his loyalty—at least for the moment. Russia had chosen its own path; now the United States must do the same. As he wrote:

> But whatever the ground for Stalin's strategic retreat, whatever advantage or delay it may gain, means nothing to us who work for a democratic reconstruction of our own country and for the preservation of peace abroad. We must not abandon our own convictions. We have no business to follow Stalin, or the Communists who cleave to him. Their recent maneuvers seem to alienate liberal and progressive men everywhere, and make it impossible for them to march with us toward common goals. . . .
>
> We must continue to hold our ground as anti-Fascists, come what may. We must also prepare to play a constructive part in the peace that must follow the war.
>
> I am for carrying on the Popular Front at home, and feel that factious quarrels among liberals, radicals, and Marxians of various kinds would serve no useful purpose.
>
> We must keep America an outpost of sanity.[7]

For most of the 1930s Josephson had been a consistent, outspoken opponent of fascism, repeatedly calling for the United States to join the other Western democracies and the Soviet Union in opposing Hitler and Mussolini. Now, however, he moderated his militancy. "I want no part in their war," he wrote in his journal of 6 September 1939. "Stalin is playing 'both ends against the middle.' It's a dangerous game. Probably not mine. I must stay with both feet in America. We have much that we can do here." He now spoke of maintaining American neutrality rather than getting involved in the European conflict. The danger was that Americans might be tricked into choosing sides. Later that month he wrote a letter to the *New Republic* in which he warned of the danger of "monopolistic-imperialistic interests" in the United States that might take advantage of the Nazi-Soviet pact to drive America into war on the side of the British Empire. "In the event that we entered such a war as now shapes itself," he maintained, "these sinister interests would certainly take power. Therefore, neutrality, abstention from war, would appear the most realistic, the most promising, and the most constructive course for progressive Americans." Josephson thus floundered for a new cause and course of action. The program he finally settled on—a rather lame one—was the revival of the Popular Front at home and the maintenance of American neutrality abroad. Such goals, however, flew in the face of the realities of the domestic and international scene.[8]

In the first few weeks following the Nazi-Soviet pact Josephson met several times at Max Lerner's house with other literary radicals, including Granville Hicks, I. F. Stone, Robert Lynd, Malcolm Cowley, Leo Huberman, and James Wechsler, in an attempt to reorganize the American Left. At the meetings Josephson criticized the "proved incompetence and ignorance" of the American Communists who remained faithful to the Soviet Union and its policies. They could never attract a wide following by constantly shifting their positions and adopting a "program of opportunism and duplicity." The American Left, he posited, "cannot win converts to purity, truth, justice and humanity by practicing deceit and compromises with evil, above all a form of self-deception." He stressed that they must "cut the umbilical cord that runs from the American Left to Moscow. The baby must learn to walk by himself." Josephson supported the idea of an independent Left in the United States—independent of Russia, that is, though not hostile to Russia. His independent Left would fully support organized labor, defend civil liberties, oppose fascism, resist war hysteria, and expose war propaganda. He was now speaking like a Fabian Socialist, urging "socialism in one country" and opposing American military intervention in Europe. Josephson wanted to organize a sort of "Jacobin Club" that would try to educate public opinion. As he remarked to Lynd, he had discovered that bourgeois writers do not make very good party organizers or workers. "The trouble with us whom you kindly call 'intelligent folk,'" Matthew noted, "is that we would give a weekend, then go back to breadwinning or paying off bills." He envisioned a loosely organized group of writers that "might gradually win authority, in a decent manner, and disseminate its opinion by various media, despite manifest difficulties; it might be able to kill by laughter, even." [9]

Thus Josephson illustrated again the genteel nature of his social and political activism. He felt that like Swift or Voltaire, writers could employ satire and pamphleteering to play a significant role in shaping public opinion and public policy. In concluding his letter to Lynd, he observed that "I like Max Lerner as a Moving Spirit. He is after all not so worldly minded that he fears or despises people who think; and on the other hand he is not a fanatic who believes in absolutes; and he has curiosity and is articulate." Josephson was less certain about working with Granville Hicks. As he wrote: "Hicks I know less well. Is he to be our Wendell Phillips? His recent apostasy, I thought, was respectably done." But all of the planning for an independent Left, or a Lonely Hearts Club, as James Farrell contemptuously referred to it, was for naught. Wechsler, in discussing the rump sessions at Lerner's, commented that "there was a good deal of ambiguity and disagreement about what was to be done next." The group could not reach a consensus about either domestic or foreign policy, and after a few meetings they dispersed. [10]

The primary reason for the failure of the independent Left group to get off the ground was the sharp difference of opinion concerning American intervention in the European war. A growing number of liberal intellectuals believed that the United States should abandon its isolation and actively intervene against fascism. During this period Lewis Mumford emerged as one of the most vehement and articulate of the interventionist liberals. In 1940 he wrote *Faith for Living*, an emotional polemic in which he assaulted liberals and fellow travelers for being innocent and timid, for placing too much emphasis on the economic and rational side of man and ignoring the "dark forces" of the irrational in shaping human events. Mumford especially lashed out at those who placed a "childish" trust in the essential goodness and perfectibility of man, thereby overlooking the revelations of modern psychology and the insights of Christian theology. He reflected his admiration for Reinhold Niebuhr when he wrote that "the most old-fashioned theologian, with a sense of human guilt and sin and error, was by far the greater realist." The intellectual fantasies of American liberals, Mumford contended, resulted in their inability to act forcefully in a crisis, especially the crisis at hand in Europe. American liberals and fellow travelers could not stand up against Hitler; they were "too noble to surrender; too sick to fight." [11]

Mumford shared with Josephson a hatred and fear of Nazism. His fears, however, were more immediate; they caused him to suggest extraordinary measures to deal with the threat. For instance, he advocated the partial suppression of democratic rights and civil liberties of "subversive" elements in the United States. Free speech must be limited. "Democracy must be prepared," he asserted, "to play the human game with the same ruthless consistency that fascism plays the anti-human game." Mumford also joined Niebuhr, Archibald MacLeish, Sidney Hook, and other intellectuals in calling for immediate military intervention against fascism. His impassioned call to arms quickly became a source of lively discussion among American liberals and fellow travelers.[12]

Mumford's book was especially disturbing to Josephson, who confessed to a friend that he had been "doing a heap of thinking on this whole question of the war and *Faith for Living*, and my own thoughts are not fully resolved. I have a very real friendship and high regard for Lewis; he has written some powerful criticisms into his book, which is a very passionate book. But I want to wait a while and then go over to him direct with my own questions." Mumford's polemic perplexed Josephson not only because he respected the author as a friend and thinker but also because the book's thesis directly challenged his own mode of thinking, his twentieth-century version of Enlightenment rationalism.[13]

In late August 1940, after the fall of France and the Low Countries, Mumford visited the Josephsons at Sherman, and he and Matthew engaged in an animated debate about liberal humanism as a philosophy and military intervention as a policy. Josephson freely admitted that he and others like him may have been too roseate in their rational, optimistic view of man and society. But he argued that in a time of crisis intellectuals must still think logically and rationally rather than go off half-cocked in a frenzy of emotionalism and anger. Moreover, he posited, the fact that one may have been too rational and optimistic did not warrant jumping to the other extreme and adopting the Augustinian Freudianism of Niebuhr. Mumford responded by accusing the literary Left of being "cowards and degenerates." He suggested that Josephson back up his passionate antifascist rhetoric with a willingness to use military force to stop Hitler.[14]

Like Mumford, Max Lerner also found Josephson's passivity disturbing. In August he asked Matty: "Do you really feel now that America ought not to use its power and prestige to stop that expansion and keep it from smashing a world within which you and I might still have a chance to advance our own ideas of life? I'll confess that there is a shrug-of-the-shoulder about your remarks on the war which bothers me a great deal." Josephson's continued isolationism was also discomforting to Malcolm Cowley, who after the fall of France decided that American military intervention was imperative in order to save Great Britain. He and Matty engaged in a bitter argument on the subject. Josephson insisted that he was no pacifist; he favored resisting aggression and intervening against Hitler, but only if absolutely necessary for American security. Cowley remembered that his friend "sat on the fence, though his legs hung down on the side of isolation." As their discussion continued their words grew sharp, leaving scars that stayed with both men many years afterward.[15]

In September 1940 Josephson wrote a note to Mumford that he never mailed, in which he again tried to explain his abstentionist position. *Faith for Living*, he began, was the most passionate and eloquent book that Mumford had written. Josephson agreed with its "spirited attacks upon our culture and political direction. But for the rest, recipe, prescription, I would not take it. No sir I do not agree." He then reiterated his own beliefs:

> I hope you will bear with me, Lewis, this once. I have sincerely esteemed you as a character, as a writer of real intelligence and spirit, above 99 out of 100 of my contemporaries. I have felt in you a good friend, even, as was often the case, from afar. But I feel that in a kind of sickness of soul, in an anguish of fear and passion, you have taken the tone and method of the enemy. This does not surprise me or necessarily shock me; because in making war . . . the principle is the same. . . . However, I do believe that there are possibilities of *democratic* mobilization against external dangers—I am really no pacifist—which you unfortunately have passed over, and which would help our people to make a far stronger fight of it when the time comes to fight.

Josephson agreed that American democracy must be defended, but it must be done without sacrificing the ideals of democracy. Since he himself was unfit for military duty, he would leave to others "of unimpaired physique and more youth the decision for war or peace." He would continue to do what he did best—write—and he cited a story about Goethe to illustrate his point. When asked to write an anthem commemorating a victory over Napoleon, Goethe supposedly answered that he was too busy with his writings and experiments. "Let Koerner do it," he replied.

Josephson added that Koerner was the Archibald MacLeish of his time. He could write adequately, but he was a "dope." In concluding his letter to Mumford, he affirmed: "What buoys me up, is my faith in human nature; there will be Koerners enough here; also would-be Goerings, generals, recruiting sergeants, killers. But you certainly threw a lot of stuff overboard that I want to keep."[16]

Josephson simply could not bring himself to advocate military intervention. The memory of World War I, his assumption that wars primarily benefit imperialists and capitalists, his hostility to the further concentration of monopoly capital, and his distrust of the rising martial spirit in the United States, all combined to make him wary of urging America into a war that would be fought for the wrong reasons and that would produce the wrong results. All the long-needed social reforms of the New Deal would be sacrificed to rearmament and mobilization. The same day that he wrote Mumford he also sent a letter to Kenneth Burke in which he again tried to explain his obviously uncomfortable intellectual position:

> There are enough others with the spirit of Responsibility and Authority for the times, so that they devote themselves already to telling the rest of us what our "duty" is and how many Huns we should kill before breakfast. They may be perfectly right. But I feel more right when I leave these stern tasks to them and occupy myself elsewhere. I had been saying here, just as you say, that we should go on doing the same things we thought ourselves a little competent for as long as possible up to the last minute.

Josephson, who had long played the role of the writer turned public man, was turning away from involving himself in an American war. Behind his curious refusal to involve himself was his almost paranoid fear that American intervention would result in the collapse of liberal reform and the emergence of fascism at home. Nor was he eager to rush to the aid of England, the world's largest colonial power. Hitler's invasion of Russia did little to change his thinking. He remained optimistic that Stalin and the Russian people would eventually turn the tide; he also continued to abstain from supporting American involvement. "Of Russia," he told his son Eric in the fall of 1941, "I persist in a long-range hopefulness. . . . I count on their endurance, will-to-suffer, and power of recuperation. . . . I persist in my unwillingness to ask or urge others to fight in my place." For the moment Josephson was willing to wait until the United States was directly threatened before advocating military action. But by then it might be too late.[17]

The dramatic events taking place in Europe in 1940 and America's response to them influenced Josephson to revise at the last minute his latest book, *The President Makers*, a history of politics during the Progressive era. Initially he had planned to conclude the study with "the tragic floundering of the great reform movement under Wilson in the world-war intervention." After Hitler invaded Poland, however, Josephson told his publisher that he must revise his book:

> I have thought there will be all the greater need for pamphleteering, for books of all sorts on public questions. I must alter my own; I believe that half of what I wrote is still timely, indeed urgent. But the altered perspective will require a different method of treatment.

He intended to place more stress upon the domestic and diplomatic pressures leading to American intervention in World War I, since it seemed to him that the same situation was developing in 1940. Josephson wanted *The President Makers* to relate directly to the exigencies of the present, to an even greater degree than either *The Robber Barons* or *The Politicos*. As he observed at the time, the book "seems more pertinent, more 'timely' and more sympathetic in its subject than the last study." [18]

Published in the fall of 1940, *The President Makers* ostensibly examines the men who between 1896 and 1919 developed the art of manipulating national party politics, men who with consummate skill "made" presidents. Josephson describes in great detail the characters, methods, and purposes of such political kingpins as Mark Hanna, George Cortelyou, George B. Harvey, George Perkins, and Colonel Edward House. And again he displays his skill at portraiture. His description of Hanna is typical: "His dictatorial temper, his blunt epithets, his shocking candor about the use of money, made men fear him, as they feared the red-nosed Morgan. Men of gentle feeling, at sight of the paunchy figure, the jowled face, the heavy mouth and piercing eye of the Ohio boss, would be taken aback. He seemed feudal, warlike; a man who would crush or buy out all those who stood in his way." [19]

But Hanna and the other backroom politicos are not the men who dominate the pages of *The President Makers*. Instead, the Progressive leaders, the presidents or the near-presidents—Bryan, Roosevelt, LaFollette, and Wilson—clearly stand out as the protagonists of the study. To Josephson the twenty years or so after the election of 1896 represented an "age of enlightenment" when courageous political reformers sought to curb the power of the political machines and the industrial trusts. It was a period "both enlightened and repentant in contrast with the age of the 'robber barons' and the spoilsmen." Ultimately, however, the reformers were only partially successful. Although he recognizes Roosevelt's and Wilson's positive achievements, Josephson accuses them of compromising with entrenched corporate and political interests, of not taking advantage of their tremendous popular support to restructure the capitalist system. "At its best," he insists, "Wilsonian liberalism had been slowly extending the influence of political democracy over increasing areas of American life, without of course changing the basic relations of property or the real disposition of economic and social power." [20]

Josephson's interpretation of national politics during the Progressive era was not original; others before him had emphasized the "conservative" nature of Roosevelt's and Wilson's reform programs. John Chamberlain, for instance, had presented the same thesis in his *Farewell to Reform*, published in 1932. Josephson, however, succeeded in substantiating Chamberlain's interpretation in a fashion that was a marked improvement over that earlier work. Despite its lack of originality, Josephson's treatment of the Progressive era in *The President Makers* was by far the best synthesis of the period to that time. Had Josephson concluded his book with the election of 1916, he would have written an excellent study of domestic political life during the first decade and a half of the twentieth century. But he chose to cover the American entry into the Spanish-American War and World War I in order to shed light on the situation facing the United States in 1940. And it was in his treatment of foreign affairs that Josephson offered his most dubious interpretations.

In 1898, Josephson claims, jingoists such as Roosevelt, Lodge, and Beveridge decided that war with Spain was necessary for "*internal domestic reasons.*" Along with other leading Republicans, they feared the party was on the verge of disintegration, that the Western silverites would bolt unless war was declared. With McKinley's war message, the "baffled passions of a long period of depression . . . had been safely channeled away." The Republicans thus focused public attention on Spain, the common enemy, and thereby drew "attention from the domestic demons troubling the American family." Such an interpretation of America's entry into the Spanish-American War, while no doubt accurate to some degree, falls far short of explaining the complex interaction of events, policies, and personalities that led to war. By concentrating on certain phrases or speeches of the jingoists and ignoring others, Josephson fails to provide a balanced view of the issue. Roosevelt and the jingoists, on several occasions that he does not cite, did argue for intervention on humanitarian grounds or for reasons of national security. Moreover, by again portraying national political decisions as resulting from a "conspiracy" of a few leaders, he shows little appreciation of the genuine desires of the masses.[21]

As in his treatment of the Spanish-American War and Roosevelt's foreign policies, Josephson concludes that Wilson turned his attention from domestic reform to international relations because of the internal political situation. By 1916, he argues, the New Freedom had been carried to its limits. Progressivism ended not in 1919, as many observers had maintained, but three years earlier, before America entered the war. Wilson had accomplished his major goals by the end of his first term. Thereafter, he was "then in the position of a man who wields great power, yet feels convinced that his mission has nearly been completed, or has reached its natural limits. For beyond the limits set by the statesmanship of equilibrium . . . there remained all the work of revolution, the overturning of all property and social relations." At this point Wilson halted. "Such a moment is dangerous," Josephson asserts, for Wilson had an acute desire to exert "positive leadership" in large affairs. The war in Europe provided Wilson with an opportunity to play a leadership role in world affairs. He turned to foreign policy and eventually to war primarily because of the "growing conviction that the program of domestic reform and renovation encountered ever-narrowing limits." Yet Josephson offers little substantive evidence to support this claim. Later he adds that the immediate cause of intervention was America's increasing involvement in "worldwide imperialist competition and struggles." Thus he accepts much of the "revisionist" view of the war espoused by scholars such as Hartley Grattan, Charles Beard, Walter Millis, and Charles Tansill. He lists the patently pro-British sympathies of Wilson and his advisers, the one-sided, lucrative war trade and financial ties with the Allies, and the effective propaganda campaign against the Germans as the forces contributing to intervention.[22]

Josephson clearly intended his interpretation of Wilson's actions and America's intervention in World War I to speak to the contemporary situation in 1940, as he admitted in the foreword:

> Historical parallels may be vastly instructive, though they must be used with caution. For example, early in the second term of President Franklin Delano Roosevelt, toward 1938, the movement of progress showed signs of reaching its natural limits, halting before apparently insurmountable obstacles, in a manner nearly identical with the stoppage of President Wilson's New Freedom program. . . .

> Once more, by a historical "coincidence" in the midst of a domestic crisis, unfinished and unsolved, we turn as a nation to confront the world's wars, the dangers and opportunities they offer (At such times there are always wars on hand). . . . The clock may be turned back, the large social gains abandoned, as decaying monuments to forgotten victories of peace time.

Josephson considered his book a "parable" for the present. The events of 1898 and 1917 anticipated those of 1940—propagandists, bankers, and politicians were conspiring to involve the country in another war in order to serve their selfish interests. His thesis that American reformers eventually turn to war as an alternative to carrying out true social revolution at home illustrated his personal concern in 1940 that the country appeared ready to forsake the New Deal and embark on another Great Crusade. FDR had exhausted his bag of tricks on the domestic front and was now prepared to solve the depression through massive military spending.[23]

Like Beard, moreover, Josephson feared a repetition of the domestic consequences of World War I, when social inequalities and the suppression of civil liberties became more marked than ever. The large industrial units, hugely overexpanded, "when peace came were compelled to merge with each other into still greater combinations in very self-defense, fixing more completely and irrevocably than ever the system of monopoly which Wilson had promised to abolish." The description Richard Hofstadter applied to Beard's approach to foreign policy applies equally to Josephson's method: "In discussing foreign policy he would often begin with a sound statement about some of the sobering realities—the limitations of American power, the problems of foreign markets and investments, the dangers of overreaching idealistic aims—and then suddenly emerge with a cranky thrust at the big bankers or their countryside allies among the village skinflints." Josephson's economic determinism and political cynicism blinded him to the myriad of factors relating to American intervention in 1917—and 1940. Superficially, history may seem to repeat itself. But in actuality, no two historical events are identical.[24]

Just before *The President Makers* was published, Josephson wrote a letter to one of the editors at Harcourt, Brace in which he discussed the problem of finding capable reviewers for his new book. He noted that the staff at the *Nation* had unfairly attacked his other books for partisan reasons. Apparently, he surmised, they thought that by shooting at me they could get at Mr. Stalin too. They had a rat named Hacker, who had been following my books for years, sometimes reviewing them in two papers at once. I enjoy "attacks" thoroughly, when I feel that I and others are learning something from them. But when it gets to be a clique job it is too tiresome.

Josephson added that the *New York Herald-Tribune* habitually asked Henry Steele Commager to review his books, a historian "who sees no use in me, since long ago." Josephson's fears concerning the fate of *The President Makers* were not unfounded. He was indeed viewed by many critics as a muckraking fellow traveler. While the *New Yorker* described his new book as a "superb job" and Robert Morss Lovett observed in the *New Republic* that Josephson had written a "brilliant and illuminating history," most critics rejected his reductionist interpretation of World War I and Wilson's foreign policies. The now conservative Whittaker Chambers remarked in *Time*: "Matthew Josephson continues to tell Americans that their administrators and respectable citizens are a bunch of crooks." As Josephson expected, Commager wrote a critical review in which he questioned the author's historical ability. After praising Josephson's literary skill, he sarcastically concluded that *The President Makers* was a "first rate piece of journalism." [25]

Josephson's undisguised preoccupation with the current domestic and international scene did indeed color his historical judgment. But *The President Makers* was much more than just a "journalistic" exercise; it also represented a valuable contribution to the political history of the Progressive era, as its recent reprinting attests. Counterbalancing Josephson's questionable interpretation of foreign affairs were the positive attributes that continually won him praise as a popular historian. He again demonstrated a superb ability to personalize history, to make characters live and breathe for the reader. In addition he wrote in a clear, crisp style that evoked a real sense of the drama of American political life. His treatments of Roosevelt's New Nationalism and Wilson's New Freedom provided students of the period with concise, accurate accounts of those political philosophies. Robert Wiebe has described *The President Makers* as the best introduction to the Progressive era, and Robert Engler asserted in 1979 that the book "remains valuable for those concerned about understanding when American politics offered genuine choices." [26]

With the publication of *The President Makers* Josephson's trilogy of historical works was complete. For most of the rest of his career he would return to writing biography, his favorite genre. Now, however, he decided to take up free-lance journalism again. In the spring of 1940 the editors of the *New Yorker* asked him to go to Washington and write a number of profiles of leading national figures. Josephson readily accepted the offer, not only because it was lucrative, but also because it would give him the opportunity to be in the "center of things" as the nation readied itself for a possible war. He wanted to see at first hand whether the concerns he had expressed to Lewis Mumford about the danger posed to domestic reform by preparedness and intervention were valid. Josephson's assignments for the *New Yorker*, as well as similar ones for the *Saturday Evening Post*, kept him in Washington during much of the hectic prewar period.

Washington in 1940–41 was throbbing with activity. The economy's transformation from stagnation to the dynamic pace of war production had already begun when Josephson arrived in the city in the late spring of 1940. On May 26, 1940, President Roosevelt ordered the immediate construction of 50,000 airplanes and 10,000 tanks. But the question that concerned Josephson was how this great transformation would be managed. As one of his first articles for the *New Yorker* on the subject, he chose to write an extensive profile of William Knudsen, the former head of General Motors who had recently been appointed to the newly formed National Defense Advisory Commission (NDAC). Among the other members of the commission were economist Leon Henderson and labor leader Sidney Hillman. Knudsen was placed in charge of production planning.

During the summer and fall of 1940, while the Battle of Britain dominated the headlines and the presidential campaign got under way, Josephson met and mingled with a variety of political and labor officials. He attended several parties given by Max Lowenthal, a left-wing lawyer closely affiliated with organized labor. Lowenthal, who also had a home near Sherman, had become one of Josephson's closest friends. Through him Matthew met a number of influential political activists in Washington, as he reported to Hannah in October:

> I have had some parties at the Lowenthals, who utterly spoiled me. I now love them both. I have seen I. F. Stone—and met a good many of the more serious men on the left, such as young Lee Pressman, counsel to the C.I.O. [Congress of Industrial Organizations]—and others such as Nathan Witt, secretary of the N.L.R.B. [National La-

bor Relations Board]—but I end by detesting Washington—It's too mad.

During the daytime Josephson doggedly prepared his articles for the *New Yorker*, haunting the offices of the NDAC. There he interviewed Knudsen, Hillman, Henderson, Robert L. Patterson, the former corporate lawyer who was undersecretary of war, Robert A. Lovett, former partner of Harriman Brothers and now undersecretary of air, and a number of other businessmen turned government officials who were managing the preparedness program. He was disturbed at the potential danger of so many "dollar-a-year" businessmen now gaining control and influence in Washington.[27]

In March 1941 Josephson published his profile of Knudsen in the *New Yorker*. In it he revealed the disorganization, stumbling, and bickering that characterized the early days of the NDAC as it attempted to prepare the nation for war. His tone, however, was uncharacteristically objective and detached throughout the piece. It was not so by choice. The editors at the *New Yorker* had gone over the article with a sharp blue pencil. They felt that he was too critical of the preparedness effort and its leaders. They also feared that some of his information was classified. Josephson strongly objected to their tampering. In a memo to the editors he wrote: "I yield to no one in my sense of loyalty to this country and its people. I think that my implied criticisms of the organizers of supply defense, a much less delicate subject than the military arm criticized in *Harper's* and *Time*, give no secret information that was otherwise unavailable to the German intelligence service." Josephson charged in his complaint that Roosevelt's policies would "lead us to future Flanders and Dunkerques" because "we are too prone to muffle self-criticism." But his protests had little effect. The edited version was printed in the magazine.[28]

In his article on Knudsen, Josephson noted that the problems confronting the NDAC in trying to facilitate a smooth transition from a peacetime economy to one based on a war footing

derived from the fact that they are functioning within a true democracy. Our businessmen were free to attack the head of state. Everyone was free to plunge into an election campaign which tore the country apart for three months. Unemployed citizens were free to do nothing for their country in an emergency. The New Dealers, the dollar-a-year men, and the Army and Navy officers were free to bicker, and congressmen were free to be long-winded.

As he pointed out, however, such limitations were more than compensated for by the positive qualities of American democracy. The United States had the greatest industrial plant in the world. "She loved money," he observed, "but she loved liberty, too." He concluded that the American people and the government had made mistakes in preparing for a possible conflict, they had moved slowly and sometimes grudgingly, "but they could never make some final, fateful mistake with the brilliant rapidity of a Mussolini or a Hitler." Although he still hoped that American intervention in the European war could be avoided, Josephson was optimistic that the American tortoise could overtake the fascist hare.[29]

During most of the 1930s Matthew Josephson had been "a relatively detached" fellow traveler. Consequently, the turbulent events of 1939–41 had an impact on his state of mind much different from their effect on Cowley, his close friend and neighbor. The difference between the two men's experiences helps illuminate Josephson's position as a writer on the Left as well as indicating that there were different degrees of fellow-traveling. As literary editor of the *New Republic* for most of the thirties, Cowley was much more directly and emotionally involved in the politics and quarrels of the literary Left than was Josephson. Thus, the revelation of the Nazi-Soviet pact, followed soon thereafter by the Russian invasions of Poland and Finland, had a devastating effect upon Cowley's outlook. The fall of France in June was a still more telling blow. Like many writers on the Left he was plagued by a "sense of guilt," by a feeling that his intellectual sense had betrayed him and that he in turn had betrayed his literary craft. After the fall of France he became convinced that the United States must enter the war and keep Britain from falling in turn. He resigned from the League of American Writers in July 1940, and at the end of the year he vacated his desk at the *New Republic*. When he later joined the Office of Facts and Figures in Washington in an effort to support the American preparedness campaign, he was immediately set upon by the Dies committee, was vilified as a Communist and Stalinist stooge, and was forced to resign after only two months on the job.[30]

By the spring of 1942 Cowley wanted out—out of the "movement," out of the public arena, out of sight. He returned to his home in Sherman, and while literally tending his garden, he made a number of resolutions: "Not to join anything in the future. Not to write statements. Not to sign statements written by others. Not to let my name appear on letterheads." The once-involved Cowley was now determined above all else to be nonpolitical. It was time to leave the ramparts and return to literary criticism, pure and simple. His initial attraction to communism had been analogous to a religious conversion, and he now experienced the alienation of the apostate. "Anyone who was as close to the radical movement as I was," he told Burke in December 1940, "is going to be deeply shaken by breaking connections with it. At that point the religious metaphor is absolutely accurate. You leave a church, and like a defrocked priest you can't think about anything else for a while." [31]

Unlike Cowley and others on the literary Left, Matthew Josephson did not experience such a "sense of guilt" about his political activity during the thirties, nor did he withdraw from the arena of social and political activism after the catastrophes of 1939–41. Although he too resigned from the league and moved further away from the CPUSA, he did not feel the need to turn inward and return to a life of pure literature. He revealed this difference in letters to Kenneth Burke in the early 1940s. In the fall of 1940 he wrote: "Malcolm departed for Nova Scotia to begin the second volume of his confessions, errors of the last ten years. . . . We hope M. C. will get into a calmer state." A year and a half later, when Cowley was drawn and quartered by the Dies committee, Josephson commented to Burke about their friend's plight: "This brings up poor Malcolm, our neighbor who art gone to the heaven of the Office of Facts and Figures, whither I hope you will have not yet landed. The pathetic thing is that he has been used as a Political Goat; they know quite well that he repented and turned into sort of a 'Christian Counterrevolutionist' as Cantwell now defines it, over two years ago." Josephson's comments reflected the fact that he had never been as directly involved as Cowley in the politics of the revolutionary Left. He had remained *au dessus de la mêlée*. Although he had occasionally fired a partisan volley, he had for the most part stayed behind the front lines of the literary and political wars, especially after 1935. Preferring to express his social convictions through his books and essays, he never reached the point of staking his personal and literary reputation on the success of the "movement," as Cowley and others had done. This helps explain the lack of understanding and compassion in his attitude toward Cowley—and toward all repentant leftists, for that matter. [32]

According to Josephson, however, the primary reason for his ability to maintain an active, critical stance on the Left after 1939 was that he had never linked his personal philosophy of the "writer turned public man" to the performance of Russia, the CPUSA, or Marxism in general. He always viewed himself as a humanist first and a Marxist second. Writers, he had long maintained, had a duty to speak out against social and political injustice. Whether they did so as socialists, Marxists, or liberals was really insignificant, as long as they did not turn their backs on society. During the thirties Josephson had supported a Communist program because it seemed the right approach at the time. As the times changed, so did his perception and use of Marxism. His concept of his role as a literary intellectual, however, did not change; it transcended ideological boundaries. Even after the events of 1939–41 he remained optimistic and involved. He would never subscribe to the "tragic" liberalism of Niebuhr, Mumford, and others. Nor did he ever accept the charge that the writers on the Left had failed the cause of democracy. He emphasized this point in a letter to Burke in 1940:

> Through sheer ignorance, I remained sane in 1917–1918, and hope to do so again. I simply don't know yet about the end of civilization. I suspect that it must be one of those illusions like Inevitable, Constantly Rising Progress. I refuse to get religion with Waldo Frank, or go berserk with Lewis Mumford, or blame the liberal intellectuals and artists for letting everything go wrong, as Archie MacLeish does. I never saw, in all my 41 years, the Liberals and Artists work so hard, as they did lately to fight Fascism. Every other fellow was passing a hat, and not a few shouldering a gun. But when in history did artists and intellectuals run the state, the army, the counting houses?

Unlike so many literary radicals who during and after World War II became ideologues of the New Right, Josephson was determined not to abandon his liberal humanism in the face of the Nazi-Soviet pact and the collapse of the Popular Front. Instead of feeling guilty about his activities during the thirties, he was proud of them.[33]

Much of what Josephson said about his activities on the Left was certainly true. But what he did not explain, either then, or later in his memoirs of the decade, is equally revealing. One cannot help but wonder, for example, how a self-described humanist could repeatedly minimize or casually dismiss the growing body of evidence pointing to Stalin's repeated violation of civil liberties and basic human rights in the Soviet Union. For a literary intellectual so genuinely indignant at the tyranny of fascism, Josephson was remarkably contained about similar activities in Russia. His continued rationalization of Stalin and Stalinism as necessary evils promoting the creation of a democratic collectivist state badly soiled his claim to being a forthright defender of individual freedom. Rather than viewing essential human rights as inviolable under any system of government, he seemed to adhere to a double standard. Oppression under a socialist regime was unfortunate but understandable; under a fascist system it was intolerable.

Josephson was certainly not alone in adopting such a relativist position. Scores of other writers on the Left in the United States and Europe did the same. Why they did so is a question that has puzzled and frustrated observers then and since. And it is a question crucial to an understanding of the mentality of the literary fellow travelers. Some scholars and former literary radicals have emphasized the insecurity and naivete of the writers on the Left. Others have pointed to their muddleheadedness. No doubt many of the fellow travelers, including Josephson, were at times muddled and naive in their thinking. In Josephson's case, however, a more complete explanation is that which David Caute has presented in his study *The Fellow Travelers*. There he argued that the reason why so many Western fellow travelers, with all their passion for civil liberties, freedom of thought, and judicial safeguards, were blithely able to overlook Stalinist terror was because of their fundamental elitism. For the most part they did not build their social and political philosophies upon Marxism but upon the tradition of the Enlightenment. They never felt comfortable identifying with the toiling masses. They even rebelled against proletarian literature. Most of them at heart felt quite ill at ease around the common people. Nor did they truly believe that the masses were capable of carrying out Marx's historical scenario, bringing about revolutionary change on their own. Change, therefore, would have to occur as Lenin and Stalin had shown—from the top down. Thus, Caute concluded, it was fairly easy for the fellow travelers in the West to gloss over the plight of the masses under Stalin's totalitarian regime. His actions were supposedly in the best interest of the populace.

It is curious that Caute does not mention Josephson in his study, for the author of *The Robber Barons* would have provided a convincing example of his thesis. As discussed earlier, Josephson was strongly influenced by the Enlightenment credo. He placed great faith in rational social progress through the enlightened use of social engineering. Like Voltaire, he also never really trusted the masses. His suggestion in 1932, for instance, that writers should form their own radical political party instead of combining with the workers illustrated his queasiness. Consequently, he tended to emphasize the positive achievements and glorious potential of the collectivist experiment in Russia rather than dwell on its current horrors. In this sense, then, Josephson was being truthful when he characterized himself as being a "humanist first and a Marxist second." His humanism, however, was of the eighteenth-century variety, Girondist much more than Marxist. His commitment to civil liberties and intellectual freedom, as he would demonstrate in the postwar era, was indeed fervent. But it was a commitment most easily stimulated by threats posed to the freedoms of his own intellectual and artistic community, not to the man in the streets or to literary intellectuals of opposing political factions. For example, he later would strongly protest against the imprisonment of Communist party leaders under the Smith Act, yet there is no evidence that he did likewise when a group of Trotskyists were sent to jail for the same reason several years earlier. Like so many fellow travelers, Josephson sincerely wanted the people to be both equal and free. But if both goals could not be achieved, he would regretfully accept equality for the masses and freedom for the "right" thinking literati. In this sense he was probably correct when he insisted to a friend that he was "never virtuous enough to be a true Communist."

12   THE TROUGH OF A WAVE

The Japanese attack on Pearl Harbor ended a lot of intellectual uncertainty for Josephson and many other intellectuals concerned about whether or not the United States should intervene in the war. America's official involvement in the conflict also contributed to the continuing disintegration of the literary Left. The Popular Front was disconcerted and disunited. More and more writers withdrew from the activism of the political arena into the solitude of the artistic imagination. Others rushed to assert their nationalism and martial fervor. As William Phillips remarked in 1944, "In the last few years . . . most American writers have done nothing so much as display their capacity to conform, by draping themselves in the official doctrines of All-America anti-fascism and knuckling under the chest-thumping nationalism now rampant." [1]

Josephson was also concerned about the negative impact the war had upon the literary Left and its ideals. He commented to Robert Lynd in 1943 that the war years seemed like the "trough of a wave" in which the progressive Left lay becalmed. "To be sure," he emphasized, "there would be an upswing—but when?" Between 1941 and 1945 the war understandably monopolized the attention of literary intellectuals. But even though much of the literary Left lost its cohesion and sense of social purpose, Josephson did not abandon his own support of a more collectivist social program. He marked time during the war, waiting for a resurgence of an independent political organization on the Left. As he told Lynd, "At a time when there seem to be no organized groups to work with, I've simply used my literary and technical ability to keep afloat, to do work of a passing interest even if it didn't give me the satisfaction of moving together with the constructive forces toward some socially desirable objective." The events of 1939–41 had dealt the literary Left a severe body blow, and it would take time for it to recover. Josephson was willing to wait. [2]

After Pearl Harbor Josephson supported the American and Allied cause, although he reserved the right to criticize those who sought to take personal or corporate advantage of the national emergency. He generally shared the attitude toward the war expressed by Hannah in a letter to Eric the day after the Japanese attack:

> Either the Japs are plumb crazy, or you and I are. . . . The President has got us into this war by the back door, for no one can say that he left the Japs any alternative but to undo everything they have been fighting for the last ten years or else go to war with us. And yet, although I see clearly what he has done, I have always felt that they needed a lesson for their crimes in China. Oh dear, I hope we can give it to them quickly, and stop this nightmare that we have all been living through for so long. But I fear the incompetence of our own crowd so greatly that I have grave doubts.

Like their friend Charles Beard, Matthew and Hannah feared that the exigencies of the war effort would place power in the wrong hands, the hands of military specialists and business leaders. And such men would be reluctant to give up their power and influence once the war ended. Three days after the Japanese attack Matthew voiced his fears in a letter to Kenneth Burke. "It's not that I'm afraid of the outcome, in the long run," he stressed, "but I am sure that the kind of life we will have during that long run will be wholly changed, infinitely less agreeable than the recent past, before Dec. 7, 1941." In February he told Burke that he saw the conflict as two wars: "1) against the enemy at home, and 2) against the one outside, the latter a shade less detestable to me because more distant—though I promise to go for him as hard as any other patriot." [3]

Josephson emphasized much the same message in letters to his son Eric and to Charles Beard in the months following Pearl Harbor. When Eric, then a freshman at the University of North Carolina, expressed misgivings about the fate of the Japanese and German people, his father's response was surprisingly militant: "I don't see why any of the boys at Chapel Hill should worry too much in advance about our hurting the poor Jappies and Nazis. I don't pretend that we are much purer and more virtuous; but there are degrees of evil." The Japanese assault had changed Beard's attitude to the war as well. In response to a letter from Josephson he affirmed early in 1942: "With you I am hoping that the Japs, the Heinies, and the Musso boys get hell fire and destruction as quickly as is humanly possible. The more of them that are blasted to pieces the better for poor bedeviled humanity." Beard also agreed with Matty that it would be foolish to join "Dorothy Thompson and company" in praising all things American; they must support the war effort, but at the same time retain their critical faculties and fundamental principles. Beard remarked that when he returned to Connecticut they could "sit under the vine and fig tree and discuss the hypothetical questions which now engage the captains and the kings. Until I see a way for a man of my age to help destroy Japs, nazis, and fascists, I shall keep on working at something I 'feel' competent to do." [4]

Like Beard, Josephson continued during the war years to do what he felt competent to do—write. In 1942 he returned to biography and to French literature, publishing a comprehensive study of Victor Hugo. As he had done with his other works, he stressed in *Victor Hugo* the "timeliness" of his subject. He wanted to speak through Hugo to the French people, to remind them of their ability as a nation to survive the rule of tyranny. The inspiration for the biography came from Josephson's correspondence with several of his French friends, especially Louis Aragon and Philippe Soupault. Aragon, who had been such a strong influence on Josephson in the early 1920s, served in a French armored division and was captured by the Nazis in the early fall of 1940. He escaped a few weeks later. Aragon related his war experiences in a letter mailed in September:

> I found myself on the front line of the first French troops that entered Belgium, and I served through the whole campaign of Flanders under conditions that were extremely adventurous. They gave me the Croix de Guerre for that, can you imagine? It was a rapid and romantic war for me, but its consequences for the country are more terrible than you can ever imagine.

Despite the calamity that had befallen France, Aragon refused to despair. "I believe on the contrary," he affirmed, "that God moves in a mysterious way and that the gate is straight through which we must pass. In my country, even when it is unfortunate, even when it is crushed, I have a confidence that there is no way of expressing except by deeds."[5]

Aragon's letters profoundly affected Josephson. He wept as he read of the courage and faith of his friend and other members of the French Resistance. Here were writers, artists, and historians leading the fight against Nazi and Vichy tyranny despite overwhelming odds. Aragon's example stirred in him the desire to do something to help his friends and the cause of France, his second home. Matthew and Hannah organized a fundraising campaign to help writers such as Soupault get out of France. But the Vichy government thwarted such efforts. Josephson then decided that if he could not help his French friends directly, he might at least use his pen on their behalf. And in his view Hugo provided the prime example of the heroic man of letters who served as the conscience of France during the mid-nineteenth-century reign of Louis Napoleon and after.

Victor Hugo, like Josephson's earlier studies of Zola and Rousseau, tells as much about the biographer as the subject. Josephson is again primarily concerned with portraying the writer as citizen. How does the artist, he repeatedly asks, reconcile his private work with his public duty? He places Hugo in the same tradition as his other "heroes"—Voltaire, Rousseau, and Zola. Victor Hugo, he asserts, provides "one of the greatest examples of the sedentary, meditative man turning from his study to service in public life." Josephson then presents a succinct description of his own attitude toward the writer's role in society:

> For a long time I have been absorbed in the problem of the relation of the artist to society, the problem of his participation in public life. . . . To me it has always seemed that the artist, the creative man generally speaking, has two functions: one is to do his duty as a craftsman, unequivocally, disinterestedly, without regard to contemporary parties or regimes. The second function begins when the first has been obstructed, as often occurs in a time of social crisis. This touches the creative man's function as citizen. To fulfill this he leaves his study and takes part in political campaigns, or fights in a war, or in a revolution, by the side of his fellow citizens, if only that he and his people may be able, later, to return to their civilized and creative tasks.

Here, finally, was the credo he had begun developing in 1927 and had adopted by 1942. Its sentiments were as compelling as they were sincere.[6]

Victor Hugo's varied and colorful career offered Josephson a perfect opportunity to display again his gift for spirited narrative and keen characterization. He skillfully traces Hugo's conversion from literary great to political hero. Along the way he adds texture to his portrait by interweaving the fascinating components of Hugo's personal life—his marriage to Adèle Foucher, his fifty-year liaison with Juliette Drouet, and his friendship and betrayal by Sainte-Beuve. Throughout the study, however, Josephson consistently focuses on Hugo's development as the writer turned public man.

In the biography Josephson indicates that despite the failures of the literary Left during the 1930s, he still believes that writers have a duty to speak out, to serve as the conscience of the nation. Whatever faults Hugo may have had, he exclaims,

> he seemed heroic and gigantic, compared to the indifferent, the writers who stayed in bed, the sheep who quietly did what they were told. By his exaltation he kept a flame burning, which he fed steadily and fervently with his boundless indignation, a flame that glowed beyond the border of France, whose lights had gone out. For twenty years, long after other men had cravenly made their peace, accepting the best terms they could, and had crawled back to their places of submission, that flame burned on brightly.

Victor Hugo's life was a success story without parallel, and it provided an apotheosis of Josephson's point about the duty of writers in times of social and political crisis. The critics again praised Josephson's talents as biographer. André Maurois found the book "well informed, well constructed, and very fair." Writing in the New York Times Herbert Gorman called the book Josephson's best biography yet. Other reviewers referred to Josephson as one of the best American biographers of the day.[7]

After completing his study of Hugo in 1942, Josephson again returned to free-lance journalism. With Eric in college and Carl about to enter a boarding school near Philadelphia, Josephson needed, as he told Kenneth Burke, to build up his bank account, "which had gone down during long years of completing disinterested historical research." In the early 1940s he wrote a series of lengthy profiles for the New Yorker and Saturday Evening Post. His subjects included such diverse figures as Leon Fraser, John Marin, Edward Steichen, J. B. Matthews, Arthur Krock, and Juan Trippe, the controversial president of Pan American Airways. As always, however, Josephson privately considered such "slick" journalism a necessary evil. He anguished over having to make his articles "moderate and palatable in tone." Nevertheless he felt he needed the money. He always wanted to be able to return to writing about subjects that he felt were significant and "timely." [8]

During the war years Matthew corresponded regularly and frankly with his son Eric, who had entered the University of North Carolina in 1941 to study sociology under Howard Odum. Josephson's letters to his son between 1941 and 1945 provide an intimate record of his intellectual personality as he reached middle age. In March 1942 Eric proudly informed his father that he had joined a campus study group made up of Communists and fellow travelers. Matthew was less than overjoyed at his son's ideological associations.

> I think communist fellows are fine fellows all right; but nowadays I take them (the American satellite variety) with much salt. You see I've been following them in my mind in a friendly way for some 12 years. There are 48 million wage workers in America and the com's have got 100,000 of them roundly in the fold in about the last 20 years. At this rate they may capture the rest of the workers about the year 2,742 A.D.—if nothing turned up to interfere with them.

Josephson suggested that his freshman son "investigate the glowing possibilities of Buddhism" or some other less totalitarian cult. "Why grab only at the same old recipe that somebody in the neighborhood happens to dish up? I feel you ought to keep an open mind at this stage. Not take up one scheme and lose your mind to the rest." Josephson had seen enough of the CPUSA in action during the 1930s to convince him that his inexperienced son would do better to shop around before aligning himself with the "comrades" in Chapel Hill. But Eric had inherited his father's stubborn streak, and he persisted in his left-wing political activity. By May he had become quite a campus radical. That month he complained to his father about the incessant squabbling he had discovered among the comrades and the vigor with which he and his group were vilified on campus. Although he appreciated Eric's idealism, Matthew had little consolation to offer his son: "If you want to be a leaflet pusher that's the kind of nuisance you are going to experience all the time." What bothered the bourgeois father most was that Eric's academic performance had suffered because of his political commitments. "I think you or any friends of yours who are exclusively interested in politics, public questions, rescuing Earl Browder, or Revolution would be more honest if they ceased being non-studying *rentiers* and pursued their non-studying activities at their own expense." The issue of Eric's college associations, however, soon became a moot question; early in 1943 he entered the army.[9]

Eric Josephson had a difficult time adjusting to life as an army recruit. Growing up in a literary household in Sherman and Manhattan, he had been surrounded by books and ideas, politics and social activism. He had attended an innovative, progressive boarding school near Sherman with few regulations and no formal curriculum. Most of the other students there were intelligent, inquisitive, and opinionated—as was Eric. Thus from an early age he had become accustomed to an intellectually stimulating environment. Army life, therefore, was quite a new and in many ways disillusioning experience for the younger Josephson. He grew exasperated trying to relate to his fellow recruits, most of whom seemed to be uneducated or unthinking souls, full of prejudice and vulgarity and devoid of ideas or inquisitiveness. His first letters home from boot camp reflected his malaise and sense of isolation.

In a lengthy response to Eric, Matthew offered some pointed fatherly advice. He found it ironic that his son, the aspiring sociologist, should have so much difficulty relating to people of different backgrounds and tastes:

> the men in your encampment represent a cross-slice of our society. If you are going to be an effective social scientist or improver those are the boys you have to work over, not the subscribers of *The New Republic* or the enlightened colony in Sherman or Martha's Vineyard. And yet what are you doing about them? You are peeved at them. You think it is not worth helping or taking with them. They discourage you. And you go your way talking Beethoven and Harold Laski while they, the vast unwashed, uncultured majority, who ARE American go on being Ku-Kluxers, anti-semites, bigots, ignoramuses, and "sex-fiends". . . . I have often said that our intellectuals are too widely separated from the great masses of common ordinary Americans and have failed to "sell" their ideas to the real people. I am aware of my own failure.

Josephson emphasized that as intellectuals they must constantly try to relate to the masses, even if on a different level. "As a scholar, writer, an artist," he observed, "I am really much attracted by low company and love to observe them as a scientist observes different kinds of crabs and insects, analyzing them and classifying them. But you seem to close up." Josephson challenged Eric to grow up and face the responsibilities of his intellectual role: "Well I give you the Amurrican Peepul. . . . You are an embryonic sociologist. Go ahead; work with them; they're your material. If you can't learn them some democracy and justice and humanity, how are you going to get anywhere? And yet if intellectuals like you can't make a dent in them during the next 20 yrs., there's going to be another war, etc. sure as fate." [10]

While Eric learned to be a soldier, Matthew kept up his writing and political activity. When not writing articles for the *Saturday Evening Post* or the *New Yorker*, or working on biographies of Juan Trippe and Stendhal, he remained actively interested in the political questions of the day. He spent considerable time in Washington during the war years, and while there he became friends with a number of lawyers active in organized labor and with ties to the Communists. Through his friend Max Lowenthal, he grew close to Nathan Greene, John Abt, and Nathan Witt. He found them extremely interesting and able men, as he reported to Eric:

> Two nights ago I ran into my lawyer friend Greene staying at Lowenthal's with Nathan Witt, formerly a sparkplug of the NLRB, i.e. executive secretary, and banished by the opposition. Both these men give me the feeling of being happy soldiers in the cause of humanity, though lawyers. One is a theoretician, the other, Witt, is a trial and court fighter, now counsel to the biggest CIO unions. Their work is so realistic and interesting that I often wonder whether you still might not want to go to Harvard or Yale Law . . . and move into that field.

Josephson's association with such men drew him into working with the organized labor movement. At the same time, his friendships with Malcolm Cowley, Kenneth Burke, and Charles Beard continued to lapse. In 1944 Josephson began supporting the newly formed political action committee (PAC) of the CIO. The CIO had made great strides in organizing industrial workers since its creation in the 1930s. In the process it had benefited greatly from the prolabor New Deal legislation. By 1943, however, the political temper in Washington had changed, and Republicans and conservative Democrats made significant gains in the off-year elections. In 1943 Congress overrode Roosevelt's veto to pass the War Labor Disputes Act, which severely restricted organized labor's activities. Such setbacks prompted the CIO to form a group to bolster labor's political position in Congress and around the country. Sidney Hillman, the highly esteemed and effective union leader, whom Josephson had come to know in the 1930s, was asked to head the political action committee.[11]

When Josephson learned of the formation of the PAC he offered his services, writing political pamphlets and encouraging prominent writers to support labor candidates. He explained to Eric that the CIO "represents only a slightly more politically conscious trade union movement, resembling the British labor organization more than our AFL [American Federation of Labor] (which, however, has also been a little more progressive)." Josephson surmised that the "progressive" labor movement was growing steadily in the United States and "will play a larger part in future plans." A few months later he gleefully reported that there had been an "upsurge in the pro-labor tide, the pro New Deal goes forward." He added that Hillman's PAC had done "an amazing job of political education," as indeed it had. Largely through that organization's efforts, Martin Dies, the archconservative, antilabor chairman of the House Un-American Activities Committee (HUAC), was ousted from his Texas congressional seat. Josephson had played no small part in discrediting Dies and his committee. In April 1944 he had published in the *Saturday Evening Post* a sharp attack on Dies, his committee, and J. B. Matthews, the former Communist and editor of *Time* who reversed himself during the war years and became the committee's "expert" informer on Communists and fellow travelers. After Dies decided not to run for reelection, Josephson informed Eric, "The Tories are hysterical." He buoyantly announced that "collectivism" seemed on the rise in England, Canada, and Australia. "Even our leading capitalists now admit that government controls must be used to guarantee employment and a good standard of living and education for our nice guys who are doing such a great job." Josephson's glee over the ouster of Dies and the upsurge in labor support thanks to the PAC was unrestrained. "Yes sir," he concluded in his letter to Eric, "I am hopeful: this is a great country and you are going to have your own happy place in it some day."[12]

During the war the Josephsons established their practice of spending the winter months in Manhattan and then returning to Sherman in the late spring. Carl, their younger son, attended the George School near Philadelphia before entering Harvard in 1947. In New York Matty and Hannah lived in an apartment on East Twenty-second Street. Josephson would do his research and writing, however, in a small rented studio on East Twenty-third Street at the south side of Madison Square. There he fell into a regular routine of reading and writing in the mornings and afternoons, eating lunch with literary friends or associates, and carrying on an active social life in the evenings, entertaining frequently at their apartment.

Josephson had always thrived on the social life of literary New York. Indeed, it was the stimulating contact with fellow writers and intellectuals that most attracted him to the city. But by the mid–1940s he was growing disenchanted with the social scene in Manhattan. In March 1945 he described the situation to Eric:

> New York is divided into sects. Some people, professing to be intellectuals and writers, seek me out—as a matter of fact there have been many parties and cocktail gatherings. But usually they want me to review one of their books or give them something for nothing and are just as practical and determined about their little affairs as the Juan Trippes about theirs. I am in a misanthropic mood. Enjoying human company heartily, I nevertheless do not enjoy the specimens that come and go in my proximity, and fall to studying their motives coldly, or asking myself why they say certain things.

Until now Josephson had delighted in playing cicerone and mentor to young writers. Now, however, he did not suffer supplicants kindly. He frequently grumbled about other writers trying to use him. He also betrayed a sense of feeling both displaced and out of place among the new generation of literary intellectuals.[13]

In his frank way Eric suggested to his father that his criticism of Manhattan's literary and social life probably reflected a feeling of insecurity on his part, a feeling that he and his group of writers no longer held center stage. They were no longer the young writers on the move, being watched with keen interest by the critics and reading public. The younger generation had become the older generation. Matthew strongly denied his son's psychological interpretation. "In truth," the elder Josephson argued, "we had a most intense social life; saw hundreds of people; were given numerous parties or dinners, some of them very lively occasions, at which I 'throned' as much as I cared to." He further maintained that his "misanthropy" derived not from any sense of insecurity or jealousy but "from the feeling that too few of the peope I see are worthy of much esteem, or have something to 'give' mentally." Josephson cited his talks with Aragon's friend Jean-Paul Sartre, then visiting New York, as some of the few stimulating discussions he had had in the city. But his explanation seems forced; it seems to confirm as much as refute Eric's charge.[14]

Despite his claims to the contrary, Josephson was indeed uncomfortable with the new breed of writers appearing in New York in the 1940s. A changing of the guard was taking place, as a group of writers somewhat younger than Josephson and with sharply different political views began to dominate the cultural scene. The most energetic and articulate of the young Turks tended to coalesce around the Partisan Review. In the 1940s the Partisan Review offices located just east of Greenwich Village at 45 Astor Place housed the most dynamic and controversial literary organ in the city. Its staff and contributors included some of the brightest intellectuals in the country, men such as Phillip Rahv, William Phillips, Sidney Hook, James Burnham, Harold Rosenberg, Fred Dupee, Paul Goodman, Lionel Trilling, Clement Greenberg, Delmore Schwartz, William Barrett, and Irving Howe. They held in common a love for modern literature and a hatred for Stalinists and fellow travelers. Such a volatile combination of attitudes, needless to say, caught the attention of the reading public—including Matthew Josephson.[15]

Partisan Review had a colorful and fluctuating history. The magazine had been founded in 1934 as a cultural arm of the New York City John Reed Club. One of its primary goals was to provide a forum for literary criticism, a forum that was lacking in the New Masses. In 1937, in the shadow of the Spanish Civil War and the Moscow trials, the magazine declared its independence of the Communist party and any other organized political group, including the League of American Writers. Editors Rahv and Phillips were now joined by Dwight Macdonald, and the magazine entered its Trotskyist phase. An editorial in December 1937 announced the severance of ties with the Communists: "Any magazine, we believe, that aspires to a place in the vanguard of literature today, will be revolutionary in tendency; but we are also convinced that any such magazine will be unequivocally independent." They wanted to be radical but not regimented. Bitterly opposed to the partinost conception of art espoused by the Stalinists and more and more attracted to Trotsky's example, they vigorously asserted the autonomy and permanence of art regardless of politics. As Phillips later remarked, they "were for purity in politics and impurity in literature."[16]

After Pearl Harbor the Partisan Review continued to emphasize culture over politics. Although its detestation of Stalin, Russia, and the CPUSA remained steadfast, its Trotskyism waned as Phillips and Rahv strongly supported the war effort and welfare capitalism. The contents of the magazine during the war years tended to be much more ontological than ideological; essays argued more about aesthetics than dialectics. Rather than issuing political manifestos, the editors concentrated on formal literary criticism. During the early 1940s *Partisan Review* increasingly concerned itself with the plight of the alienated intellectual, the disenchanted writer, the man in retreat from politics. Kafka, Koestler, Orwell, and even T. S. Eliot were put forth as guides to follow. But as the conflict neared its end and Americans speculated about the postwar world, the editors felt compelled to express their political opinions once again. The threat of Stalin and the Soviet Union abroad and the resurgence of the Popular Front at home came to dominate their attention in 1945–46. In numerous articles in the mid–1940s, Rahv, Phillips, Burnham, Hook, and others lashed out at Stalinism, Russia, and American fellow travelers.[17]

One former fellow traveler of the 1930s was Matthew Josephson, and he took special interest in the crusade launched by the *Partisan Review*. In the early 1940s he had come into contact with the magazine's staff through his newly formed friendship with Delmore Schwartz, who had joined the editorial board in 1943. He was impressed with Schwartz's poems and especially his short stories. "There was the charm of the unexpected; and l'humeur noir." During 1945 Schwartz and Josephson met occasionally for lunch and their discussions were wide-ranging, stimulating, and not always genteel. In March 1945 Schwartz and Phillip Rahv attended a cocktail party hosted by the Josephsons at their Essex House suite. Matthew engaged the two "*Partisan Review* boys" in a friendly debate, admonishing them for their growing political conservatism and anti-Soviet mania. The conversation grew quite animated and extended, prompting them to agree to continue it over lunch the next day. Matthew described the luncheon meeting in his journal. He noted that the *Partisan Review*, although started by Communists, was now a predominantly literary review with "political overtones that are pessimistic and defeatist." He asked the two editors why they kept saying that the United States was winning the war but losing the peace. Russia, they responded, represented a totalitarian monstrosity which would destroy America unless stopped soon. To them, Soviet communism was the same as nazism—a terrible menace. The three then waged a heated argument that resulted only in hardening positions.[18]

Josephson's discussion of the luncheon debate in his journal was bitter. He observed that the main contention of the "poor partisans" against fellow travelers like himself was that Stalin and Russia "are not *pure* enough; they have become disillusioned." They now had abandoned all hope of a socialist solution and offered "nothing but reading good books" as an alternative. Such a course, if followed, would lead to a wave of reaction. Josephson penned a sharp description of the *Partisan Review* group:

> The former Trotskyists have been the most effective reactionaries. They are experts in proletarian movements and eagerly lend their services to the Henry Luces, who accept them as intimate advisers at high compensation. It seems to be increasingly an easier transfer. Though they accuse Soviet Sympathizers of "immoralism" it is they who have adopted it with facility. Disillusioned, they devote themselves even to red-baiting, are well paid for it.

He wondered why they were so shocked to discover that Stalin as politician was less than pure. "When," he asked, "has there been anything else?" He suggested that they examine their own government first, since they were so concerned about power politics.[19]

At their suggestion Josephson wrote a letter to the editors of *Partisan Review* in which he elaborated on his critique of their position. He first acknowledged that he had always admired "small literary reviews that have few readers and high intentions." Young writers, he insisted, should attack "older writers, stuffed shirts, pundits, academicians, jobholders, and all that." After commenting that *Partisan Review* seemed "more alive" than most other literary journals, he began analyzing their editorial philosophy. And in the process he revealed his criticism of the emerging new breed of writers. He struck hard at the growing emphasis upon New Criticism and *explication du texte*. "The Curse of the present crop of younger writers . . . seems to me its aestheticism, its bookishness and its imitativeness. I should guess that for every one boy or girl who tries to do something imaginative or creative there are now five or ten who stand ready to provide a 'line by line' criticism." Josephson bemoaned the loss of interest among the younger writers in social themes and their hostility toward literary realism, as well as their lack of concern with the sources of a work or its social or moral effects. *Partisan Review*, he contended, "shows this disposition to playing the 'literary critick,' and placing perfection of form (which I see very little of) above having new ideas, or creating something that has power and truth." He also wondered why readers should trust the magazine's writers, who were so unstable in their own political convictions. After all, they had started as Communists, then turned to Trotsky, and now were headed in a variety of different directions, some even crawling belatedly, Josephson observed, into their "Ivory towers." Moreover, they seemed preoccupied with the supposed menace of Stalinist Russia, repeatedly linking Soviet communism with nazism. Josephson concluded his letter with a lesson in history:

> History is like the Perils of Pauline weekly serial thriller in the movies. The trouble with some of your circle is that they always expect the end next week and are continually being surprised when the darn thing continues.
>
> Those who have studied history earnestly have learned to be humble about their prophecies and not anticipate next week's developments with arrogance. Thus your face need not be so red when it turns out afterward that Soviet Communism and German nazism are not the same thing but are fighting each other to the death; or that Russia will fight Japan also.

Josephson had yet to be convinced that Russia was the imperialist menace that Rahv, Phillips, Hook, Burnham, and others maintained it was.[20]

Josephson's attitude toward Stalinist Russia had been tempered a great deal since his early enthusiasm for the Soviet experiment in the 1930s. However, he could not easily turn his back on the country that had offered the greatest hope to the world, even if that hope had been betrayed. In the 1940s he continued to clarify his attitude toward Stalinist Russia. Early in 1944 he wrote a letter to Eric, now stationed in France, in which he revealed that his affection for the Russian people and their social experiment remained steady. His opinion of their leader, on the other hand, had diminished considerably. He explained that on principle he was opposed to Stalin, but he saw no point during "these delicate times" in carping at him. Josephson continued to place his faith in the Russian people, hoping that they would "see the light themselves—re political democracy." He made it clear to his son, however, that he was not at all satisfied with Russian collectivism in its current mold:

> I want the Russians to have whatever political system suits them best—provided they don't harm other peoples, which I think they don't want to do—but also I want them to add on political democracy, the "rights of man," the writ of habeas corpus which the American and British constitutions provide for. Someday, in my opinion, they must come to this. But they think economic security and justice come first. Perhaps they are right. But I will never be content until they do add those other great human privileges encouraging freedom of thought, individual rights before the law to fair trial, etc.

If such reforms did occur, he pragmatically maintained, there should be no fundamental conflict between Russia and the United States. "What the hell is the difference what system we call ourselves, so long as it works, produces, keeps people busy and happy and progressing." Josephson still harbored a persistent, if politically naive, faith that the Russian masses would assert themselves and their human rights. In 1945 he commented: "In Russia I see beyond Stalin and the totalitarian communism and nationalism. The people are on the march, and they have always been apocalyptic."[21]

Josephson's commitment to the Russian social experiment exercised an almost hypnotic effect upon his thinking; it caused him to adjust his stance time and again. As had been the case in the late 1930s, after the Nazi-Soviet pact, he tended when discussing Russia to shelve temporarily his humanitarian idealism and adopt a pragmatic perspective. In April 1945 he reflected on the increasing number of former radicals who were assuming the role of disillusioned Jeremiahs, complaining of the power politics employed by Stalin in running the war. He wondered why all the sudden shock and indignation. "Russia is not pure and we never were. . . . When was there ever politics without power? Power to get the votes, run a machine, write the laws your crowd wanted." Using a rather strained historical analogy, Josephson implied that he still believed that Stalin was doing more good than harm:

> But the wonder is that the world does move. That great leaders like Lincoln, Lenin, and even the rather corny Roosevelt, or the harsh Stalin, include tremendous human gains with their power-drives. Did not Abe Lincoln play power-politics plenty? All the purists of his time were sick of him because he would not emancipate the slaves. A trimmer and a coward he was called. But when the hour struck he wrote the famous Emancipation Proclamation.

When the emergency of conducting the war was over, he suggested, Stalin would turn his attention to improving Russian domestic life; he would issue his own Emancipation Proclamation.[22]

Josephson still believed that the Russian social system, while admittedly flawed, served a useful purpose. He refused to give up on it. Instead he saw "some gains out of the rise of Soviet Russia to a place in the sun, as a victorious great power moving toward vast constructions. How can we or England remain Tory, with cycles of depression, and old soldiers selling apples in the streets, when Russia is building up socialism. It will affect our policy internally. Against others' gloom here, I remain hopeful." Josephson was correct in one of his predictions. Russia would certainly affect domestic life in the United States. But not exactly in the positive way he envisioned.[23]

During the war years Josephson spent his free time planning, researching, and writing a biography of Stendhal, for many years his "favorite" author, which he had planned ever since completion of the study of Zola in 1928. During the thirties Josephson's publisher had preferred for him to concentrate on historical studies. Not until 1944, after years of deferment, did Josephson confront Harcourt and announce that he was going to write the biography of Stendhal next. His publisher, however, thought that a study of Balzac would have wider appeal. The discussion quickly turned into an argument. Harcourt could not understand why Josephson insisted on writing about Stendhal, a subject already covered by two recently published works. After citing many reasons for the timeliness of his project, Josephson charged that Harcourt seemed to care more about sales than literary art. At that point the discussion ended. Josephson informed his long-time publisher that he would find someone else to print his Stendhal. Within a few days Doubleday agreed to publish the book.[24]

Josephson found in Stendhal a writer and a man who was even more attractive to him than Zola or Hugo. As a psychologist and a moralist Stendhal seemed particularly relevant both to Josephson's own life and situation and to the larger problems of twentieth-century society. Stendhal had even prophesied that future generations would find him so. As the times grew darker and many grew pessimistic about the outlook for Western civilization during the late 1930s, Josephson thought often of Stendhal and read further in his papers, letters, and journals. The more he learned about the amazingly introspective French writer, the more devoted he became. For in Stendhal Matthew thought he had discovered the meaning of his own life. Stendhal felt himself alienated, ever in conflict with the society of his time. This conflict runs through all his novels, in which the central problem, Josephson came to believe, is always the same: the education of a youth for life in a world that has lost its old values and has found no new goals; the formation of the youth's mind and character under the blows of experience; his pursuit of success, of "happiness," in a maze of snares, pitfalls, and self-doubt.

For most of his career Stendhal was the writer turned adventurer. Born in 1783, when Louis XVI still had his kingdom and his head, Stendhal was a child of the French Revolution. After witnessing the coup d'état of Napoleon, he became for a time an ardent follower of the military dictator who rose out of the revolution and conquered most of Europe. He served as a soldier and as one of Napoleon's young administrative aides, both participating in and describing in his journals the whole turbulent era of the Napoleonic wars. Then after Waterloo a disastrous period of reaction set in for Stendhal as well as for France and Europe. Fervent Jacobin that he was, liberal in politics, materialist in religion, it seemed to him that the imposition of Bourbon rule in France by means of foreign conquerers was a return to the Dark Ages. Rather than live under the rule of the restored Bourbons he left for Italy, where he took up residence in exile. In his early thirties, he, along with the rest of Europe, passed into a long "age of darkness," the Metternichean peace of 1815–48, with its Jesuitical politics, its feudal bureaucracy, its police rule, and its spies. Yet just as Stendhal maintained his critical balance under Napoleon, he exhibited in the age of Metternich a similarly independent and critical spirit. He neither conformed to the slogans and etiquette of the changed order, nor gave way to despair. In considerable intellectual solitude and obscurity he continued to write, laboring to perfect the expression of the cruelly realistic philosophy by which he lived and survived and through which he addressed himself, as he often said, to those who would come fifty or a hundred years after him. Steadfastly he protested at his times, holding that they, and not he, were out of touch with realities. Stendhal was a philosopher of human freedom. But he taught that such values as freedom and justice do not come easily; they must be fought for with enthusiasm, will, and energy.

Josephson particularly identified with Stendhal's war against cant, hypocrisy, Jesuitism, respectability, conventionalism, and romanticism during a time when he felt not only alone but also hounded and persecuted. In 1941 he told Christian Gauss, the Princeton scholar, of his interest in Stendhal: "To me Stendhal, who refused to be engulfed by a 'wave of darkness' of the Metternichean kind, with his hardy philosophy, is peculiarly a man for this time. . . . He has been my companion and guide, over and over again." He described his planned biography of the French novelist as "my labor of love" because it enabled him to return to the "eternal things of literature from the social questions that have absorbed—not leave the latter, in any sense, but to seek renewed strength before returning to them." The ideological warfare of the 1930s and his historical writing had wearied Josephson; he needed both a respite from the politics of literature and renewed contact with creative writing. In the spring of 1943 he confessed to Kenneth Burke:

> I still hold to these truths: that men in Literary and Artistic circles know all too little about the real world outside their purlieus. That's why I enjoy leaving those circles for intervals. It is nonetheless true that I also enjoy coming back to 'em. I am neither all black nor all white. . . . As for me I am really a Stendhalian, as I will demonstrate in my next volume. It has been more or less under way since 1937 and will have part of seven years' reflection woven into it.

Increasingly during the war years Josephson feared that the United States might experience a conservative postwar reaction similar to the one that had swept over France after Waterloo. As he explained to Robert Lynd in 1943: "What I fear most now is the shadow of Metternich. On all sides the old regime will try to reconstitute to itself and postpone all threats— this time for the sake of monopoly capitalism instead of church and throne."[25]

There is much of Matthew Josephson in his portrait of Stendhal. He took pains to make his work speak directly to contemporary issues and circumstances. Repeatedly he emphasizes the timeliness of his subject. When the conservative reaction set in after 1815 in France, Stendhal refused to be "right-thinking" and for long periods exiled himself from Bourbon France. "At this period, after Waterloo," Josephson writes, "one might say that Stendhal was 'underground' in Italy, as men would take to the 'underground' more than a century later in the odious times of Hitler, Mussolini, and Marshal Pétain." He proudly notes the popularity of Stendhal among the young French writers of the Resistance, who read his works "with almost religious fervor, for countless pages of his novels, essays, and particularly of his autobiographical and epistolary writings, breathed an intellectual revolt that was subtle and resourceful as well as stubborn."[26]

Josephson is even more direct in relating Stendhal's situation in the age of Metternich to that of America at war's end. Both were periods of war-weariness and confusion; both witnessed the emergence of conservative movements intent upon destroying radicalism and heedless of civil liberties. "But then, as now," Josephson observes, "society was divided fundamentally into 'Reds' and 'Blacks': those who believed that the progress, the liberation of man must be carried on endlessly and by revolution if need be; those who desired, above all, the conservation of the old order and the old faith." As in the United States during the 1940s, society then "lived in fear, fear even of ideas." Stendhal, who loved liberty, refused to make his peace with the counterrevolution of the "men in black," the new Jesuitical order after Waterloo. He refused to turn chameleon and become a supporter of the new regime. This intellectual courage and honesty, this refusal to go along with the crowd, was for Josephson Stendhal's greatest attribute. "He too might have been a 'success' if he had brought himself to write and think like others. But he had been stubborn in his quarrel with his age, its fashions, conventions, and its mariage de convenance with despotism. At bottom he had never sold out."[27]

Nor would Josephson. He makes it clear that as the United States entered the postwar era he would continue to fight for those principles he had espoused for years. Again he speaks through his biographical subject. Guided by his sense of history, Stendhal clung stubbornly to his convictions as a man of the Enlightenment:

> Stendhal tenaciously believed in the eighteenth-century concepts of reason and progress, by whose lights we still struggle to advance again; but he also warns us that besides having humane ideals we must have will, enthusiasm, and energy in order to realize them. This exponent of extreme individualism, hating the reaction that dominates Europe in his time, is no political retrograde but a realistic democrat whose minimum demands are for the free press, the jury trial, a parliamentary system, and universal education.

Like Stendhal, Josephson still placed his faith in reason, scientific knowledge, and the march of the common man toward self-improvement. He also retained his emphasis on the role of the writer turned public man. Just because he and others had made mistakes in the past was no reason to abandon ideals or activism. Stendhal's "political convictions," he maintains, "despite frequent changes of emphasis, were always predominantly those of radical democracy." Politics "never ceased to interrupt the concert of his imagination with its pistol shots." In quoting Stendhal Josephson clearly indicates his own perception of the ideal role for the writer: "Writers are the hussars of liberty. And always in action, sometimes they retreat, but only to advance again." In the long run, he emphasizes in concluding, it would be such literary activists, not the despots and economic royalists, who would control the future.[28]

Josephson's portrait of Stendhal, published in 1946, is a fine literary biography, a comprehensive, sympathetic, richly detailed, and dramatic study of undoubtedly one of the strangest men in literary history. Yet despite Josephson's zeal for his subject, his *Stendhal*, while in many ways superb, still falls somewhat short of his *Zola*, which remains his best literary biography. It does so primarily because of the significant difference between the two subjects. His biography of Zola beautifully reveals a writer and a man with a clearly delineated personality and a cohesive personal philosophy. In *Zola* Josephson's structural motif of the writer turned public man dramatically dominates the work and neatly defines the subject's development from naturalist to activist. Stendhal, however, defied such straightforward treatment or interpretation. His was a complex, deeply layered personality at odds with his environment, vainly trying to understand his sense of isolation yet never really succeeding. Like his biographer, he was a bundle of paradoxes and false starts. Instead of a tightly woven progression, the carpet of his life was full of frayed threads and a complicated pattern, replete with vivid contrasts from start to finish. Where Zola's life was crystal clear and readily perceived, Stendhal's was fuzzy, full of subtleties and shadows. In short, Stendhal posed quite a challenge for any biographer.

In writing about Stendhal, Josephson tries to portray all facets of the man, to clarify every nuance, to leave nothing out. The overall result is a blurred image. Stendhal's essential character, if he ever really had one, gets somewhat lost among his many roles and fluctuating attitudes. Josephson devotes considerable attention to Stendhal the soldier, lover, diarist, musicologist, mathematician, wit, raconteur, archeologist, tour guide, precursor of Freud, duelist, diplomat, rake, novelist, republican, and exile. Finally, near the end of the book, he does point out that the key to Stendhal's life was actually very simple—his goal had always been the creation of a literary masterpiece. Josephson quotes Stendhal confessing, "The true occupation of my soul has always been the same: to make *un chef d'oeuvre*." Such a revelation prompts Matthew to exclaim: "O admirable consistency! In those thirty and more years, despite every temptation or interruption, he had continued the same stern chase, as unswerving as that of Captain Ahab in pursuit of the White Whale." Josephson, however, unlike Ahab, keeps changing course, veering away from Stendhal's elusive chase in order to chart in minute detail the "temptations" or "interruptions" that he surmounted along the way. In fact, he spends more time discussing Stendhal's numerous love affairs than his literary works. He also exaggerates Stendhal's proletarian sympathies and political activism, foisting upon the complex Frenchman the social consciousness of a modern fellow traveler. For all his opposition to entrenched political conservatism, Stendhal, like Josephson himself, was fundamentally bourgeois. Thus the ruling metaphor of Stendhal's literary quest becomes blurred as the study progresses.[29]

Despite its somewhat blurred focus, Josephson's *Stendhal* represented a major contribution to the growing body of writing about the long neglected French novelist. And the critics recognized it as such. The *New York Post* characterized Josephson's latest book as a "brilliant, highly readable and becomingly modest biography." The reviewer for *Time* magazine, while noting the author's penchant for "tinkling trifles," concluded nevertheless that "like Josephson's *Victor Hugo* it is the best and most comprehensive English study of its subject, a careful collection of material, skillfully assembled and organized." The Book Find Club thought *Stendhal* good enough to select as its monthly offering. But the high point in the reception given *Stendhal* was a review by John Erskine, Josephson's former professor at Columbia. He asserted that Matthew Josephson "is on the way to be, if he isn't already, our ablest American biographer." In a letter to his former rebellious student, Erskine was even more effusive:

> When I read your fine biography of Victor Hugo I had the impulse to tell you at once what a splendid piece of work I think it is. Some inertia made me postpone writing. Now with your *Stendhal* in my hands I feel the same impulse, and this time I must not let the occasion slip by.
>
> You must know what a delight it is to find an American scholar writing biography of such character—all the more delight because you deal with great figures in those early decades of the 19th century. . . .
>
> During the last few days I have been reading Stefan Zweig's Balzac. It seems to me that your biographies challenge comparison with Zweig's work—and mind you, I have always thought of him as the prince of biographers.

Josephson had truly mastered the difficult art of literary biography. But he had little chance to reflect on his latest success. The war was now over, and the age of darkness that he had long feared quickly began to engulf the American scene. Soon he himself would feel its chilling effects.[30]

13 A DIVIDED SOUL

With the end of World War II and the onset of the Cold War and McCarthyism, Matthew Josephson entered what he himself might have called the Stendhalian phase of his life. He self-consciously identified with Stendhal both as a critic of a reactionary political system and as an introspective, middle-aged writer nagged by personal doubts and frustrations. Josephson believed that the peace was ushering in a new era of repression in which the authorities, much like those in France after Waterloo, would try to force intellectuals to conform or be silent. And like Stendhal he was determined to cling stubbornly to his convictions and to his right to speak out in defense of them. After the war Josephson also subjected himself and his literary career to a probing analysis reminiscent of Stendhal's famous self-scrutiny. As he reached and passed his forty-fifth year he assessed his professional career and his private life and found both wanting. His analyses of his frustrations and anxieties, while typical of writers of his age and circumstances, were distinctive for their frequency and intensity.

Since the 1920s Josephson had grappled with three frequently conflicting desires. He wanted to strike a balance between his art and his politics, to combine his bohemian inclinations and his bourgeois tastes, and to write a novel of great power and merit. Of course, he had more success in achieving the first two goals than the last. And for most of his career he had been able to accept such a mixed performance. During his middle years, however, he anguished more and more over his failure to produce a work of fiction. Like many people entering the second half of life Josephson had attained success and some affluence only to discover that he was not satisfied. Ever since his unsuccessful attempt in the 1920s he had remained a frustrated novelist. Although pleased with his accomplishments as journalist, biographer, and historian, he had always considered such fields subordinate to imaginative literature. His study of Stendhal only intensified the problem, since it once again brought him into contact with one of the great novelists. Now, approaching fifty, he still wondered what he was to do with his life.

In his journal of March 1946 Josephson reflected on his situation. "Endowed with some little funds, property," he observed, "I am nevertheless obsessed with the need for security—in order to have some rope to feel 'free' someday. To 'pursue happiness,' to read or do what I like, to write what I most enjoy, for the pleasure of writing it." Josephson wanted desperately to again try his hand at creative writing. In April 1946 he explained his dissatisfaction with his career:

> When I am melancholy I am chiefly troubled by the fear that, for several years—while improving my circumstances in the material sense—my position of literary influence over my contemporaries has gone down. How to correct this? I wish to write imaginative prose, moral tales, essays of such value that they cannot be by-passed as I fear some of my books have been in recent years by those I would prefer most as my readers. This thought always stays with me. "Il faut se secouer l'âme." Sometimes I think of planning a novel of dramatic treatment.

A few months later he confessed that he craved "true literary fame, nay 'glory.' But where can I go that my influence and skill might be fully displayed, used, esteemed?" In these Stendhalian observations Josephson disclosed, perhaps without even realizing it, the irony of his situation. He repeatedly told himself that he wanted enough material security to enable him to write what he wanted to write, for the public he wanted to address, yet he was so concerned about money that he never felt he had enough to stop his commercial writing and take the risk of producing a novel. And to him such a step was indeed a risk. His earlier failure as a novelist left doubts about his creative ability that always remained with him.[1]

By June of 1946 Josephson was beginning to recognize that his mate-

234 A Divided Soul

rial concerns had markedly affected his literary decisions. At that time he had just finished a lucrative article on the longshoreman's union for *Collier's* and was again kicking himself for doing such "hackwork." In a lengthy journal entry he took inventory of himself and his career. What precipitated his analysis was his reading of George Gissing's *New Grub Street*, published almost sixty years before. In that work the English novelist reflected on the angst of working at the writer's trade in a society that viewed literature as a commodity. Gissing portrayed the protagonist, Edwin Reardon, attempting to preserve some vestige of literary integrity while at the same time making a living as a professional writer. Josephson noted in his journal that in Gissing's era writers feared the vulgarizing effect of the popular press and the circulating library upon literary craftmanship. And the situation had since worsened considerably. "Now without self-questioning we deliberately write to order for a public regimented by book clubs and multimillion reader magazines dominated by advertising. The game of literature is openly directed toward mass audiences and mass production." He then turned his attention to himself:

> And what of myself? It seems to me that I have been a divided soul. I have particularly adapted my original impulse to that of a semi-popular writer. My hope is that I have not yet been ruined or debased beyond repair. I feel a considerable resilience in myself. But to examine myself truthfully is to perceive that I have mingled ideas of partly commecial utility, e.g., the biography as popular medium, with ambitions of a higher sort.

Now he had just published *Stendhal*, his "work of love." He wondered, however, whether he had waited too long to do so, remarking that its quality might have been adversely affected by the "strain of journalism for the *New Yorker* and the *Saturday Evening Post*." [2]

Josephson found Gissing's insights into the struggle between literature and commercialism particularly relevant to his own circumstances and "divided soul." *New Grub Street*, ending with Reardon's defeat at the hands of cant, commercialism, and corruption, provided a "serious warning to me." He resolved henceforth to write "only that which appeals to me naturally, that which invites me. Then let the earnings or consequences be what they may." Josephson pointed to his recent article in *Collier's* as an example of what to avoid in the future. "I should have weighed what was truly possible for me. I did not really need the money, and should have begun to retreat from the money-system." He then grew serious and stern with himself. He was not through baring his soul; there was more to confess, more flagellation to endure, more resolutions to make. "I must," he affirmed, "rid myself of anxiety over money, provided there is enough to eat with and live simply. In many ways I have followed after false gods, inasmuch as I feverishly hoped to win by speculation a considerable fortune; and also desired to keep adding to my funds by writing of a popular sort. It was a form of greed that possessed me. I feel chastened now." He also regretted his loss of influence among the younger generation of writers. "For a long time I enjoyed being regarded as one of those who gave direction to the advance guard, even in currents of thought. My influence seems to have declined."[3]

As he concluded that day's lengthy discussion in his journal, Josephson turned to the subject that underlay so much of his growing malaise. He was getting old. "I have also," he admitted, "the gnawing problem of growing middle-aged: I am not happy anymore; and my family does not give me much joy at present. I feel at times constraint in the presence of my children; I feel myself unable to speak or act with freedom, to be myself." Josephson was now forty-seven, and he began to experience a rather conventional mid-life crisis of doubt. The often gregarious man turned inward; even in the company of his family he rarely exhibited his true feelings. In September 1946 he noted that he was becoming "a terrific grumbler at my family. This is curious, because I am not considered such by persons outside; or seldom. To the ladies I am all sweetness and light." At social occasions Josephson played the misanthrope, convinced that those around him were unthinking or uncaring companions. In 1948, while wintering in Manhattan, he discussed in his journal the considerable social life of the season. In assessing some of the people he had recently seen he wrote: "Some men lack intelligence, though they have character. Brooks has character but he is not really interested in what he is writing. This goes for Dos Passos also, whom I saw by chance in an art gallery. He is more cultivated than most other writers; but he is frantic and wrong-headed in his politics to my mind. . . . Lionel Trilling, critic turned novelist, seems disgusting."[4]

Josephson also saw less of Malcolm Cowley and Kenneth Burke, both of whom were spending much of their time teaching and lecturing at universities around the country. When he did see them he realized that they were different, both artistically and politically. There had always been rivalry as well as friendship between them. For several years after the war Josephson and Cowley were particularly at odds. Matthew believed that his long-time friend and neighbor had overreacted to the political events of 1939–45 and had become "conservative." At another party at the home of Van Wyck Brooks in 1948 Josephson bluntly revealed his disgust at Cowley's political quietism. Cowley was at the gathering and began talking about Archibald MacLeish, with whom he had recently been collaborating on some literary work. "I said," Josephson reported to Burke, "'Malcolm, how could you play with a boy like that who let you down when you had a job under him in Washington?'" He was referring to Cowley's short-lived job with the Office of Facts and Figures in 1942, before he was hounded out by the conservative press. "And Malcolm said," Matthew continued, "'He was nice to me.' At which I became wild and said: 'Oh the more they kick you around the more you like it.' He was somewhat disturbed and left the room." That Cowley no longer was active in social or political causes was true to a degree. During the postwar years he admittedly suffered from a "sense of guilt" about his political past and tended to immerse himself in literature and criticism. In 1948, for example, he refused to support Henry Wallace's candidacy, while Josephson played an active role in the campaign. But he was not apathetic, as Matthew in his less understanding moments charged.[5]

What bothered Josephson most about his old friends, as he noted repeatedly in his journal after 1945, was the suspicion that neither Burke nor Cowley was interested in his political and journalistic writings. This dealt him a far more damaging blow than either of them realized. They were not so much opposed to what Matty was writing as they were disappointed in how he was writing. Cowley believed that Josephson, in pursuing lucrative commercial assignments and in involving himself in politics, was not doing justice to his art. "Kenneth and I felt," he recently recalled, "that Matty was doing too much commercial journalism—and political journalism too, which was decidedly noncommercial, but in which he didn't pay enough attention, so we thought, to the simple craft of writing."[6]

Nor did Josephson find much comfort among his family. His obligations as husband and father gave him a sense of "individual constraint" and aroused "anxieties on pecuniary grounds." Moreover, his dominant position within the family was eroding. Ever since his childhood, when he had been the focus of his mother's adoring attention, Matthew had become accustomed to playing center stage at home. "As a father," his son Carl remembered, "he sometimes behaved more like a jealous sibling than a parent, demanding everyone's attention, but particularly my mother's." In the postwar years, however, Josephson began to lose his favored status. Hannah and the children were now immersed in their own activities. The boys were grown up and had opinions and directions of their own. Nevertheless, Matthew frequently worried about their future. "My relationship with my sons," he observed in 1947, "is overcast by anxiety for their success in life." He feared that they would always look to him for financial support, that they would continue "to lean upon their parent and his sense of Family Duty, and his breadwinning power." And such dependence, he felt, directly threatened his personal and artistic freedom. "To 'carry' them, I must go on being a hack-writer of magazine articles."[7]

Matty's relationship with Hannah was increasingly ambivalent. Still vivacious and attractive at middle age, Hannah was an amazing woman, at once a caring wife, concerned mother, efficient house manager, gracious hostess, research assistant, and intelligent conversationalist. She had long been a source of strength and support for Matthew, far more so than he realized. By the 1940s, however, she was becoming a career woman, getting involved in her own interests and in the process demonstrating her own independent personality and feisty nature. She refused to let Matty dominate her. During and after World War II she gained more intellectual independence of him, and in the process some of the romance faded. Hannah began a literary career of her own, first as a translator of some of Aragon's works and then as a historian and biographer. Moreover, in 1949 she would become the busy librarian of the American Academy of Arts and Letters, as well as editor of its publications. Thus she was away from home a great deal. And away from Matty. He had always depended on her for assistance and attention, and he did not welcome her new career. In December 1947 he remarked: "Hannah also aspires to be an 'author.' As a consequence I have three *dichter* to carry, for her help to me is removed. Nor is she of help in meeting the practical problems of our life, like traveling to a better climate or finding a home in the city for the winter." A year later he again complained that Hannah's literary interests interfered with his own freedom, as well as affecting their relations together. "She is always fatigued, and distracted, and even ill at times. . . . The truth is that I do very little with her; she follows her own ideas and yields very little to mine."[8]

In his heart Josephson loved Hannah dearly. But he still had a penchant for other women, and he succumbed to it more easily as Hannah pursued her new career interests. During 1945 Matthew began another affair, this time with a woman considerably younger than himself. He had always been attracted by charming and intelligent women, and he was also attractive to them. A succession of women in some measure supplied the admiration and recognition that he felt the world at large denied him. No woman, not even Hannah, could supply all the attention he needed. Like Stendhal he desired both *l'amour amitié* and *l'amour passion*. His ideal, as he explained, was to have both a wife and a mistress:

> Many men, in middle age or earlier, tire of the little wife, the same record being played. They dream of a Concubine. With the wife there are associated not only sexual activity, but responsibilities, demands of family, economics, children, diapers, dishes. Nevertheless the Concubine is also not enough. The wife is sister, buddy, mother to the children and the man; and in truth the man likes all the scrambled *vie de famille* too.

Just as Josephson wanted to enjoy both the pastoral serenity of country life in Sherman and the cosmopolitan excitement of city life in Manhattan, he also wanted the advantages of middle-class family life and the adventure of a bohemian affair. He discovered, however, that maintaining such a dual life-style was not a simple task.[9]

During the 1940s the "other woman" was not a writer like Katherine Anne Porter but an unhappily married art curator living in New York. They had first met in 1941, but it was not until three years later that their relationship grew close. That year she approached Matthew at a party. He remembered that she was "troubled, her life was a struggle. Amid the noise of others talking I tried to give her counsel, to help her deal with her problems. My counsel was 'Stendhalian.' I felt how, in her own uninhibited state, she was drawn to me, hung on my words, and showed her affection." He was drawn to her. She seemed "young-looking, beautiful, clever, strong (my type)." Six years younger than he, she had a striking figure, blue eyes, a deep, but soft voice, and a quick wit. To him she was full of life and, imprévu, "feminine and warm and demonstrably affectionate with me." By 1945 they were lovers, and they saw each other frequently during the rest of the decade. "I have never," Josephson admitted at the time, "felt the appeal of any woman so long, in a romantic sense (different from my marriage). Usually they have pursued me, and I, after a brief interlude, have tired of the role I played before them. But here I have been remarkably constant. Merely to see her for an hour, at a cafe, was a consolation." That they both were dissatisfied with the progress of their careers and with their family lives provided a common thread binding them together. They engaged in ingenious subterfuges to keep their relationship a secret from their spouses. Josephson admitted that they were "very hypocritical," but he could not help it. He was "mad for her." Well into middle age, uncertain about his career, and clinging desperately to his youth and his sexuality, he felt that she was exactly what he needed at that turbulent period in his life. The affair, he observed in July 1947, "has been as good for my hopes as for my *amour propre*. In effect, all joy is not lost. Life need not be a routine affair." The bohemian in Josephson had again come to the fore.[10]

Josephson's resolution to rid himself of his monetary concerns and write imaginative literature was short-lived. He soon accepted another assignment from the *Saturday Evening Post* to write a series on A. P. Giannini, the California financial tycoon. The articles took six months to research and write but were quite profitable. Matthew again felt guilty for doing them. He was earning money but not living up to his own expectations as a writer. Commercial journalism, with its periodic injections of money and success, was a medication he could not refuse. By the end of 1947 his mood again was dark. "I have continued in poor spirits," he wrote, "with little stomach for resumption of regular writing. Everything seems to vex me. My sons home for the holiday, my wife. They neither understand nor enjoy my moodiness." He confessed, however, that "reason tells me that my emotional difficulties should not be laid to them." At times he seemed to admit his own weaknesses and deficiencies. He questioned whether it was possible for him to return to serious writing at his advanced age. What he feared most, he confessed, was that "my potential for writing has been declining. The truth may be that I have fallen into arrears; in trying to change directions, I find all sorts of unexpected difficulties." Six months later, in July 1948, he complained that he found writing "pot-boiling" magazine articles "more arduous than ever, each successive one. (The others seemed bad, the next always worse.)" He thus felt trapped, wanting desperately to climb out of his rut and write something of significance but unable to do so.[11]

During 1947 and 1948 Josephson still talked of writing a novel, one that would examine the pressing problems of modern society. In his journal he suggested that his own "middle-aged neurosis" might serve as the structure of the work. He then described the two primary causes of his melancholia: the anxiety of money and the anxiety of age and impotence, both sexual and literary. The fear of growing old and impotent "hung over me." The more he considered the subject, the more obsessive his anxiety became. "If one is calculating, introspective, detached," he recognized, "one goes round and round the problem, seeing no satisfactory solution. Panic seizes one. A terrible weight of foreboding, of self-pity; a waiting for death." He lingered over his sense of loneliness, frankly noting that this was especially keen "in the presence of others because they are less intelligent than I, or have less brains at any rate, and so resent me." After remarking how "galling" it was not to have gained more recognition in the literary world, Josephson conceded that for the most part his melancholy resulted from his not having achieved the expectations he had set for himself. He had not made his mark in creative literature. Like Stendhal he longed for a chef d'oeuvre.[12]

One of the primary reasons for Josephson's failure during the postwar years to find the time to write the novel of his dreams was that he felt compelled to devote his pen and his time more to political questions than to literature. In 1946 he commented, "I veer between turning to write prose fiction and going into the political arena." The contemporary situation in the United States revolted him; the forces of reaction and intolerance held the upper hand. "Our politics," he stressed, "smacks of mediocrity enthroned, of small venal men. Our press is cowardly and horribly biased, even 'censored' against dissenters." The economy in his view was quickly returning to its uncontrolled and monopolistic ways. Corruption was rampant in business, labor, and politics, and American foreign policy seemed imperialist and aggressive. The wartime alliance with Russia quickly turned into a struggle for international influence and markets; the Cold Warriors, he believed, had gained control of Washington.[13]

Josephson was determined to do what he could to combat such ills, even though he risked retaliation. For an address to a conference on Cultural Freedom and Civil Liberties in New York, sponsored by the Progressive Citizens of America (PCA), a group formed in support of Henry Wallace, Josephson chose as his subject the relationship of the writer to society, using Stendhal as his primary example. In preparing the speech he observed that he "feared that this would expose me to political and economic retribution, and knew most other liberal writers feared that greatly now. For this reason I decided to take part and 'stick my neck out.'" At the conference he commented that Stendhal's current appeal and timeliness reflected the fact that "throughout his life and in nearly all his writings he was profoundly interested in politics." Yet many American writers were abandoning any political involvement. Josephson wondered how anyone in the modern world could not be interested in politics. There were no longer any ivory towers to provide refuge. Where, he asked, "are there any garden walls high enough to afford immunity from the atom bomb?"[14]

Josephson then cited the numerous parallels between Stendhal's situation in post-Waterloo Europe and the American writer's position after

World War II. The age of Metternich was an age of reaction against the eighteenth-century Enlightenment and the French Revolution; similarly, postwar America seemed intent upon dismantling the structure of New Deal liberalism and the philosophy of the welfare state. Public opinion was being regimented by columnists and radio commentators who stupefied the masses with their own fears and prejudices:

> We are told that we must all join in a great conflict of ideologies, the underlying assumption of our own ideology being that there is something divine in our system of free enterprise while those who are opposed to it are all the children of the Devil. We are told this a hundred times a day over the radio and through the newspapers; and as writers we are urged and prodded to conform to this view of the world or pay the penalty. If we do not conform we are liable to be—well—investigated by the grand inquisitors of a committee of Congress that now sits permanently in judgment of what thoughts are patriotic and what are disloyal, what is American and what is un-American.

Independent writers who remained sympathetic to collectivism and who urged cooperation with the Soviets were being intimidated and isolated. To maintain one's principles under such conditions demanded a measure of courage and stoicism, and Josephson appreciated those who stood firm. As he surveyed his audience he noted that there "are some among us who have the honor of being singled out for prosecution by the Un-American Committee of the Congress."[15]

Josephson admitted in his speech that conditions in 1947 were not as bad as those in France after the Congress of Vienna. But the situation was getting worse, not better. More and more left-liberals were growing afraid to speak out. In the process they were betraying both their political ideals and their intellectual roles. He concluded by detailing several lessons to be drawn from earlier writers who had also lived under oppressive regimes. First of all, like Voltaire and Zola, writers "must have the courage to hang on to our power of reasoning when others around us are confused or emotionally stampeded by propaganda." Secondly, he suggested, the examples of Voltaire, Swift, and Stendhal demonstrated the power of humor and satire as weapons of ridicule. Instead of being defensive, writers should go on the attack. Finally, he warned against growing calloused and indifferent toward social and political issues. American writers, he stressed, must "reassert our feeings of humanity and our capacity for indignation."[16]

Josephson especially disliked those writers who had been active among the radical Left in the 1930s but who were now ideologues on the Right, writers such as Max Eastman, James Burnham, Richard Rovere, John Chamberlain, and Robert Cantwell.[17] He recognized that it would be difficult to make much headway against such entrenched conservatism. "I certainly feel myself," he told Kenneth Burke in April 1947, "driven underground mentally by all the incredible nonsense that is propagated everywhere and particularly through the medium of ex-men of light. The James Burnhams have the facilities of Life Magazine and an audience of twelve millions." His distaste for the "apostates" was intense and long-lasting. Several years later he analyzed them for Murray Kempton:

> The trouble is that the repentant liberals overwhelmed with guilt at having sent $5 to Loyalist Spain prematurely, now try to hang on to the coat-tails of the McCarthy's. They say: we know better than anyone else how to save the country from the few wretched Communists still surviving. And each outdoes the other in repenting, recanting, or whining or offering to commit atrocities against Communists or any other shameless and unrepenting heretics, however few their numbers.

Josephson harbored a similar disgust for the Americans for Democratic Action (ADA), the newly formed liberal political organization that combined a passionate support for the New Deal reform philosophy with a passionate hatred both for the Soviet Union and for the Popular Front mentality at home. He portrayed the ADA as "symptomatic of this Age of Cant. Or shall we call it the Age of Whiners?"[18]

At the same time, however, Josephson had little sympathy for orthodox Marxism and its few remaining literary advocates. His own fellow-traveling days with the CPUSA were now clearly over. Yet he saw no reason for badgering the American comrades. In September 1946 the press reported a purge of several literary Marxists from the party, including Ruth McKenney, Albert Maltz, and Isidor Schneider. Upon learning of this development Josephson commented in his journal that he had "always thought most of these literary Marxians rather foolish and no account. As a 'literary school' I did not rate them highly enough even to dispute with them. Now they are finished. (On the other hand I never believed in baiting them as James Farrell has done)." Josephson then reflected on his attitude toward the Communist party in general. He characterized his position as essentially the same one he held toward orthodox Christians and all orthodox persons. "Au fond I am scornful of orthodoxies and dogmatism. But I am willing to refrain, often enough, from mockery of such people if they seem truly convinced that they work good through their orthodoxy." [19]

If Josephson was reluctant to snipe at the Communists, he had no such reservations about lashing out against Cold War liberalism and Truman, who in Josephson's view had not only betrayed the New Deal but was also primarily responsible for starting and intensifying the Cold War with the Soviet Union. In 1947 Josephson delivered a speech in which he gave a sharply critical assessment of Truman's presidency. His opening remarks indicated the tone of the address:

> It is now nearly three years since President Franklin Roosevelt died and Harry Truman succeeded him. Three years that to many of us have seemed like a bad dream—a period in our national history that I would define as one of drift and muddle. Indeed I would say further that it was distinguished by its very absurdity, its highly comic qualities, even its sheer idiocy.

Josephson's analysis then grew more specific. He first commented on the disturbing erosion of civil liberties in the country. Truman's loyalty program was now in operation, and leftist liberals found themselves subject to questioning and harassment by the government. "Who would have believed that less than three years after the end of our war against German and Japanese tyranny, we ourselves would be trembling in fear for our right to freedom of thought, freedom of speech and freedom of peaceful petition and assembly?" Leftists lived in fear, Josephson maintained, because politicians, militarists, and commentators constantly warned that "we are in mortal danger of being ravished by a few communists." [20]

What the country needed was a leader courageous enough to be different and intelligent enough to provide a practical political alternative. Josephson found such a man in Henry Wallace. In September of 1946 Secretary of Commerce Wallace made national headlines when he gave a speech in Madison Square Garden in which he openly criticized the Truman administration's hard-line policy toward Russia. He saw no reason why the wartime collaboration with the Soviet Union could not be maintained. In his view Russia was not an imperialist power bent on conquering the world, but rather a country understandably concerned about its safety and seeking security by developing spheres of influence in Eastern Europe. The United States should recognize such realities, show goodwill toward its former ally, and thereby restore the spirit of trust that had developed between Roosevelt and Stalin. A few days later Truman clumsily dismissed Wallace from the cabinet. Since that time Wallace had attracted a considerable grass-roots political following made up primarily of militant trade unionists, disaffected left-liberals, and Negroes. In December 1946 the PCA was founded to reflect and espouse Wallace's political philosophy. After leaving the Truman administration Wallace accepted the editorship of the *New Republic* and soon used that influential platform to hammer away at Truman, the ADA, and the Republicans. By the end of 1947 he was ready to leave the Democratic party and start his own independent campaign for the presidency. As he explained, "There is no real fight between a Truman and a Republican. Both stand for a policy which opens the door to war in our lifetime and makes war certain for our children." [21]

In Josephson's eyes Henry Wallace was both an inspiring idealist and a practical politician, possessed of both overpowering earnestness and a moral austerity that clearly distinguished him from his peers in Washington. As early as January 1947 he was following Wallace's political fortunes with keen interest. In that month he expressed his admiration for the idealistic political maverick in a letter to Angus Cameron, a leftist editor at Little, Brown:

> I believe, at present, that Wallace—despite all the obstacles to be run—is doing a great thing whose values consist in what may be created five years hence. He has helped clear the air already. The run-of-the-mill liberals have only one counter-proposal: to buy a piece of a bet in Truman's crap game and hope to win a little bit at least. It did not work in 1946. It seems best to start clearing ground and setting up a sound structure. We must go into training and build the local organizations for a true Opposition Party, thus preparing ourselves for opportunities that may develop suddenly, on a big scale, some years hence.

Always the political optimist, Josephson believed that in the long run Wallace and the PCA could provide a genuine alternative to the politics of reaction and stalemate that had come to dominate the country. Toward the end of 1947 he reflected on Wallace's developing organization. When Wallace spoke out against the anti-Russian policy of Truman and Secretary of State Byrnes, Josephson "felt a great hope go through me. . . . There was someone who would speak the truth, who would say what we believed inside, that you cannot go threatening people with an atom bomb in one hand and a bankroll in the other and build world peace that way!" He compared Wallace's courageous stand to that of Zola in the Dreyfus case. He, too, "for a moment was the conscience of all mankind." [22]

As the fall presidential campaign got under way in 1948, Josephson debated what role he should play. He knew that Wallace had no chance of winning; in fact the net result of his candidacy would probably be to guarantee the election of Dewey. In September he discussed the problem in his journal:

> I like to think in terms of realities—Wallace and Co., are advocating all sorts of good things. The fact is that it is a campaign to build up a little, persecuted opposition party which must travel in the wilderness for long years. It will begin by insuring the election of Dewey. The negroes will not have their rights any sooner; the people without homes will not get decent housing any sooner.

The short term looked bleak, but what was the alternative? He could not in good conscience vote for Truman, nor could he sit idly by. "It all depends," he explained, "on whether you believe in working with a long-range 'visionary' party in this kind of world, and feel that such action may have some weight." But Josephson remained uncertain about what his personal role in the campaign should be. "I am troubled about what action to pursue: to conserve energy, holding that my brains and vision may be of use again if not crushed out? Or to undertake agitation and pamphleteering against l'Infame?" He recognized that his talent was "not for political action in the direct sense . . . but through the word." [23]

Josephson finally decided to act, to use his pen and his time as best he could to support Wallace and oppose the Red scare mentality that he felt was coming to dominate Washington and the country. He wrote pamphlets for the PCA, attended Wallace rallies, and donated money to the campaign. He also helped organize the Committee of 1,000 to Abolish the Thomas Committee (House Un-American Activities Committee, or HUAC). Josephson particularly enjoyed working with this group because it cut across the political spectrum. Its supporters included Republicans, ADA members, fellow travelers, and Wallaceites. Moreover, there were not any orthodox Marxists to stir up trouble. As he told his friend Thomas Cochran, the respected economic historian, "There have not been any hard-boiled little comrades in the boiler-room to speed organization along. This makes the organization a little softer than usual; but the results have been encouraging. Again the experience of people of opposing political affiliations working together may help cure the terrible wounds of schism in the liberal ranks."[24]

Of course the schism in the liberal ranks was not healed; it only widened. Truman's unexpected victory and Wallace's surprisingly poor showing in November 1948 represented a triumph for the Cold War liberalism of the ADA and a disastrous setback for the postwar popular front that Josephson envisioned. By the end of 1948 left-liberals were hopelessly divided and disorganized. Some had turned conservative, some had joined the ADA, others had withdrawn from politics altogether. In addition, within weeks after Truman's inauguration, the Red scare at home and the Cold War abroad created a climate of anticommunist hysteria unparalleled in American history. The Alger Hiss case dominated the headlines early in 1949, then came the shattering news of the fall of China, followed shortly thereafter by disclosure of the first Russian atomic bomb. The age of darkness began to enshroud the United States, just as Josephson had feared.[25]

In the wake of the Wallace debacle the Josephsons left for an extended vacation in Europe. Matthew's reason for doing so, however, was not so much political as personal. 1948 had been a difficult year for him in several respects. He had done little writing of importance, had made no progress on his long-planned novel, and had seen the secret upheavals of his domestic life grow more turbulent. "The past twelve months," he maintained in July, "can be thrown out the window virtually, with the exception of l'amour. And in that regard I am aware of regrets and confused results." While he continued to enjoy seeing his mistress, Matthew grew weary of the strain of maintaining such an affair. He also grew more disenchanted with his relations with Hannah. Such a development was not surprising. As he pointed out, "you cannot have an affair without losing ground in the old relationship." Husband and wife had both grown more set in their ways, they both had hardened, and as a result there was more friction between them. Hannah, who for so long had deferred to Matty, now increasingly stood her ground, and he found it difficult to adjust to her new attitude. "A man doesn't need a wife," he remarked in frustration, "who is so clever, so intelligent, that she can always tell him when he is wrong." Josephson believed that a year in Europe would improve his outlook. There he hoped to "come to terms with my work, travel, distract my mind, gain perspective, and write something worthwhile, worthy at any rate of my own self-respect."[26]

Matthew and Hannah sailed from New York in December 1948. Once in Europe they traversed the continent in leisurely fashion, spending four months in Italy and several weeks in Czechoslovakia and Germany before settling down in Paris for the summer of 1949. There Matty renewed old friendships and associations. In a lengthy letter to Malcolm Cowley in July he described the Parisian scene. Louis Aragon was now a great French hero on the Left, a "communist saint." At political rallies women stood enraptured as he spoke and rushed up afterward to touch his hand. But success and attention had not gone to Aragon's head. He remained, Josephson reported, "still a pretty nice feller." His old foe Breton, on the other hand, was simply "silly." Tristan Tzara had mellowed, "his humor is sweet rather than malicious." Turning to the French political situation Josephson felt that the presence of the Communist party had been helpful: "It has always potential power and its pressure perhaps prevents things from being worse, under the drive of the dollar." He did not have such a favorable opinion of De Gaulle. After attending a Gaullist rally, he observed that he "didn't like what I heard and saw of the big arm-flapper." Josephson found the art and literature of postwar France inferior in quality, even though the cultural life remained active and diverse. The cafes in the St. Germain quarter had "now gone Montparnasse" and were full of young "*littérateurs* speaking French with a Harvard accent." He no longer felt comfortable among the bohemians in Paris. "I feel too old for them." Josephson told Eric that he had enjoyed several conversations with Jean-Paul Sartre, "who is so fabulously rich now he ought to be genial. . . . He's intelligent and a charmer." Sartre was much friendlier than Josephson had been led to believe. "His pose is to be sweet and agreeable to everyone, which makes things so pleasant; and he is such a smart cookie, too."[27]

During the summer of 1949 Matthew's relationship with Hannah grew increasingly strained. He was not making any headway on the novel he intended to write while in Paris, and he vented his frustrations on her, claiming that the "new Hannah" was impeding his work. Hannah, whose supply of patience had always seemed limitless, now decided she had heard enough criticism from her husband the "artiste." In July she told Matty that since he considered her such a burden, she would take up residence in the south of France while he remained in Paris. Thus they began their first trial separation. It did not take Matthew long to realize how much he depended on Hannah's companionship. The night she left on the train he wrote her that he "was very moved when the train left the Gare de Lyons. Do you miss me enough to forget how naughty I am at times? And to forgive me? I miss your drive and your vitality, and your outspoken, almost painful honesty." A few days later he admitted that his solitude had revealed that it was not Hannah who impeded his writing. He was not getting much done without her either. "Will you come back to these aching arms?" he pleaded. "It is dull without you even in Paris." Hannah, however, was not yet ready to return. Thus Matty wrote again:

> I've hardly been away from you for a week in several years. But when I am alone and feel the inertia of my deafness stop me from telephoning anyone I know, or simply sense that there is no one I care enough to see to make a formal request, then I miss you very much. And I surely dread the idea of going on a long while without you around.

By the end of July Hannah relented and returned to Paris, hoping that he had learned his lesson. Matthew was an extremely difficult man to live with, but she found him even more difficult to live without.[28]

14   THE GREAT FEAR

After spending several weeks in England the Josephsons returned to the United States in November 1949. Events soon caused them to wish they were still in Paris. In Eric Goldman's words, 1949 was a "year of shocks." To Arthur Miller it was "the year it fell apart." Henry Wallace and the Progressive movement had been routed; the liberal Left was divided and disorganized; China fell to the Communists; and the Russians exploded an atomic bomb. That same year the pursuit of political heretics began in earnest. The "great fear," as David Caute has demonstrated, began to haunt the American mind. In January 1950 Alger Hiss was convicted of perjury. That same month Truman announced the development of the hydrogen bomb. On February 3 Klaus Fuchs was arrested for passing atomic secrets to the Russians. A few days later the anticommunist crusade acquired its pied piper when Senator Joseph McCarthy made his notorious speech attacking the State Department for harboring Communists. By the spring he was in full stride, and "McCarthyism" began to fasten its frenzied grip upon American society.[1]

In such an atmosphere of superheated patriotism and anti-intellectualism, Josephson felt himself more and more isolated. The HUAC was not eliminated; instead, he discovered on his return to the United States, it was more powerful than ever. Even the CIO had turned conservative and intolerant. It now wholeheartedly endorsed Truman's policies and systematically expelled the left-wing unions from its membership. Josephson was especially concerned over the growing popularity of the new Cold War liberalism. Prominent intellectuals such as Reinhold Niebuhr, Lionel Trilling, and Arthur Schlesinger, Jr., horrified by the atrocities of World War II and the specter of Stalinist Russia, abandoned many of the traditional assumptions of liberalism and the Old Left—faith in progress, in man's essential goodness, in popular democracy—and instead replaced them with a more "realistic" philosophy recognizing the flawed nature of man's character, the inevitability of international conflict, and the dangers of mass rule. Unlike their counterparts in the 1930s, the Cold War liberals self-consciously positioned themselves at the center of the political spectrum rather than on the Left.[2]

Josephson could not understand the appeal of such a gloomy and tepid political philosophy. In January 1950 he read Schlesinger's *The Vital Center*, a passionate defense of the new liberalism and a stinging critique of the Old Left and Popular Front mentality. Josephson found the book's argument less than convincing. He wrote in his journal: "Poor young Schlesinger, Junior. Russia won't do, Marx won't do, Wallace neither; and so he has whipped himself into a frenzy of enthusiasm for the 'Vital Center,' which is the same as the Middle of the Road." Josephson worried that if the youthful Schlesinger was already adopting such a mundane political philosophy, he would be verging on the reactionary by the time he reached middle age. "I have always believed," he chided, "that one registered some gains only by exerting pressure from the Left. Even from the extreme Left. . . . But I hold, if you start out at twenty-five or thirty in the Middle, where are you going to wind up, when you are fifty—somewhere to the right of Herbert Hoover?"[3]

By the end of 1950 Josephson had lost all patience with the politics of the "vital center." In a splenetic letter to Thomas Cochran, he revealed the depth of his rancor: "The Me-and-Truman liberals make me puke. With Truman going broke, they too are running around in circles." Josephson was especially upset about America's involvement in the Korean conflict. Again the United States hurried to defend a corrupt, reactionary government. "I always said," he told Cochran, "the whole Truman Doctrine was cockeyed." He was also concerned about the reconversion of the economy once the war in Korea ended. The United States would be "stuck with our big tanks and guns and nowhere to go with 'em. Also, if armament (vide Hitler) is the health of the modern late-capitalist state, then de-armament may mean depression of some sort."[4]

Josephson meanwhile stepped up his own journalistic efforts to combat McCarthyism at home. He reported to Cochran that when he was not working on his latest book, a biography of labor leader Sidney Hillman, he was collaborating with "a circle of writers and publicists, to put in our two cents for civil rights where we can." Along with Paul Sweezy, Max Lowenthal, Carey McWilliams and others, he wrote pamphlets and articles attacking the excesses of the Red scare. After completing his biography of Hillman in 1952, he informed Eric that he had "decided to 'cut loose' for a period and quarrel with everyone. I am taking up the cudgels again. Otherwise I see no alternative save to conform and write some innocuous stuff." His sizable commission for writing the Hillman book provided him with enough financial security to turn polemicist for a while: "I can survive for a couple of years, by living mostly in the country, and can engage in pamphleteering, which is what my heart desires." In the summer of 1952 Josephson contributed an article entitled "Battle of the Books" to a special edition of the *Nation*. Throughout the late 1940s and early 1950s that magazine remained a persistent supporter of New Deal liberalism and Popular Front cooperation. Its editor, Carey McWilliams, met Josephson in the spring of 1951. He recalled that he and Matty "became and remained the best of friends." Josephson impressed him as "a forceful, resolute, highly intelligent person; he knew what he thought." [5]

Josephson and McWilliams feared that civil liberties in the country were being flagrantly disregarded. McWilliams was so concerned about McCarthyism that he decided to devote an entire issue of the *Nation* to the subject. In his contribution Josephson described with a sense of shock and foreboding the numerous attempts throughout the country to censor, suppress, or destroy teaching materials or books considered "subversive" by local authorities. America's fear of the enemy within, he noted, was imperceptibly transforming the country into a totalitarian state itself. In a statement typical for its satire and hyperbole, Josephson compared the current Red scare with that of 1919:

> Today's breed of super-patriots is a good deal better organized, less given to physical violence, and pretends to be literate. These people do not beat up women marching in labor union parades, as in 1919. Instead, they go trooping into little Carnegie libraries or bookshops or high schools to spy out "Red-slanted books" and administer the anti-Communist "treatment." They know Karl Marx well and the "infiltration" methods of his votaries.

He cited several examples of textbook authors revising their products "so that the most bigoted reader need find nothing to offend him." New editors were conspicuous for their "extreme political neutrality and dullness." He then examined the "smearing" of book publishers, devoting most of his attention to the forced resignation of his friend Angus Cameron from the editorship of Little, Brown.[6]

Josephson suggested that such an anti-intellectual crusade resulted from politicians and government agencies conditioning the masses to believe that there really was a Red menace lurking behind every editor, schoolteacher, and writer. During the Korean War, he pointed out, "federal and state loyalty boards, Congressional committees aiming at thought control, and our big Drummer Boy Joe in the Senate have created a veritable panic over the alleged internal danger offered by a few Communists—a panic that has particularly affected our less sophisticated citizenry." He compared the move to censor the publishing houses to that of Nazi Germany, when the people were reduced to reading only what Goebbels wanted them to read. "Will American publishers and their authors," he asked, "also wait patiently until everyone is 'coordinated,' that is, made to think the same thoughts and read the same few books?" He concluded that there was need for a few Zolas among America's prominent writers, writers willing to lift their voices and their pens against the "self-appointed thought police."[7]

Josephson may have exaggerated the degree of censorship then taking place in the country. But he was playing the role of pamphleteer, not objective commentator. He exaggerated for effect, trying to impress upon his readers the fact that there was a dangerous movement afoot to stifle free speech and free thought. Judging by the response his and other articles in the issue provoked, he certainly aroused interest in the subject. The *New Leader*, a journal reflecting the virulently anticommunist ideology of the "vital center" liberals, offered a lengthy rebuttal to the charges contained in the issue of the *Nation*. "In the name of fighting censorship," the editorial maintained, "Josephson would not have us unmask any Red wolf in sheep's clothing." A few months later the *New Leader* stepped up its assault on his character and professional integrity when an editorial referred to him as a "Stalinist shill."[8]

Such charges did not deter Josephson. As the 1950s progressed he continued to play the role of Zola and Stendhal in opposing the "reign of terror" he saw being waged in the United States. In September 1953 he wrote an article for the *Nation* in which he decried the attempts to censor modern art. "The trouble is," he opened the piece, "that our triumphant

Babbitts, in this time of witch-hunting and scapegoats, have at last turned their attention to art and culture." Representative George A. Dondero of Michigan led the campaign against modern art, especially abstract art. Dondero, reported Josephson, believed that modern art is "communistic because it is distorted and ugly, because it does not glorify our beautiful country, our cheerful and smiling people." Dondero and other self-appointed guardians of the national taste waged a relentless battle in the Congress, depicting modern painters and art critics as "enemies within," breeding "dissatisfaction" or disseminating "sinister ideas opposed to our government." As he had done earlier Josephson noted that Hitler and the Brown Shirts had engaged in similar censorship campaigns. At the same time, he stressed that Stalin had likewise abhorred modernism in the arts. Thus, Josephson wondered, if modern art was communistic, as Dondero, Nixon, and others claimed, why do the communists oppose it? "We seem to be losing many freedoms nowadays," he concluded. "Will our artists lose the freedom to paint as they please?"[9]

Another aspect of the Cold War mentality that Josephson found repugnant was the growing movement to "rewrite" American history, to emphasize the essential unity and harmony of the American past in the face of the ideological war against the Soviet Union. Until 1945 the Progressive historians such as Charles Beard had dominated historical scholarship with their emphasis upon the conflicts between economic interest groups in American society. Now they came under blistering attack. Samuel Eliot Morison, one of the pillars of the professional historical community, told the American Historical Association in 1950, "We need a United States history written from a sanely conservative point of view." And many scholars heeded his call. Instead of class conflict and social progress, the "neoconservative" historians such as Morison and Daniel Boorstin stressed that consensus and continuity characterized America's development. In their view the United States had been for the most part a homogeneous nation prospering under a beneficent capitalism.[10]

Some of the revisionist historians in the postwar period particularly glorified the achievements of America's business community. Appreciative of the contributions of businessmen and industrialists to the war effort and to the postwar prosperity, scholars such as Louis Hacker, Edward Saveth, and Allan Nevins launched a well-organized crusade to polish the tarnished image of American capitalists. The ex-Marxist Hacker accused American historians of displaying an openly "anticapitalist bias." In an article in *Fortune* Saveth chastised his peers for portraying businessmen in an unfavorable light. But it was left to Nevins to lead

254 The Great Fear

the campaign to transform the "robber barons" into "industrial statesmen." In the summer of 1951, about the time he published his second
biography of John D. Rockefeller, Nevins delivered an address at Stanford University in which he sharply criticized the way historians had
treated the country's business leaders. American historians, he maintained, were given to a "feminine idealism." They felt guilty about their
country's material prosperity and took out their frustrations by label-
ing businessmen "robber barons, who were not robber barons at all."
He concluded that scholars—apparently the masculine ones—must
set about redressing the damage done to the "leaders of our material
growth—the Rockefellers, Carnegies, Hills, and Morgans." [11]

Two years later Nevins stepped up his attack on the "robber baron"
stereotype and its popularizers. Speaking to the American Petroleum Institute, he cited Josephson's *Robber Barons* along with Gustavus Myers's
History of the Great American Fortunes and Lewis Corey's *House of Morgan*, "all written by avowed socialists," as contributing a great deal "to
color the attitudes of more careful writers and teachers of history." Nevins regretted that these leftist authors "stated the case against capitalism with vigor, eloquence, and an apparent buttress of documented
thought—and they were not answered!" He went on to extend a left-
handed compliment to such muckrakers:

> Everybody who reads Josephson's or Corey's books carefully per-
> ceives that they are tendentious, one-sided, and meant to serve the
> Marxian cause. But they are entertaining; they have an air of ver-
> isimilitude; they are placed on history reading shelves in colleges
> and universities; they affect the thought of young men and women.
> They did something to give even sober, conservative historians a
> prejudicial attitude toward business.

Nevins admitted that no one had written "an impartial account of the
business era after the Civil War as swift-paced, colorful, and entertaining
as Josephson's book." Now, he emphasized, was the time to set the record straight, and he called for a concerted effort by his fellow historians
to write books about the constructive aspects of American business leaders, books that would be just as "exciting, convincing, and inspiring as
those of earlier socialist scholars." [12]

Josephson watched with more than a little interest as Nevins and others sought to transform the robber barons into knights in shining armor.
He responded to the revisionist movement with characteristic vigor and
choler. In May of 1952 he ran into Nevins and Henry Steele Commager at

a dinner party at the American Academy of Arts and Letters. Josephson afterward wrote Thomas Cochran that the three of them engaged in a "solemn discussion of my intended reply to Nevins' animadversions on *The Robber Barons*, when I get around to it." He reported that Commager "must be more the fool than Nevins," since the former had earned "much discredit by writing that frightful stuff in *Collier's* about the war to liberate the Rooshians." Historian Merle Curti learned of Josephson's planned rejoinder to Nevins and encouraged his efforts: "I am glad you are going to reply to the boys who have been building up beyond their due the big business outfit. That these fellows contributed a great deal to the American economy and standard of living, no one has ever doubted. But to make great heroes and utterly blameless giants out of them is certainly going a bit too far."[13]

The much talked about confrontation between Nevins and Josephson finally took place in the pages of the *Saturday Review* in February 1954. They debated the question "Should American History Be Rewritten?" Nevins argued strongly in the affirmative. The time had come, he again contended, for scholars to rescue the reputations of American businessmen. After all, the United States had emerged from World War II as the leading power in the world. Now the country was engaged in an ideological struggle with the Russians. It was no occasion for self-doubt or self-criticism. Americans "can henceforth be more confident, and more energetic, in asserting that our way of life, called decadent by our enemies, has proved itself historically to be freer, more flexible, and more humane than any other in history." Accompanying this new confidence and self-esteem should be a more frank appreciation of the country's material growth:

> In the past our historians were apologetic about this. They condemned our love for the dollar, our race to wealth, our interest in material objects; they deprecated our worship of size, and deplored our boastfulness about steel tonnage, grain production, and output of machinery. Clio, with her tradition of moral value, was scornful of any others. Our writers in general . . . intimated that America had grown too fast, too coarsely, too muscularly; they exalted the rarefied air of the study as against the smoky atmosphere of the mill.

Nevins branded the interpretations set forth by Josephson and others as erroneous and asserted that America "grew none too fast." He then stretched the chain of logic to its limits in arguing that without the efforts of John D. Rockefeller in the nineteenth century, the United States would not have won either World War I or World War II. Nevins boldly predicted that eventually a "scientific" appraisal of the Gilded Age entrepreneurs would prove that the waste of natural resources and the human misery caused by rapid industrialization and mass production were not "a tremendous price to pay for their benefits." The Rockefellers, Carnegies, Mellons, Whitneys, and the rest would yet "stand forth in their true stature as builders, for all their faults, of a strength which civilization found indispensable."[14]

In his reply to Nevins, Josephson noted that the nation, obsessed by its fears of communism, had developed a spirit of mental conformity. Academic scholars were now reluctant to criticize American values or institutions. Since the end of World War II the United States had assumed "some of the character of a Restoration, with our Stuarts and Bourbons coming in where they left off," and Nevins and the advocates of historical revisionism would have Americans view the "economic royalists" as the "architects of prosperity." He imagined large numbers of historians responding like helots to the call for a favorable portrait of big business and hurriedly reversing their "liberal" interpretations: "Where only a decade or two ago they, like Mr. Nevins himself, were fairly strong for the New Deal, we may fancy them, henceforth, writing panegyrics on the wisdom, courage, and moral beauty of FDR's enemies, the economic royalists." Josephson wondered whether in the new histories FDR would be "trimmed down to size—say that of Calvin Coolidge—and Henry Ford be given wings and a harp? Will the art of Tacitus, Voltaire, and Gibbon be reduced to a public relations job?"[15]

Responding to Nevins's contention that the robber barons were not "morally worse" than their Gilded Age contemporaries, Josephson suggested that such moral relativism went against the grain of America's democratic tradition. If, he stressed, "Dr. [sic] Nevins is going to teach us to 'appreciate' or condone the moral ruthlessness of our older captains of industry, if he is going to let the end always justify the means, then I fail to see what arguments we can bring to bear against the Russian Communists." Nevins asserted that had it not been for the Rockefellers, Carnegies, and Fords, the United States would have lost both world wars; Josephson charged that this view represented a "fairly *simpliste*, big business version of the American Century." Actually, he pointed out, many of the leading industrial titans had stubbornly resisted the conversion of their manufacturing plants to military production.[16]

What Josephson feared most was a witch-hunt. The talk about revising and rewriting American history had menacing overtones. It recalled the

Federal Institute for the History of the New Germany established by the Nazis and the rewriting of the history of Soviet Russia directed by Stalin. He worried that "the new history of this country, too, [might] be rewritten as crude propaganda for the party in power." Josephson correctly recognized that Nevins would "be the last person to recommend such a program." But Nevins's proposal for the rewriting of American history, he concluded, was "ill conceived and ill timed," coming in a period when "overheated patriots" were busy banning books and intimidating writers. The last thing the country needed, in Josephson's view, was a respected scholar like Allan Nevins leading a vigilante assault upon historians who espoused the "robber baron" interpretation.[17]

Josephson's rebuttal to Nevins was extremely effective. Through the use of hyperbole and historical allusion he laid bare Nevins's sloppy argumentation. After the debate appeared he received numerous letters supporting his position. Van Wyck Brooks was especially effusive in his praise:

> The trouble with A. N. is that he is a Philistine. What interests the non-Philistine is the quality of a country's life, its measure of humaneness, culture, what you will; and I think it's a fact that the quality of life goes down the more the element of "power" rises. . . . Nevins never asks himself whether or not it is good for a country to be a "great power," though it seems to me the opposite is plain enough. The attempt to defend the "robber barons," so well called by you, is also to destroy all feelings for decent morals.

Brooks added that Josephson had been correct in observing that the "robber barons" had never captured the popular imagination. He remarked that he had never known one American writer "who didn't say with E. A. Robinson, 'Business be damned.' If we didn't all unite in feeling and saying that, what room would there be in the country for imagination?"[18]

In reply to a congratulatory letter from Thomas Cochran, Josephson reported that there "has been a very good response, as if many felt these things ought to be said out loud." He knew that he had exaggerated things a bit in his reply to Nevins, but only for a good purpose: "To be sure I wasn't trying to be a Foolosopher of History, like Nevins—who gave us such pompous twaddle there—but simply directing some rocks at the new conformists. I was raising questions." Nevins, he concluded, "is naive, unwary, self-contradictory whenever he lets go of his 'little facts' and tries to think and generalize." Such was the distinction Josephson drew between his own historical perspective and that of Nevins and other "professionals." He was concerned primarily with interpreting within a moral and ideological framework the broad sweep of events, while the academic scholars were bogged down in detail and pedantry.[19]

During the Eisenhower-Dulles years American foreign policy continued to revolve around the Cold War and the need to stay ahead of the Russians in the expanding arms race. The "military-industrial complex" had become a reality, a development Matthew Josephson had long feared. As early as 1940 he had worried that the coming war would inextricably bind together the military and big business in an unholy alliance. By 1955 he viewed the situation with growing alarm.

In an attempt to educate the public to the dangerous growth of the military establishment, Josephson wrote a number of articles for the *Nation* in 1956 and 1957 on the subject. "The Big Guns" was a series of three articles that appeared in January 1956. In them he lashed out at the foolish and costly "atomic rat race" with the Soviet Union. "For too long," he maintained, "we have lived in a mood of existentialist dread. Civilization has been sleeping badly, with its weekend case packed, ready to take off at any moment to the caves or ruins." Josephson observed that Americans had always been suspicious of a large, permanent military force. But now the country was developing into what Harold Lasswell called a "garrison state." Government subsidies for military research and development were rapidly taking over wider areas of scientific and educational activities. Thus, he believed, the drive for internal security was spreading into more segments of American life: "From the repression of the partisans of communism in America we move on to that of other dissenting groups of Socialists, religious pacifists or liberals— and sometimes simply of persons whose opinions are considered 'unsound' (e.g., 'disloyal') by men vested with new and unaccustomed powers of surveillance."[20]

In addition Josephson focused on the disquieting connection between corporate America and the defense establishment. Since World War II, he observed, "there has been a long marriage festival between the men of the sword and the men of the factories." Generals and admirals were retiring from military service only to take up positions as executives of large corporations. At the same time, many business leaders were going to Washington to serve as administrators within the Defense Department. As a result of such interaction the corporate giants tended to win most of the military contracts, thereby increasing their institutional size and influence. The size of corporations was growing dramatically in the 1950s, and Josephson attributed such growth to the bloated defense budgets.

But unlike other observers such as David Lilienthal, A. A. Berle, and John K. Galbraith, he did not welcome the centralization of corporate America. Nor did he see much to praise in the activities of big business. He felt that too many commentators were exaggerating the achievements of American business enterprise:

> That American capital should have recovered and grown rich under the economy of the greatest of world wars and the long cold war should be, in itself, no occasion for lavishing praises upon our present-day entrepreneurs for "vim," "vision," and "venture." Indeed, the distinctive thing about the American system is the manner in which, year by year, its resemblance to "free enterprise" is disappearing. Today the system leans increasingly on government paternalism, direct and indirect subsidies and tax remissions so encouraging to capital investments.

The business leaders remained "robber barons" in Josephson's eyes. He still denied to them the qualities of vision and daring that people like Nevins sought to praise.[21]

Josephson's "Big Guns" articles provoked considerable interest among the *Nation*'s readers, so much so that the editors decided to reprint the three pieces in pamphlet form for public sale. He reached sympathetic ears with his attack on the inefficiency and waste within the Defense Department. He also found some support for his plea to end the arms race through bilateral negotiations with the Soviets. In addition he won praise for his insights into the alarming connection between big business and the Defense Department, insights that preceded C. Wright Mills's influential work on the same subject, *The Power Elite*. Josephson, however, at times painted the picture of the military-industrial complex with too broad a brush. The growing defense budgets of the 1950s resulted more from the general atmosphere of the Cold War than from the collusion between business and the military. As William Leuchtenburg has demonstrated, "Swollen military budgets represented less the machinations of malevolent men than the obsessions of ideological conflict, the tragic incapacity of nation-states to develop institutions of accommodation, and the headlong pace of technology that made costly weapons systems obsolete before they left the factory." Josephson's disdain for American capitalists continued to blind him to such larger, more complex realities. The imprint of Beard and an economic interpretation of history and events remained etched on his critical conscience, as it always would.[22]

Josephson was proud of his political writing during the 1950s. He regarded the "Big Guns" series as "a piece of serious polemical journalism." In his own mind he was fulfilling his role as "public man," speaking out in Stendhalian fashion against the forces of reaction. Josephson was naturally fitted for polemical writing, and he basked in the controversy and heated exchanges he provoked with his journalism. Yet he still regretted the personal and artistic sacrifices that he had made in concentrating on political and commercial journalism. He also remained frustrated by his failure to write creative literature. "Looking back at the mid-thirties," he wrote in his journal, "I realize that I have grown much lonelier, more isolated, the circle of friendships greatly narrowed. It seems to me many persons loved me then. My potentialities appeared to be larger than they seem now." His artistic friendships meant much more to him than those who knew him realized. "I derived great pleasure from friendships. Now this pleasure seems rarer. It is almost as if one anticipates increasingly less pleasure from this source." Two months later, in December 1954, after publishing a commissioned history of the Hotel and Restaurant Employees Union, Josephson again expressed his disgust at doing such hackwork. He wondered if he would ever change his literary direction. Would he ever write the novel that so dominated his private thoughts? "I must leave some sort of record before I go, n'est-ce pas? Better than the last ten years or so." [23]

But money matters, family concerns, and his own inertia and lack of ability prevented Josephson from doing so. Consequently the frustrations that he had expressed in 1946 continued to plague him at the end of the 1950s. "I am irked by the problems of property, of adjusting myself to my wife's schedule of work, living in the city where I do not feel as well as in the country, the burdens of importunate children, in short the lack of freedom of movement." Josephson obviously wanted to break out of the mold he had cast for himself. In moments of wistful reflection he still longed for a purely artistic career. Yet the writer turned public and family man eventually realized that the professional career role he had long ago chosen for himself was a permanent one. His novel, his chef d'oeuvre, would always elude him. No matter how much he tried to be like Stendhal, he would always come up short. Stendhal was always able to involve himself in contemporary political affairs without becoming immersed in them. His creative writing transcended the historical moment. Josephson, however, chose to be a political and commercial journalist. And in doing so he inevitably restricted his artistic choices. [24]

15 LAST BOOKS AND LAST YEARS

Although Josephson would remain actively concerned with political and social issues, he came to feel by 1957 that the crisis period had passed.[1] The age of darkness had lightened considerably. He could now in good conscience leave the arena of political journalism and return to writing for its own sake. His initial inclination was to begin work on the novel that had for so long eluded him. But again a more attractive project intervened. In 1957 he accepted a lucrative offer from McGraw-Hill to write a biography of Thomas Edison. Despite Edison's significance there was no first-rate biography of him. Literally hundreds of articles, books, and pamphlets had been written about him, but most of them were inflated popular accounts, full of myths and hero worship. The authorized biography published in 1910 remained the standard work, but it was sketchy and uneven. Thus Josephson had the opportunity to write a sorely needed definitive account of the enigmatic Edison.

And he did. Josephson's study, published in 1959, represented one of his most challenging, but also most successful, biographical efforts. It was a challenge in that understanding the prolific inventor and his work meant understanding unfamiliar scientific principles and research techniques. Josephson therefore had to educate himself in a new field. In doing so he again demonstrated his uncanny ability to write confidently about subjects initially foreign to him. Along with Norbert Wiener, Josephson sees Edison as a "transitional figure" bridging the gap between the isolated inventor of the nineteenth century and the huge industrial research centers of the modern era.[2]

Unlike Josephson's earlier biographies *Edison* contains no pressing contemporary message. Its subject was not a prominent social or political activist; in fact, Edison was decidedly conservative. Josephson certainly admires Edison's scientific achievements and his unquestioned integrity, but he does not reveal that sense of personal identification with his subject that highlighted his literary biographies. The book, therefore, is written with uncharacteristic objectivity. Seldom does Josephson overtly intrude between reader and subject. A close reading of the text, however, reveals that while indeed telling the story of Edison's life and career with praiseworthy detachment, he also takes the opportunity to reaffirm the central themes of *The Robber Barons*. His own feelings about the great business leaders and the materialist atmosphere of the Gilded Age had changed very little since 1934.

In *The Robber Barons* Josephson had echoed Veblen in portraying the captains of industry as vultures waiting to pounce on the technological discoveries of unsuspecting inventors. The true men of genius, the inventors who actually created something new and tangible for society's benefit, "were used and flung aside by men of ruse and audacity who had shown gifts for the accumulation of capital, who were skilled at management . . . and who, far from sharing the hazards of applied science, tended to enter a new affair only when its commercial character had been established beyond a doubt." In the introduction to *Edison*, Josephson presents the same view of the relationship between entrepreneur and inventor. Edison, he asserts, "was above all creative, hence one of the real builders of America. During a long era when America seemed dominated by men who were great acquisitors, Edison typified the Spirit of Workmanship." He then sets out to maintain such a distinction between Edison the disinterested tinkerer and the robber barons of industry and finance with whom he came into contact.[3]

Josephson portrays young Tom Edison as certainly thrifty, but not greedy, in his outlook on things material. He had "no disposition for money accumulation and could be gloriously 'impractical'. . . . the passion for glory, rather than money, and the desire to gain preeminence through *acts of skill* are usually the ruling motives for the inventor type." Later Josephson repeats this theory, arguing that "no one to whom money was the primary consideration would have spent his whole life tormenting himself to invent things." He repeatedly insists that money was for

Edison always a secondary motive at best. No one was more satisfied, he contends, "once there was a little money on hand, to make that little do for his needs and to live for the joy of inventive work." Not only was Edison uninterested in money for money's sake, he also possessed a personality far more appealing than the Jay Goulds, Jim Fisks, and Daniel Drews of the era. The captains of industry, Josephson writes, were "cold fish, who knew only the icy pleasures of the market place in which they perpetually swam. . . . By contrast, a creative being like Edison seems to us full of the joy of life."[4]

But as Edison's inventions and prestige mount, Josephson finds it more and more difficult to distinguish his subject from the sordid "robber barons." He is forced to admit that Edison's social philosophy was just as Social Darwinian as theirs: "To be sure his social thinking was far less original than his workmanship and seemed to stop at the belief . . . that the acquisitive were the fittest to survive and that the rights of capital, as well as those of the individual, were sacred." During Edison's middle years, as the inventor turned manufacturer and entrepreneur, he grew ever more infatuated with building larger laboratories, factories, and research facilities. "His ambitions nowadays were unlike those of a typical man of science and bore a resemblance rather to those of the Carnegies and Rockefellers, the ruthless captains of industry who were his contemporaries." Edison drove his workers hard, paid them only average wages, and hated labor unions. In the process he himself became a wealthy man, although he frequently squandered his money on impractical schemes.[5]

Josephson thus traces the decline of Edison from disinterested inventor to scheming businessman, the moral being that men of science should beware of mixing business with research. But as the book ends he steadfastly maintains that Edison's career as a whole was much more admirable than that of his "robber baron" peers. Far "from being an exploiter, Edison, as inventor and engineer, regarded himself as a creator of new wealth for all men, new tools, new industries." His interests were as much social as selfish, and to Josephson such mixed motives placed Edison above the crass money men whose single-minded devotion to self characterized their behavior.[6]

Josephson's comprehensive biography of Edison represented a significant contribution to the history of American science and industry. It did indeed take its place as the definitive study of Edison and remained so for almost twenty years. The book was an immediate best-seller and was soon republished in England, Germany, Japan, and Spain. By 1968 it had sold well over 100,000 copies. Not ony did the book sell widely, but parts of it were bought for publication in magazines like *Scientific American*, *High Fidelity*, and *American Heritage*. Josephson had again reached the wide public he had always pursued. But to him the most gratifying result of his latest book was the winning of the Francis Parkman Prize in American history and biography, awarded by the Society of American Historians. The book was nominated for the award by none other than Allan Nevins, his old nemesis.

As the century entered its sixth decade, so did Matthew Josephson, and like many aging authors he turned to reminiscent writings, publishing two volumes of memoirs in the 1960s—*Life among the Surrealists* (1962) and *Infidel in the Temple* (1967). The former dealt with the 1920s and the latter with the 1930s. Neither told very much about Matthew Josephson. In general they contain far more incident than insight. There is little pretense at autobiographical reflection, with only sketchy references to the author's inner feelings. His memoirs are not so much confessionals but galleries, group portraits of his friends and associates. He shows what he saw but not what he thought. And much of what Josephson does say about himself is selective and superficial. In 1969 he confessed in his journal that he had "unconsciously tended to conceal the truth about myself and my contemporaries in my two books of memoirs. My inconsistencies, the contradictions in my character, and the episodes of lâcheté; of meanness, of cowardice, or hypocrisy even, or at least of comforting self-deception are passed over."[7]

Although Josephson's memoirs lack forthrightness and self-analysis, they do contain thoroughly entertaining reminiscences about the literary, business, and political figures he had known in the interwar years. In the introduction to *Life among the Surrealists* he announces that instead of "presenting only an apologia for myself in these pages, I would attempt to make a group portrait of the circle of my friends and acquaintances who were active in the literary and art movements of the 1920s." Unlike *Exile's Return*, Malcolm Cowley's classic study of the lost generation, Josephson's volume has no connecting theme. Nor is there much attention given to the works of the painters and poets he discusses. Instead he takes the reader on a lively guided tour of the cafes of Paris and Berlin, the boardrooms of Wall Street, and the boisterous parties in Manhattan and Connecticut, pausing frequently to give incisive character portraits of Kenneth Burke, Malcolm Cowley, Hart Crane, Allen Tate, E. E. Cummings, Edmund Wilson, André Breton, Jean Arp, Tristan Tzara, Max

Ernst, Robert Desnos, Paul Eluard and, of course, Louis Aragon. He seemed to have known or encountered almost every major figure in modern art and literature. But in trying to include them all in *Life among the Surrealists*, Josephson at times produces a catalogue of names whose sheer number blurs their identity and significance.[8]

After *Life among the Surrealists* was published, Matthew discovered that many of his friends did not appreciate his characterization of them. The aristocratic Allen Tate was furious about his depiction as a janitor-poet. Muriel Cowley was not flattered by her neighbor's offhand reference to her as a "younger woman who, besides having other virtues, kept her household in beautiful order." The maddest of them all, however, was Edmund Wilson. He took heated exception to Josephson's account of a party at which Wilson supposedly got into a tussle with Burton Rascoe and bit him on the leg. Wilson threatened to sue if the offending passage were not removed. The crusty pundit vented his spleen to Allen Tate:

> My copy of Mattie's book is at my lawyer's. At first I had the idea of writing him a letter which should begin as follows: "Cher faux dadaiste démodé, [illegible word] immonde, farci de merde, dans les entrailles de Rousseau et de Stendhal." I also conceived the project of writing a letter to the literary papers which should commence: "When I first met Matthew Josephson in the early twenties, he persuaded me to read the manuscript of a novel unusually lacking in promise. He has now written another inferior work of fiction which he has attempted to make more interesting by giving the characters the names of real people."

Wilson later dropped the matter when Josephson's publishers promised to delete the offensive reference.[9]

Josephson's second volume of memoirs is similar in structure to the first, focusing primarily on the famous personalities and important events he encountered in the 1930s. He combines his considerable talents as biographer, historian, and journalist to provide a vivid picture of literary and intellectual life during the Great Depression. His far-ranging journalistic and political activities, as he notes, brought him into close "contact not only with writers and painters, but also with politicians, social workers, economists, labor leaders, radical agitators, and conservative capitalists as well." But like *Life among the Surrealists*, *Infidel in the Temple* casts more light on his glittering circle of friends and acquaintances than on Josephson himself. The book for the most part is an inhibited and unreflective series of profiles of John Dos Passos, Charles Beard, Sidney Hook, Theodore Dreiser, John Chamberlain, William Z. Foster, Erskine Caldwell, Jerome Frank, Hugh Johnson, Ernest Hemingway, and others.[10]

The tone of *Infidel in the Temple*, however, is markedly different from that of *Life among the Surrealists*. The first volume is a rather lighthearted account of the pranks and parties of the "lost generation." In the second volume, on the other hand, Josephson has a score to settle, and he uses his memoirs as a weapon. His target is the group of ex-radicals of the 1930s who in the postwar years spent their time repenting, recanting, and informing. After Pearl Harbor, Granville Hicks, Leslie Fiedler, Sidney Hook, James Burnham, John Chamberlain, Daniel Bell, and others castigated themselves and their friends for succumbing to the lure of communism during the Great Depression. They portrayed the decade as one infested with moral betrayal and intellectual stupidity. Josephson bristled at such "revisionist" history written by the new ideologues on the Right. As early as 1953 he had pledged to set the record straight one day. In that year he wrote in his journal: "The present is one of the low-water-marks for American civilization. Our history is being rewritten. The recent past is being buried under a heap of lies and slanders." Young Americans, he feared, would grow up knowing nothing of the "true" atmosphere of the 1930s, the hopes and disappointments, advances and defeats of the literary Left. Instead they would be told that it was a disgraceful period in the history of American thought and culture, one that scarcely merited attention. Josephson took it upon himself to tell his side of the story: "I must endeavor to leave behind me some record of the truth, at least insofar as I was able to see something of it, so that men who come to read books in future times will be able to know and judge what we really were."[11]

In describing the way things "really were" in the 1930s, Josephson begins *Infidel in the Temple* by announcing that the Great Depression was not really depressing. He chastises Alfred Kazin for writing of the "grim thirties" and joins Edmund Wilson in emphasizing the lively ferment of ideas that bubbled up among intellectuals and gave them real hope for a fundamental change in American society. "I would like to cross my heart and deny," Josephson affirms, "that the mood of the intelligentsia of the 1930s was in any way as melancholy or grim as later revisionists of our literary history . . . have represented it." On the face of it Josephson's statement is certainly true. Neither he nor Wilson was depressed during the 1930s; nor were many other successful writers. But there were other artists and scholars who had no secure contract with a major publisher like Alfred Harcourt, who had no inheritance to tide them over, who owned no peaceful country estate immune from the aftershocks of the economic crisis. To a younger group of writers just beginning their careers, men such as Erskine Caldwell, Robert Cantwell, and Alfred Kazin, the economic aspects of the depression were much more real and devastating. Instead of having an agent handle their writing assignments, they often, as in the case of Kazin, spent the day sitting in the anteroom of magazine offices waiting for a review to write in order to pay the rent. In his zeal to counter the critical studies of the decade, Josephson seems surprisingly insensitive to the precarious position of such writers.[12]

In addition to emphasizing the upbeat mood of the writers on the Left, Josephson also goes to great lengths to defend them against the charges of the "revisionist" histories of the decade. He emphatically denies that they were hoodwinked by the Communists:

> In the light of later recantations and "revelations" by some of the persons involved in the left-wing activities here described, and their later claims that it was part of a vast underground "conspiracy" to use writers and scholars as "dupes" who would deliver the people into the hands of the Bolshevists, I should like to deny all such allegations with all my heart. I cannot for the life of me recall anything partaking of the nature of a conspiracy.

Josephson sees no evidence, for example, that the writers who supported Foster and Ford in 1932 were manipulated into doing so by the comrades. Neither his group nor "the younger men were deceived, driven, or duped into taking the stand they did in September 1932." Later he mentions the books by Fiedler, Bell, and Peter Viereck that characterized the fellow travelers as naive idealists who in supporting the Communists betrayed their liberal heritage. Josephson wonders how they could have been both "innocent" and "traitorous" at the same time. He stresses that there were all types represented among the literary Left. Some were indeed evangelical, others were certainly capable of being fooled. But many writers, he insists, did not fit either category: John Dos Passos, for instance, was never as innocent in the 1930s as he later pictured himself, and Malcolm Cowley throughout the 1930s remained realistic about the chances of revolution. Cowley had never thought the proletariat capable of mass action.[13]

Josephson portrays his own thoughts and activities on the Left in a similar manner. He knew full well that capitalism was firmly entrenched in the United States. He never really believed that communism had a chance. But he supported the objectives of the radical Left because he felt that a strong showing by the American Communists would force the two major political parties to adopt more sweeping reform programs. Matthew time and again maintains that as a fellow traveler he "was by temperament relatively detached." He held "orthodox communists and heretics alike at arm's length," struggling to maintain his own independence and freedom of action. Certainly that was the case, but he repeats it too much:

> "I was able to rove freely 'between the lines' from one camp to the other, which I always found diverting."

> "I always found it amusing to rove between the two camps."

> "It seems to have been my destiny in those days to rove back and forth between the different camps."

That Josephson was so disengaged and "above the battle" helps explain his inability to understand the mentality of the former radicals turned conservatives. He himself never experienced the anguish of the disillusioned true believer and therefore saw no reason to abandon his political principles in disgust.[14]

For those who did make such a political reversal, Josephson has only contempt. His portraits of the "apostates" are etched in venom. Fellow traveler Max Lerner, for instance, turned solidly anti-Stalinist and anti-Russia after the signing of the Nazi-Soviet pact. "For him," Josephson writes, "the future would be anticommunist, and it would be a fairly prosperous future. But then Max Lerner was an amiable liberal who never pretended that he was out to sacrifice himself for the human race." His description of James Burnham is similarly caustic. Burnham shifted so far to the ideological right that "even Trotsky, his former master, denounced him as a 'witch doctor' forever concocting different theoretical broths, each stronger than the last. (By 1947 Burnham's shift to the extremism of the right would lead him to theoretics about starting an unprovoked nuclear war against the communist nations.)"[15]

Josephson saved his sharpest barbs for Whittaker Chambers, with whom he spent one evening in March 1933 at Robert Cantwell's Manhattan apartment. Cantwell introduced them, but Josephson already knew of the man who "lived an underground life full of real or imaginary dangers, always under cover or on the run." He had also heard that Chambers carried a gun because he suspected the FBI of following him. Josephson's image of Chambers before they met was that of a "clown or an eccentric." At Cantwell's the two of them sat down with a bottle of bootleg whiskey and began discussing the banking crisis. According to Matthew the apocalyptic Chambers was convinced that the end of capitalism was near. Josephson disagreed and noted the rumors about Roosevelt's New Deal program, intended to ease the depression and defuse the revolutionary temper. Chambers then began screaming that Josephson was crazy and that the revolution would begin that week. Matthew raised his voice as well, exclaiming that there would be no revolution in the United States. Chambers grew hysterical and branded his listener a "capitalist stooge" and a "spy." The two were about to exchange blows when Cantwell and his wife entered the room and asked Chambers to leave. In assessing the incident Josephson declares that Chambers was a "thoroughgoing paranoiac." The only cause that such neurotic rebels "really cared about was that of their own ill-adjusted personalities."[16]

Through such descriptions and others, Josephson made his point about the instability of the ex-radicals. But his portraits contain more heat than light. They represent Josephson the vengeful polemicist rather than Josephson the detached historian. There is little attempt to understand or analyze the psychology of metronome radicalism, only criticism and caricature. Consequently, many of his reminiscences tell more about the 1950s than about the 1930s. Josephson's repeated attacks on the neoconservatives mar the otherwise praiseworthy aspects of the book, such as his excellent reporting of the plight of the unemployed he visited in Hoovervilles and his vignettes of life in Washington under the New Deal. As Daniel Aaron remarked, *Infidel in the Temple* represents a curious mixture, "part history, part meditation, a factual, opinionated, gossipy, polemical record of the times, never dull, often illuminating, and occasionally irritating."[17]

After completing *Infidel in the Temple*, Josephson would write two more books during his career, one a biography of Al Smith coauthored by Hannah and published in 1969 and the other a sequel to *The Robber Barons*, entitled *The Money Lords*, which appeared in 1972. They both were solid, competent works, but they lacked the verve, polish, and involvement of his earlier writings. He did not put as much time or effort into them as into his previous books. This in part reflected the fact that both books were commissioned; he viewed them primarily as commercial ventures.[18]

That Matthew was advancing in years also affected the quality of his last books. As he reached and passed his sixtieth year it grew more and more wearing for him to keep to his normally prodigious literary pace.

While writing *Infidel in the Temple* in 1963 he admitted to his brother Murray, "I still have the habit of undertaking very long and difficult projects, of my own will, and feel the strain more than when I was younger." The next year he turned sixty-five, and he took the opportunity to reflect on his situation. In his journal Josephson noted how lucky he was to have lived so long, considering the close calls he had had earlier in life. Now, however, age was beginning to creep up on him. He was increasingly bothered by bouts with chronic asthmatic bronchitis that sapped his energy and impeded his writing. "Now I don't look particularly old," he commented, "but have to think of slowing down." [19]

When Josephson surveyed his long career he again seemed less than satisfied: "I want to say I have no regrets—but cannot. Certainly I have lost time, lost my road at periods, and wasted opportunities." But he reminded himself to keep quiet about such regrets. "I must never annoy or bore the younger people by admitting that I am old and sad, or feel that way!" Four years later he repeated many of the same sentiments on the occasion of his sixty-ninth birthday. He especially regretted his failure to write creative literature. "In the sixties," he confessed, "one reckons bitterly how little of what one hoped to do or accomplish or win has come through. And more so, more ruefully so, in the seventieth, beginning of the septuagenarian decade." Josephson still spoke of the same unfulfilled desires that had long frustrated him. "I would like to write fiction based on recollection and reflection. . . . I would like to occupy myself in leisurely reading according to my tastes: and also in philosophical reading." As before, however, he never got around to writing creative literature. He would sketch out ideas, spend several days thinking about the structure of a novel, then get distracted by some other project. For all his self-assuredness and drive in other areas, Josephson lacked confidence in his imaginative abilities. [20]

In the winter of 1969–70, after completing the biography of Al Smith, Josephson accepted an offer made by Professor Jay Martin to teach a seminar at the University of California at Irvine. Although his friends Cowley and Burke had been regularly teaching and lecturing at colleges and universities across the country, he had shied away from such academic commitments, preferring to spend the time writing on his own. Now the prospect seemed more appealing. Still, he was skeptical at first. He worried about his lack of experience in such a setting. He had never taught a class. How would the rebellious students of the late 1960s, he wondered, respond to an aging, nearly deaf writer? In addition, some of his friends in Sherman expressed concern for his physical safety. After all, students were taking over college campuses around the country, frequently by force. But the more Josephson thought about such a "novel and exciting undertaking," the more attractive the offer seemed, and he finally decided that he was certainly capable of handling the job. As he told his concerned friends in Connecticut, "Oh, I used to be a bit of a rebel myself in college days, and some consider I have never changed very much. And I used to torture some of my teachers too." [21]

Josephson decided to organize the course around his two recent memoirs, focusing on the young American and French writers in Paris during the early 1920s and the literary Left in the United States during the 1930s. His students were quite a varied lot, as he noted in his journal: "Several of the young men were huge fellows, with long hair down to their shoulders, and a couple of them wore luxuriant beards. The girls were highly miniskirted; except that one was a wife and mother forty years old." The campus was then alive with political activity. There were, it seemed to him, "daily mass meetings, mill-ins, and sit-ins." Josephson was surprised to discover that the student activists were not simply "hotheads." Instead he found them politicaly mature, revealing "considerable intelligence about political action—and [they] were aware of their own power." [22]

Josephson was quite popular with the students, who found his colorful personal experiences directly relevant to their own literary, social, and political concerns. Professor Martin remembered that Matty and Hannah "both became favorites with the students, especially the radical ones." In discussing Dada, Josephson described it as essentially a fierce protest of youth against the corrupt civilization responsible for the mass slaughter of World War I, just as the student revolt of the sixties seemed to result from disgust with American involvement in Vietnam. He emphasized, however, that Dada was carried off with wit and inventiveness, unlike the current movement. "If you are going to be revolutionaries," Josephson insisted to his students, "at least be humorous revolutionaries." After the term ended he reported to Ivan von Auw, his literary agent, that he had "had a ball." Even though he was seventy years old, he "bridged the Generation Gap and became a popular figure with the boys and co-eds. . . . We were on the verge of uprisings here, but it was mainly marching around and big rallies but bloodless. I was amused and formed some ideas about the big student movement. I found the students most likeable." [23]

One suspects that Josephson's experience at Irvine was an enjoyable one largely because of the atmosphere of political activism and radicalism on campus. He remained in his seventh decade intensely interested in national politics. In the spring of 1970, for instance, he wrote a letter to the editors of the *New York Times* in which he expressed support for the Church-Cooper and Hatfield-McGovern bills intended to restrict American military involvement in Vietnam and Cambodia. "What no one has noticed," he pointed out, "is that the real intention behind those proposed measures is to compel the President of the United States to keep his word to the American people." He then expanded on this point.

> For six years now, under two Presidents, we have been wandering through Credibility Gap; after succeeding Mr. Johnson, Mr. Nixon has shown no sign of becoming the Moses who will lead us out of that wilderness region. Therefore some of the more public-spirited members of Congress have begun a struggle to induce the President to keep his pledges, and especially those concerning the withdrawal of our forces from Southeast Asia. We have no assurance that such bills will be passed by both Houses of Congress, or that, if passed, they may not be vetoed. But even so they give us the measure of the disillusionment and the growing resentments of millions of Americans who have seen two Presidents in succession compile a bad credit record.[24]

Josephson could not abide Nixon. In 1973, when the International Telephone and Telegraph scandal made national headlines, he wrote Kenneth Burke: "The bourgeois are livid against Milhous. No decent man of business is safe while the sneaks of ITT bug all the secrets of his affairs. The same is true of civil liberties. Well, I warned them back in 1952 that Nixon was one of the 'vandals.'" Josephson supported McGovern's candidacy in 1972 in the hope that the liberal senator could "manage a real confrontation with Milhous, of No against Yes, instead of me-too." As the campaign progressed, however, he was shocked to discover that Nixon, "one of the least likeable politicos that have held his high office," retained widespread support among the voters. The president had clearly been shown to be "secretive, power-hungry, deceptive, and 'tricky.'" Yet the voters seemed not to care. They preferred an incumbent conservative to an idealistic outsider. Thus he resigned himself to the Nixon landslide, blaming the two-party system for preventing minority views from carrying any weight.[25]

As the Watergate scandal unfolded along with the Spiro Agnew affair, Josephson viewed the events as only confirming his long-held opinion of Nixon and his cronies. In May of 1973 he told his son Eric, "We've survived some pretty rotten Presidents with our lumbering Ship of State, but this is really the low man, and full of animal cunning." He characterized Nixon as "a man without ideology and without values." His aides appeared as "unfeeling, unscrupulous versions of Stendhal's Julien making their careers." Josephson told Maxwell Geismar that he did not mind Nixon's "being so tricky, many politicos are thus; but I resented his extreme vulgarity. We have lots of Americans of lovely character and this creep was not representative at all." Nor was Josephson impressed with Gerald Ford as Nixon's replacement. He remarked to Burke that the White House attempts to build Ford into a great leader had been laughable:

> I thought him one of the lowliest characters in the Lower House these many years. I kept saying: but my god we are changing from Iago-Machiavelli-Nixon to a Bag of Sheet. Thus tragedy is turned into farce—the multitude of voters is twice diddled. . . . nowadays we get mediocrities who have never been elected, or who could never have won a presidential nomination, and after that won an election even against some dog, or dog-catcher![26]

If Watergate and Nixon's shenanigans had any positive effect at all on Josephson, it was in providing the stimulus for renewing his correspondence with Kenneth Burke, which had lapsed in recent years. They both hated Nixon with equal vigor and communicated frequently about the president's declining fortunes. In doing so they rediscovered the dynamic intellectual byplay that had made their relationship so vigorous and durable through the years. Burke confessed to Matty in February of 1973 that "it suddenly occurred to me how absurd is the fact that we communicate so seldom, when you are my second oldest friend. We must figure out something. For we're closing ranks, and it's a gloomy bizz." He emphasized how much their relationship had meant to him over the years, commenting that "you don't have the slightest idea of what you did for me, by your act of bringing us together." Josephson felt much the same way, despite their occasional arguments. He confided to Kenneth that he was "full of fraternal feelings for you. Hannah loves you also. She fully agrees with me that without Kenneth Burke our life would not have been as enjoyable." The two friends had taken markedly different literary directions since their early days together at Columbia and in Greenwich Village. But they both respected and perhaps envied each other's work. Josephson admitted as much when he told Burke in July 1973, "I must say in your honor that, while others in the republic of letters manipulated their way onward to publicity-glory-shekels, you did it the hard way, without wirepulling or cheating." [27]

By the mid–1970s the Josephsons had slowed their pace considerably, although their basic interests and activities remained unchanged. Matthew and Hannah continued to enjoy the social life of Sherman and Manhattan, and they continued to travel a great deal. In his peaceful retreat at Sherman Josephson tried to maintain his lifetime habits of regular work, despite declining health. Each morning he would rise early and head for the study, where he would keep up with correspondence and work on his latest literary projects. During the 1970s he published in the *Southern Review* a number of lively portraits of writers he had known, including John Brooks Wheelwright, Evan Shipman, Dawn Powell, Leane Zugsmith, and Edmund Wilson. When he finished his morning work he would then join Hannah for lunch on the terrace overlooking the brook and afterward either read or spend the afternoon tending the garden or walking along the brook up the ridge. In the evenings they might occasionally see the Cowleys or the Peter Blumes, who lived nearby.

Beginning in 1974 the Josephsons regularly spent several months a year in Sarasota, Florida. The balmy climate was good for Matthew's bronchitis and for his spirits. He also enjoyed the social life among the small community of writers and artists from the North who had settled in Sarasota. Even at his advanced age, Matty remained a strikingly handsome man, still an inexhaustible causeur, full of manly charm and capable of entertaining others for hours with stories of his colorful career and acquaintances. He reported to Burke in 1975 that physically he felt much better after a lengthy stay in Florida. He still noticed, however, the creeping effects of old age. "I look well with a white moustache in a red face, but we are slowing down here along with the other valetudinarians struggling to write their last commercial novels." In an interview for a local newspaper Josephson explained that he and Hannah were "not only resting here, but continuing to work—work being an escape undertaken for fear of not doing anything. We go on, even we old people are afraid to stop working." [28]

What Josephson was working on during his last years was a subject that had long fascinated him—Alger Hiss. He planned to write a book on the famous case that would expose the investigation and trial of Hiss as a miscarriage of justice, just as his hero Zola had done in the Dreyfus Case. In the Hiss affair, Josephson saw another "*cause célèbre* which could lend itself to the dramatic treatment I had given earlier to the Dreyfus affair." He intended to set forth "a new version and more accurate one of the hearings and two trials." As in the Dreyfus case, secret government documents were used by the prosecution to great effect. Although Hiss and his lawyers had argued that the evidence was forged, they were not believed. Now, at last, Josephson contended, the truth would come out, as the "horrors of the Watergate affair gave full exposure to the dark side of Richard Nixon and brought about his ruin." Moreover, he noted, a recent amendment to the Freedom of Information Act promised to open up the files of the Federal Bureau of Investigation to interested scholars.[29]

When he began the Hiss project in 1974 Josephson had no specific knowledge of new evidence that would exonerate Hiss. Largely his assumptions reflected his long-held personal conviction that Hiss must be innocent, considering the character and vehemence of his two notorious accusers, Chambers and Nixon. He admitted that like "thousands of Americans who lived through the thirties, under the New Deal, I 'identified' with Hiss, followed every new development touching him, read everything on the affair." Like many supporters of Hiss, Josephson believed that the former State Department official had been the victim of the witch-hunt atmosphere that pervaded American society in the postwar years. Hiss was a symbol of all that the extreme Right hated: he was an Ivy League New Dealer devoted to the welfare state and sympathetic to Soviet communism. At the same time, he was a symbol for left-liberals like Josephson, appearing as a scapegoat, suffering for the supposed sins of thousands of others. During the second Hiss trial, late in 1949, Josephson had approached the defense lawyers and had offered to testify about his stormy encounter with the "unstable" Whittaker Chambers in the 1930s. Hiss's harried attorneys, however, refused the offer. Matthew later met Hiss when he was released from prison. They became casual friends, several times meeting for lunch in New York. In 1974 Josephson wrote him, announcing that he was starting the project. After noting the plethora of Hiss biographers already on the scene, he explained, "I had the idea that your turn had finally come—as others have no doubt suggested, or you must have sensed." His intention, he informed Hiss, was to write not a full-length biography but rather a concise, hard-hitting account of the two trials. Hiss offered his complete cooperation.[30]

Thus Josephson embarked on what to him would be his most important literary work. A book clearing the name of Alger Hiss would serve both his craft and his conscience well. In the midst of his research, however, disaster struck. On July 3, 1976, the Josephsons hosted a holiday party at their home in Sherman. While serving her guests Hannah suddenly began to limp noticeably. By the next day she could hardly walk. The doctors initially diagnosed a stroke, but as the numbness continued to spread during the next several weeks, they conducted more tests, finally discovering malignant tumors on her brain and lung. The cancer caused paralysis and a deterioration of the motor system. Hannah was too weak to undergo surgery, which would have been risky at best. All that could be done was to make her comfortable.

The inevitable was slow in coming. Hannah fought on for more than three months. She had always been a strong, courageous woman, and now such qualities came to the fore as she literally willed herself to live a few days, then a few weeks more. Matthew was at her side daily during the agonizing last three months of her life, comforting her, urging her on, recounting with her their experiences together. Their relationship during the past fifty-six years had frequently been turbulent, strained by Matthew's numerous liaisons, but in the past decade their feelings for each other had deepened considerably. In August 1975 Josephson had confessed to Eric, "Your mother and I made a good marriage, thanks to her (I say)." Matthew had always looked to Hannah for support, far more so than most people knew. In 1933, while on board ship headed for Russia, he had written her, "Besides being my darling, and my sweetheart and my snooky-snookums and all that, you are my public utility, my vehicle or vessel of confidences, whims, inspirations, moods, notes, impressions. My business in life is sadly incomplete without you." Hannah probably had mixed feelings about being called a "public utility," but it was an accurate description of his attitude toward her. Since then he had come to realize that his feelings for her were far more profound. She alone, during their later years, could speak to him and make herself understood without raising her voice. Now the thought of losing her threw him into a panic. "I had planned," he observed in his journal, "and even counted on her kindly laying me in my bier. We had come to a stage, in recent years, of beautiful understanding mixed with compassion for the weakness of age in each other, and I reckoned on continuing to enjoy for some years this marvelous love-friendship." As he watched her struggle with cancer, he marveled at her grace under pressure, her humility, and her devotion. He not only loved her; he esteemed her. "She fairly overwhelms me with her expressions of joy and gratitude for the ordinary kindness I have shown her in her extreme illness, which is perhaps terminal. She exudes love as if from every pore. Few others can be as loving as she. I run to her every day because of her greatness of heart, her prodigies of affection."[31]

By September, two months after the initial seizure, Hannah's condition had stabilized, with one side immobile. She was unable to sit or stand or walk, just able to eat with one good arm, and living on drugs that soothed her pains and controlled her spasms. Watching her struggle day after day was almost more than Matthew could bear. "Pity for her literally tears at me when I think of her pain, her helplessness, and her humiliation. . . . What a dreadful way to die." Matthew lost all sense of direction. He could not work, think, or relax as long as Hannah battled on. As he explained, he had arrived at the age "when a man is much disposed to slow down activities and try to evaluate and review things. Now this human disaster, this tragic happening, leaves me as if transfixed. I am occupied all the time, and going nowhere." Malcolm Cowley reported early in October that Josephson "is distraught. Poor dear Hannah is on the point of death, and can't die, though she has pretty well passed beyond the point of communicating with Matty and her sister Felicia, who have kept daily vigil at her bedside."[32]

Late in October the doctors indicated that the end was near. Hannah had gradually lost the ability to talk and had difficulty staying awake. On the 25th Josephson concluded his journal entry: "So we are coming to the end of the chapter." Four days later Hannah was dead. Even though her death had been long in coming, the finality of the event was a shattering blow for Matthew. In attending to the funeral arrangements, he proceeded like a "mechanical drone, still uncomprehending, not measuring the enormity of what happened. At home I kept looking for her nearby, or listening. Now I am truly and terribly alone." Hannah had been his steady companion and friend for well over fifty years, always providing a stable support for his own insecurity and need for attention. Her departure left a vacuum that was impossible to fill. Josephson later recalled that during the period after the funeral, "My mind was so distracted, because everything seemed so disastrously changed. She gave me so much, she was all grace and generosity—our later years were especially wonderful—as I told her. . . . She protected me a good deal while I went on alone in my long hours of work; and I was surprised at how many loved and came to mourn her, while our intimates believed, as I do, that she was the making of me."[33]

For several months after Hannah's death, Matthew was only a walking shadow of his old self, his spirit gone and his health deteriorating. Cowley observed that Hannah's death "was a blow to us, and of course vastly more of a blow to Matty, who is emotionally and physically exhausted—bad heart, bad lungs, high blood pressure, fever." Kenneth Burke, whose own wife had died a few years before, tried to console his friend: "There is the one solace that dear Hannah is now beyond the need to die. Those of us who were close companions with our wives must now do some cruel improvising. In feeling sorry for you, I but feel sorry for myself all over again. . . . But our education must go on." Fortunately for Josephson, Eric was there to help. He invited his father to come live with him in New York, which he did for four months. As time passed Matty's health and spirits improved, but he remained a changed man. Friends noticed that he was quieter, less inclined to make the witty remarks or engage in the heated discussions that had characterized him for so long. He simply could not stop dwelling on Hannah's death. She had been, as he told Malcolm Cowley, "my eyes and hands." [34]

Gradually Josephson returned to his research and writing, immersing himself in the Hiss project in an effort to forget the pain and sense of loneliness. He also spent a great deal of time responding to inquiries from scholars working on studies of Katherine Anne Porter, John Brooks Wheelwright, and other writers he had known. The winter of 1977 he spent in Sarasota. "I'm working again," he reported, "and learning to cook for myself, though numerous friends treat me as their favorite sponger." That spring he returned to Sherman for the first time since the death of his wife, "residing alone in this rambling old house to which Hannah and I first came in 1930." [35]

In January 1978 Josephson accepted an offer to be a scholar-in-residence at the University of California at Santa Cruz. He found it "a lively academic center, a small version of Berkeley." There he was made to feel quite at home by Page Smith, the Pulitzer-Prize winning historian. They frequently had lunch or dinner together. Josephson doggedly continued to work on the Hiss project, even though plagued by intermittent bouts with ill health. In February he received the proofs of *Perjury*, the controversial new study of the Hiss case by Allen Weinstein. "Wish I could review it somewhere," Matthew wrote Eric, "Heavy-handed. It's amazingly partisan and full of 'loaded dice' plays. He's made fantastic efforts to destroy the cult of Alger Hiss and preserve the Chambers myth. If Chambers forgets something or is proven wrong, Weinstein doesn't mind it; but if Hiss has a memory lapse 'it's thirty years lying.'" Josephson had come to view his study of the Hiss case as a moral obligation. He wrote in March that he had been "working at his labor of love for Hiss' sake mainly." But

Josephson was never to finish the book. On March 13, the day he planned to return to Sherman, he suffered a pulmonary seizure and died at age seventy-nine. Josephson's last journal entry revealed at least one of the factors contributing to his death: "More than sixteen months have passed since Hannah died, and I can never put her out of my mind." Carl had the body cremated and returned the ashes to Sherman, where they were strewn in the brook below the house.[36]

16   CONCLUSION

Any judgment of Matthew Josephson's life must inevitably reflect the ambivalent nature of his personality and his career. He was a fascinating, often paradoxical man, a combination of nobility and smallness, innocence and guile. He could be stubborn, vain, disagreeable—and a good hater. Quick to discern other people's errors, he was often slow to recognize his own. Josephson himself admitted as much in 1977 when he remarked: "I was a rather indiscreet person. I made a lot of enemies. I offended many people. I have enjoyed that. I never pulled my punches. Some people like me for that, others are down on it." Nearly thirty years before, he had made a similar observation, describing himself as a "high-willed man—full of temperament—rationalizing his temperamental qualities—dominating, pounding at everyone. Living often in a storm—spreading a certain subdued terror in others." Behind this self-confident facade, however, there resided an often troubled man, torn between rival obligations, rival callings, and rival passions, insecure among his friends, and uncertain about his career. Once, when Kenneth Burke complained of insomnia, Matthew replied that he himself was "usually a sound sleeper, because I have a good conscience." He quickly added, however, "In reality my conscience is no better than your own guilt-laden one."[1]

Yet if Josephson was arrogant, anxious, and petulant, he could also be warm and convivial, witty and ubane. He had an ironic sense of humor and a cosmopolitan charm that served to disarm much of his bluster. Despite the occasionally turbulent relationships they had with Matty, Kenneth Burke and Malcolm Cowley always held him in high esteem. Burke remembered him most clearly as a "spontaneously, charmingly sociable man." Cowley, while admitting that Josephson could at times be quarrelsome and dogmatic, thought of him most often as a "delightful and stimulating companion with a sweep and swoop of imagination, more than any other of my friends."[2]

It was Hannah, however, who knew Matthew best and who provided the most accurate analysis of him. To her his good qualities more often than not outweighed the bad. Like many other women who knew him well, she was able to overlook his domineering personality and his posturing. Of course, even Hannah at times grew impatient or irritated with Matty. But she found it difficult to maintain such a posture for long. In 1935, when Matty faced a serious operation, she wrote a thoughtful description of him and their relationship:

> His conversation is at its best when it is a monologue, and I call it conversation because he must have a listener, and preferably an intelligent one. I have been an intelligent listener for fifteen years. He can be charmingly ribald, delicate in his approach to limited persons, indulge in wild flights of Rabelaisian fancy (to his children), logical as a screwdriver fitting the screw into the hole, caustic and bitter. His gaiety is terribly infectious—no long-standing grudge can hold out against it.

"Headstrong, affectionate, thoughtless, cruel at times," she concluded, "he is the most interesting and lovable man I have ever met."[3]

During the 1940s and after, as Hannah painfully witnessed, Matthew fell into a pattern of blaming his family situation for his failure to write creative literature, often bemoaning in his journal the personal and artistic sacrifices he was forced to make in order to maintain their standard of living and to fulfill his duties as husband and father. This was more rationalization than explanation. Josephson failed to produce a work of fiction not so much because of his family obligations but because he lacked the spark of creativity, as well as the imaginative self-confidence, required of the novelist. These personal limitations help explain why after the 1920s he made the transition from poetry and fiction to biography, history, and journalism. "Biography," Harold Nicolson once remarked, "is the preoccupation and solace not of certainty, but of doubt." Josephson lacked the introspective certainty of the poet or novelist. He found it much easier to write about someone else's life and about some other historical era than to create original characters and to develop a believable fictional world. He was better at eliciting the meaning in a historical subject, a real-life hero or villain, than at conjuring up a subject on his own. Writing literary biography for Josephson was a vicarious experience; it allowed him to study the great creative writers turned social activists whom he so genuinely wanted to emulate. As Malcolm Cowley once observed, Matty literally "became" his subject, living the life of another in order to know himself better.

If Josephson lacked the imaginative certainty of a successful poet or novelist, he was admirably suited for writing biography and history. He needed his characters and incidents ready-made, he needed the mask of another life to hide behind, but once he discovered his subject, he then effectively combined the creative abilities he did have with a superb capacity to discern significance in a life, to discover in a mass of seemingly complex material the unifying theme in a life and then to humanize and vitalize the material. Biography was an art, he maintained, "requiring the intuition of the man of letters to achieve form and significance, and above all, to create life out of the materials given." It was not enough to recite a life's details; the biographer must use the techniques of creative literature to integrate vividness and cumulative drama into the narrative, thereby making his subject come alive and grasp the imagination of the reader.[4]

Josephson believed that the biographer must discover a guiding theme to give his study focus. Too few American biographers, he felt, made the effort to "seize the pattern which underlies any worthwhile life, by means of some consistently upheld criterion, measuring the relative importance of evidence and fact." This was what Josephson tried to do. Although he read into his subjects' lives his own attitudes and concerns, allowing them to serve as vehicles for the satisfaction of his own longings, he was generally accurate in isolating their dominant characteristics. Viewed in this light his biographies of Zola, Rousseau, Hugo, and Stendhal share a common pattern: they present heroic, enlightened literary men who cherished their integrity enough to attack entrenched convention and authority, who possessed the creative ability to develop original ideas, and who risked established reputations and sometimes their lives to defend a noble cause. Josephson not only portrayed them as courageous men of letters and moral successes but also as human beings heir to all the ills and foibles of human flesh—as he himself was. His literary biographies were successful largely because they have a coherent and sustained argument, grounded upon a persistent theme, an explicit historical vision of the subject's social environment coupled with skillful analyses of inner conflicts.[5]

While Josephson's historical studies share many of the same qualities that distinguished his biographies, they reveal a much greater sense of urgency. He once described the situation he confronted during the 1930s:

> Faced with unforeseen social-political problems, compelled to take unprecedented measures, our contemporary politicians seemed to grope for new values, new interpretations of the relationship of the present epoch to the continuity of the past. Yet the conventional historians, with their antiquated Spencerian individualism and their Chamber of Commerce mentalities, yielded neither nourishment nor counsel.

Josephson sought to provide such new interpretations of the past in order to help stimulate social and political change. Consequently, he decided to write *The Robber Barons*, *The Politicos*, and *The President Makers* because he considered them "timely" studies; he hoped that by shedding light on the past, he could illuminate problems in the present.[6]

Josephson's historical orientation resembled that of the *philosophes* he so admired. Like the eighteenth-century writers, he wrote history with "rage and partisanship." He likewise believed that history should be written by moralists, not pedants. Late in his life he explained his perspective as historian:

> The essence of the historian's art is to recreate the past as it truly was and the motivation of past times also; but surely this cannot be accomplished well by persons who are fish-blooded, without moral fibre, without any sense of human values, without human compassion or the capacity for "noble indignation." The game is to make history come alive, and impress us as true.

Josephson recognized the virtue of Ranke's dictum to portray the past as it actually was, but he thought it more important to use history to express one's moral indignation at corruption and injustice. For this reason he never intended to write as an "objective" historian. As he pointed out in 1975, "When a man sees someone about to murder his wife he doesn't stop to look at 'both sides' of the question." Such was the crisis psychology he acted under during the depression years. The need for reforming

or even revolutionizing the country's socioeconomic system was immediate; he must do what he could to spur such change.[7]

It is true that Josephson was, as many critics have charged, a "popular"
historian. He selected his subjects for their intrinsic appeal and their relevance to contemporary concerns. Moreover, he wrote not for scholars
but for the general reading public, a public that wanted the results of
scholarship without its tedious paraphernalia. His purpose was to expose
as much as to understand. While admitting the significance of careful research, he gave more attention to "the equipment of a philosophy of history, to a point of view, a compass by which one may navigate the oceans
of documents and facts." At the same time, however, he believed that
history should never be so dominated by an interpretive scheme that it
becomes dry or mechanical. The unpardonable sin for any writer was to
be boring. He saw "no compulsion under the heavens, no conceivable
reason why writing, historical or otherwise, should deliberately seek to
be dull." He was a popular historian, therefore, but not in the pejorative
sense of the term, for he never wrote in a vulgar style, nor was the content of his books superficial or trivial.[8]

In his stress upon history as literary art, in the boldness and vigor of his
style, and in his sense of personal involvement with his material, Josephson resembled the Romantic historians of the nineteenth century. Although he freely used theories of Marx, Veblen, Weber, and others to
help explain the past, he centered his historical studies on the activities
of dominant men, as did Prescott, Parkman, Carlyle, Macaulay, and
Motley. Like them he structured his narratives in the form of a drama.
Each work is built around a dramatic buildup of tension that leads to a
climax followed by some form of resolution. In *The Robber Barons* he
traced the industrialists and financiers from their humble beginnings
through their early struggles and successes at pooling and monopoly formation until eventually the whole country was "trustified." For *The Politicos* he chose as his dramatic theme the evolution of a well-organized,
centralized, and ruthlessly efficient national party system that demonstrated its clout in the climactic election of 1896. Finally, in *The President Makers*, Josephson described the growth of the Progressive movement, which reached its climax in 1916; then he traced its dissolution
after America's intervention in the Great War and Wilson's physical and
political collapse two years later.

Josephson thus wrote muckraking literature as much as history. There
is no doubt that in the process his partisanship caused him to make villains of men who deserve greater understanding. It is equally apparent

that he sometimes derived his history from his personal opinions. He was also occasionally amateurish and casual about documentation and generalization. Despite such defects, however, Matthew Josephson wrote much undeniably good history—and it was never dull. As Geoffrey Blodgett recently noted, Josephson's historical works "surpassed all previous studies in density of narrative detail and vivid identification of villains and heroes." His books remain in print and continue to excite interest in robber barons, politicos, and president makers. Judged by his own criteria and purposes, Josephson was remarkably successful in "making history come alive and impress us as true."[9]

In the final analysis, the success of Josephson's biographies and histories is based chiefly on their use as a vehicle for his ideas and his indignation. Perhaps the most salient aspect of his literary career was his emphasis on the ethical nature of his task. "The merits of my work," he wrote in 1934, "have been skill in presentation; a vigorous and elastic style; good organization toward the dramatic; a penchant for irony and some humor; a freshness of approach." His list of weaknesses was considerably shorter: "Wants: lack of real depth or exhaustiveness—almost a universal vice." It was hard for Josephson to admit weakness, especially to himself. But he was remarkably accurate in his self-analysis. He later observed that his "style is best when I am moved and write with a sweep of conviction." He was pleased with the "passionate accent" of his writings. Josephson was never a timid writer; he wrote energetically and emotionally. In a revealing comparison, Malcolm Cowley recently discussed his two friends Josephson and Burke. Matthew, he wrote, "wasn't as good a stylist as Kenneth. His thought didn't go as deep. But he had a broader grasp of conception." He was never as profound or analytical in his thinking as Burke. Josephson always placed more emphasis than Burke did on the larger social and political implications of literature, organizing his material for dramatic impact, and seeking to promote reform and concern directly through his writings. He judged men, both past and present, by their moral qualities, and these judgments gave his writings verve and appeal.[10]

Like his personality, Josephson's political views were a mixture of admirable and questionable elements. "There is no such thing," he contended in 1937, "as a writer without ethical principles and political opinions." He himself was certainly a principled and opinionated writer—sometimes too much so. Until his death Josephson remained an unreconstructed, unapologetic left-liberal. His attempt to assume the responsibilities of the writer turned public man occasionally exposed the shallowness and inconsistency of his political opinions. He never developed an appreciation for the complexity of human nature or of causation; nor did he ever satisfactorily resolve the conflict between his bourgeois aloofness and his support of an egalitarian social program.[11]

Josephson was also the victim of moral blind spots. One feels impatient with his prolonged attachment to the Russian version of communism, long after its excesses had been revealed. He was so preoccupied with exposing the crimes of American capitalism that he tended to ignore or minimize the crimes and moral bankruptcy of Stalinism. How an independent liberal so concerned with basic human values and the protection of civil liberties could regard the Soviet state with such complacency for so long remains a puzzle. Certainly his natural stubbornness was a factor in his remaining silent. That some of the more vocal of the former literary radicals during the postwar era were screaming for blood and insisting that everyone join in their apostasy was probably reason enough for Josephson not to do so. He felt that there were plenty of anti-Communists to carry the banner of neo-orthodoxy. But his silence was not based solely on an unwillingness to conform. There was some wishful thinking at work. Josephson remained optimistic that the Soviets and their American supporters, despite their dogmatism and authoritarianism, were pursuing noble objectives. Criticizing them would only endanger the ultimate success of the liberal Left. It was not until 1962 that he could admit that "in my later years, I am more strongly impressed with the failings of the Soviet version of Communism—though I was never a dupe."[12]

Josephson may have erred in his complacent attitude toward Stalinist Russia and in his roseate view of man's nature; he may have placed too much emphasis on reason and progress and too little on the tragic reality of modern life. But the choices that he and other literary intellectuals of his generation faced were neither clear nor easy. "Alas," as Josephson recognized late in life, "our choices . . . are seldom as clear or morally satisfying as we would wish them to be; neither are they often as ideologically consistent or as perfectly attuned to our finer sentiments as we might hope." Whatever the defects of the individual decisions Josephson made, he did not give in to a gloomy pessimism or to the worst excesses of Left radicalism. Maxwell Geismar fondly remembered him as an "old-fashioned radical democrat who never recanted during the worst phases of the cold war epoch and McCarthyism; this must be stressed about him."[13]

Josephson was genuinely a man of good hope, and his generation may have been the last capable of sustaining such faith in man and his future. His was a humanism strengthened and given a sense of urgency by his hopes for mankind—and his fears. Despite an occasional lapse into cynicism, he consistently felt that the attainment of a better, more humane, and more collectivist social order was possible in the United States if intellectuals would only continue to strive for it. As the twentieth century has progressed, literary intellectuals have increasingly assumed a more detached pose and a more "realistic" view of society and its capacity for improvement. From such a perspective Josephson's outlook no doubt seems naive and outdated. Yet art without such humane faith and involvement represents an abdication of responsibility. If Josephson was led astray, it was by his own indignation and sense of social duty. "I am proud," he once wrote, "of the small effort I made . . . to encourage social relief—through pressure from the Left—and I am not proud of the people today who would never permit any human emotions to lead them to anything that wasn't right-thinking, respectable." [14]

Viewed in retrospect Matthew Josephson's career followed the pattern of alienation, exile, return, and reintegration common to so many middle-class writers of his generation. But his reconciliation with American society was never complete. Instead of reintegrating himself into his native culture, he remained in a state of creative tension with his homeland, unable either to embrace or reject it fully. America, he believed, did not provide as fertile an environment for the writer turned public man as did France. This attitude can be seen in the dualistic nature of Josephson's literary subjects. On one hand he wrote about French writers like Zola, Hugo, and Stendhal, men who displayed both superior literary ability and admirable social and political involvement, and on the other hand he wrote about American businessmen, politicos, and inventors. The one exception to this pattern was *Portrait of the Artist as American*, in which he did discuss American writers. The discussion, however, was not a happy one. Josephson's conscious choice of French writers to portray and emulate reflected his belief that European culture offered a wider possibility for the writer to play the role of public man without sacrificing his art in the process. American culture, by contrast, favored robber barons and politicos, men of crass action rather than artistic sensitivity. Instead of providing artists with a congenial atmosphere in which to combine their creative and social impulses, it forced them to struggle for mere survival. Josephson came to realize that making a living in America by commercial journalism in order to have the freedom to make a statement through literature was not easy.

Hannah recognized that Matthew was a split personality, torn between being a bohemian rebel and being a bourgeois social reformer. That is how she explained his love affairs. They resulted from his innate artistic rebelliousness. As she suggested: "He would willingly be unsteady; he has a passion to be footloose and free of responsibility—perhaps a hang-over from his career as a poet." At the same time, however, Hannah pointed out that he also found "the regularity of responsibility most conducive to habits of work." In this way she laid bare the dualism that provided the dynamic for Josephson's life and career. As he once told Kenneth Burke, "I am neither all black nor all white." He wanted to be both a successful, serious, somewhat bohemian writer, with all the personal freedom and social detachment that such a life entailed, and a successful bourgeois with the benefits and responsibilities of middle-class life—a home in the country, a family, a sense of material security and social involvement. That he chose for most of his life to maintain both a homestead in the Berkshires and an apartment in Greenwich Village illustrates his divided loyalties. Such ambivalence, of course, was not unique to Matthew Josephson; it was common among writers of his generation. In 1952 William Phillips observed that the American writer was no longer totally alienated but "suspended between tradition and revolt, nationalism and internationalism, the aesthetic and the civic, and . . . belonging and alienation."[15]

Josephson persistently tried to balance such conflicting tendencies only to discover that to emphasize one he had to sacrifice the other. His anxieties about such decisions dogged him increasingly through the years. Yet one must beware of painting his portrait in too somber hues. While the frustrations Josephson faced in trying to be both a bohemian and a bourgeois were real and persistent, his life was also in many respects a rich and rewarding one. The dynamic tension created by the clash of such opposed tendencies may have been a necessary catalyst in his literary and personal development. Reflecting on his career he once remarked that despite occasional disappointments, he had "few regrets. I have thoroughly enjoyed my life, activities, friendships, and enmities; I have been alive, have been aware of the moments of high pleasure and beauty which the mind knows through the body, either for things seen or felt, music heard, words spoken or the play of emotions within." It makes a fitting epitaph to a remarkable life.[16]

KEY TO ABBREVIATIONS

AH	Alfred Harcourt
AL	Amy Lowell
ALP	Amy Lowell Papers, Houghton Library, Harvard University
AS	Alfred Stieglitz
ASP	Alfred Stieglitz Papers, Beinecke Library, Yale University
AT	Allen Tate
ATP	Allen Tate Papers, Firestone Library, Princeton University
CA	Charles Allen
CAP	Charles Allen Papers, Beinecke Library, Yale University
CB	Charles Beard
CP	Charles Pearce
EJ	Eric Josephson
ER	Malcolm Cowley, *Exile's Return: A Literary Odyssey of the 1920s* (New York: Viking/Compass, 1956)
EW	Edmund Wilson
GM	Gorham Munson
HC	Hart Crane
HCF	Harcourt Brace Jovanovich, Incorporated, Correspondence File, New York
HJ	Hannah Josephson
HL	Harold Loeb
HLP	Harold Loeb Papers, Firestone Library, Princeton University

HM	Harriet Monroe
IT	Matthew Josephson, *Infidel in the Temple: A Memoir of the 1930s* (New York: Knopf, 1967)
JBW	John Brooks Wheelwright
JBWP	John Brooks Wheelwright Papers, Brown University Library
Journal	Matthew Josephson's personal journals, in the possession of his son Eric, Sherman, Connecticut
KAP	Katherine Anne Porter
KB	Kenneth Burke
LAS	Matthew Josephson, *Life among the Surrealists: A Memoir* (New York: Holt, Rinehart and Winston, 1962)
Letters	*The Letters of Hart Crane*, ed. Brom Weber (Berkeley: University of California Press, 1965)
LM	Lewis Mumford
LRP	*Little Review* Papers, University of Wisconsin—Milwaukee
MC	Malcolm Cowley
MCP	Malcolm Cowley Papers, Newberry Library, Chicago
MJ	Matthew Josephson
MJP1	Matthew and Hannah Josephson Papers, Beinecke Library, Yale University
MJP2	Matthew Josephson Papers in the possession of Eric Josephson, Sherman, Connecticut. The Josephson family have since transferred most of these letters and manuscripts to the Josephson collection at Yale University
NR	*New Republic*
PMC	*Poetry* Magazine Collection, University of Chicago
Speech	Unidentified and untitled speech, probably delivered by MJ at the Conference on Cultural Freedom and Civil Liberties, 25–27 October 1947, New York (MJP2)
TC	Thomas Cochran
TCP	Thomas Cochran Papers, Van Pelt Library, University of Pennsylvania
WF	Waldo Frank

NOTES

Chapter 2: Growing Up in Brooklyn

1. General background information concerning Julius and Sarah Josephson was obtained through personal interviews and correspondence with Matthew Josephson, his brother Murray K. Josephson, and his sister Essie Weinstein.

2. MJ to author, 20 September 1975.

3. Irving Howe, *World of Our Fathers* (New York: Harcourt, Brace, 1976), p. 131. On Brownsville see Alter F. Landesman, *Brownsville: The Birth, Development, and Passing of a Jewish Community in New York* (New York: Bloch, 1969); Alfred Kazin, *A Walker in the City* (New York: Harcourt, Brace, 1951).

4. MJ to author, 25 January 1976.

5. *LAS*, p. 26.

6. MJ to author, 7 February 1976.

7. Henry Adams, *The Education of Henry Adams*, Riverside edition (Boston: Houghton Mifflin, 1973), p. 457.

8. *LAS*, p. 15.

9. "A Growing Village," *New York Herald-Tribune*, 30 August 1899, p. 7; Kazin, *A Walker in the City*, p. 8.

10. MJ, "My Friend Oliver and the New Freedom," manuscript, p. 3, MJP2.

11. MJ to Alfred Kazin, 29 November 1967, MJP2; Journal, 30 November 1967.

12. *LAS*, p. 24.

13. Elias Ginzberg, autobiographical manuscript in the possession of Joel Freeman, Tuckahoe, New York, pp. 338–39.

14. MJ discussed his relationship with Winner in "My Friend Oliver and the New Freedom." See also *LAS*, pp. 19–22 (MJ uses "Clarence Newman" as a pseudonym for Winner).

15. *Las*, p. 19; MJ; "My Friend Oliver and the New Freedom," p. 13.

16. MJ, "My Friend Oliver and the New Freedom," pp. 14–15.
17. MJ to author, 25 August 1976; personal interview with MJ, 16 August 1976.
18. *LAS*, p. 23; *ER*, pp. 21–23.
19. *LAS*, p. 24.
20. MJ, "Walk over Jersey Meadows," manuscript, pages unnumbered, MJP1.
21. *LAS*, p. 25.

Chapter 3: Columbia and Greenwich Village

1. Lloyd Morris, *A Threshold in the Sun* (New York: Harper, 1943), p. 42. On the intellectual atmosphere of the period, see Morton White, *Social Thought in America: The Revolt against Formalism* (Boston: Beacon, 1947).
2. Henry May, *The End of American Innocence* (New York: Knopf, 1959), p. 63; Max Eastman, *Great Companions: Critical Memoirs of Some Famous Friends* (New York: Farrar, Straus, 1959), p. 281; Randolph Bourne to Dorothy Teall, 23 October 1913, Randolph Bourne Papers, Columbia University.
3. John Erskine, *My Life as Teacher* (New York: Lippincott, 1948), p. 93; MJ, "Charles Beard: A Memoir," *Virginia Quarterly Review* 25 (October 1949): 586; Irwin Edman, *Philosopher's Holiday* (New York: Viking, 1938), p. 253.
4. Alan Trachtenberg, ed., *Critics of Culture: Literature and Society in the Early Twentieth Century* (New York: Wiley, 1976), p. 3. See also Arthur Wertheim, *The New York Little Renaissance: Iconoclasm, Modernism and Nationalism in American Culture, 1908–1917* (New York: New York University Press, 1976).
5. Floyd Dell, *Intellectual Vagabondage* (New York: Doran, 1926), p. 106.
6. *ER*, pp. 52–73; James Oppenheim, "The Story of the *Seven Arts*," *American Mercury* 20 (June 1930): 157.
7. Richard Hofstadter, *The Progressive Historians: Turner, Beard and Parrington* (New York: Vintage, 1970), p. 185.
8. Joseph Freeman, *An American Testament: A Narrative of Rebels and Romantics* (New York: Farrar, 1936), p. 32; AL, *Some Imagist Poets* (Boston: Houghton Mifflin, 1915), p. ii.
9. MJ to AL, 12 February 1917, ALP; AL to MJ, 17 February 1917, ALP.
10. AL to MJ, 29 May 1917, ALP.
11. *LAS*, pp. 30–31.
12. Personal interview with KB, 17 July 1977.
13. KB, "A Commemorative Tribute to MJ," National Academy of Arts and Letters, New York City, 15 November 1978; MJ, "Notes for a Memoir," MJP2; Burke's description of MJ is quoted in JBW, "Comment on Malcolm's Letter from Giverny," manuscript dated 9 May 1923, p. 10, JBWP.
14. KB to author, 20 April 1979; JBW, "Comment," p. 10; MJ, "Notes for a Memoir," MJP2; MJ to KB, 10 June 1917, MJP2.
15. MJ to Theodore Dreiser, 20 June 1917, Theodore Dreiser Papers, Van Pelt Library, University of Pennsylvania.
16. John Dos Passos to Rumsey Marvin, 20 February 1917, in *The Fourteenth Chronicle: Letters and Diaries of John Dos Passos*, ed. Townsend Ludington (Boston: Gambit, 1973), p. 67; Miles Colean to author, 23 June 1977.
17. Floyd Dell, *Love in Greenwich Village* (New York: Doran, 1926), p. 15. On Village life, see Allen Churchill, *Improper Bohemians: A Recreation of Greenwich Village in Its Heyday* (New York: Dutton, 1959).
18. *LAS*, pp. 41, 50; MJ to KB, 25 July 1917, MJP1.
19. *Columbia Spectator*, 7 February 1917, p. 4.

20. *LAS*, pp. 53–54.

21. MJ, "The Decadents," unpublished notes, MJP2.

22. MJ to KB, 25 July 1917, MJP1.

23. *LAS*, p. 55.

24. Ibid., p. 43.

25. Ibid., p. 47; MJ to KB, 30 June 1918, MJP2.

26. MJ, "The Last Lady," *Poetry* 17 (October 1920): 20; MJ to KB, 7 September 1919, MJP2.

27. MJ to HM, 28 September 1918, PMC.

Chapter 4: The Making of a Writer

1. William Leuchtenburg, *The Perils of Prosperity, 1914–1932* (Chicago: University of Chicago Press, 1958), p. 8; Roderick Nash, *The Nervous Generation: American Thought, 1917–1930* (Chicago: Rand McNally, 1973), p. 41.

2. MJ, "'Grundyism' at College: 1919," Journal, undated (probably 1950s), unnumbered.

3. Personal interview with MJ, 26 July 1976; *ER*, p. 48; MC to KB, 8 July 1919, MCP; MJ to KB, 16 July 1919, MJP2.

4. GM, "The Fledgling Years, 1916–1924," *Sewanee Review* 11 (January–March 1932): 29.

5. *LAS*, p. 51; *ER*, p. 72; MJ, "Walk over Jersey Meadows," unnumbered, MJP1.

6. May, *The End of American Innocence*, pp. 219–32.

7. The literature on Symbolism is voluminous. Especially useful are Anna Balakian, *The Symbolist Movement: A Critical Appraisal* (New York: Random House, 1967); A. G. Lehmann, *The Symbolist Aesthetic in France, 1885–1895* (Oxford: Blackwell, 1950); Arthur Symons, *The Symbolist Movement in Literature* (New York: Dutton, 1958).

8. *ER*, p. 142. On Cowley see Eleanor Bulkin, "Malcolm Cowley: A Study of His Literary, Social and Political Thought to 1940" (Ph.D. diss., New York University, 1973), pp. 17–43.

9. *LAS*, pp. 60–62.

10. MJ to KB, 18 March 1919, MJP1.

11. MJ to HM, 13 March 1919, PMC; MJ to AL, 10 November 1919, ALP.

12. AL to MJ, 25 November 1919, ALP; MJ, "Variations on a Theme of Baudelaire," *Gargoyle* 1 (December 1921): 28–29; May, *The End of American Innocence*, p. 275.

13. MJ to AL, 1 December 1919, ALP; Josephson quoted in HC to GM, 13 December 1919, *Letters*, p. 61; personal interview with MJ, 26 July 1976.

14. HC to GM, 13 December 1919, *Letters*, p. 25; HC to MJ, 15 March 1920, *Letters*, p. 36. On the relationship between Josephson and Crane, see John Unterecker, *Voyager: A Life of Hart Crane* (New York: Farrar, Straus, 1969), pp. 158–59.

15. HC to GM, 13 December 1919, *Letters*, pp. 26–27.

16. MJ to KB, 21 September 1919, MJP2; *LAS*, p. 27; MJ, undergraduate transcript, Columbia University.

17. HC to GM, 14 April 1920, *Letters*, p. 37; Percy Winner to MJ, 26 May 1920, MJP1.

18. HJ, untitled portrait of MJ, Fall 1935, p. 1, MJP2.

19. Personal interview with MJ, 26 July 1976.

20. Louis Untermeyer, *From Another World: The Autobiography of Louis Untermeyer* (New York: Harcourt, Brace, 1939), pp. 90–91.

21. MJ to KB, undated (October? 1920), MJP1; MJ to KB, undated (November? 1920), MJP1; MJ to KB, 10 January 1921, MJP1.

22. *LAS*, pp. 67–70.

23. HC to GM, 19 September 1921, *Letters*, pp. 64–65.

24. Frederick Lewis Allen, *Only Yesterday: An Informal History of the 1920's* (New York: Harper, 1931), p. 237.

25. Harold Stearns, ed., *Civilization in the United States* (New York: Harcourt, Brace, 1922), pp. 9, 135–50.

26. MJ to CA, 25 July 1944, MJP1; MJ, "Notes for a Memoir," unnumbered, MJP1.

27. MJ, "Walk over Jersey Meadows," unnumbered, MJP1; Frederick Hoffman, *The Twenties: American Writing in the Postwar Decade* (New York: Free Press, 1962), pp. 444–48. The most thorough study of the literary expatriates remains Warren Susman, "Pilgrimage to Paris: The Background of American Expatriates" (Ph.D. diss., University of Wisconsin, 1958).

28. MJ, "Walk over Jersey Meadows," unnumbered, MJP1.

29. MC, "Matthew Josephson," *Book-Find Notes* (January 1947): p. 13; Wallace Stegner, *The Uneasy Chair: A Biography of Bernard DeVoto* (Garden City, N.Y.: Doubleday, 1974), p. 7.

30. Nichols quoted in John Garraty, ed., *Interpreting American History: Conversations with Historians* (New York: Macmillan, 1970), p. 270; *ER*, pp. 7, 9, 27, 80, 206, 213–14.

31. As Frederick Hoffman observed, the "concern with form was basically a concern over the need to provide an aesthetic order for moral revisions." See *The Twenties*, pp. 434–38.

32. Daniel Aaron, *Writers on the Left* (New York: Avon, 1961), p. 92.

Chapter 5: A European Adventure

1. MJ to KB, 4 November 1921, MJP1.

2. Ibid.

3. Ibid.; MJ, in foreword to *The Left Bank Revisited: Selections from the Paris Tribune, 1917–1934*, ed. Hugh Ford (University Park: Pennsylvania State University Press, 1972), p. xxii.

4. MJ to MC, 5 December 1921, MCP; John Dos Passos, *The Best Times: An Informal Memoir* (New York: New American Library, 1966), p. 144.

5. MJ to KB, 4 November 1921, MJP1; MJ to KB, 10 December 1921, MJP1.

6. GM, "The Fledgling Years," p. 29; HC to GM, 5 December 1921, *Letters*, p. 74.

7. Percy Winner to MJ, 26 May 1920, MJP1; MJ to KB, 10 September 1920, MJP2; HC to MJ, 14 January 1921, *Letters*, p. 50.

8. *LAS*, p. 113.

9. MJ to KB, 15 December 1921, MJP1.

10. MJ to MC, 5 December 1921, MCP; *LAS*, p. 116.

11. *ER*, p. 165; Aragon quoted in M. Adereth, *Commitment in Modern French Literature* (New York: Schocken, 1968), p. 65.

12. MJ to MC, 5 December 1921, MCP; MJ to KB, 10 December 1921, MJP1; KB to MJ, 27 December 1921, MJP1; HC to GM, 23 January 1922, *Letters*, pp. 78–79.

13. MJ to KB, 4 February 1922, MJP1.

14. Philippe Soupault, *The American Influence in France* (Seattle: University of Washington Press, 1930), pp. 13–14.

15. *LAS*, p. 125; MJ to KB, 4 February 1922, MJP1.

16. MJ to KB, 24 May 1922, MJP1; MJ to KB, 4 February 1922, MJP1; MJ to HL, 3 February 1922, HLP.

17. MJ to Alfred Kreymborg, undated, HLP; MJ to KB, 13 November 1921, MJP1.

18. MJ to KB, 4 February 1922, MJP1.

19. MJ to KB, 15 December 1921, MJP1; *LAS*, p. 154; MJ to KB, 28 February 1922, MJP1.

20. *Secession* 1 (Spring 1922): 19.

21. Ibid., pp. 9–13. MJ used the pseudonym "Will Bray."

22. Ibid.

23. Ibid., p. 13. In an illuminating study, Dickran Tashjian examines in detail this concept of a machine-age aesthetic, which developed among American writers and artists between 1910 and 1925. He devotes considerable attention to Josephson's ideas and activities, particularly in chapter 6. See *Skyscraper Primitives: Dada and the American Avant Garde, 1910–1925* (Middletown, Conn.: Wesleyan University Press, 1975).

24. EW, "The Aesthetic Upheaval in France," *Vanity Fair* (February 1922), p. 100.

25. MJ to KB, 10 April 1922, MJP1; MJ to MC, 25 April 1922, MCP.

26. HC to GM, 19 April 1922, *Letters*, p. 84; HC to GM, 16 May 1922, *Letters*, pp. 86–87.

27. MJ to HL, March 1922, HLP; MJ to KB, 26 April 1922, MJP1; MJ to KB, 18 June 1922, MJP1; MJ to KB, 24 May 1922, MJP1.

28. *New Age*, 21 September 1922, p. 6; Gertrude Stein to HL, 15 February 1922, HLP.

29. *Broom* 2 (May 1922): 178, 179, 181.

30. *Broom* 2 (June 1922): 269, 270.

31. Harold Loeb, *The Way It Was* (New York: Criterion, 1959), pp. 109, 118.

32. MJ to KB, 18 June 1922, MJP1.

33. HC to GM, 7 August 1922, *Letters*, p. 95.

34. MJ to Wallace Stevens, 22 February 1922, quoted in Robert Buttel, *Wallace Stevens: The Making of Harmonium* (Princeton, N.J.: Princeton University Press, 1967), p. 246; Maxwell Bodenheim, to HL, 30 January 1923, HLP.

35. WF to HL, 15 July 1922, HLP; WF to HL, 25 September 1922, HLP; AT to HC, 23 July 1922, HCP; HC to GM, 12 October 1922, *Letters*, p. 102; MJ to KB, 4 July 1922, MJP1.

36. MC to KB, 2 June 1922, MCP.

37. *ER*, p. 133; MC to KB, 27 August 1922, MCP.

38. MC to KB, 17 December 1922, MCP.

39. The quarrel between Josephson and Munson is explained in detail in several sources, though with varying nuances. See David E. Shi, "Munson vs. Josephson: Battle of the Aesthetes," *Lost Generation Journal* 5 (Spring 1977): 18–19; Alvin Rosenfeld, "John Wheelwright, Gorham Munson, and the 'Wars of *Secession*,'" *Michigan Quarterly Review* 14 (Winter 1975): 22–32; *LAS*, pp. 231–38; *ER*, pp. 179–85; GM, "The Fledgling Years," pp. 40–51.

40. JBW, "Comment on Malcolm's Letter," p. 7. On JBW see MJ, "Improper Bostonian: John Wheelwright and His Poetry," *Southern Review* 7 (April 1971): 509–40; Alan Wald, "From Antinomianism to Revolutionary Marxism: John Wheelwright and the New England Rebel Tradition," *Marxist Perspectives* 10 (Summer 1980): 44–68.

41. JBW, "Comment," pp. 11–13.

42. Ibid., p. 3. See also *LAS*, p. 235.

43. *Broom* 4 (December 1922): 53, 55.

44. *Broom* 3 (November 1922): 305, 310.

45. Ibid., p. 310.

46. WF to HL, 13 December 1922, HLP; HC to GM, Thanksgiving Day, 1922, *Letters*, pp. 105–06.

47. Louis Untermeyer, "The New Patricians," *NR*, 6 December 1922, pp. 41–42; Julius W. Friend, "Innocents Abroad," *The Double-Dealer* (October 1922): 203.

48. MC to KB, 11 January 1923, MCP; MC to KB, 16 January 1923, MCP; HC to GM, 5 January 1923, *Letters*, p. 113.

49. MJ to HL, 22 May 1923, HLP.

50. MC to KB, 4 June 1923, MCP.

Chapter 6: Dada in New York

1. MC to author, 4 April 1975.

2. MJ to HL, 16 May 1923, HLP.

3. MJ to MC, 12 July 1923, MJP1; MJ to MC, 26 June 1923, MCP.

4. HC to GM, 2 March 1923, *Letters*, p. 129; HC to AS, 26 May 1923, ASP; Unterecker, *Voyager*, pp. 305–06.

5. MJ, "Encounters with Edmund Wilson," *Southern Review* 11 (Summer 1975): 733.

6. MJ to HL, 16 May 1923, HLP; MJ to HL, 7 June 1923, HLP.

7. MJ to HL, 7 June 1923, HLP.

8. HL, "*Broom*: 1921–1923," *Broom* 5 (August 1923): 57.

9. *Broom* 5 (September 1923); *Broom* 5 (October 1923).

10. *Broom* 5 (August 1923): 49–50.

11. MJ, "Comment," *Broom* 5 (September 1923): 123, 120.

12. MJ, "The Brain at the Wheel," *Broom* 5 (September 1923): 96.

13. "Comment," *Dial* 74 (September 1923): 312; EW to John Peale Bishop, 15 January 1924, *Letters on Literature and Politics*, ed. Elena Wilson (New York: Farrar, Straus, 1977), p. 119.

14. EW, "An Imaginary Conversation: Mr. Paul Rosenfeld and Mr. Matthew Josephson," *NR*, 9 April 1924, pp. 179–82.

15. Ibid.

16. AS to HC, 27 October 1923, HCP; Burton Rascoe, "Josephson and the Modern Aesthetic," *New York Herald-Tribune*, 17 September 1923.

17. MJ to HL, 15 July 1923, HLP.

18. *LAS*, p. 244.

19. Ibid.; MJ to HL, 3 June 1923, HLP.

20. MJ to HL, 26 April 1923, HLP; MJ to HL, 15 July 1923, HLP.

21. MJ to HL, 3 September 1923, HLP.

22. HC to GM, 20 December 1923, *Letters*, pp. 161–62; MJ to AS, 12 September 1923, ASP; MJ to HL, 20 October 1923, HLP.

23. Cited in Unterecker, *Voyager*, p. 314.

24. *ER*, p. 181; MJ to HL, 23 October 1923, HLP.

25. MC to GM, 14 November 1923, MCP.

26. GM, "The Fledgling Years," pp. 50–51; personal interview with KB, 9 August 1979.

27. GM to CA, 29 January 1929, CAP; MJ to CA, 9 March 1938, CAP; MJ to HL, 30 November 1923, HLP.

28. *ER*, p. 185; MJ to HL, 30 November 1923, HLP.

29. Burton Rascoe, "Bookman's Daybook," *New York Herald-Tribune*, 27 January 1924; Eugene O'Neill to Postmaster-General Harry S. New, undated, MCP; *LAS*, p. 261.

30. *ER*, p. 196; *LAS*, p. 261.

31. Rascoe, "Josephson and the Modern Aesthetic"; MC to KB, 18 November 1923, MCP.

32. GM to MC, 20 February 1923, MCP.

33. AL, "Two Generations in American Poetry," *NR*, 5 December 1923, p. 3.

34. Kenneth Rexroth, *American Poetry in the Twentieth Century* (New York: Herder, 1973), p. 91; Tashjian, *The Skyscraper Primitives*, p. 230.

Chapter 7: From Grub Street to Wall Street

1. *LAS*, p. 278.
2. Robert Sobel, *The Great Bull Market: Wall Street in the 1920s* (New York: Norton, 1968), p. 65.
3. MJ, *The Money Lords: The Great Finance Capitalists, 1925–1960* (New York: Weybright and Talley, 1973), p. 9; MJ, "Confessions of a Customer's Man," manuscript, 1931, p. 7, MJP1.
4. MJ to KB, 4 February 1924, MJP1.
5. MJ, "Confessions of a Customer's Man," p. 8.
6. Ibid., p. 10.
7. Ibid., p. 11; MJ, *The Money Lords*, p. 12.
8. MJ, "Confessions of a Customer's Man," p. 12.
9. MC, *Blue Juniata* (New York: Viking, 1968), p. 74.
10. MJ to HL, 25 July 1924, HLP.
11. MJ to KB, 15 August 1924, MJP1.
12. MJ to HL, 13 October 1924, HLP.
13. MC, *A Second Flowering: Works and Days of the Lost Generation* (New York: Viking, 1956), p. 195; *ER*, pp. 222–23.
14. MJ to HL, 13 October 1924, HLP; MJ to KB, 9 November 1924, MJP1.
15. MJ to KB, 9 November 1924, MJP1; MJ, "Confessions of a Customer's Man," p. 32.
16. MJ to HL, 13 October 1924, HLP.
17. MJ to KB, 23 November 1924, MJP1.
18. Ernest Boyd, "Aesthete: Model 1924," *American Mercury* 1 (January 1924): 51, 53.
19. Burton Rascoe, "'Aesthete: Model 1924'—Timeless and Universal," *New York Herald-Tribune*, 30 December 1923; H. L. Mencken, "A Modern Masterpiece," *American Mercury* 1 (March 1924): 378.
20. MC to JBW, 22 November 1924, JBWP; William Carlos Williams to MJ, 1 December 1924, MJP1.
21. *Aesthete 1925* (February 1925), inside cover.
22. Ibid., pp. 29–31.
23. MJ to KB, 6 February 1925, MJP1.
24. MJ, "Confessions of a Customer's Man," p. 34.
25. Ibid., pp. 35–36.
26. Henry James, *The American* (Boston: Houghton Mifflin, 1887), pp. 31–32; MJ to MC, 2 August 1925, MCP.
27. MJ, "Confessions of a Customer's Man," p. 38.
28. *LAS*, p. 309.
29. AT to MC, 20 October 1925, MCP.
30. MJ to MC, 14 January 1925 (letter dated 1925 but was probably written in 1926), MCP; AT to MC, 23 December 1925, MCP; Slater Brown to MC, undated, MCP; MJ to MC, 14 January 1925 (1926), MCP.
31. MJ to JBW, 28 November 1925, JBWP.
32. MJ to Jane Heap, 13 November 1926, LRP.
33. *LAS*, p. 513.

Chapter 8: The Poet Transformed

1. MJ, "Letter to My Friends," *Little Review* (Spring 1926), p. 18.
2. Will Bray (MJ), "Exordium to Ducasse," *Broom* 3 (August 1922): 3; MJ, "Letter to My

Friends," p. 18. The Riffs are natives of Morocco who revolted in 1925 against French colonial rule.

3. MJ to KB, 10 April 1926, MJP1; *LAS*, p. 314.

4. MJ to KB, 4 November 1926, MJP2.

5. MJ, "Matthew Josephson," *Book-League Monthly* (November 1928), p. 341.

6. MJ to MC, 30 May 1927, MJP2.

7. MJ, "Matthew Josephson," p. 341.

8. MJ to KB, 10 August 1927, MJP2.

9. MJ to KB, 8 September 1927, MJP2.

10. MC, "Matthew Josephson," *Book-Find Notes* (January 1947), pp. 6, 13; *LAS*, p. 351.

11. MJ, *Zola and His Time* (New York: Macaulay, 1928), pp. 63, 73.

12. Ibid., p. 429.

13. Ibid., pp. 436, 446–47; *LAS*, p. 348.

14. MC, "Excessive and Colossal," *New York Herald-Tribune Books*, 14 October 1928, p. 3; Van Wyck Brooks, "Introduction," *Book-League Monthly* (November 1928), pp. v–vi; Herbert Gorman, "Zola's Life," *New York Times Book Review*, 28 October 1928, p. 5; MJ to Van Wyck Brooks, undated (1928), MJP2.

15. Edward H. O'Neill, *A History of American Biography* (1935; rpt., New York: Russell, 1968), p. 239; *LAS*, p. 351.

16. See Dougald McMillan, *transition: The History of a Literary Era* (New York: Braziller, 1976).

17. KB to MJ, 8 November 1927, MJP1.

18. William Slater Brown, "Seven Occasional Poems," *transition* 13 (Summer 1928): 86.

19. MJ, "Open Letter to Ezra Pound and the Other 'Exiles,'" *transition* 13 (Summer 1928): 99–100, 102.

20. William Carlos Williams to Ezra Pound, 11 August 1928, *The Selected Letters of William Carlos Williams*, ed. John C. Thirlwall (New York: McDowell, 1957), p. 105; MJ to KB, 15 June 1928, MJP2.

21. MJ, "American Letter: Some Contemporary Themes," *transition* 13 (Fall 1928): 57–59, 62–63; Aaron, *Writers on the Left*, p. 131.

22. MJ, "The Militant Intellectual," *New Masses* 4 (January 1929): 19; *LAS*, p. 362.

23. MJ, "Detroit: City of Tomorrow?" *Outlook and Independent*, 13 February 1929, p. 244; MJ, "Chicago: A Modernistic Portrait," *Outlook and Independent*, 30 January 1929, p. 164; MJ, "Mass Civilization and the Individual," *Outlook and Independent*, 5 June 1929, pp. 206–07, 238.

24. *New York World*, 19 December 1928, p. 18.

25. KB to AT, 15 March 1929, ATP.

26. Personal interview with MJ, 17 July 1976.

27. MJ to JBW, 4 April 1929, JBWP.

28. MJ, *Portrait of the Artist as American* (New York: Harcourt, Brace, 1930), p. 16.

29. Ibid., pp. xx, xiii.

30. Ibid., p. 303.

31. Ibid., p. 306.

32. MJ to KB, 3 August 1929, MJP2; Murray Godwin, "Portrait of the Artist as American," *Plain Talk* (August 1930), p. 252.

33. See James Radcliffe Squires, *Allen Tate: A Literary Biography* (New York: Pegasus, 1971), pp. 61–62; *LAS*, pp. 305–07.

34. MJ to Marianne Moore, 4 December 1925, MJP1.

35. MJ to AH, June 1929, HCF.

36. *LAS*, pp. 352–54; Journal, 27 October 1976.

37. Journal, 27 October 1976.

38. Ibid.

39. KAP to MJ, undated (1928), MJP2.

40. KAP to MJ, December 1928 (Tuesday), MJP2; KAP to MJ, December 1928 (Thursday), MJP2.

41. Journal, 27 October 1976.

42. KAP to MJ, undated (1929), MJP2; KAP to MJ, 16 March 1929, MJP2.

43. MJ to Joan Givner, undated (1974; supplied by the recipient).

44. John K. Galbraith, *The Great Crash* (New York: Houghton Mifflin, 1955), pp. 60–92.

45. *IT*, p. 23.

46. LM to author, 11 December 1975.

47. "Burned Trying to Save Manuscripts," *New York Times*, 1 February 1930; "Writer Burned Hunting Son," *New York Evening Sun*, 31 January 1930.

48. Personal interview with KB, 24 July 1977.

49. *LAS*, p. 385.

Chapter 9: Fellow Traveler

1. *IT*, p. 36.

2. John Chamberlain, "The Frustrated Creature, the American Writer," *New York Times Book Review*, 29 June 1930, p. 2; Gamaliel Bradford to MJ, 8 May 1930, MJP1; LM to MJ, 30 May 1930, MJP1; James Thurber to MJ, undated, MJP2.

3. KB to MJ, 27 May 1930, MJP1.

4. Max Lerner to author, 4 March 1977; *IT*, p. 38.

5. MJ to KB, 22 August 1930, MJP2.

6. MJ, "On Liberty," *NR*, 10 September 1930, p. 104.

7. Ibid., p. 105.

8. Gerald Johnson, "The Average American and the Depression," *Current History* 35 (1932): 673.

9. EW, "An Appeal to Progressives," *NR*, 31 January 1931, pp. 235–36. On the relationship between liberalism and communism, see Richard Pells, *Radical Visions and American Dreams: Culture and Social Thought in the Depression Years* (New York: Harper, 1973), pp. 43–95; Frank Warren, *Liberals and Communism* (Bloomington: Indiana University Press, 1966).

10. George Soule, "Hard-Boiled Radicalism," *NR*, 21 January 1931, pp. 261–63.

11. MJ to JBW, 26 January 1931, JBWP.

12. MJ, "Encounters with Edmund Wilson," p. 742; MJ, "The Road of Indignation," *NR*, 18 February 1931, pp. 13–14.

13. MJ, "The Voice of No Man," *NR*, 3 June 1931, pp. 76–77. See the chapter on Chase in R. Alan Lawson, *The Failure of Independent Liberalism, 1930–1941* (New York: Capricorn, 1971), pp. 75–85.

14. MJ to JBW, 26 January 1931, JBWP; MJ to KB, 7 May 1931, MJP.

15. Interview with MJ (1963), LaFollette Civil Liberties Committee File, p. 75, Columbia Oral History Collection, Columbia University; *IT*, p. 45; MJ, "The Voice of No Man," p. 77.

16. *IT*, p. 42.

17. Alfred Kazin, *Starting Out in the Thirties* (New York: Little, Brown, 1962), pp. 10–11; *IT*, pp. 47–71.

18. MJ, "Encounters with Edmund Wilson," p. 733.

19. MJ, "The New Era: Its Rise and Fall," *NR*, 4 November 1931, p. 317; MJ to MC, August 1931, MCP.

20. Journal, undated (1962).

21. MJ, "Confessions of a Customer's Man," p. 12; MJ, "Notes on a Memoir," Journal (1962), p. 34. Some of his journalistic pieces included "Groton, Harvard, Wall Street," *New Yorker*, 2 April 1932, pp. 19–22; "Jolly Bear," *New Yorker*, 14 May 1932, pp. 21–25; "The Red House," *New Yorker*, 17 September 1932, pp. 39–44; "Fifty Years on Wall Street," *New Yorker*, 1 October 1932, pp. 22–26.

22. MJ, "Evan Shipman: Poet and Horseplayer," *Southern Review* 9 (Fall 1973): 837–38.

23. MJ, *Jean-Jacques Rousseau* (New York: Harcourt, Brace, 1931), pp. vii–viii.

24. MJ to KB, 4 December 1939, MJP2; MJ quoted in MC to JBW, 28 November 1925, JBWP.

25. *IT*, p. 467. David Caute has written a penetrating study of the fellow travelers in which he notes their affinity with the philosophes. See *The Fellow Travelers: A Postscript to the Enlightenment* (New York: Macmillan, 1973).

26. MJ, "The Road of Indignation," *NR*, 18 February 1931, p. 14.

27. MJ to *Pravda*, undated (1932), MJP2; MJ to John Dos Passos, 21 March 1932, John Dos Passos Papers, Alderman Library, University of Virginia.

28. *New York World Telegram*, 12 March 1932.

29. Charles Yale Harrison to Harry Hansen, March 1932 (no day), MJP2.

30. *New York World Telegram*, 21 March 1932, p. 12.

31. MJ, "Revolution: The First Phase," *NR*, 16 March 1932, p. 131; Wilson quoted in Caute, *The Fellow Travelers*, p. 263.

32. "Form Group to Back Foster," *New York Times*, 12 September 1932. See also Aaron, *Writers on the Left*, p. 213; "Writers in Support of Communists," *Daily Worker*, 14 September 1932, p. 1.

33. "2,000 Professionals, Writers, Artists, Pledge Support to Communists in Elections," *Daily Worker*, 14 October 1932, p. 1.

34. *Culture and Crisis* (n.p., 1932), p. 29; MJ to HJ, October 1932, MJP1.

35. *New Masses*, 8 April 1933, p. 11.

36. MJ, *Nazi Culture: The Brown Darkness over Germany* (New York: John Day, 1933), p. 32.

37. *IT*, p. 162.

38. Smith quoted in Aaron, *Writers on the Left*, p. 262; Bernard Smith, "The Liberals Grow Old," *Saturday Review*, 30 December 1933, p. 377.

39. MJ to John Chamberlain, 18 May 1932, MJP1; MJ, "The Younger Generation: Its Young Novelists," *Virginia Quarterly Review* 9 (April 1933): 261.

40. MJ, "Citizen Zola," *NR*, 8 February 1933, p. 355.

41. Karl Schriftgiesser, "The Criticism of Matthew Josephson," *Boston Evening Transcript*, 23 January 1932, Book Section, p. 1; Austin Warren, "Kenneth Burke: His Mind and His Art," *Sewanee Review* 41 (Spring 1933): 229; *Boston Evening Transcript*, 1 April 1933, Book Section, p. 1.

42. MJ, "In the Country," Journal, undated (1962).

43. MJ, "Improper Bostonian," p. 526.

44. David Caute has emphasized that fellow-traveling was "remote-control radicalism," involving commitment at a distance that is not only geographical but also emotional and intellectual." See *The Fellow Travelers*, p. 3.

45. See for example Eugene Lyons, *The Red Decade* (New York: Bobbs-Merrill, 1941); Daniel Bell, *The End of Ideology: On the Exhaustion of Political Ideas in the Fifties* (New York: Collier, 1961); Peter Viereck, *Shame and Glory of the Intellectuals* (Boston: Houghton Mifflin, 1953); Leslie Fiedler, *An End to Innocence* (Boston: Houghton Mifflin, 1955).

46. *ER*, pp. 9, 27, 80, 206, 213–14, 244–45, 284–85, 291, 305. See also MC, *The*

Dream of the Golden Mountains: Remembering the 1930s (New York: Viking, 1980), pp. 36–50.

47. *IT*, pp. 157, 358; WF, quoted in *Memoirs of Waldo Frank*, ed. Alan Trachtenberg (Amherst: University of Massachusetts Press, 1973), pp. 184–85.

48. *IT*, p. 108; Murray Kempton, *Part of Our Time: Some Monuments and Ruins of the Thirties* (New York: Dell, 1955), p. 118.

49. MJ, "Norman Thomas: Enraptured Socialist," *NR*, 10 August 1932, p. 32; Journal, July 1932; MJ to MC, June 1932, MCP.

50. T. B. Bottomore, *Critics of Society: Radical Thought in North America* (New York: Pantheon, 1968), p. 39.

51. *IT*, p. 108; Caute, *The Fellow Travelers*, p. 250.

52. John Dewey, *Freedom and Culture* (New York: Harper, 1939), p. 96. James Gilbert is one of the few scholars to have emphasized that the seed of literary radicalism was planted long before the Great Crash. See *Writers and Partisans: A History of Literary Radicalism in America* (New York: Wiley, 1968), p. 90.

Chapter 10: A Writer on the Left

1. CB, "Written History as an Act of Faith," *American Historical Review* 39 (January 1934): 219–23.

2. MJ to AH, 13 April 1932, HCF.

3. Ibid.; MJ, *The Robber Barons: The Great American Capitalists, 1865–1901* (New York: Harcourt, Brace, 1934), p. viii; MJ to AH, 31 May 1933, HCF; MJ to CP, 21 July 1933, HCF.

4. William Leuchtenburg, *Franklin D. Roosevelt and the New Deal* (New York: Harper and Row, 1963), p. 22.

5. MJ to Lewis Corey, 29 August 1934, Lewis Corey Papers, Columbia University.

6. MJ, *The Robber Barons*, pp. 275, 38, 59, 158.

7. Ibid., pp. 14, 101, 108.

8. Ibid., pp. 181, 87, 90, 91.

9. Ibid., pp. 344, 346.

10. Ibid., pp. 54, 236, 264, 217, 270.

11. Ibid., p. 280.

12. Ibid., pp. 452–53.

13. "Peter Quince Radio Book Review," Station WRVA, Richmond, Virginia, 27 March 1934, MJP2; Henry Hazlitt, "Money and the American Scene," *New York Times Book Review*, 4 March 1934, p. 1.

14. Allan Nevins, "Malefactors of Great Wealth," *Saturday Review*, 3 March 1934, p. 517.

15. Hal Bridges, "The Robber Baron Concept in American History," *Business History Review* 32 (Spring 1958): 7. Useful bibliographical essays on the "robber baron" interpretation include David E. Shi, "Matthew Josephson: The Evolution of a Historian," (Ph.D. diss., University of Virginia, 1976), pp. 316–36; Thomas C. Cochran, "The Legend of the Robber Barons," *Pennsylvania Magazine of History and Biography* 74 (1950): 307–16; Edward C. Kirkland, "The Robber Barons Revisited," *American Historical Review* 66 (October 1960): 68–73; Allen Solganick, "The Robber Baron Concept and Its Revisionists," *Science and Society* 29 (Summer 1965): 257–69; William Woodruff, "History and the Businessman," *Business History Review* 30 (September 1956): 241–59. In 1970 Thomas Brewer wrote in the introduction to an anthology of writings about the "robber barons" that the majority of scholars "still adhere to the 'robber baron' interpretation that the beliefs and policies of the

post–Civil War businessmen were detrimental to the nation." Thomas Brewer, ed., *The Robber Barons: Saints or Sinners?* (New York: Holt, Rinehart, 1970), p. 1.

16. Arthur Koestler, *Arrow in the Blue* (New York: Macmillan, 1952), p. 278. Peter Filene has traced the evolution of the American fascination with the Soviet system in *America and the Soviet Experiment, 1917–1933* (Cambridge, Mass.: Harvard University Press, 1966).

17. *IT*, p. 191; MJ to HJ, 10 December 1933, MJP2; MJ to HJ, 16 December 1933, MJP2.

18. *IT*, p. 367; Caute, *The Fellow Travelers*, p. 111.

19. MJ to CP, 30 March 1934, HCF.

20. MJ, "The Literary Life in Russia," *NR*, 6 June 1934, pp. 90–91; Max Eastman, "Artists in Uniform," *Modern Monthly* (August 1933), p. 399. On Eastman's position see William O'Neill, *The Last Romantic: A Life of Max Eastman* (New York: Oxford University Press, 1978), pp. 154–62.

21. MJ, "The Literary Life in Russia," p. 90.

22. Ibid.; EW to Louise Bogan, 20 August 1934, *Letters on Literature and Politics*, p. 251.

23. MJ, "Roosevelt and the New Deal," manuscript, August 1934, pp. 6, 9, MJP2; Journal, 29 October 1934; Journal, 8 September 1935.

24. *IT*, pp. 356–57.

25. Richard Hofstadter observed that American liberals have "tried to be good and believing citizens of a democratic society and at the same time to resist the vulgarization of culture which that society constantly produces." *Anti-Intellectualism in American Life* (New York: Vintage, 1962), p. 407.

26. Journal, 1 October 1934.

27. Ibid.; Journal, 12 January 1938.

28. Journal, 19 January 1935.

29. Journal, 12 May 1935.

30. James Gilbert, *Writers and Partisans*, p. 75; Granville Hicks, "The Crisis in American Criticism," *New Masses*, 12 February 1933, p. 5.

31. *New Masses*, 22 January 1935, p. 20.

32. *IT*, p. 359; MJ, "For a United Literary Front," *New Masses*, 30 April 1935, pp. 22–23; John Dos Passos to MJ, 6 February 1935, MJP2.

33. MJ, "The Role of the Writer in the Soviet Union," in *American Writers' Congress*, ed. Henry Hart (New York: International, 1935), pp. 41, 45.

34. Ibid., pp. 41–42.

35. MJ to KB, 15 September 1935, MJP1.

36. "A Conversation with Malcolm Cowley," *Southern Review* 15 (April 1979): 278; MJ to MC, 8 November 1935, MJP1.

37. KB to MJ, 11 September 1935, MJP1; KB to MJ, 20 June 1933, MJP2.

38. Journal, 1 October 1934.

39. Journal, 10 November 1935; MC to MJ, 27 March 1936, MJP2.

40. Journal, 15 March 1935; Journal, 25 January 1935.

41. MJ to HJ, 8 July 1935, MJP2.

42. Ibid.

43. MJ to HJ, 14 December 1936, MJP2; MJ to HJ, undated (December 1936), MJP2; MJ to CP, 28 December 1936, HCF.

44. MJ to HJ, 17 December 1936, MJP2; *IT*, p. 421.

45. MJ to KB, 5 February 1937, MJP2.

46. Allen Guttmann, *The Wound in the Heart: America and the Spanish Civil War* (New York: Free Press, 1962), p. 82. See also Frederick R. Benson, *Writers in Arms: The Literary*

Impact of the Spanish Civil War (New York: New York University Press, 1967).

47. Journal, 27 August 1936. MJ, "Viva Espagne Libre," *New Masses*, 18 August 1936, p. 13.

48. MJ to CP, 26 February 1937, HCF; MJ to CP, 28 January 1937, HCF.

49. MJ, "Russia and Some Utopians," *NR*, 1 December 1937, pp. 105–08.

50. Ibid.

51. Upton Sinclair to MJ, 30 November 1937, MJP1; Eugene Lyons, Letter to the editor, *NR*, 29 December 1937, pp. 229–30; MJ, Letter to the editor, *NR*, 29 December 1937, p. 230; Aaron, *Writers on the Left*, p. 350.

52. MJ to CP, 11 July 1936, HCF; MJ to AH, 15 August 1936, HCF; MJ to AH, 3 February 1938, HCF; Journal, 28 June 1938.

53. MJ to Helen Taylor, 11 April 1938, HCF; *IT*, p. 439.

54. MJ, *The Politicos, 1865–1896* (New York: Harcourt, Brace, 1938), pp. 80, 88, 211, 98, 275.

55. MJ, research notes for *The Politicos*, undated, MJP1; *The Politicos*, p. vii.

56. *The Politicos*, p. vii.

57. Ibid., pp. 287, 637, 385, 365. More recent studies have demonstrated that voter interest was much higher during the Gilded Age than MJ indicated. See Richard Jensen, *The Winning of the Midwest: Social and Political Conflict, 1888–1896* (Chicago: University of Chicago Press, 1971); Paul Kleppner, *The Cross of Culture: A Social Analysis of Midwestern Politics, 1880–1900* (New York: Free Press, 1970).

58. MJ to CB, 12 January 1938, MJP2; CB to MJ, 30 January 1938, MJP2.

59. *New York Sun*, 9 April 1938, p. 16; Henry Steele Commager, *New York Herald Tribune Books*, 10 April 1938, p. 5; Louis Hacker, "The Politics of Reconstruction," *Nation*, 14 May 1938, p. 563.

60. MJ to Max Lerner, 16 May 1938, MJP2.

61. Journal, 26 April 1938, MJP2; MJ to CP, 12 May 1938, HCF; MJ to CP, 7 October 1938, HCF.

62. MJ to CP, 7 October 1938, HCF; C. Vann Woodward to MJ, 26 August 1938, MJP2.

63. MJ to Charles Hastings, 11 December 1938, HCF; Vincent P. DeSantis, "The Political Life of the Gilded Age: A Review of the Recent Literature," *History Teacher* 9 (1975–1976): 73–105. For a more detailed discussion of *The Politicos*, see David E. Shi, "*The Politicos*: A Modern Look at a Muckraking Classic," *South Atlantic Quarterly* (forthcoming).

Chapter 11: The Forked Road to War

1. Journal, 4 October 1938; Hamilton Basso to MJ, 24 October 1938, MJP2; MJ to Hamilton Basso, 29 October 1938, MJP2.

2. "How to Fight Fascism," Journal, 3 December 1938.

3. MJ, "Fascism's Seventh Veil," *New Masses*, 18 April 1939, pp. 5–7.

4. MJ to Chester B. Kerr, 25 July 1939, HCF; MJ, "No Panic before Fascism," manuscript, p. 17, MJP2.

5. MJ, "No Panic before Fascism," manuscript, pp. 24–25, MJP2.

6. Carey McWilliams, *The Education of Carey McWilliams* (New York: Simon and Schuster, 1979), p. 93; Granville Hicks, *Where We Came Out* (New York: Viking, 1954), p. 80; "In Reply to a Committee," *Nation*, 23 August 1939, p. 63.

7. Journal, 26 August 1939; Koestler quoted in Richard Crossman, ed., *The God That Failed* (New York: Vintage, 1949), p. 66; Journal, 26 August 1939; Journal, 6 September 1939.

8. Journal, 6 September 1939; MJ, "Open Letter: On the Russian-German Pact," manuscript, p. 1, MJP2.

9. Journal, 16 November 1939; MJ to Robert Lynd, 7 November 1939, MJP2.

10. MJ to Robert Lynd, 7 November 1939, MJP2; James Wechsler, *The Age of Suspicion* (New York: Random House, 1953), p. 153.

11. LM, *Faith for Living* (New York: Harcourt, Brace, 1940), pp. 117–18, 56.

12. Ibid., pp. 95, 100, 105–06. For a thorough discussion of Mumford and other interventionist liberals, see Pells, *Radical Visions*, pp. 330–64.

13. MJ to Helen Taylor, 15 August 1940, HCF.

14. *IT*, pp. 489–90.

15. Max Lerner to MJ, 2 August 1940, MJP2; MC to author, 18 July 1979.

16. MJ to LM, 17 September 1940, MJP2.

17. MJ to KB, 17 September 1940, MJP2; MJ to EJ, 30 October 1941, MJP2.

18. MJ to Chester B. Kerr, 12 September 1939, HCF; MJ to Chester B. Kerr, 30 November 1939, HCF.

19. MJ, *The President Makers: The Culture of Politics and Leadership in an Age of Enlightenment, 1896–1919* (New York: Harcourt, Brace, 1940), p. 11.

20. Ibid., pp. 31, 496.

21. Ibid., pp. 82, 83.

22. Ibid., pp. 506, 503, 518. For the revisionist account see CB, *The Rise of American Civilization* (New York: Macmillan, 1927); Walter Millis, *Road to War: America, 1914–1917* (Boston: Houghton Mifflin, 1935); Charles Tansill, *America Goes to War* (Boston: Houghton Mifflin, 1938).

23. Ibid., p. xi.

24. Ibid., pp. 541–42; Richard Hofstadter, *The Progressive Historians* (New York: Vintage, 1970), p. 322.

25. MJ to Helen Taylor, 16 September 1940, HCF; Robert Morss Lovett, "The Men Behind the President," *NR*, 14 October 1940, pp. 846–47; Whittaker Chambers, "Ballot Barons," *Time*, 21 October 1940, p. 97; Henry Steele Commager, "Age of T. R., Wilson, LaFollette," *New York Herald Tribune Books*, 10 November 1940, p. 2.

26. Robert Engler, introduction, *The President Makers* (New York: Putnam's, 1979), p. vi.

27. MJ to HJ, 19 October 1940, MJP2.

28. MJ, memo to *New Yorker*, undated, MJP2.

29. MJ, "Production Man," *New Yorker*, 15 March 1941, p. 36.

30. MC, *And I Worked at the Writer's Trade: Chapters of Literary History, 1918–1978* (New York: Viking, 1978), pp. 133–52. See also Aaron, *Writers on the Left*, pp. 347–55.

31. MC, *And I Worked at the Writer's Trade*, p. 158; MC to KB, 17 December 1940, MCP.

32. MJ to KB, 30 September 1940, MJP2; MJ to KB, 28 February 1942, MJP2.

33. MJ to KB, 29 May 1940, MJP2.

Chapter 12: The Trough of a Wave

1. William Phillips, "Portrait of the Artist as a Middle-Aged Man," *Partisan Review* 11 (Winter 1944): 120.

2. MJ to Robert Lynd, 23 December 1943, MJP2.

3. HJ to EJ, 8 December 1941, MJP2; MJ to KB, 10 December 1941, MJP2; MJ to KB, 28 February 1942, MJP2.

4. MJ to EJ, 31 January 1942, MJP2; CB to MJ, 16 January 1942, MJP2.

5. Louis Aragon to HJ and MJ, 5 September 1940, MJP1.

6. MJ, *Victor Hugo: A Realistic Biography of the Great Romantic* (Garden City, N.Y.: Doubleday, 1942), pp. vii–viii.

7. Ibid., p. 364; André Maurois, "Sonorous Echo of France," *Saturday Review*, 24 October 1942, p. 17; Herbert Gorman, "Victor Hugo: A Great Fighter as Well as a Great Writer," *New York Times Book Review*, 18 October 1942, p. 3.

8. MJ to KB, 3 January 1943, MJP2. Some of his articles included "Production Man," *New Yorker*, 8, 15 March 1941, pp. 22–32, 26–36; "The Hat on the Roll-Top Desk," *New Yorker*, 14, 21 February 1942, pp. 24–28, 22–26; "Leprechaun on the Palisades," *New Yorker*, 14 March 1942, pp. 26–30; "Columbus of the Airways," *Saturday Evening Post*, 14 August 1943, pp. 9–14; "Commander with a Camera," *New Yorker*, 3 June 1944, pp. 30–34; "Typewriter Statesman," *Saturday Evening Post*, 5 August 1944, pp. 9–10; "Daring Young Man of Wall Street," *Saturday Evening Post*, 11 August 1945, pp. 12–13.

9. MJ to EJ, 10 March 1942, MJP2; MJ to EJ, 2 May 1942, MJP2.

10. MJ to EJ, 18 September 1943, MJP2.

11. MJ to EJ, 22 August 1943, MJP2.

12. MJ to EJ, 8 April 1944, MJP2; MJ to EJ, 13 June 1944, MJP2; MJ and Russell Maloney, "Testimony of a Sinner," *New Yorker*, 22 April 1944, pp. 30–34.

13. MJ to EJ, 6 March 1945, MJP2.

14. MJ to EJ, 30 March 1945, MJP2.

15. On the *Partisan Review* see Gilbert, *Writers and Partisans*; Alan Wald, "Revolutionary Intellectuals: *Partisan Review* in the 1930s," *Occident* 8 (Spring 1974): 118–33.

16. William Phillips, "What Happened in the 1930s," *Commentary* 34 (September 1962): 204–12.

17. See Gilbert, *Writers and Partisans*, p. 257.

18. MJ to James Atlas, Easter Sunday 1975 (supplied by the recipient); Journal, 23 March 1945.

19. Journal, 23 March 1945.

20. MJ to *Partisan Review*, contained in Journal, 19 April 1945. The letter was apparently never mailed.

21. MJ to EJ, 16 January 1944; MJ to EJ, 22 February 1945; MJ to EJ, 1 April 1945, MJP2.

22. MJ to EJ, 8 April 1945, MJP2.

23. MJ to EJ, 23 May 1945, MJP2.

24. MJ to John Erskine, 10 November 1946, MJP2.

25. MJ to Christian Gauss, 10 March 1941, MJP2; MJ to KB, 19 May 1943, MJP2; MJ to Robert Lynd, 23 December 1943, MJP2.

26. MJ, *Stendhal, or the Pursuit of Happiness* (Garden City, N.Y.: Doubleday, 1946), p. 391.

27. Ibid., pp. 330, 234, 381.

28. Ibid., pp. 437, 388, 237.

29. Ibid., p. 391.

30. *New York Post* review quoted in *Book-Find News* 2 (December 1946), p. 2; "Crystallized Romantic," *Time*, 21 October 1946, p. 106; John Erskine, "The Realm of Books," *Los Angeles Examiner*, 15 December 1946; John Erskine to MJ, 5 November 1946, MJP2.

Chapter 13: A Divided Soul

1. Journal, March 1946 (no day), 12 April 1946, 7 September 1946.

2. Journal, 12 June 1946.

3. Ibid.

4. Ibid.; Journal, 9 February 1948.

5. MJ to KB, 31 October 1948, MJP2.

6. MC to author, 5 August 1979.

7. Carl Josephson to author, 17 March 1980; Journal, 11 August 1947.

8. Journal, 26 December 1947.

9. Journal, undated (1967).

10. Journal, 7 June 1945, 2 June 1945, 3 July 1947.

11. Journal, 29 December 1947, 16 July 1948.

12. Journal, October 1948 (no day).

13. Journal, 23 September 1946.

14. Journal, 22 October 1947; MJ, "Stendhal Takes the Stand," *New Masses*, 25 November 1947, pp. 15–16.

15. MJ, "Stendhal Takes the Stand," pp. 15–16.

16. Ibid.

17. A fascinating study of the intellectuals who made the transition from Left to Right is John Diggins, *Up from Communism: Conservative Odysseys in American Intellectual History* (New York: Harper and Row, 1975).

18. MJ to KB, 1 April 1947, MJP2; MJ to Murray Kempton, 8 March 1955, MJP2.

19. Journal, 19 September 1946.

20. Speech, p. 1.

21. On Henry Wallace see Norman D. Markowitz, *The Rise and Fall of the People's Century: Henry A. Wallace and American Liberalism, 1941–1948* (New York: Free Press, 1973).

22. MJ to Angus Cameron, 1 January 1947, MJP2; Speech, p. 9, MJP2.

23. Journal, 28, 29 September 1948.

24. MJ to TC, 16 October 1948, TCP.

25. Useful studies of postwar liberalism and radicalism include Mary S. McAuliffe, *Crisis on the Left: Cold War Politics and American Liberals, 1947–1954* (Amherst: University of Massachusetts Press, 1978), and Joseph R. Starobin, *American Communism in Crisis, 1943–1957* (Cambridge, Mass.: Harvard University Press, 1972).

26. Journal, 16 July 1948, 18 September 1948, 28 November 1948, 22 December 1948.

27. MJ to MC, 8 July 1949, MCP.

28. MJ to HJ, 9 July 1949, 14 July 1949, 20 July 1949, MJP2.

Chapter 14: The Great Fear

1. See David Caute, *The Great Fear: The Anti-Communist Purge under Truman and Eisenhower* (New York: Simon and Schuster, 1978).

2. McAuliffe, *Crisis on the Left*, pp. 48–62.

3. Journal, 31 January 1950.

4. MJ to TC, 27 December 1950, TCP.

5. Ibid.; MJ to EJ, 4 May 1952, MJP2; letter from Carey McWilliams, 28 June 1979. See also McWilliams, *The Education of Carey McWilliams*, pp. 147–48.

6. MJ, "Battle of the Books," *Nation*, 28 June 1952, pp. 619–24.

7. Ibid., p. 624.

8. "Meet the 'Nation' Experts on Civil Liberties," *New Leader*, 14 July 1952, pp. 14, 22; "Whose Liberties," *New Leader*, 26 January 1953, p. 31.

9. MJ, "The Vandals Are Here," *Nation*, 26 September 1953, pp. 244–48.

10. Samuel Eliot Morison, "Presidential Address," *American Historical Review* 56 (1951): 261–75. On the "consensus" school of American historians, see John Higham, "The Cult of the 'American Consensus': Homogenizing Our History," *Commentary* 27 (February 1959): 93–100.

11. Louis Hacker, "The Anticapitalist Bias of American Historians," in *Capitalism and the Historian*, ed. F. A. Hayek (Chicago: University of Chicago Press, 1954), pp. 62–90; Edward Saveth, "What Historians Teach us about Business," *Fortune* 45 (April 1952): 118–19; Nevins quoted in *Fortune* 45 (April 1952): 118.

12. Allan Nevins, "Business and the Historians," *American Petroleum Institute Proceedings* 33 (1953): 85–89.

13. MJ to TC, 1 May 1952, TCP; Merle Curti to MJ, 12 September 1953, MJP2.

14. MJ and Allan Nevins, "Should American History Be Rewritten?" *Saturday Review*, 6 February 1954, pp. 8–10, 44–49.

15. Ibid., p. 10.

16. Ibid., p. 44.

17. Ibid., p. 10.

18. Van Wyck Brooks to MJ, 7 August 1955, MJP1.

19. MJ to TC, 22 February 1954, TCP. Allan Nevins was by no means himself a detached observer of the business process. In May 1954, for example, he was paid to appear in advertisements for the American Petroleum Institute. In addition, several of his business histories were subsidized by the corporations themselves. He proposed to the Ford Corporation, for instance, that it contribute half the cost of publishing his biography of Henry Ford. See letter from Scribner's Publishing Company to Nevins, 12 November 1954, Allan Nevins Papers, Columbia University.

20. MJ, "Big Guns: Pentagon Power," *Nation*, 14 January 1956, pp. 30–31.

21. Ibid., p. 33, MJ, "Big Guns: Billions for Insecurity," *Nation*, 28 January 1956, p. 70.

22. William Leuchtenburg, *A Troubled Feast: American Society since 1945* (Boston: Little, Brown, 1973), p. 28.

23. Journal, October 1958, 2 December 1958.

24. Ibid.

Chapter 15: Last Books and Last Years

1. His articles during the period include "Big Bomber Symington: Aiming at the Presidency," *Nation*, 26 May 1956, pp. 442–46; "The Hydrogen Balance," *Nation*, 26 January 1957, pp. 82–83; "Military Model for America," *Nation*, 6 April 1957, p. 299–300; "Fantasy for Limited War," *Nation*, 31 August 1957, pp. 89–91.

2. MJ, *Edison* (New York: McGraw-Hill, 1959).

3. *The Robber Barons*, p. 101; *Edison*, p. ix.

4. *Edison*, pp. 67, 126, 138, 294.

5. Ibid., pp. 138, 311.

6. Ibid., p. 463.

7. Journal, 15 July 1969.

8. *LAS*, p. 4.

9. EW to AT, 9 February 1962, in Wilson, *Letters on Literature and Politics*, p. 625.

10. *IT*, p. xi.

11. Journal, July 1953 (no day).

12. *IT*, p. 153.

13. Ibid., p. 151.

14. Ibid., pp. 158, vi, 84.

15. Ibid., pp. 481, 460.

16. Ibid., pp. 169–81.

17. Daniel Aaron, *New York Times Book Review*, 26 November 1967, p. 6.

18. *Al Smith: Hero of the Cities* (New York: Houghton Mifflin, 1969); *The Money Lords: The Great Finance Capitalists, 1925–1950* (New York: Weybright and Talley, 1972).

19. MJ to Murray Josephson, 23 December 1923 (supplied by the recipient); Journal, 17 February 1964.

20. Journal, 15 February 1968.

21. Journal, June 1969 (no day).

22. Ibid.

23. Jay Martin to author, 10 September 1979; Journal, June 1969 (no day); MJ to Ivan von Auw, 12 March 1969, Harold Ober Associates Papers, Princeton University.

24. Letter to *New York Times*, 18 May 1970, MJP2.

25. MJ to KB, 18 June 1973, 5 August 1972 (supplied by the recipient); Journal, 31 October 1972.

26. MJ to EJ, 23 May 1973, MJP2; MJ to Maxwell Geismar, 5 June 1973, Maxwell Geismar Papers, Boston University; MJ to KB, 18 September 1974 (supplied by the recipient).

27. KB to MJ, 18 February 1973, 3 March 1973 (supplied by the writer); MJ to KB, 31 October 1973, MJP2; MJ to KB, 20 July 1973 (supplied by the recipient).

28. MJ to KB, 13 March 1975 (supplied by the recipient); Marcia Corbino, "Visiting Authors' 'Rest' Was Work," *Sarasota Journal*, 19 May 1976, p. 10-A.

29. MJ, "The Hiss Case," memorandum, MJP2.

30. Ibid.; MJ to Alger Hiss, 24 January 1974, MJP2.

31. MJ to EJ, 21 August 1975, MJP2; MJ to HJ, 4 December 1933, MJP2; Journal, 10 September 1976, 23 July 1976.

32. Journal, 10 September 1976; Journal, September 1976 (no day); MC to author, 7 October 1976.

33. Journal, 25 October 1976; MJ to Joan Givner, 7 May 1977 (supplied by the recipient).

34. MC to author, 4 November 1976; KB to MJ, 1 November 1976 (supplied by the writer).

35. MJ to author, 10 February 1977.

36. MJ to Joan Givner, 3 January 1978 (supplied by the recipient); MJ to EJ, 20 February 1978, MJP2; MJ to EJ, 5 March 1978, MJP2; Journal, 10 March 1978.

Chapter 16: Conclusion

1. Recorded interview with MJ, 6 July 1977; Journal, 21 February 1948; MJ to KB, 31 July 1961, MJP2.

2. KB, "Commemorative Tribute to MJ," p. 3; MC to author, 5 August 1979.

3. HJ, "Description of MJ (untitled), 1935, p. 1, MJP2.

4. MJ, "Historians and Mythmakers," *Virginia Quarterly Review* 16 (January 1940): 97.

5. Ibid., p. 104.

6. Ibid., p. 102.

7. MJ to author, 11 May 1976.

8. MJ to author, 18 May 1975; MJ, "Historians and Mythmakers," pp. 95, 101.

9. Geoffrey Blodgett, "The Mugwump Reputation, 1870 to the Present," *Journal of American History* 66 (March 1980): 872.

10. Journal, September 1934 (no day); "A Conversation with MC," p. 282.

11. MJ, "A Banquet of Literature—With Intruders," *NR*, 22 September 1937, p. 122.

12. Journal, undated (1962).

13. *IT*, p. 412; Maxwell Geismar to author, 26 March 1978.

14. MJ to Michael Straight, 31 July 1953, MJP2.

15. HJ, Description of MJ, p. 1; Phillips quoted in Gilbert, *Writers and Partisans*, p. 281.

16. MJ to HJ, 8 July 1935, MJP2.

Index

N5